D0209371

Digital Fascism

This fourth volume in Christian Fuchs's *Media, Communication and Society* book series outlines the theoretical foundations of digital fascism and presents case studies of how fascism is communicated online.

Digital Fascism presents and engages with theoretical approaches and empirical studies that allow us to understand how fascism, right-wing authoritarianism, xenophobia, and nationalism are communicated on the Internet. The book builds on theoretical foundations from key theorists such as Theodor W. Adorno, Franz L. Neumann, Erich Fromm, Herbert Marcuse, Wilhelm Reich, Leo Löwenthal, Moishe Postone, Günther Anders, M. N. Roy, and Henry Giroux. The book draws on a range of case studies, including Nazi-celebrations of Hitler's birthday on Twitter, the 'red scare 2.0' directed against Jeremy Corbyn, and political communication online (Donald Trump, Boris Johnson, the Austrian presidential election). These case studies analyse right-wing communication online and on social media. Fuchs argues for the safeguarding of the democratic public sphere and that slowing down and decommodifying the logic of the media can advance and renew debate culture in the age of digital authoritarianism, fake news, echo chambers, and filter bubbles.

Each chapter focuses on a particular dimension of digital fascism or a critical theorist whose work helps us to illuminate how fascism and digital fascism work, making this book an essential reading for both undergraduate and postgraduate students of media and communication studies, sociology, politics, and political economy as well as anyone who wants to understand what digital fascism is and how it works.

Christian Fuchs is a critical theorist of communication and society. He is co-editor of the journal *tripleC: Communication, Capitalism & Critique*. He is author of many publications, including the books *Digital Capitalism* (2022), *Foundations of Critical Theory* (2022), *Communicating COVID-19: Everyday Life, Digital Capitalism, and Conspiracy Theories in Pandemic Times* (2021), *Marxist Humanism and Communication Theory* (2021), *Social Media: A Critical Introduction* (3rd edition 2021), *Communication and Capitalism: A Critical Theory* (2020), *Marxism: Karl Marx's Fifteen Key Concepts for Cultural and Communication Studies* (2020), *Nationalism on the Internet: Critical Theory and Ideology in the Age of Social Media and Fake News* (2020), *Rereading Marx in the Age of Digital Capitalism* (2019), *Digital Demagogue: Authoritarian Capitalism in the Age of Trump and Twitter* (2016), *Digital Labour and Karl Marx* (2014), and *Internet and Society* (2008).

Digital Fascism

Media, Communication and Society
Volume Four

Christian Fuchs

Routledge
Taylor & Francis Group

LONDON AND NEW YORK

Cover image: © mauritius images GmbH / Alamy Stock Photo

First published 2022
by Routledge
4 Park Square, Milton Park, Abingdon, Oxon OX14 4RN

and by Routledge
605 Third Avenue, New York, NY 10158

Routledge is an imprint of the Taylor & Francis Group, an informa business

British Library Cataloguing-in-Publication Data
A catalogue record for this book is available from the British Library

Library of Congress Cataloging-in-Publication Data
Names: Fuchs, Christian, 1976- author.
Title: Digital fascism / Christian Fuchs.
Description: Abingdon, Oxon ; New York, NY : Routledge, 2022. |
Series: Media, communication and society; volume 4 | Includes bibliographical references and index.
Identifiers: LCCN 2021039497 (print) | LCCN 2021039498 (ebook) |
ISBN 9781032187617 (hardback) | ISBN 9781032187600 (paperback) |
ISBN 9781003256090 (ebook)
Subjects: LCSH: Fascism. | Communication in politics--Technological innovations. | Digital media--Political aspects. | Internet--Political aspects.
Classification: LCC JC481 .F834 2022 (print) | LCC JC481 (ebook) |
DDC 320.53/3--dc23
LC record available at https://lccn.loc.gov/2021039497
LC ebook record available at https://lccn.loc.gov/2021039498

ISBN: 978-1-032-18761-7 (hbk)
ISBN: 978-1-032-18760-0 (pbk)
ISBN: 978-1-003-25609-0 (ebk)

DOI: 10.4324/9781003256090

Typeset in Univers
by MPS Limited, Dehradun

Contents

Figures

Tables

Acknowledgements

Chapter 2 was first published as a journal article. Reprinted with permission of the journal *tripleC*. Christian Fuchs. 2017. The Relevance of Franz L. Neumann's Critical Theory in 2017: "Anxiety and Politics" in the New Age of Authoritarian Capitalism. *tripleC: Communication, Capitalism & Critique* 15 (2): 637–650. DOI: https://doi.org/10.31269/triplec.v15i2.903.

Chapter 3 was first published as parts of a journal article (sections 1, 4, 5, 6). Reprinted with permission of the journal *tripleC*. Christian Fuchs. 2017. Günther Anders' Undiscovered Critical Theory of Technology in the Age of Big Data Capitalism. *tripleC: Communication, Capitalism & Critique* 15 (2): 584–613. DOI: https://doi.org/10.31269/triplec.v15i2.898.

Chapter 4 was first published as sections 1, 5, and 6 of the following article: Christian Fuchs. 2019. M. N. Roy and the Frankfurt School: Socialist Humanism and the Critical Analysis of Communication, Culture, Technology, Fascism and Nationalism. *tripleC: Communication, Capitalism & Critique* 17 (2): 249–286. DOI: https://doi.org/10.31269/triplec.v17i2.1118. Reprinted with permission of the journal *tripleC*.

Chapter 5 was first published as a journal article. Reprinted with permission of the journal *tripleC*. Christian Fuchs. 2015. Martin-Heidegger's anti-Semitism: Philosophy of Technology and the Media in the Light of the "Black Notebooks". Implications for the Reception of Heidegger in Media and Communication Studies. *tripleC: Communication, Capitalism & Critique* 13 (1): 55–78. DOI: https://doi.org/10.31269/triplec.v13i1.650.

Chapter 6 was first published as a journal article. Reprinted with permission of the journal *tripleC*. Christian Fuchs. 2015. Anti-Semitism, Anti-Marxism, and Technophobia: The Fourth Volume of Martin Heidegger's Black Notebooks (1942–1948). *tripleC: Communication, Capitalism & Critique* 13 (1): 93–100. DOI: https://doi.org/10.31269/triplec.v13i1.677.

Chapter 7 was first published as a journal article. Reprinted based on a contractual agreement that permits reuse of the article in a collected volume of the author's own works. Christian Fuchs. 2017. Fascism 2.0: Twitter Users' Social Media Memories of Hitler on his 127th Birthday. *Fascism: Journal of Comparative Fascist Studies* 6 (2): 228–263. DOI: https://doi.org/10.1163/22116257-00602004.

Chapter 8 was first published as a journal article. Reprinted based on a contractual agreement whereby the author retains the right to use the article or parts of it in future works under his own name. Christian Fuchs. 2016. Red Scare 2.0: User-Generated Ideology in the Age of Jeremy Corbyn and Social Media. *Journal of Language and Politics* 15 (4): 369–398.

Chapter 9 was first published as a journal article using a Creative Commons CC-BY licence that allows reuse and reprint: Christian Fuchs. 2016. Racism, Nationalism and Right-Wing Extremism Online: The Austrian Presidential Election 2016 on Facebook. *Momentum Quarterly – Zeitschrift für sozialen Fortschritt (Journal for Societal Progress)* 5 (3): 172–196. Published open access: https://www.momentum-quarterly.org/ojs2/index.php/momentum/article/view/1772.

An earlier version of chapter 10 was first published on the author's Huffington Post blog. He has retained the copyright of this contribution. Christian Fuchs. 2017. How the Frankfurt School Helps Us to Understand Donald Trump's Twitter Populism. *Huffington Post*, 18 January 2017. https://www.huffingtonpost.co.uk/christian-fuchs1/how-the-frankfurt-school-_b_14156190.html.

Chapter 11 was first published online. Reprinted with permission by LA Review of Books. Christian Fuchs. 2019. Henry A. Giroux and the Culture of Neoliberal Fascism. *Los Angeles Review of Books*, August 12, 2019. https://lareviewofbooks.org/article/henry-a-giroux-and-the-culture-of-neoliberal-fascism.

Chapter 12 was first published as a journal article. It is reprinted based on SAGE's Author Archiving and Re-Use Guidelines. Christian Fuchs. 2018. Authoritarian Capitalism, Authoritarian Movements, Authoritarian Communication. *Media, Culture & Society* 40 (5): 779–791.

Chapter 13 was first published as a journal article. Reprinted with permission of the journal *tripleC*. Christian Fuchs. 2018. Fuchs, Christian. 2018. Why There Are Certain Parallels Between Joachim C. Fest's Hitler-Biography and Michael Wolff's Trump-Book. *tripleC: Communication, Capitalism & Critique* 16 (1): 260–263. DOI: https://doi.org/10.31269/triplec.v16i1.1007.

Chapter 14 was first published as a journal article. Reprinted with permission of the journal *tripleC*. Christian Fuchs. 2021. How Did Donald Trump Incite a Coup Attempt?

tripleC: Communication, Capitalism & Critique 19 (1): 246–251. DOI: https://doi.org/10.31269/triplec.v19i1.1239.

Chapter 15 was first published online. Reprinted with permission of *TruthOut*. Christian Fuchs. 2019. Boris Johnson Takes His Brexit Demagoguery to the Social Media Sphere. Op-Ed. *TruthOut*, August 31, 2019. https://truthout.org/articles/boris-johnson-takes-his-brexit-demagoguery-to-the-social-media-sphere/.

Chapter 16 was first published online using a CC-BY-ND licence that allows reprinting. Christian Fuchs. 2019. Slow Media: How to Renew Debate in the Age of Digital Authoritarianism. *The Conversation*, April 23, 2019. https://theconversation.com/slow-media-how-to-renew-debate-in-the-age-of-digital-authoritarianism-113582.

Chapter One
Introduction

1.1 This Book's Chapters

This book asks: how is fascism communicated on the Internet? It outlines theoretical foundations of digital fascism and presents case studies that involve how fascism is communicated online.

The book at hand is the fourth volume of a series of books titled *Media, Communication and Society*. The overall aim of *Media, Communication and Society* is to outline foundations of a critical theory of communication and digital communication in society. It is a multi-volume book series situated on the intersection of communication theory, sociology, and philosophy. The overall questions that *Media, Communication and Society* deals with are: what is the role of communication in society? What is the role of communication in capitalism? What is the role of communication in digital capitalism?

Digital Fascism presents and engages with theoretical approaches and empirical studies that allow us to understand how fascism, right-wing authoritarianism, xenophobia, and nationalism are communicated on the Internet. The book engages with the theories of Theodor W. Adorno, Franz L. Neumann, Erich Fromm, Herbert Marcuse, Wilhelm Reich, Leo Löwenthal, Moishe Postone, Günther Anders, M. N. Roy, Henry Giroux, and Martin Heidegger. It presents analyses of how Nazis celebrate Hitler's birthday on Twitter, how user-generated ideology constructed a red scare 2.0 directed against Jeremy Corbyn, how right-wing authoritarianism utilised social media in the context of Donald Trump, Boris Johnson, and the Austrian presidential election, and how slowing down the logic of the media ("slow media") can advance and renew debate culture in the age of digital authoritarianism, fake news, and filter bubbles.

The book is organised in the form of fifteen chapters, an introduction, and a conclusion. There are three parts. Part I (Foundations) engages with theoretical and philosophical aspects of fascism (Chapters 2–6). Part II (Applications) presents chapters based on critical theories of fascism and empirical analyses of how fascism and right-wing

DOI: 10.4324/9781003256090-1

authoritarianism are communicated on the Internet and social media (Chapters 7-16). Part III is the conclusion that presents a concept of digital fascism.

The book follows the method that Marx called the advancement from the abstract to the concrete. In the Introduction to the Grundrisse, he described this method as follows:

> Labour seems a quite simple category. The conception of labour in this general form – as labour as such – is also immeasurably old. Nevertheless, when it is economically conceived in this simplicity, 'labour' is as modern a category as are the relations which create this simple abstraction. [...] As a rule, the most general abstractions arise only in the midst of the richest possible concrete development, where one thing appears as common to many, to all. [...] The simplest abstraction, then, which modern economics places at the head of its discussions, and which expresses an immeasurably ancient relation valid in all forms of society, nevertheless achieves practical truth as an abstraction only as a category of the most modern society. [...] The categories which express its [bourgeois society's] relations, the comprehension of its structure, thereby also allows insights into the structure and the relations of production of all the vanished social formations out of whose ruins and elements it built itself up, whose partly still unconquered remnants are carried along within it, whose mere nuances have developed explicit significance within it, etc. [...] The bourgeois economy thus supplies the key to the ancient, etc. [...] the latest form regards the previous ones as steps leading up to itself [...]
>
> The order obviously has to be (1) the general, abstract determinants which obtain in more or less all forms of society, but in the above-explained sense. (2) The categories which make up the inner structure of bourgeois society and on which the fundamental classes rest. Capital, wage labour, landed property. Their inter relation. Town and country. The three great social classes. Exchange between them. Circulation. Credit system (private). (3) Concentration of bourgeois society in the form of the state. Viewed in relation to itself. The 'unproductive' classes. Taxes. State debt. Public credit. The population. The colonies. Emigration. (4) The international relation of production. International division of labour. International exchange. Export and import. Rate of exchange. (5) The world market and crises. (Marx 1857/ 1858, 103–108)

In dialectical analyses of society, there is a dialectic of the abstract and the concrete. For understanding a concrete social phenomenon such as wage-labour or a society such as capitalist society, we need to understand what is common to all forms of work and all societies and how these general categories and the forms of them that existed in preceding epochs are sublated (*aufgehoben*) in the current social and societal forms.

If we want to understand how digital fascism works, we need to understand what fascism is in general and how it has worked historically. Our analyses and understandings of digital fascism should be based on and go beyond the analysis of historical examples.

Such insights should be the basis and inform our understandings of digital fascism. The analysis of digital fascism needs to preserve and at the same time go beyond its analytical basis. There are novel aspects in digital fascism that are expressions of general aspects of fascism and go beyond previous forms of fascism. The old and the more general aspects are sublated in the new and the more concrete aspects of the world. Hegel speaks in this context of *Aufhebung*, a term that is often translated from German into English as "sublation", a term that means substitution, elimination, and preservation at the same time. The German word *Aufhebung* means at the same time elimination, preservation, and lifting something up. Digital fascism is a preservation of the general characteristics of fascism. It also is in certain ways different from previous forms of fascism. And it is fascism organised on a new level.

Part I of this book presents general analyses of fascism and related phenomena such as authoritarian capitalism, ideology, nationalism, anti-Semitism, and racism. Part II presents more concrete analyses of right-wing authoritarianism and fascism on the Internet that build on the insights from part I. The conclusion to the book (part III, Chapter 17) brings together the analyses of the book, the foundational analyses of part I and the concrete analyses of part II, at a meta-level, and works out and presents a concept of digital fascism.

Each chapter in this book focuses on a particular dimension of digital fascism or a critical theorist whose work helps us to illuminate how fascism and digital fascism works. Here are the main questions that each chapter asks:

- Chapter 2: how can Franz L. Neumann's critical theory help us to understand fascism?
- Chapter 3: how can Günther Anders's critical theory help us to understand fascism?

- Chapter 4: how can M. N. Roy's critical theory help us to understand fascism?
- Chapters 5 and 6: what are and should be the implications of the publication of Martin Heidegger's *Black Notebooks* for the reception of Heidegger in the study, theory, and philosophy of media, communication, and technology?
- Chapter 7: how did Internet users communicate about Hitler on his 127th birthday on Twitter?
- Chapter 8: how was Jeremy Corbyn during the Labour Leadership Election framed in discourses on Twitter in an ideological manner and how have such ideological discourses been challenged?
- Chapter 9: how did supporters of the far-right Freedom Party (FPÖ) express their support of the party's candidate Norbert Hofer in the 2016 Austrian presidential election on Facebook?
- Chapter 10: how does the Frankfurt School help us to understand Donald Trump's Twitter authoritarianism?
- Chapter 11: how does the critical theorist Henry Giroux assess Donald Trump?
- Chapter 12: why is it that right-wing authoritarian populism in recent times has become much more popular than left-wing movements? How do right-wing authoritarian movements communicate? Why is it that right-wing political communication strategies seem to garner and result in mass support?
- Chapter 13: how did Donald Trump incite a coup attempt (the storm on the Capitol on 6 January 2021)?
- Chapter 14: what parallels are there between Joachim C. Fest's Hitler biography and Michael Wolff's book *Fire and Fury: Inside the Trump White House*?
- Chapter 15: how did Boris Johnson communicate about Brexit on social media?
- Chapter 16: how can the logic of the media be decelerated ("slow media") in order to advance debate and the public sphere in the age of digital authoritarianism, fake news, and filter bubbles?

In this book the readers encounter a number of theorists who will now be introduced:

Theodor W. Adorno, Franz L. Neumann, Erich Fromm, Herbert Marcuse, Wilhelm Reich, Leo Löwenthal, Moishe Postone, Günther Anders, M. N. Roy, Henry Giroux, and Martin Heidegger.

Theodor W. Adorno (1903–1969) was a German philosopher and sociologist who together with Max Horkheimer shaped the approach of Frankfurt School critical theory. Among Adorno's most well-known works are *Dialectic of Enlightenment* (written together with Horkheimer), *The Authoritarian Personality, Minima Moralia: Reflections from Damaged Life, Introduction to the Sociology of Music, Hegel: Three Studies, The Jargon of Authenticity, Negative Dialectics,* and *Aesthetic Theory.* Chapter 3 (Adorno and the Media in Digital Capitalism) analyses how Adorno's works can inform the critical analysis of digital capitalism.

Franz Leopold Neumann (1900–1954) was a political theorist associated with the Frankfurt School. He obtained a doctoral degree in legal studies at the University of Frankfurt with the dissertation *A Legal-Philosophical Introduction to A Treatise on the Relationship between the State and Punishment* (Neumann 1923). After that, he worked as assistant of Hugo Sinzheimer, who was a professor of legal studies at Frankfurt University. Neumann was a practising advocate who specialised in labour law. In 1927, Neumann together with Ernst Fraenkel started a lawyer's office in Berlin. They both worked for trade unions: Neumann specialised on legal cases for the construction workers' union, and Fraenkel focused on support for the metal workers' union. Neumann became the German Social Democratic Party's main legal advisor at a time when the Nazis and Hitler gained strength in Germany. When Hitler came to power in 1933, the legal office had to be closed. Neumann had to flee from Nazi Germany and went first to London, where he completed a second PhD, and then to the USA. His main book *Behemoth: The Structure and Practice of National Socialism, 1933–1944* analyses the connection of capitalism and fascism.

Erich Fromm (1900–1980) was a Marxist-humanist philosopher, psychoanalyst, and sociologist. He coined the notion of the authoritarian character. He was a member of the Frankurt School in the 1930s. Fromm's approach combines Marx's theory and Freud's psychoanalysis. He is one of the main representatives of Marxist psycho-analysis and Marxist humanism. Among his most important books are *Escape from Freedom, The Sane Society, Marx's Concept of Man, The Anatomy of Human Destructiveness,* and the collected volume *Socialist Humanism.*

Herbert Marcuse (1898–1979) was together with Theodor W. Adorno and Max Horkheimer the major thinker in the first generation of the Frankfurt School. He was a philosopher and political theorist who contributed to the development of Marxist humanist philosophy and the critique of ideology. He was influenced by Hegel, Marx, and Freud. His major books are *Reason and Revolution: Hegel and the Rise of Social Theory, Eros and Civilization: A Philosophical Inquiry into Freud, One-Dimensional Man: Studies in the Ideology of Advanced Industrial Society, An Essay on Liberation,* and *Counterrevolution and Revolt.*

Wilhelm Reich (1897–1957) was a psychoanalysts, political economist, sociologist, and sexologist. Reich was interested in the analysis of sexuality in capitalism and the connection of fascism, capitalism, ideology, sexuality, and the human psyche. In his book *The Mass Psychology of Fascism*, Reich analyses how fascists, especially the Nazis, gained power. He saw the authoritarian family is the cell form of the fascist state and fascist society. Reich anticipated and influenced the notion of the authoritarian personality that was developed by Erich Fromm and Theodor W. Adorno.

Leo Löwenthal (1900–1993) was a philosopher, sociologist, and cultural theorist. He was associated with the Frankfurt School. He had to flee from Nazi Germany to the USA. After the Second World War, he became a professor of sociology at the University of California Berkeley. Among Löwenthal's books are *Literature and the Image of Man; Literature, Popular Culture, and Society; Prophets of Deceit: A Study of the Techniques of the American Agitator* (together with Norbert Guterman); *Literature and Mass Culture;* and *False Prophets: Studies on Authoritarianism.*

Moishe Postone (1942–2018) was a historian, political economist, and critical theorist. He was a professor of history at the University of Chicago. Postone contributed to the reinterpretation and reactualisation of Marx's theory. Postone gave special attention to Marx's concepts of value that he used for grounding a critical theory of time in capitalism and to Marx's notion of commodity fetishism that he used for the critical analysis of ideology, anti-Semitism, and fascism. His major work is *Time, Labor and Social Domination: A Reinterpretation of Marx's Critical Theory.*

Günther Anders (1902–1992) was a philosopher and critical theorist of technology. He analysed how contemporary technologies are used by capital and bureaucracy for advancing alienation and destroying humans' control of society. Anders's most well-known book is the two-volume *Die Antiquiertheit des Menschen* (*The Outdatedness/ Antiquatedness of the Human Being*). Anders analysed the problems of technology in 20th-century society, the impacts of the media on human beings, destructive technologies such as the atom bomb, and the logic of fascism.

Manabendra Nath Roy (1887–1954) was a philosopher, political theorist, and anti-Stalinist communist activist who founded the Mexican Communist Party and the Communist Party of India. Roy was influenced by both humanism and Marxism. Among his major works are *Reason, Romanticism and Revolution, New Humanism: A Manifesto, Science and Philosophy, Fascism: Its Philosophy, Professions and Practice, Revolution and Counter-Revolution in China.* At the Second Congress of the Comintern in 1920, Roy presented supplementary theses to Lenin's *Theses on the National and Colonial Questions* and convinced Lenin to agree with his position. Roy put the interaction of capitalism, imperialism, and racism on the agenda of the international communist movement.

Henry Giroux (born in 1943) is one of the founders of critical pedagogy, an approach that combines critical theory and pedagogy. He has worked on the development of a critical theory of education that helps advance citizens' critical thinking and democracy. He is professor, Chair for Scholarship in the Public Interest, and the Paulo Freire Distinguished Scholar in Critical Pedagogy at McMaster University. Among his books are *Theory and Resistance in Education: A Pedagogy for the Opposition; Ideology, Culture, and the Process of Schooling; On Critical Pedagogy; Theory and Resistance in Education: Towards a Pedagogy for the Opposition; Disturbing Pleasures: Learning Popular Culture; Terror of Neoliberalism: Authoritarianism and the Eclipse of Democracy; Neoliberalism's War on Higher Education*.

Martin Heidegger (1889–1976) was a German philosopher who contributed to the development of phenomenology and existentialism. He was a professor of philosophy at the University of Marburg from 1923 until 1946. He was a member of the Nazi Party from 1933 until 1945 and welcomed Hitler's ascendance to power in 1933. *Being and Time* is Heidegger's major work. Heidegger's *Schwarze Hefte* (*Black Notebooks*) was published as part of the German complete edition of Heidegger's works. The first three volumes were published as one book in 2014 and unleashed a debate about Heidegger and anti-Semitism. Among Heidegger's students were the philosophers Herbert Marcuse, Hannah Arendt, Karl Löwith, Hans Jonas, and Hans-Georg Gadamer.

1.1 This Book's Chapters

Chapter 2 ("The Relevance of Franz L. Neumann's Critical Theory Today: *Behemoth* and *Anxiety and Politics* in the New Age of Authoritarian Capitalism") asks: how can Franz L. Neumann's critical theory help us to understand fascism? It provides some background of Neumann's life and works and shows how in the age of new nationalisms, rising right-wing authoritarianism, and authoritarian capitalism, Neumann's works can help us to understand society based on critical theory. There is a special focus on his essay Anxiety and Politics and the book *Behemoth: The Structure and Practice of National Socialism, 1933–1944*.

This Book's Chapters

Chapter 3 ("Günther Anders's Critique of Ideology") asks: how can Günther Anders's critical theory help us to understand fascism? Günther Anders (1902–1992) was an Austrian philosopher, critical theorist, political activist, and a writer of poems, short stories, and novels. Anders sees capitalism as having catastrophic potentials. This chapter analyses Anders' letters to Adolf Eichmann, the SS commander who played a major role in the Nazis' extermination project of the Jews; his exchange of letters with Claude Eatherly, who was involved in dropping the nuclear bomb on Hiroshima; his concept of annihilism (annihilation as nihilism); and his relationship to his former teacher and Nazi Party member Martin Heidegger.

Chapter 4 ("M. N. Roy's Critique of Ideology, Fascism, and Nationalism") asks: how can M. N. Roy's critical theory help us to understand fascism? Manabendra Nath Roy (1887–1954) was the founder of the Communist Parties of Mexico and India and a socialist-humanist philosopher. In the Western world, his works are today widely ignored and forgotten. This chapter introduces some philosophical aspects of Roy's thought. Frankfurt School thinkers such as Theodor W. Adorno, Max Horkheimer, Herbert Marcuse, and Erich Fromm were interested in similar topics as Roy. This chapter also compares the approach of Roy and the Frankfurt School. It shows parallels between Roy and the first generation of the Frankfurt School with respect to themes such as the dialectic of technology and society, the dialectic of the Enlightenment, fascism, nationalism, and authoritarianism. In the age of new nationalisms and authoritarian capitalism, global environmental crises, capitalist crisis, and the digital crisis, socialist-humanist theories such as the one of M. N. Roy can inspire struggles for a humanist and socialist society as antidotes to the acceleration and deepening of society's crises.

Chapter 5 ("Martin Heidegger's Anti-Semitism: Philosophy of Technology and the Media in the Light of the *Black Notebooks*. Implications for the Reception of Heidegger in Media and Communication Studies") asks: what are the implications of the first three volumes of Martin Heidegger's *Black Notebooks* (published as one book in 2014) for the reception of Heidegger in the study, theory, and philosophy of media, communication, and technology? In spring 2014, three volumes of the *Schwarze Hefte* (*Black Notebooks*), Heidegger's philosophical notebooks, were published in the German edition of his collected works. They contain notes taken in the years 1931–1941 and have resulted in public debates about the role of anti-Semitism in Heidegger's thought.

This chapter discusses Theodor W. Adorno and Moishe Postone's contributions to the critical theory of anti-Semitism and applies these approaches for an analysis of

Heidegger's *Black Notebooks*. The analysis shows that the logic of modern technology plays an important role in the *Black Notebooks*. This chapter therefore also revisits some of Heidegger's writings on technology in light of the *Black Notebooks*. There is a logical link between the *Black Notebooks'* anti-Semitism and the analysis of technology in *Being and Time* and *The Question Concerning Technology*. The first publication provides the missing link and grounding for the second and the third. Heidegger's works have had significant influence on studies of the media, communication, and the Internet. Given the anti-Semitism in the *Black Notebooks* and their implications, it is time that Heideggerians abandon Heidegger, and instead focus on alternative traditions of thought. It is now also the moment where scholars should consider stopping to eulogise and reference Heidegger when theorising and analysing the media, communication, culture, technology, digital media, and the Internet.

Chapter 6 ("Anti-Semitism, Anti-Marxism, and Technophobia: The Fourth Volume of Martin Heidegger's *Black Notebooks* (1942–1948)") asks: what are the implications of the fourth volume of Martin Heidegger's *Black Notebooks* (published in 2015) for the reception of Heidegger in the study, theory, and philosophy of media, communication, and technology? The fourth volume of Martin Heidegger's *Schwarze Hefte* (*Black Notebooks*) was published in March 2015. It contains philosophical notes written in the years 1942–1948. This chapter discusses the role of anti-Semitism, the hatred of modernity, democracy, Marxism and socialism, the belittlement of the Nazi system, and the opposition to modern media and technologies that can be found in the book.

Chapter 7 ("Fascism 2.0: Hitler's Birthday on Twitter") asks: how did Internet users communicate about Hitler on his 127th birthday on Twitter? This chapter analyses how Twitter users communicated about Hitler on his 127th birthday. It employs an empirical critique informed by critical Marxist theories of fascism. The analysis is based on a dataset of 4,193 tweets that were posted on 20 April 2016, and that used hashtags such as #Hitler, #AdolfHitler, #HappyBirthdayAdolf, #HappyBirthdayHitler. The results provide indications about how fascism 2.0 works. There are various strategies that fascism 2.0 uses, such as online authoritarianism, online nationalism, an online friend-enemy scheme, and online patriarchy and naturalism. The growth of fascism 2.0 is a consequence of a "fascism-producing" crisis of society that requires adequate anti-fascist responses and strategies.

Chapter 8 ("Red Scare 2.0: User-Generated Ideology in the Age of Jeremy Corbyn and Social Media") asks: how was Jeremy Corbyn during the Labour Leadership Election framed in discourses on Twitter in an ideological manner? How have such ideological discourses been challenged? The chapter uses ideology critique as method for the investigation of tweets mentioning Jeremy Corbyn that were collected during the final phase of the Labour Party's 2015 leadership election. The analysis shows how user-generated ideology portrays Jeremy Corbyn by creating discourse topics focused on general scapegoating, the economy, foreign politics, culture, and authoritarianism.

Chapter 9 ("Racism, Nationalism and Right-Wing Extremism Online: The 2016 Austrian Presidential Election on Facebook") asks: how did supporters of the far-right Freedom Party (FPÖ) express their support of the party's candidate Norbert Hofer in the 2016 Austrian presidential election on Facebook? The 2016 Austrian presidential election saw a run-off between the Green Party candidate Alexander Van der Bellen and the Freedom Party of Austria's (FPÖ) far-right candidate Norbert Hofer. This chapter presents the results of a qualitative ideology analysis of 6,755 comments about the presidential election posted on the Facebook pages of FPÖ leader Heinz-Christian Strache and FPÖ candidate Hofer. The results reveal insights into the contemporary political role of the online leadership ideology, online nationalism, new racism online, the friend/enemy-scheme online, and online militarism. Right-wing extremism 2.0 is a complex problem that stands in the context of contemporary crises and demagoguery.

Chapter 10 ("A Frankfurt School Perspective on Donald Trump and His Use of Social Media") asks: how does the Frankfurt School help us to understand Donald Trump's Twitter authoritarianism? This chapter uses the approach of the Frankfurt School for the analysis of how Donald Trump used Twitter. It utilises the concepts of the culture industry, authoritarianism, nationalism, the friend/enemy-scheme, militarism, and patriarchy.

Chapter 11 ("Donald Trump and Neoliberal Fascism") asks: how does the critical theorist Henry Giroux assess Donald Trump? Henry A. Giroux's book *The Terror of the Unforeseen* studies the contemporary negative dialectic of American capitalism and how this dialectic brought forth an authoritarian version of capitalism. This chapter provides a discussion of Giroux's analysis of Trump. *The Terror of the Unforeseen* analyses the conditions that have enabled and led to Donald Trump's rule, its consequences, and possible ways out.

Chapter 12 ("Authoritarian Capitalism, Authoritarian Movements, Authoritarian Communication") asks: why is it that right-wing authoritarian populism in recent times has become much more popular than left-wing movements? How do right-wing authoritarian movements communicate? Why is it that right-wing political communication strategies seem to garner and result in mass support? The critical theory of authoritarianism advanced by the Frankfurt School and related authors on fascism, Nazism, and the authoritarian personality helps us to critically analyse the communication of authoritarianism. In this context, particularly the works by Franz Leopold Neumann, Erich Fromm, Theodor W. Adorno, Herbert Marcuse, Leo Löwenthal, and Willhelm Reich are relevant.

Chapter 13 ("Why There Are Certain Parallels Between Joachim C. Fest's Hitler-Biography and Michael Wolff's Trump-Book") asks: what parallels are there between Joachim C. Fest's Hitler biography and Michael Wolff's book *Fire and Fury: Inside the Trump White House*? The US journalist Michael Wolff in 2018 published the book *Fire and Fury: Inside the Trump White House*, which is one of the most widely read and discussed books about Trump. In the 1970s, the German historian Joachim C. Fest published a biography of Hitler. This chapter discusses if there are parallels between the way Fest portrays Hitler and Wolff analyses Trump.

Chapter 14 ("How Did Donald Trump Incite a Coup Attempt?") asks: how did Donald Trump incite the storm on the Capitol on 6 January 2021? On 6 January 2021, supporters of Donald Trump stormed the Capitol after a Trump rally. The presented research analyses parts of a dataset consisting of Trump's most recent 8,736 tweets as well as Trump's speech given at the rally that preceded the storming of the Capitol. The chapter shows how Trump's speech and use of Twitter triggered violence and that the coup was the consequence of a long chain of events that unfolded as a consequence of Trump's authoritarian ideology, personality, and practices.

Chapter 15 ("Boris Johnson Takes His Brexit Demagoguery to the Social Media Sphere") asks: how did Boris Johnson communicate about Brexit on social media? Boris Johnson makes use of popular culture and social media as tools of populist communication. This chapter analyses how Johnson uses social media and what the implications of this use are for the public sphere.

Chapter 16 ("Slow Media: How to Renew Debate in the Age of Digital Authoritarianism") asks: how can the logic of the media be decelerated ("slow media") in order to advance debate and the public sphere in the age of digital authoritarianism, fake news, and filter bubbles? The rise of authoritarian capitalism has been supported by the capitalist media's logic of tabloidisation and acceleration. This chapter discusses how decelerating and decommercialising the media could help to overcome the culture of fake news, filter bubbles, and fragmented publics that have helped advance authoritarianism.

This Book's Chapters

Chapter 17 ("Conclusion: What is Digital Fascism?") draws conclusions to the book *Digital Fascism*. It engages with definitions of fascism and provides an understanding of digital fascism.

Reference

Marx, Karl. 1857. Introduction. In *Karl Marx: Grundrisse*, 81–111. London: Penguin.

Part I

Foundations

Chapter Two
The Relevance of Franz L. Neumann's Critical Theory Today: Behemoth and Anxiety and Politics in the New Age of Authoritarian Capitalism

2.1 Who was Franz Leopold Neumann?[1]

Franz Leopold Neumann (1900–1954) was a German, Jewish political theorist associated with the Frankfurt School. He was born in Kattowitz/Katowice. He was part of the left wing of the German Social Democratic Party SPD. Neumann was influential in the organisation of the Socialist Students in Frankfurt and participated in the 1918 November revolution. He received training in legal studies in Breslau, Frankfurt, Leipzig, and Rostock. He obtained a doctoral degree in legal studies at the University of Frankfurt with the dissertation *A Legal-Philosophical Introduction to A Treatise on the Relationship between the State and Punishment* (Neumann 1923). After that, he worked as assistant of Hugo Sinzheimer, who was a professor of legal studies at Frankfurt University. Neumann was a practising advocate who specialised in labour law. In 1927, Neumann together with Ernst Fraenkel started a lawyer's office in Berlin. They both worked for trade unions: Neumann specialised on legal cases for the construction workers' union, and Fraenkel focused on support for the metal workers' union. Neumann became the German Social Democratic Party's main legal advisor at a time when the Nazis and Hitler gained strength in Germany. When Hitler came to power in 1933, the legal office had to be closed. Neumann had to flee from Germany and went to London, where he started studying political science and sociology at the London School of Economics (LSE).

At the LSE, Neumann held a PhD scholarship and worked under the guidance of Harold Laski and Karl Mannheim on a second dissertation. As a result, in 1936 he obtained his

DOI: 10.4324/9781003256090-2

second doctoral degree with the work *The Governance of the Rule of Law* (Neumann 1936b). He moved to New York in 1936, where he became a member of the Institute of Social Research (also known as the "Frankfurt School") that was then in exile in the USA and associated with Columbia University. In 1942, he started working for the Office of Strategic Service (OSS), where he together with Herbert Marcuse and Otto Kirchheimer analysed Nazi Germany. After the War, he contributed to writing indictments in the Nuremberg trials. Neumann stayed in the USA. In 1948, he was appointed professor of political science at Columbia University. He died in 1954 in a car accident.

Alfons Söllner (2001) distinguishes three periods in Neumann's works and life:

1) The Weimar period up until 1933 when he had to flee from Nazi Germany;
2) The time of the Nazi regime and the Second World War (1933–1945);
3) The post-war time until Neumann's death in 1954.

It is "Neumann's unusual tripartite course – his path fro legal practice via confrontation with Nazism to political science – which is of general significance" (Söllner 2001, 123). In the Weimar phase, Neumann focused on legal practice and theory. The time of the Nazi regime and the Second World War was, according to Söllner (2001, 125), Neumann's most materialistic phase. Neumann certainly was always a materialist thinker, but this phase, in which he wrote and published *Behemoth*, certainly was one where he heavily engaged with and made use of Marxist theory. In the post-war years, Neumann contributed to the establishment of political science as a field in general and West German political science, and he also worked on foundations and various elements of a theory of modern dictatorship (Söllner 2001, 131). In the third phase, Neumann increasingly combined political theory, the materialist theory of alienation, and political psychology. *Anxiety and Politics*, the essay that *tripleC* republishes in 2017, was written during Neumann's third phase.

2.2 *Behemoth*: Franz Neumann's Analysis of the Structure and Practice of the Economy, the State, and Ideology in Nazi Germany

Neumann's (2009/1944) main book is *Behemoth: The Structure and Practice of National Socialism, 1933–1944*. It was first published in 1942. Neumann brought out an updated and expanded version in 1944. Herbert Marcuse (1941, 410) writes that Neumann's book shows that the "roots of Fascism are traceable to the antagonisms between growing industrial monopolization and the democratic system".

One of the book's basic hypotheses is that Nazism is not a state, but a form of political violence that Neumann based on Thomas Hobbes terms the Behemoth. Neumann argues that Nazism repealed the rule of law and substituted it by irrationality. "Behemoth, which depicted England during the Long Parliament, was intended as the representation of a non-state, a situation characterized by complete lawlessness" (Neumann 2009/1944, 459). For Neumann, Nazism was a lawless and irrational monster that he termed "the Behemoth".

Peter Hayes argues in the book's introduction:

> Like the Behemoth in Jewish mythology and the writings of Thomas Hobbes, Hitler's regime was a chaotic, lawless, and amorphous monster. Its policies expressed the sometimes overlapping and sometimes contending drives of the four symbiotic but separate power centers (the Nazi party, the German state bureaucracy, the armed forces, and big business) that composed it. Both the enormous might and the inherent vulnerability of Nazi Germany stemmed, according to Neumann, from its very nature as a conspiracy among these four self-interested groups, each of which sought to expand German power and territory without ceding authority or status to any of the other parties.
>
> (Neumann 2009/1944, vii)

In *European Trade Unionism and Politics*, Neumann (1936b, 85) defines fascism as "dictatorship of the fascist (National Socialist) party, the bureaucracy, the army and big business – dictatorship over the whole of the people, for the complete organization of the nation for imperialist war". Neumann here identifies some core characteristics of fascism:

1) Fascism is based on authoritarian leadership;
2) Fascism is nationalist; it propagates that "employers and workers work together in perfect harmony" (39) although class society and the division of labour continue to exist;
3) Fascism is a dictatorial form of capitalism;
4) Fascism uses militaristic means (such as war, terrorism, and imperialism).

A feature that is missing is that (5) fascism uses the friend-enemy scheme for creating imagined enemies and scapegoats in order to distract from social problem's foundations in class inequality and power asymmetries. In *Behemoth*, Neumann worked out the critical theory of fascism in more detail.

Behemoth: Franz Neumann's Analysis of the Structure and Practice of the Economy, the State, and Ideology in Nazi Germany

Neumann argues that Nazism consists of four groups all functioning based on the leadership principle: monopoly capital, the party, the military, and bureaucracy.

> Under National Socialism, however, the whole of the society is organized in four solid, centralized groups, each operating under the leadership principle, each with a legislative, administrative, and judicial power of its own. Neither universal law nor a rationally operating bureaucracy is necessary for integration. Compromises among the four authoritarian bodies need not be expressed in a legal document nor must they be institutionalized (like the "gentlemen's agreements" between monopolistic industries). It is quite sufficient that the leadership of the four wings agree informally on a certain policy. The four totalitarian bodies will then enforce it with the machinery at their disposal. There is no need for a state standing above all groups; the state may even be a hindrance to the compromises and to domination over the ruled classes. The decisions of the Leader are merely the result of the compromises among the four leaderships.
>
> (Neumann 2009/1944, 468–469)

Friedrich Pollock (1941a, 1941b) argues that Nazism was a totalitarian state capitalism, where "the profit motive is superseded by the power motive" (1941b, 207) and that it was based on the "masochistic submission to all kinds of commands, to suffering, sacrifice, or death" (1941a, 449). Totalitarian state capitalism would have been a new order that succeeded private capitalism (450). "The recognition of an economic sphere into which the state shall not and cannot intrude, so essential for the era of private capitalism, is being radically repudiated. In consequence, execution of the programme is enforced by state power and nothing essential is left to the functioning of laws of the market or other economic 'laws.' The primacy of politics over economics, so much disputed under democracy, is clearly established" (Pollock 1941a, 453). Max Horkheimer (1940, 1941) followed Pollock's state capitalism approach, although he more foregrounded aspects of ideology and instrumental reason. "*State capitalism is the authoritarian state of the present.* [...] The self-movement of the concept of the commodity leads to the concept of state capitalism" (Horkheimer 1940, 96, 108)

Neumann disagreed with Friedrich Pollock's assessment that Nazism was a new order of state capitalism that had replaced monopoly capitalism. In state capitalism, according to Pollock, there would be a primacy of politics over the economy. Horkheimer largely followed Pollock's approach. Neumann did not share the assumption that state power strongly limited capital's power in Germany. He rejected the term state capitalism and characterised Nazism as totalitarian monopoly capitalism. Neumann argued that Nazism combined monopoly capitalism and a command economy and did thereby not bring about a new order and did not replace monopoly capitalism. "The German economy of today has two broad and striking characteristics. It is a mono-polistic economy – *and* a command economy. It is a private capitalistic economy, regimented by the totalitarian state. We suggest as a name best to describe it, 'Totalitarian Monopoly Capitalism'" (Neumann 2009/1944, 261). There were both ca-pitalist and state interests (the latter involving the Nazi Party, bureaucracy, and the military) in Nazism that converged in the war economy: the Nazi regime wanted to arm Germany for an imperialist World War in order to accumulate power. Germany's large industry welcomed such efforts because armament meant its expansion and possibi-lities for capital accumulation. Whereas Pollock stresses more on the discontinuities between capitalism and fascism, Neumann tends to foreground the continuities.

Underlying Neumann's critique of the term totalitarian state capitalism is the as-sumption that "a state is characterized by the rule of law" (Neumann 2009/1944, 467) and that Nazi Germany was therefore not a state. Certainly not everyone will agree to such a concept of the state. Neumann (1936b) argues that the state in Nazi Germany was a racist state (559) and a leadership state (562), in which the "law is the will of the Leader in the form of law" (562). The rule of law did not exist (571). Instead Hitler and his cabinet passed laws per decree. The independence of the judiciary did not exist, the judge was "the absolute servant of the law, i.e., of the will of the Leader. [...] The judge was to serve the Leader" (573–574). There was no separation of legislative, executive, and judiciary power. Hitler had "supreme legislative and ex-ecutive power" and also took on "judicial functions" (577). Neumann therefore con-cludes that the Nazi state was "in no way a Rechtsstaat" (570). He here differentiates between the state and a state under the rule of law, and makes clear that Nazi Germany was a state without the rule of law. This does not imply that it is not a state. It was not an *Unstaat* (non-state), but rather an *Unrechtsstaat* (state of injustice, unjust/tyrannical state).

Herbert Marcuse and Franz Neumann were close friends. Marcuse's first wife died in 1951. Franz Neumann died in 1954. Marcuse married Neumann's widow Inge in 1956. Neumann and Marcuse's works also resonated in many respects. Marcuse shared Neumann's view that Nazi fascism was totalitarian monopoly capitalism: "For in the totalitarian theory of the state the foundation of this society, i.e. the economic order based on private property in the means of production, are not attacked. Instead, they are only modified to the degree demanded by the monopolistic stage of this very economic order" (Marcuse 1934, 21). In the manuscript *State and Individual Under National Socialism*, Marcuse (1942, 69) refers to the first edition of *Behemoth* and argues that Neumann has shown that Nazi fascism has not abolished monopoly capitalism. Marcuse writes based on Neumann that big capital, the Nazi Party, and the army divided power in Nazi Germany.

Some authors stress that there were major differences between the approaches of Neumann, Kirchheimer, Gurland, and Marcuse on the one side and Pollock, Horkheimer, and Adorno on the other side (Held 1990, 52–53). So for example Martin Jay in his book *The Dialectical Imagination: A History of the Frankfurt School and the Institute of Social Research* argues: "Franz Neumann's general indifference towards psychology was one of the factors preventing his being fully accepted by the Institut's inner circle" (Jay 1996, 87). "Behemoth did contain short section on the psychology of charisma, but it ignored the Institut's earlier work on the authoritarian personality entirely. There was scarcely anything in Behemoth's more than six hundred pages (including an appendix added in 1944) to suggest that Neumann accepted Fromm's notion of the sado-masochistic character type" (Jay 1996, 162). It is certainly true that Behemoth does not contain any discussion of Freud, which however does not imply that the book ignores psychology. Jay's criticism cannot be upheld. Neumann (2009/ 1944, 402) for example writes in Behemoth that in "terms of modern analytical social psychology, one could say that National Socialism is out to create a uniformly sado-masochistic character, a type of man determined by his isolation and insignificance, who is driven by this very fact into a collective body where he shares in the power and glory of the medium of which he has become a part".

It is an idiosyncratic critique to say that Neumann represents an orthodox Marxism (Jay 1996, 165) and "minimized the independent importance of anti-Semitism and racism in general" (162). Quite to the contrary, Neumann (1943, 27–28) stressed that anti-Semitism was "the most constant single ideology of the Nazi Party. [...] We may, indeed, say that anti-Semitism is the sole ideology that can possibly cement the Nazi Party [...] Anti-Semitism is thus the spearhead of terror".

In contrast, Rolf Wiggershaus in his book *The Frankfurt School: Its History, Theories, and Political Significance* argues that not only Neumann but also Adorno voiced criticism of Pollock's approach on Nazism (Wiggershaus 1995, 282), whereas Horkheimer defended Pollock. Adorno thought that Pollock politically assessed state capitalism too positively. Wiggershaus stresses the parallels between Neumann and Pollock and that their differences were rather at the level of words than of a fundamental theoretical nature: "Neumann's analysis of the relations between the party, the state, the armed forces and the economy made it clear that his differences of opinion with Pollock were basically quibbles about words. The development which Neumann described clearly pointed in the same direction as that for which Pollock had chosen the unhappy term 'state capitalism'" (Wiggershaus 1995, 288–289). The basic difference between Neumann on the one side and Pollock and Horkheimer on the other was that "Neumann insisted on the basically capitalist character of the Nazi system, and therefore thought the notion had been disproved that an unexpected new social formation and a fundamental anthropological transformation had forced their way ahead of socialism, overtaking all the hopes which had been raised in the previous decades" (289–290). Horkheimer thought that *Behemoth* left out the cultural-anthropological dimension of analysis.

A prejudice about the Frankfurt School is that it reduced Marxism to culture and ideology and ignored Marx's political economy. The way Marx understood political economy is evident in *Capital* Volume 1 (see Fuchs 2016). Marx starts the analysis of capitalism with the analysis of the commodity form. This analysis involves aspects of value, labour, and fetishism. Value and labour form the level of the productive forces, whereas fetishism deals with the way that subjectivity and intersubjectivity in a commodity-producing society appear as things and objects as well as with the subjective experience of humans in a society shaped by the commodity form. So a true critical political economy-analysis focuses on economy, politics, and ideology/culture. The Frankfurt School under Horkheimer's leadership advanced interdisciplinary studies that brought together many different perspectives. The works of Neumann, Kirchheimer, Gurland, and Pollock show that the analysis of the capitalist economy was an important element of the Frankfurt School at the time of Horkheimer and Adorno. "The work of Pollock, Neumann and Gurland is often ignored by critics of the Frankfurt school. If it were properly addressed, the charge that the school neglected political economy would lose a great deal of its force" (Held 1990, 360).

Behemoth is a good example: it brings together economic, political, and ideological analysis. Neumann starts the analysis with an introduction that focuses on Nazism's pre-history and context in the Weimar Republic. The book's first part ("The Political Pattern of National Socialism)" starts with remarks on Nazi ideology. Neumann (2009/1944, 38) argues that it is opposed to "all traditional doctrines and values", including liberalism, democracy, and socialism. The second part focuses on the "Totalitarian Monopoly Economy". The third part is about "The New Society" and focuses on Nazism's class structure.

Neumann shows how politics, economy, and ideology interacted in the Nazi system. In his analysis of Nazism's political system, he analyses how the leadership ideology, anti-Semitism, and racist imperialism shaped politics under Hitler. "The justification of this [leadership] principle is charismatic: it rests on the assertion that the Leader is endowed with qualities lacking in ordinary mortals. Superhuman qualities emanate from him and pervade the state, party, and people" (Neumann 2009/1944, 99). Nazism is ideologically an "Anti-Semitic movement" that advocates "the complete destruction of the Jews" (111). The compulsory acquisition of Jewish property and the Jews' deprivation of rights strengthened big business (117) and satisfied "the anti-capitalistic longings of the German people" (121). So terroristic state power had both economic and ideological dimensions and was driven by the political-ideological motive to annihilate the Jews. Nazism ideologically justified the Second World War as a war against "plutocratic-capitalistic Jewish democracies" (187). Imperialist warfare was justified as a "proletarian" warfare of the "Aryan race" against an imagined unity of capitalism, democracy, liberalism, socialism, and Marxism. Neumann speaks of the ideology of racial proletarianism (188). Nazism's military strategy both had an ideological aspect (the destruction of perceived enemies) and an economic dimension (the creation of *Lebensraum* for the biological expansion of "Aryans" and the biological and economic expansion of Germany).

In part two, Neumann shows that Nazism's economy featured compulsory cartellisation, the organisation of the entire economy based on the leader, the growth of monopolies via "Aryanisation", Germanisation, technological progress in the heavy industries, and the elimination of small and medium businesses, state intervention into the economy via the control of prices, investments, trade, and the labour market (the abolishment of workers' rights, the ban of trade unions and collective bargaining, compulsory labour). Neumann shows how ideology (leadership ideology, anti-Semitism), militarism, the command economy and totalitarian politics were fused into a total system of control, annihilation, accumulation, expansion, and imperialist warfare.

For the economic part of the book, Neumann could draw on knowledge by Arkadij R. L. Gurland, who like Neumann had fled from Nazi-Germany to the USA and was a researcher at the exiled Institute of Social Research. Gurland (1941) published, for example, an analysis of Nazi Germany's technology and economy in the Institute's journal. With respect to section 2.III (The Monopolistic Economy), Neumann mentions in an endnote that he "discussed all the problems of this section" with Gurland (Neumann 2009/1944, 503, footnote 38). Neumann writes in the preface that Gurland "placed his comprehensive knowledge of German industry at my disposal" (Neumann 2009/1944, xx).

In section three, Neumann shows how Nazism's ideology and class system interacted. Ideologically, Nazi fascism "claims to have [...] created a society differentiated not by classes but according to occupation and training" (367). But in reality it, under the ideological guise of racism and nationalism, would have "deepened and solidified" class antagonisms (367). Nazism organised society in "a monistic, total, authoritarian" (400) manner that was ideologically presented as an "abstract 'people's community,'" which hides the complete depersonalization of human relations and the isolation of man from man" (402). "The essence of National Socialist social policy consists in the acceptance and strengthening of the prevailing class character of German society, in the attempted consolidation of its ruling class, in the atomization of the subordinate strata through the destruction of every autonomous group mediating between them and the state, in the creation of a system of autocratic bureaucracies interfering in all human relations" (367). Nazism's totalitarian monopoly capitalism deepened capitalist class structure via a terroristic state that driven by anti-Semitic and racist ideology abolished the rule of law and exercised upmost violence.

2.3 *Anxiety and Politics* and its Relevance in 2017

Franz Neumann's article *Anxiety and Politics* was first published in German as *Angst und Politik* in 1954. The English translation was published in the volume *The Democratic and the Authoritarian State: Essays in Political and Legal Theory* that Herbert Marcuse edited in 1957 after Neumann's death in a car accident in Switzerland. *Anxiety and Politics* has again become of key importance in the times we live in today, which forms the background for the republication of the article in the journal *tripleC: Communication, Capitalism & Critique* in the year 2017.

In the article *Approaches to the Study of Political Power*, Neumann argues: "The devices and forms for the translation of economic power into political power thus vary considerably and yet patterns are discernible which ought to be more sharply defined on a comparative basis" (Neumann 1957, 14). Neumann here stresses that political economy is contextual and that the interaction of economic, political, and ideological power depends on specific societal conditions. We today live in a conjuncture of economic and political crisis that opens us power to changes and is shaped by two main tendencies.

On the one hand there is a tendency of the de-globalisation of the economy and the rise of more nationally contained economies, in which state intervention favours national capitalist interests and monopolies. To a certain degree one can here speak of some elements of state capitalism. Examples are the British decision to leave the European Union, which takes Britain out of a major regional free trade association, and the election of Donald Trump as US president. Trump has voiced criticisms of free trade agreements such as NAFTA (North American Free Trade Agreement) and TPP (Trans-Pacific Partnership) because he thinks that Mexico and China are threatening US jobs. Trump's critique is not a critique of capitalism, but a nationalist critique that pits nations against each other and disregards the underlying conflict between global capital and labour (Fuchs 2017). He seems to aim at a more nationally contained US capitalism that features low capital taxation and a high exploitation of labour as well as state power that is partly directly controlled by the billionaires and thereby intervenes in favour of US capital interests (Fuchs 2017). He also argues in favour of a "Keynesian neoliberalism" that makes public investments into infrastructure projects that are controlled, carried out, and whose results are owned by private for-profit corporations.

On the other hand we have in different parts of the world experienced an increase of nationalism and authoritarian power. Since the mid-1970s, neoliberal capitalism has become the dominant capitalist model and form of governance. It massively strengthened capitalist interests and weakened working-class interests by commodi-fication, privatisation, market liberalisation, deregulation, financialisation, international competition states, and a regime of low/no capital taxation. As a result, inequalities have been rising throughout the world. The world economic crisis that started in 2008 was a turning point: states turned towards state-capitalist measures in order to bail out banks and auto companies. At the same time, hyper-neoliberal austerity measures were launched. Right-wing demagogues used political fetishism for blaming migrants, refugees, welfare recipients, and other nations for the crises. Although there were some forms of progressive rebellion (such as the Occupy movements and the rise of Syriza, Podemos, Bernie Sanders, and Jeremy Corbyn), nationalism and authoritar-ianism have tended to be far stronger tendencies. They distract attention from class questions by presenting social questions in terms of nationalism and xenophobia.

For Neumann (1957, 2017), democracy is the unity of personal/civil, political, and social rights. Neumann experienced the rise of Nazism in Germany and how democratic rights were thereby undermined. Writing in the USA in the early 1950s, the time of McCarthyism, he feared the rise of a dictatorship and therefore warned that dicta-torships emerge when civil, political, and social rights are undermined and suspended.

The "transformation from democracy into dictatorship seems to arise when the political system discards its liberal element and attempts to impose a creed upon its members, ostracizing those who do not accept it" (Neumann 1957, 194).

> The real difference between democracy and dictatorship consists first in the boundlessness of political power of dictatorship in contrast with the voluntary restrictions which democracy imposes upon itself – that ant nothing else is the meaning of the rule of the rights of man; secondly, in the responsibility of the holders of political power to the people, for democracy is not direct popular rule, but responsible parliamentary or governmental rule in contrast with the theory and practice of the irresponsibility of a political power that rests upon the leadership principle. Thirdly, in a democracy political power is to be rationally employed, not only negatively to keep down private social power, but positively to shape a decent existence. This is often ignored.
>
> (Neumann 1957, 269)

Neumann distinguishes between simple dictatorship, caesaristic dictatorship, and totalitarian dictatorship (Neumann 1957, 233–256). Although it is untrue that Neumann ignored aspects of subjectivity in Behemoth, it can certainly be said that the book is more a combination of institutional analysis and ideology critique. The interesting aspect of his late work, including the essay *Anxiety and Politics*, is that it combines the institutional analysis of political economy with ideology critique and the analysis of subjectivity and socio-psychology. Neumann asked himself how it could be that authoritarianism existed as ideological and political movement and how it could be that citizens followed it. One can say that in his late work, Neumann tried to combine Marx and Freud and took up Freudo-Marxian elements. This becomes evident by the fact that Neumann in *Anxiety and Politics* discusses, quotes, and engages with Freud, whereas in *Behemoth* any such reference is missing. "Compared with the *Behemoth*, the emphasis on the economic determinants has receded, but only in order to place these determinants in a more concrete framework. [...] One of the problems with which he was most concerned was the support for dictatorship among the underprivileged masses" (Herbert Marcuse, in: Neumann 1957, ix). *Anxiety and Politics* tries to unite the objective and the subjective analysis of politics and capitalism. One could say it combines the analysis of Behemoth with Adorno and Fromm. It takes into account aspects of capitalist development, the state, ideology, and socio-psychology (see also Erd 1985, 200–206, 218–220).

Based on Freud, Neumann argues that fear can take on the role of warning, protection, or destruction. When in a society, where societal anxiety prevails, a larger number of

Anxiety and Politics and its Relevance in 2017

individuals identifies with a caesaristic leader and projects their anger and aggressions into an imagined enemy who has been constructed by ideology and a conspiracy theory, then the danger of dictatorship or even fascist dictatorship, according to Neumann, becomes real.

Destructive collective anxiety can emerge when one or several of the following factors are present (Neumann 1957, 288–293; Neumann 2017, 624–628):

a) The alienation of labour;
b) Destructive competition;
c) Social alienation: a group fears or is threatened by the decline of "its prestige, income, or even its existence" and "does not understand the historical process or is prevented from understanding it" (Neumann 1957, 290; Neumann 2017, 624);
d) Political alienation in respect to the political system;
e) The institutionalisation of anxiety (for example in the form of a totalitarian movement, propaganda or terror);
f) Destructive psychological alienation and persecutory anxiety.

Neumann gives the following summary of these six dimensions:

> Neurotic, persecutory anxiety can lead to ego-surrender in the mass through affective identification with a leader. This caesaristic identification is always regressive, historically and psychologically. An important clue for the regressive character is the notion of false concreteness, the conspiracy theory of history. [...] The intensification of anxiety into persecutory anxiety is successful when a group (class, religion, race) is threatened by loss of status, without understanding the process which leads to its degradation. Generally, this leads to political alienation, i.e., the conscious rejection of the rules of the game of a political system. The regressive mass movement, once it has come to power must, in order to maintain the leader-identification, institutionalize anxiety. The three methods are: terror, propaganda, and, for the followers of the leader, the crime committed in common.
>
> (Neumann 1957, 293–294; Neumann 2017, 628)

Neumann's analysis is so topical today because many of these factors are present in various parts of the world: neoliberal capitalism has intensified the alienation of labour, destructive competition, large-scale fear of social decline, political apathy, and a lack of trust in the political system, political parties, politicians and democracy, the institutionalisation of anxiety in the form of demagogic, nationalist, xenophobic far-right movements, and the large-scale psychological desires for not just social change, but destructive social change. At the same time, we have seen a relative weakness and fractioning of the political Left and a shift of social democracy towards the right and neoliberalism that has been going on for decades. Contemporary societies may as a combination of these conditions be at a tipping point, where quantity turns into a new quality. Neumann argues that persecutory anxiety can take on three methods: "terror, propaganda, and, for the followers of the leader, the crime committed in common" (Neumann 1957, 294; Neumann 2017, 628). In many parts of the world, anxiety has taken on at least one of these elements, namely right-wing propaganda. In some, it has also already taken on others too.

Consider the following two examples of political communication on Twitter:

Donald J. Trump: "It is time for DC to protect the American worker, not grant amnesty to illegals. Let's Make America Great Again! donaldjtrump.com". (Twitter, @realdonaldtrump, 23 April 2015)

Donald J. Trump: "We should be concerned about the American worker & invest here. Not grant amnesty to illegals or waste $7 billion in Africa". (Twitter, @realdonaldtrump, 1 July 2013)

How can *Anxiety and Politics* help us to understand the political-economic, ideological, and psychological dimensions of such social media postings? Trump appeals in his political communication to those who feel or fear the negative impacts of capitalism, neoliberalism, inequalities, unemployment, social decline, or de-industrialisation. He speaks to those who feel or have the fear that their labour is or could become highly alienated (a) and that capitalism's new-imperialist globalisation has resulted in destructive competition that brings about precarity and unemployment (b), to those who feel or fear that their social status declines (c), and to those who are fed up with the existing political parties, politicians, and politicians whom they see as corrupt elites (d). Trump himself is as a political leader and represents an institutionalisation of such anxieties (e). He communicates simple nationalist solutions to complex problems by using right-wing ideology as destructive political response to anxiety (f).

Trump's nationalist ideology claims he will bring about change that means a return to a better past. It says it will "make America great again". He says that the USA's national greatness is under attack by China, Mexico, illegal immigrants, Africans, the transfer of taxes to foreigners, and development aid. He identifies Americanness and the American interest with the American working class and un-Americanness with developing countries and immigrants.

Trump combines two semiotic chains: the chain of negative associations (amnesty, illegals, waste, Africa) is ideologically set into a relation to the chain of positive associations (protect, invest, concern, workers, America, greatness). The total message is that the USA is under attack and threatened by immigrants, the developing world, and everything foreign. Trump identifies US labour and US capital as having a joint national interest that is under external attack. He presents political-economic conflict as an antagonism between nations and thereby deflects attention from the class contradiction between capital and labour and power inequalities that are at the heart of contemporary crises. Trump communicates a state of exception and constant crisis that would require his political leadership in order to "make America great again". What is missing and what he tends not to mention is that US capital is transnational; it not just exploits US workers, but also migrant workers and workers in developing countries.

Right-wing authoritarianism responds to political-economic crises with ideologies that speak to disenfranchised individuals' psychology. Those who feel politically anxious have an ambiguous relationship to love and hate. They seek for an alternative and identity that promises them hope and they want to express their anger and aggression. Figures like Trump on Twitter and in other forms of public communication institutionalise anxiety by offering opportunities to these individuals for loving the nation and the leader and expressing hatred against scapegoats. Right-wing authoritarianism works on the level of psychological anxieties, desires, emotions, affects, and instincts. It often does not use rational arguments, but post-truth political psychology and ideology. A key question for progressive movements is how to respond to such movements. Rational arguments and statistics that deconstruct far-right claims are often not enough. The question arises what political strategies are best suited for turning the love for the leader and the nation into the love for humanity, democracy, and socialism and the hatred against immigrants and refugees into the critique of capitalism.

2.4 Axel Honneth on *Anxiety and Politics*

Axel Honneth (2009, 146–156) focuses in his essay *Anxiety and Politics: The Strengths and Weakness of Franz Neumann's Diagnosis of Social Pathology* in some detail on the article by Neumann that *tripleC* republished. Honneth is interested in Neumann's essay because it deals with social pathologies of society, a key theme in Honneth's theory of recognition. Honneth (2009, 150) claims that Neumann "distinguishes emotional or affective types of identification from those free of affective components. [...] He is convinced that this second type of identification is exclusively rational and, hence, does not constitute an example of individual regression". The implication would be that there is "an affect-free identification" (Honneth 2009, 151).

It is on the one hand true that Neumann distinguishes between affective and non-affective identification and considers the second one less regressive (Neumann 1957, 278; Neumann 2017, 618). But he considers the non-affective identification as operating for example between lovers and small groups and says that there is a co-operative form of affective identification. These considerations seem somewhat paradoxical because lovers certainly always have an emotionally driven relationship and Neumann characterises small group relations as both affective and non-affective. It seems therefore more likely what he has in mind is a Freudian distinction between an identification that is based on a dominance of the death drive and aggression on the one hand and one that is based on the life instincts on the other hand. The first has caesaristic and authoritarian potentials, the second co-operative potentials that can contradict authoritarianism. Both forms certainly involve emotions.

Honneth (2009, 151) continues by saying that Neumann assumes that all forms of ego-boundary dissolution are reactionary and irrational. He here seems to misread Neumann (1957, 278; 2017, 618), who says that the identification of the masses with leaders means "a nearly total ego-shrinkage". Neumann is in his essay only concerned with the love to a leader that comes along with persecutory hatred against a constructed enemy. He does not analyse co-operative love that is free of hate and the role of the ego in it. He rather leaves open this question. A fascist group always demands total subsumption of the ego to the nationalist collective and its leader. Collectivism and the collective identification with the leader as individual trump the individual. In a social relationship that is driven by co-operation, love, and eros without persecutory and annihilatory hatred against an ideologically constructed enemy and by the belief in a world of equal humans without the friend/enemy-logic, a dialectic of the individual and the group becomes possible (see Johanssen 2016).

Honneth argues that Neumann bases his analysis on a "Freudian orthodoxy" (Honneth 2009, 152) as represented by Adorno and Horkheimer at the Institute of Social Research (he forgets to add Marcuse). Honneth thinks that "psychoanalytic 'revisionism'"

(Honneth 2009, 155) as represented by Erich Fromm is more appropriate. As a consequence, Honneth (2009, 154) criticises that Neumann's approach would be "tailored so much to the exceptional case of German National Socialism". Honneth misjudges the strengths of Neumann's approach: by pointing out the role of conspiracy theories, anti-Semitism, terror, genocide, and annihilation, Neumann does not say that authoritarianism always and with necessity leads to Auschwitz, but that negative factories of mass annihilation are the negative potential of authoritarianism and can be its final consequence, which is why we better ought to be critical of it.

2.5 Franz Neumann Today

If Franz L. Neumann were alive today, he would stress that nationalism, xenophobia, and right-wing authoritarianism pose threats to democracy and the rule of law and that the key political task is to defend the civil liberties, political rights, *and* social rights that constitute democracy. The very problem is that neoliberal capitalism has so much undermined social rights that civil and political rights have become endangered by a negative dialectic that has advanced destructive political forces. The only feasible alternative is a democratic front that defends social, political, and cultural rights against the threat of right-wing authoritarianism.

Neumann's article *Anxiety and Politics* reminds us that in such situation, the role of academics should be that they more than ever act as critical public intellectuals:

> "Hence there remains for us as citizens of the university and of the state the dual offensive on anxiety and for liberty: that of education and that of politics"
>
> (Neumann 1957, 294–295)

> "Politics, again, should be a dual thing for us: the penetration of the subject matter of our academic discipline with the problems of politics – naturally, not day-to-day politics – and the taking of positions on political questions. If we are serious about the humanization of politics; if we wish to prevent a demagogue from using anxiety and apathy, then we – as teachers and students – must not be silent. We must suppress our arrogance, inertia, and our revulsion from the alleged dirt of day-to-day politics. We must speak and write. [...] Only through our own responsible educational and political activity can the words of idealism become history"
>
> (Neumann 2017, 629)

Note

1 For a detailed discussion of Franz L. Neumann's biographical and intellectual history, see Söllner (2001), Söllner (1996, 1982), Scheuerman (1997), as well as the interviews and conversations published in Erd (1985).

References

Erd, Rainer. 1985. *Reform und Resignation: Gespräche über Franz L. Neumann*. Frankfurt am Main: Suhrkamp.

Fuchs, Christian. 2017. "Donald Trump: A Critical Theory-Perspective on Authoritarian Capitalism." *tripleC: Communication, Capitalism & Critique* 15 (1): 1–72.

Fuchs, Christian. 2016. *Reading Marx in the Information Age. A Media and Communication Studies Perspective on "Capital Volume I"*. New York: Routledge.

Gurland, Arkadij R. L. 1941. "Technological Trends and Economic Structure under National Socialism." *Zeitschrift für Sozialforschung* 9 (2): 226–63.

Held, David. 1990. *Introduction to Critical Theory: Horkheimer to Habermas*. Cambridge: Polity.

Honneth, Axel. 2009. *Pathologies of Reason: On the Legacy of Critical Theory*. New York: Columbia University Press.

Horkheimer, Max. 1941. "The End Of Reason." *Studies in Philosophy and Social Science* 9 (3): 366–88.

Horkheimer, Max. 1940. "The Authoritarian State." In *The Essential Frankfurt School Reader*, edited by Andrew Arato and Eike Gebhardt, 95–117. New York: Continuum.

Jay, Martin. 1996. *The Dialectical Imagination: A History of the Frankfurt School and the Institute of Social Research, 1923–1950*. Berkeley, CA: University of California Press.

Johanssen, Jacob. 2016. "The Subject in the Crowd: A Critical Discussion of Jodi Dean's "Crowds and Party"." *tripleC: Communication, Capitalism & Critique* 14 (2): 428–37.

Marcuse, Herbert. 1942. "State and Individual Under National Socialism." In *Collected Papers of Herbert Marcuse, Volume One: Technology, War and Fascism*, edited by Douglas Kellner, 67–92. London: Routledge.

Marcuse, Herbert. 1941. *Reason and Revolution: Hegel and the Rise of Social Theory*. London: Routledge & Keagan. Second edition.

Marcuse, Herbert. 1934. "The Struggle against Liberalism in the Totalitarian View of the State." In *Negations: Essays in Critical Theory*, 3–42. London: Free Association.

Neumann, Franz. 2009/1944. *Behemoth: The Structure and Practice of National Socialism, 1933–1944*. Chicago, IL: Ivan R. Dee.

Neumann, Franz. 2017. "Anxiety and Politics." *tripleC: Communication, Capitalism & Critique* 15 (2): 616–36.

Neumann, Franz. 1957. *The Democratic and the Authoritarian State: Essays in Political and Legal Theory*, edited by Herbert Marcuse. Glencoe, IL: Free Press.

Neumann, Franz L. 1943. "Anti-Semitism: Spearhead of Universal Terror." In *Secret Reports on Nazi Germany: The Frankfurt School Contributes to the War Effort*, edited by Raffaele Laudani, 27–30. Princeton, NJ: Princeton University Press.

Neumann, Franz L. 1936a. *European Trade Unionism and Politics*. New York: League for Industrial Democracy.

Neumann, Franz L. 1936b. *The Governance of the Rule of Law. An Investigation into the Relationship Between the Political Theories, the Legal System; and the Social Background in the Competitive Society*. Dissertation. London: London School of Economics.

Neumann, Franz L. 1923. *Rechtsphilosophische Einleitung zu einer Abhandlung über das Verhältnis von Staat und Strafe*. Dissertation. Frankfurt am Main: Johann Wolfgang Goethe-Universität.

Pollock, Friedrich. 1941a. "Is National Socialism A New Order?" *Studies in Philosophy and Social Science* 9 (3): 440–55.

Pollock, Friedrich. 1941b. "State Capitalism." *Studies in Philosophy and Social Science* 9 (2): 200–25.

Scheuerman, William E. 1997. *Between the Norm and the Exception: The Frankfurt School and the Rule of Law*. Cambridge, MA: MIT Press.

Söllner, Alfons. 2001. "Franz Neumann's Place in the History of Political Thought: A Sketch." In *German Scholars in Exile. New Studies in Intellectual History*, edited by Axel Fair-Schulz and Mario Kessler, 121–35. Lanham, MD: Rowman & Littlefield. 2011.

Söllner, Alfons. 1996. *"Deutsche Politikwissenschaftler in der Emigration." Studien zu ihrer Akkulturation und Wirkungsgeschichte*. Mit einer Bibliographie. Opladen: Westdeutscher Verlag.

Söllner, Alfons. 1982. *Neumann zur Einführung*. Hannover: Soak.

Wiggershaus, Rolf. 1995. *The Frankfurt School: Its History, Theories, and Political Significance*. Cambridge, MA: MIT Press.

Chapter Three
Günther Anders' Critique of Ideology

3.1 Introduction

Günther Anders (1902–1992) was an Austrian philosopher, critical theorist, political ac-tivist, and a writer of poems, short stories, novels, letters, and diaries. He studied art, history, and philosophy in Hamburg, Freiburg, and Marburg. His teachers included Edmund Husserl, Martin Heidegger, and Ernst Cassirer. He defended his dissertation in 1923 at the University of Freiburg. Husserl was his PhD supervisor. Just like Herbert Marcuse, Anders turned against his former teacher Martin Heidegger because of the latter's role in the Nazi regime (for a comparison of Anders' and Marcuse's works, see Fuchs 2002). Anders published texts against Heidegger, arguing that his former teacher's philosophy was pseudo-concrete. Anders was married to Hannah Arendt from 1929 until 1937.

As a son of Jewish parents, Anders, like his second cousin Walter Benjamin, had to flee from Germany after Hitler had come to power in 1933. He went first to Paris and then to the USA. The rise of Hitler, Auschwitz, and the dropping of atom bombs on Hiroshima and Nagasaki were politically formative events for Anders that he reflected in his writings. In 1950, Anders and his then-wife Elisabeth Freundlich returned to Europe. They married and settled in Vienna where he lived until his death in 1992.

In distinction to the Frankfurt School critical theorists, Anders explicitly called himself a critical theorist of technology. In his principal work *Die Antiquiertheit des Menschen*, he studied the transformations of the soul in the age of the second industrial revolution. The German version of the two-volume work consists of 818 pages. The book has until this day not been published in English. The title can be translated as *The Antiquatedness of the Human Being*, *The Outdatedness of the Human Being*, or *The Obsolescence of the Human Being*.

DOI: 10.4324/9781003256090-3

Anders (1980a, 9) characterises his approach explicitly as "philosophy of technology". Other critical theorists, such as Herbert Marcuse, also wrote about technology, but did not devote entire books to such analysis and did not define their approaches as critical theory of technology. So Anders' approach is special in that he devoted a lot of attention to the critical analysis of technology's role in society. Anders argued that there are contradictions in society that shape technology and its use (Ibid. 126). He opposed the blind belief in technological progress as well as scepticism towards all technology. A dialectical philosophy of technology has "to discover and determine the dialectical point at which our 'yes' to technology has been transformed into scepticism or into a straightforward 'no'"[1] (Anders 1980b).

Günther Anders' "genuine interest in different aspects of what he analyses as a global issue of power abuse and repression [...] established him as a transnational intellectual" (Molden 2014, 69). Konrad Paul Liessmann characterises Anders as philosophy's outsider: Anders was a truly interdisciplinary thinker, who wrote "poems, novels, fables and tales as well as philosophical essays and treatises" (Liessmann 2014, 73). Transcendence was a key feature of Anders' works, as he "did not want to commit himself: neither to a provenance, nor to a future; neither to a style, nor to a genre; neither to a philosophical school, nor to an ideology; neither to an institution, nor to an identity; neither to a discipline, nor to a category" (Liessmann 2014, 73).

Anders (1956, 8) characterises his philosophy as occasional philosophy: it takes political and other events as occasions for philosophical intervention. Exaggeration is one of his philosophical methods (1956, 15). Anders (1980a, 411–414) says that his writings do not form a system and that Hegel worked out the last systematic philosophy. Because of a lack of translation of his works into English, Günther Anders remains one of the undiscovered critical theorists of society and technology. This essay is an introduction to Anders' main works. It asks: how did Günther Anders analyse modern technology? In which respects does his thought remain relevant in digital capitalism?

This chapter proceeds by discussing Anders' analysis of Auschwitz and Hiroshima as modern catastrophes (Section 3.2) and his criticism of Martin Heidegger's philosophy (Section 3.3).

3.2 Klaus Eichmann and Claude Eatherly: Günther Anders' Engagement with the Son of the Shoah-Organiser and the Hiroshima-Nuclear Bomb Pilot

For Anders, the 20th century was an age of catastrophe epitomised by Auschwitz and the atom bomb. The apocalyptic potentials of technologies and society has become so large that the Promethean gap creates apocalyptic blindness (1956, 233–308). Blind belief in progress is one of the sources of apocalyptic blindness (276–277). New nihilistic forces have been unleashed that have created the potential for the reduction to nothingness, the "reduction ad nihil" (239). In the age of catastrophes, nihilism and annihilation have merged into what Anders terms annihilism (*Annihilismus*) (304).

3.2.1 Günther Anders and Klaus Eichmann

Adolf Eichmann (1906–1962) was a senior assault unit leader in the SS, who in the Reich Main Security Office was in charge of the organisation of the displacement and deportation of Jews. After the end of the Second World War, Eichmann as one of the main people responsible for the Shoah escaped from capital punishment in the Nuremberg Trials by first going underground and then fleeing to Argentina. The Mossad transferred Eichmann in 1960 to Israel, where he was put on trial in 1961 and found guilty of crimes against the Jewish people, war crimes, crimes against humanity, the extermination of minorities, and membership in criminal organisations (the SS, the Gestapo, and the SS' intelligence service). Eichmann was sentenced to death and hanged. Klaus Eichmann is Adolf Eichmann's oldest child. In 1964, Günther Anders (1964a, 1964b) sent a long letter to Klaus Eichmann that was published as a book.

In this letter, Anders characterises the Nazi regime and the Shoah as a monstrous machine and coins the concept of Eichmanns. Eichmanns are the "administrators and performers"[2] (Anders 1964b) of monstrosities. Eichmanns are servile (carrying out monstrosities like any other job), disgraceful (aspiring to their positions), stubborn (willing to lose their humanity for gaining total power), greedy, and cowardly (Anders 1964a, 19). Anders' characterisation of Eichmanns reminds us of Erich Fromm's analysis of the fascist as authoritarian personality: "The love for the powerful and the hatred for the powerless which is so typical of the sado-masochistic character explains a great deal of Hitler's and his followers' political actions" (Fromm 1942/2001, 200). The Eichmanns' servility, disgracefulness, stubbornness, greed and cowardice are simultaneous expressions of striving for and submitting to power and executing violence against the powerless. Adolf Eichmann strove for power and in order to be powerful submitted to the Nazi machine's logic. As one of its powerful agents, he executed the regimes terror against its victims.

Eichmann is for Anders a symbol of the monstrosities that are an immanent potential of modern society and modern technologies. Anders in his letter explicitly refers to the Promethean gap without calling this phenomenon by this name (Anders 1964a, 24). The

Klaus Eichmann and Claude Eatherly: Günther Anders' Engagement with the Son of the Shoah-Organiser and the Hiroshima-Nuclear Bomb Pilot effect of the monstrosity of technology is that "the 'outsized' leaves us cold – or rather, not even cold (since coldness would also be a kind of feeling), but completely in-different; we are becoming 'emotional illiterates'"[3] (Anders 1964b). Adolf Eichmann's trial showed that he considered the killing of six million Jews with emotional coldness as a bureaucratic act and act of obedience. He considered himself innocent and argued that he was just a cog in the machine.

Hannah Arendt (1977) argues that Adolf Eichmann was not an extraordinarily "diabolical or demonic" person (288), but one of many ordinary, banal Germans. He was "terribly and terrifyingly normal" (276) in his worship of power as fetish. Monstrosity requires what Arendt terms the banality of evil at the level of the individuals and groups carrying it out. But in considering monstrosity and evil as banal, there is a certain danger of excusing the perpetrators, which became evident in Adolf Eichmann's trial. In his final plea, Eichmann argued that he was not guilty because he only obeyed orders:

> "The guilt for the mass murder is solely that of the political leaders. [...] I accuse the leaders of abusing my obedience. [...] Obedience is commended as a virtue. May I therefore ask that consideration be given to the fact that I obeyed, and not whom I obeyed. [...] I have already said that the top echelons, to which I did not belong, gave the orders, and they rightly, in my opinion, deserved punishment for the atrocities which were perpetrated on the victims on their orders. But the subordinates are now also victims. I am one of such victims"[4]. In his final plea to be pardoned, Eichmann wrote that there "is a need to draw a line between the leaders responsible and the people like me forced to serve as mere instruments in the hands of the leaders."
>
> (Kershner 2016)

Eichmann presented himself as a cog in the Nazi-machine. The machine would have to be blamed, not its cogs. Given that Adolf Eichmann was an ordinary and banal character operating as part of a terroristic machine, Anders raises an important question for the ethics of technology: given the uncontrollability and monstrosity of technical apparatuses, can humans be blamed for the machines' negative effects? Anders' answer is that those who are creating monstrous machines do so as a conscious act they could refuse. They are therefore morally guilty. Adolf Eichmann's "guilt in regard to the monstrosity remains monstrous. Why? Because he can't be considered just another one of the millions of workers trapped in their specialization, who as part of the processes of the apparatus to which they were bound really had been completely stripped of the ability to conceptualize its ultimate and monstrous effects"[5] (Anders 1964b).

Anders argues that the whole world has turned into a machine, the world machine (Anders 1964a, 52). Accumulation, expansion, colonialism, imperialism, and maximum performance would be the very principles of the machine (Anders 1964a, 50–51). The "machines' thirst for accumulation is insatiable"[6] (Anders 1964b). "*The machines are being transformed into a single machine*[7], the "total machine"[8] (Anders 1980b).

Without explicitly acknowledging it, Anders takes up the Marxist-humanist argument that capitalism's logic of accumulation results in dehumanising and alienating effects. Global capitalism is the world machine that Anders talks about. The world machine's effect is that society and humans lose their humanity (Anders 1964a, 55). Anders' deep humanism becomes evident when he analyses how dehumanisation works. Out of Anders' examination of the deepest inhumanity speaks the political demand for a humane world, a world that accords to human essence, desires, needs and potentials.

Anders' letter ends in the suggestion that Klaus Eichmann shows solidarity with the anti-nuclear movement as a symbol for the protest against the possibilities of anni-hilation. Anders' letter remained unanswered, which led him at the age of 85 in 1988 to write a second letter to Klaus Eichmann (Anders 1964a, 76–97).

3.2.2 Günther Anders and Claude Eatherly

Claude Eatherly (1918–1978) was an officer in the US Army Air Forces. On 6 August 1945, he was the pilot of an aircraft that supported dropping the nuclear bomb "Little Boy" on Hiroshima. Eatherly commanded the Straight Flush plane that explored the weather over Hiroshima and gave the "'go ahead' to the bomb-carrying plane to bomb the primary target" (Eatherly and Anders 1962, 81). Different from others involved in the bombing, who let themselves be celebrated as heroes, Eatherly was plagued by guilt. He unsuccessfully tried to commit suicide. Eatherly and Anders (1962) engaged in an exchange of letters about Hiroshima that lasted from 1959 until 1962. Eatherly was declared mentally ill and imprisoned in a mental hospital. The exchange between him and Anders provides indications that this was done to him because he spoke out publicly against nuclear warfare.

In his first letter to Eatherly, Anders argues that the atom bomb is characteristic of the age of the Promethean gap: "we can produce more than we can mentally reproduce; [...] we are not made for the effects which we can make by means of our man-made machines" (Eatherly and Anders 1962, 3).

Paul Tibbits, pilot of the Enola Gay, the plane that dropped the atom bomb on Hiroshima, recalled: "I just hadn't even come close to imagine what the effect was. [...] One man is gonna go out with an airplane and a crew and a weapon and do what thousand airplanes used to do"[9]. Tibbits' description precisely confirms that nuclear warfare is one of the realms in which the Promethean gap operates.

Anders argues that Eatherly's doubts and criticisms of nuclear warfare show that although the pilot had been "misused as a screw" in the military machine, he "contrary to others [...] remained a human being", or became "one anew" (5). Eatherly says in one of the letters that war "is wild and inhuman. War should not be done by *us*, the head of all creatures. It seems that those sleeping under the ashes of Hiroshima were crying for peace" (31). Eatherly expressed the need for "the banishment of all nuclear weapons" (81).

When Eatherly was offered turning his life story into a Hollywood movie, Anders warned him that Hollywood's focus on profit and entertainment could portray him as "a harmless figure who does not belong to reality but only to the world of make believe" (28). Anders here draws on his theoretical analysis of broadcasting's transformation of the world into a phantom-world. He recommended to Eatherly to first write an auto-biography and to legally demand that a movie would have to closely follow the book.

For Anders, Eichmann and Eatherly are two characteristic and symbolic figures of the age of the world machine. But the difference is that Eichmann never accepted any responsibility, whereas Eatherly changed his own political position and started op-posing the military machine that he had himself been part of: "No, Eatherly is precisely not the twin of Eichmann, but his great and hope-inspiring antipode. Not the man who passes off machinery as a pretext for renouncing conscience, but, on the contrary the man who recognizes machinery as the fatal danger to conscience" (Eatherly and Anders 1962, 108–109).

"[I]f we don't accept the Eichmann arguments, we are considered – even in those countries which to-day are actually revolted by the special case Eichmann, as being disloyal or being traitors" (Eatherly and Anders 1962, 126). Authorities stigmatized Eatherly as being psychologically abnormal because he questioned imperialism's ab-normal normality. Militarist ideology that is part of the dominant ideological narrative declares demands for peace as abnormal, war as peace, pacifism as violence, etc.

Herbert Marcuse has stressed that by ideologically and linguistically declaring violence to be normal, political horror is legitimated and rationalised: "Technological progress is accompanied by a progressive rationalization and even realization of the imaginary. The archetypes of horror as well as of joy, of war as well as of peace lose their catastrophic character. Their appearance in the daily life of the individuals is no longer that of irrational forces – their modern avatars are elements of technological domination, and subject to it" (Marcuse 1964, 253). Like Marcuse, Anders criticises the one-dimensional, instrumental language used by the powerful to downplay the horrors of mass annihilation. He for example writes that the use of the term "megacorpse" for one hundred million dead human beings in military jargon indicates that "the inhibition against weapons of mass destruction has also been killed"[10] (Anders 1982, 368). Anders argues that the ideological inversions of language and facts "vilifies us as '*troublemakers*' because we *cause trouble to their troublemaking*"[11] (Anders 1982, 370).

The Enola Gay pilot Tibbits also used this one-dimensional militaristic ideology that sees absolute violence as peace and that considers pacifists to be crazy. He argued that dropping the atom bombs on Hiroshima and Nagasaki "brought peace to the world at that time. [...] The morality of dropping that bomb was not my business. [...] Morality – there is no such thing in warfare. I don't care what we are dropping, an atom bomb, or whether you are dropping a 100 pound bomb, or you are shooting a riffle. You gotta leave the moral issue out of it"[12]. By arguing that war has no morality and that nuclear war is peace, Tibbits rationalises and defends his own role as the person who commanded the plane that dropped the nuclear bomb on Hiroshima. At the same time, he ideologically declares Eatherly crazy in order to assure himself of his own "normality" and the "normality" of the military potential to create a nuclear apocalypse. He says that he "never lost a night's sleep on the deal" and that Eatherly became "unbalanced after the end of the war, but he had had a problem of mental, should we say, incapacities/disabilities leading up to the war time"[13].

3.2.3 Annihilism Today

Comparable to Horkheimer and Adorno's (1947/2002) concept of the dialectic of Enlightenment, Anders stresses that capitalism turns against the Enlightenment ideals and produces catastrophic potentials.

Capitalism creates destructive potentials for the "self-destruction of enlightenment" (Horkheimer and Adorno 1947/2002, xvi). By turning into a destructive machine, Enlightenment "mutilates people" (Ibid., 29) although it sets out to advance liberation and democracy. Konrad Paul Liessmann (2002, 50) formulates how Anders conceived of the negative dialectic: "It is precisely the triumphs of human beings that distance them from themselves, transcend the human measure and create the tendency that the human being disappears"[14].

Similar to Horkheimer and Adorno, Anders argued that the Enlightenment's individualism and freedom backfired and turned the human being "into a screw in a machine of expansion that has been constructed by a minority"[15] (Anders 2001, 277). In Nazism, this screw "was allowed to carry the brand name of the'master race'"[16] (Anders 2001, 277). For Anders, Auschwitz and Hiroshima were the consequences of carrying capitalism to the last instance. Anders adds to Horkheimer and Adorno's analysis that the destructive potentials of technology are so big that capitalism's last instance can turn into humanity's final instance.

The number of nuclear weapons has overall decreased in the past decades. At the time of the Cuban missile crisis in 1962, the number was 29,150 (Norris and Kristensen 2010). At 69,368, the amount of nuclear weapons reached a historical high in 1986 (Norris and Kristensen 2010). In 2016, there were 15,395 nuclear weapons, controlled by nine countries (USA, Russia, UK, France, China, India, Pakistan, Israel, North Korea) (SIPRI 2016). But the nuclear arsenals are continuously updated, modernised, and supported by re-investments, maintaining that the nuclear threat of human extinction will remain a reality for a long time.

We are today seeing the development of a new dialectic of the Enlightenment that is spearheaded by figures such as Donald Trump, Nigel Farage, and Marine Le Pen. Neoliberalism advanced a narrow form of freedom focused on the freedom of the market and the freedom of private ownership. As a result, inequalities have risen and welfare states, and with them basic social protections, have been dismantled. Political agendas, including the social democratic agenda, have ignored the interest of the dominated class and declared class non-existent and a thing of the past. Neoliberal ideologues' common argument is that the rise of a new middle class has eliminated traditional class society. But today we witness the return of the repressed class in negative forms. Neoliberalism's contradiction between social freedom and market freedom backfired and created new authoritarian potentials, new nationalisms, and a heavily polarised political climate. Given that also some old authoritarians (e.g. in North Korea) control nuclear and other weapons of mass destruction, the clash of old and new authoritarianism increases the risk of humanity's annihilation. Günther Anders' warning that capitalism has catastrophic potentials remains highly topical today. As long as capitalism exists, we cannot rule out a crisis that produces fascism and new forms of annihilism.

3.3 Heidegger

In the years 1921–1924, Günther Anders studied philosophy at the University of Freiburg. His teachers included Edmund Husserl and Martin Heidegger. Socialist theory was in the 1920s highly structuralist and mechanistic. Many thinkers assumed that capitalism would automatically collapse because of the tendency of the profit rate to fall and that socialism would automatically emanate from capitalism. In the world of social theory and philosophy, thinkers such as Herbert Marcuse and Günther Anders searched for alternatives that were oriented on concrete human praxis. In the 1920s, both thought that Heidegger's philosophy offered such an approach. When it became evident in the 1930s that the concrete political project that Heidegger supported was Nazism, Anders and Marcuse were among the scholars who turned against him and started realising the problematic elements in their former teacher's philosophy. "Certainly, never before has a reactionary doctrine put on such subversive clothes"[17] (Anders 2001, 28).

Anders (2001) characterises Heidegger's philosophy as nihilistic existentialism because in it, "death is the lodestar of life and being is 'being-*toward*-death'"[18] (Anders 2001, 49). For Heidegger, being is characterised by death and the circumstance that any concrete being (that Heidegger terms Da-sein) comes to its end: "Factically one's own Da-sein is always already dying, that is, it is in a being-toward-its-end" (Heidegger 1996, 235). Anders (2001, 202) also criticises that for Heidegger not the human being, but Da-sein (being-there) is the subject.

For Heidegger, most being-there is inauthentic: "Factically, Da-sein maintains itself initially and for the most part in an inauthentic being-toward-death" (Heidegger 1996, 240). For Heidegger, being-there (Da-Sein, Seiendes) becomes authentic when one accepts the possibility of death so that death does not strike one as a surprise: "Authentic being-toward-death signifies an existentiell possibility of Da-sein" (240). "One's own potentiality-of-being becomes authentic and transparent in the understanding being-toward-death as the ownmost possibility" (283).

Anders argues that Heidegger leaves out the analysis of where alienation (that Heidegger refers to as *Das Man* [the they] or *Uneigentlickeit* [inauthenticity]) comes from and simply posits it as a priori. Heidegger does not see that "the 'they' that is being supplied with principles, opinions and feelings in the commodity form, is 'inauthentic' and 'dispossessed' of its own possibilities"[19] (Anders 2001, 54). For Heidegger, "the 'they' is not the result of a historical process, but an a priori 'who of Da-sein'"[20] (Anders 2001, 55). Heidegger ignored "the social struggles of his time"[21] (Anders 2001, 61). The *"real powers that be, are not worthwhile mentioning in*

Heidegger's philosophy" (Anders 1948, 354). Heidegger would not give attention to need, hunger, and capitalism: "For the fact however, that 'Dasein' is hungry, or, in more customary words, that *men are hungry*, we are looking in vain" (Anders 1948, 346). Although Heidegger talks about *Sorge* (concern, care), he does not concern himself with the "'Sorge-tools' of today, the economic systems, industry, machines" (347). According to Anders, also Heidegger's concept of historicity (*Geschichtlichkeit*) is pseudo-concrete: "State, economy, slavery, law – nothing of it is so much as mentioned in Heidegger's philosophy of history. [...] The fact that the major portion of history is history of *power*, thus history of the un-free, history *imposed* upon people, is totally suppressed" (360).

Because of leaving out the political-economic context of society, Heidegger's concept of being is "a hopelessly amputated existence that cannot give answers to the true questions, i.e. the true difficulties of our existence, because it does not ask them"[22] (Anders 2001, 50). "The reality of industrialisation, democracy, the width of the contemporary world, and the working class did *not* enter his philosophy – because Heidegger is a provincial petty bourgeois"[23] (42–43). "It is already Heidegger's fault that he only sees the 'they' as foil for the existence of the human being and that he does not see that it could be the task of the human being to create an authentic world that corresponds to the human being"[24] (58).

Günther Anders' critique makes evident that Heidegger's philosophy leaves a theoretical void, namely the question of how the alienation of society, alienated human activity, and alienated technologies are grounded. Whereas critical theorists such as Georg Lukács, Herbert Marcuse, and Günther Anders himself see alienation based on Marx's works grounded in class, capitalism, and domination, these dimensions of heteronomous societies do not exist for Heidegger. Anders argues that this theoretical void made Heidegger unresisting to Nazi ideology. "Little wonder that he had no principle whatsoever, no social idea, in short: *nothing*, when the trumpet of National Socialism started blaring into his moral vacuum: he became a Nazi" (Anders 1948, 356).

The publication of Heidegger's (2014a, 2014b, 2014c, 2015) *Black Notebooks* shows that in his thought world, he filled the void by anti-Semitism (for a detailed discussion, see Fuchs 2015a, 2015b, Trawny 2016). For Heidegger, Jewishness is associated with instrumental reason: "Jewry's temporary increase in power is, however, grounded in the fact that Western metaphysics, especially in its modern development, furnishes the starting point for the diffusion of a generally empty rationality and calculative ability, which in this way provides a refuge in 'spirit', without being able grasp the hidden decision regions on their own. The more originary and primordial the prospective decisions and questions, the more they remain inaccessible to this 'race'"[25] (Heidegger 2014c, 46). Heidegger does not see instrumental reason as a principle of quantification associated with class rule and bureaucratic domination. Given that he filled his theoretical void with anti-Semitism, it is no surprise that Heidegger became a member of the Nazi Party.

Anders (2001, 275, 70–71) sees parallels between Heidegger's and Hitler's thought, namely anti-humanism, anti-democratic affects, the doctrine of occupation, unscrupulousness, the metaphysics of death, and anti-civilising and anti-universalist ideology. "Both metaphysics simultaneously glorify and trivialise *death*. In Nazi metaphysics, this assumption takes on the form of education for war. War is seen as realising Germany's authentic Da-sein: 'We are born to die'. In existentialist philosophy, we find the transformation of death into 'being-toward-death' that allegedly is identical with authenticity"[26] (70). "These parallels show that the model of becoming-authentic is in both cases very similar"[27] (71).

In contrast to Heidegger, Hegel's dialectic of master and slave is, according to Anders, much more concrete than Heidegger's philosophy (Anders 2001, 61). It does not conceive of existence as singularity, but as contradiction. "This is the reason why Hegel is still more topical than Heidegger. [...] Because the neutralisation of existence by positing Da-sein as singularity results in completely undialectical Da-sein"[28] (61–62). "Being-without-dialectic"[29] (62) would be a characteristic of Heidegger's philosophy. According to Anders, Marx in contrast to Heidegger in his *Economic and Philosophic Manuscripts* and *The German Ideology* understands that the worker's being is inauthentic because"as incarnated labour time, he is being-for-another and being-owned-by-another".[30]

Pseudo-concreteness is for Günter Anders also a characteristic quality of Heidegger's concept of technology. For Heidegger, "not by staring at a hammer do we know what it is, but by hammering. [...] Are modern machines really 'revealing' themselves by their operation? Is their product their purpose? Is not their purpose to be seen only by making transparent much more than the machines themselves? [...] Operating a modern machine, does not reveal it at all; its 'alienation' is obviously reckoned with in present-day society and its division of labor. [...] that at the point where Heidegger seems to become 'concrete' or 'pragmatic', he is most obsolete, shows, so to speak, a machine-smashing attitude, for all his examples are taken from the provincial

Heidegger

shoemaker workshop. The alienation produced precisely by those tools that are supposed to be revealing, is alien to him" (Anders 1948, 344).

Anders argues that for Heidegger, the world is a *Zeug*-world (a world of things and equipment) with hammer, nails, and petty-bourgeois babble, a world that "resembles the rural shoemaker's workshop"[31] (Anders 2001, 212). For Heidegger, technology is artisanal and agricultural (Anders 2001, 287). "He is not interested in machines"[32] (Anders 2001, 258). Heidegger does not take into account that technologies serve "the profit need of the class that owns the means of production"[33] (Anders 2001, 213).

In *Being and Time*, Heidegger (1996) mentions examples of *Zeug*, namely "writing, materials, pen, ink, paper, desk blotter, table, lamp, furniture, windows, doors, room", "hammering with the hammer" (64). "The shoe to be produced is for wearing (footgear), the clock is made for telling time" (65). Heidegger's analysis of technology is a romantic idealisation of pre-modern times, of a world without electricity that is dominated by rural life, agriculture, and toil. Anders' analysis of technology in contrast engages with the technologies of his time in the context of capitalism and imperialism. Whereas Heidegger analyses technologies as such, Anders focuses on the mutual shaping of technologies and political economy. Anders therefore for example analyses television and radio in the context of capitalism and the atom bomb in the context of imperialism. Capitalism and imperialism do not exist in Heidegger's philosophy or his analysis of technology.

In those instances where Heidegger mentions modern technologies such as public transport and the newspaper, it becomes evident that he sees modernity and its technologies in general as inauthentic and "true dictatorship" (Heidegger 1996, 119). Heidegger's notion of being as being-without-dialectic results in a one-dimensional notion of technology that does not see any contradictions in the relationship of society and technology.

A truly Heideggerian analysis of the computer, the Internet, the digital, and data rejects the computer as such. It disregards the potentials the computer has as a tool of co-ordination in a decentralised democratic socialist economy and society, and idealises handwriting, paper, and pencils. But computing has in fact not outdated these technologies; rather, it has updated them. The computer brings a myriad of positive effects for the simplification of our everyday life. Problems emerge when instrumental reason shapes computing and society. When computing does not substitute, but supports human activities, then it can have humanising effects.

3.4 Conclusion

The philosophy of technology is very frequently associated with Martin Heidegger. The publication of Heidegger's *Black Notebooks* has made evident that his concept of rationality has anti-Semitic characteristics. Günther Anders stressed in his analysis of Heidegger that such problems and weaknesses have to do with the pseudo-concreteness of Heidegger's approach that leaves behind a theoretical gap and is blind to political economy.

Anders has in contrast and opposition to Heidegger elaborated a critical theory of technology. For Anders, technology is not simply a world of tools. Capitalism and im-perialism are themselves world machines for the accumulation of capital and power that shape and are shaped by machines reciprocally. Anders allows us to critically analyse how the technological fetishism associated with the Promethean gap takes on new forms today, such as that of digital positivism, big data fetishism, or post-humanist ideology.

In his analysis of commercial television and radio, Anders stresses aspects of labour, ideology, and their alternatives. Today, the users of social media are what Anders termed homeworkers. Their use of platforms such as Google, YouTube, and Facebook is digital labour that produces a big data commodity that is sold for enabling targeted advertising. The world of the Internet appears to have democratised communications, but it is today shaped by new power asymmetries in the online attention economy that features new forms of banalisation, unilateralism, di-vidualism, sensationalism, and anti-sensationalism.

Anders stresses that the interaction between technology, capitalism, and imperialism generates annihilatory potentials. Given that capitalism and imperialism continue to exist and today tend to take on authoritarian forms, what Anders termed annihilism (annihilatory nihilism) remains a constant threat.

At the international level, Günther Anders' work has thus far remained rather undiscovered, which has to do with the fact that his principal work *Die Antiquiertheit des Menschen* is yet to be published in English. Anders' works remind us that confronting the negative dialectics of contemporary society requires critical intellectuals and political praxis.

Notes

1 "den dialektischen Punkt ausfindig zu machen und zu bestimmen, wo sich unser Ja der Technik gegenüber in Skepsis oder in ein unverblümtes Nein zu verwandeln hat" (Anders 1980a, 127).

2 In German original: "Leiter und Handlanger" (Anders 1964a, 19).

3 In German original: "das ‚zu Große' läßt uns kalt, nein (denn auch Kälte wäre ja noch eine Art von Gefühl) noch nicht einmal kalt, sondern völlig unangerührt: wir werden zu ‚emotionalen Analphabeten'" (Anders 1964a, 28).

4 The Trial of Adolf Eichmann, Session 120, http://www.nizkor.org/hweb/people/e/eichmann-adolf/transcripts/Sessions/Session-120-03.html (accessed on May 3, 2017).

5 In German original: "Seine Schuld am Monströsen bleibt trotzdem monströs. Warum? Deshalb, weil er jenen Millionen von Arbeitern, die zu ihren Spezialhandriffen verurteilt bleiben, und die durch die Indirektheit des Apparatsprozesses, dem sie integriert sind, der Möglichkeit, sich dessen letzte und ungeheure Effekte vorzustellen, tatsächlich beraubt sind, nicht zugezählt werden kann" (Anders 1964a, 31).

6 In German original: Der "*Akkumulationshunger der Maschinen ist unstillbar*" (Anders 1964a, 51).

7 In German original: "*Die Maschinen werden zu einer einzigen Maschine*" (Anders 1980a, 120).

8 In German original: "Totalmaschine" (Anders 1980a, 121).

9 Paul Tibbets on Dropping the Atomic Bomb, http://www.history.com/topics/world-war-ii/bombing-of-hiroshima-and-nagasaki/videos/paul-tibbets-on-dropping-the-atomic-bomb (accessed on May 3, 2017).

10 Translation from German: "dann haben sie nämlich ihre Hemmungen gegenüber den Vernichtungswaffen ebenfalls vernichtet".

11 Translation from German: "die uns deshalb als ‚*Störenfriede*' verleumden, *weil wir ihre Friedensstörung stören*".

12 General Paul Tibbits: Reflections on Hiroshima, https://www.youtube.com/watch?v=nuYBxpKIMwg (accessed on May 4, 2017).

13 Ibid.

14 Translation from German: "Es sind gerade die Triumphe des Menschen, die ihn von sich selbst entfernen, das menschliche Maß überschreiten und den Menschen tendenziell verschwinden lassen".

15 Translation from German: "zur Schraube innerhalb einer, von einer Minorität konstruierten, Expansionsmaschine".

16 Translation from German: "zu einer Schraube, die die Firmenmarke Herrenmensch tragen durfte".

17 Translation from German: "Gewiß, noch nie hat sich eine reaktionäre Lehre ein so umstürzlerisches Gewand angetan" (Anders 2001, 28).

18 Translation from German: "[d]as Sterben wird zum Leitstern des Lebens, und das Dasein ein ‚Sein *zum* Tode'".

19 Translation from German: "das ‚man', beliefert mit warenartigen Prinzipien, Meinungen und Gefühlen, seiner eigenen Möglichkeiten ‚enteignet' ist".

20 Translation from German: "Denn für ihn ist das 'man' kein Ergebnis eines geschichtlichen Verlaufs, sondern ein apriorisches 'Wer des Daseins'".

21 Translation from German: "die sozialen Kämpfe seiner Zeit".

22 Translation from German: "ein hoffnungslose amputiertes Dasein, das die wirklichen Fragen, d.h. die wirklichen Schwierigkeiten unseres Daseins schon deshalb nicht beantworten kann, weil es sie gar nicht fragt".

23 Translation from German: "Was *nicht* in seine Philosophie einging, war die Tatsache der Industrialisierung, der Demokratie, der Weite der heutigen Welt, der Arbeiterbewegung – denn Heidegger ist provinzieller Mittelständler".

24 Translation from German: "Aber daß Heidegger allein das ‚man' als Folie für die Existenz des Menschen sieht; daß er nicht sieht, daß eine dem Menschen angemessene eigentliche Welt zu schaffen auch die Aufgabe des Menschen sein könnte – das ist eben bereits die Schuld Heideggers" (Anders 2001, 58).

25 Translation from German: "Die zeitweilige Machtsteigerung des Judentums aber hat darin ihren Grund, daß die Metaphysik des Abendlandes, zumal in ihrer neuzeitlichen Entfaltung, die Ansatzstelle bot für das Sichbreitmachen einer sonst leeren Rationalität und Rechenfähigkeit, die sich auf solchem Wege eine Unterkunft im ‚Geist' verschaffte, ohne die verborgenen Entscheidungsbezirke von sich aus je fassen zu können. Je ursprünglicher und anfänglicher die künftigen Entscheidungen und Fragen werden, um so unzugänglicher bleiben sie dieser ‚Rasse'".

26 Translation from German: "In beiden Metaphysiken wird der *Tod* zugleich verherrlicht und bagatellisiert; in der nationalsozialistischen durch Erziehung zum Kriege, der das eigentliche Dasein Deutschlands verwirkliche: ‚Wir sind zum Sterben geboren'; in der Existenz-Philosophie durch Verwandlung des Todes in das angeblich mit dem Eigentlichsein identische ‚Sein zum Tode'" (Anders 2001, 70).

27 Translation from German: "Diese Parallelen zeigen, daß das Modell des Eigentlichwerdens in beiden Fällen sehr ähnlich ist".

28 Translation from German: "Deshalb ist Hegel noch immer aktueller als Heidegger. [...] Denn die Neutralisierung des Daseins im Singular hat zugleich zur Folge, daß das Dasein völlig undialektisch ist".

29 Translation from German: "Dialektiklosigkeit".

30 Translation from German: "weil er als fleischgewordene Arbeitszeit anderem Dasein zu eigen ist".

31 Translation from German: "der dörflichen Schusterwerkstatt ähnelt".

32 Translation from German: "Maschinen interessieren ihn nicht".

33 Translation from German: "dem Profitbedürfnis der die Produktionsmittel besitzenden Klasse".

References

Anders, Günther. 2016. "On Promethean Shame." In *Prometheanism: Technology, Digital Culture and Human Obsolescence*, edited by Christopher John Müller, 29–95. London: Rowman & Littlefield International.

Anders, Günther. 2001. *Über Heidegger*. Munich: C. H. Beck.

Anders, Günther. 1982. *Hiroshima is überall*. Munich: C. H. Beck.

Anders, Günther. 1980a. *Die Antiquiertheit des Menschen 2. Über die Zerstörung des Lebens im Zeitalter der dritten industriellen Revolution*. Munich: C. H. Beck.

Anders, Günther. 1980b. *The Obsolescence of Man, Volume II: On the Destruction of Life in the Epoch of the Third Industrial Revolution*. Translated by Josep Monter Pérez. https://libcom.org/files/ObsolescenceofManVol%20IIGunther%20Anders.pdf.

Anders, Günther. 1964a. *Wir Eichmannsöhne*. Munich: C. H. Beck. 3rd edition.

Anders, Günter. 1964b. *We, Sons of Eichmann*. Translation by Jordan Levinson. http://anticoncept.phpnet.us/eichmann.htm.

Anders, Günther. 1962/2014. "Theses for the Atomic Age." In *The Life and Work of Günther Anders: Émigré, Iconoclast, Philosopher, Man of Letters*, edited by Günter Bischof, Jason Dawsey, and Bernhard Fetz, 187–94. Innsbruck: Studienverlag.

Anders, Günther. 1956. *Die Antiquiertheit des Menschen 1: Über die Seele im Zeitalter der zweiten industriellen Revolution*. Munich: C. H. Beck.

Anders, Günther. 1948. "On the Pseudo-Concreteness of Heidegger's Philosophy." *Philosophy and Phenomenological Research* 8 (3): 337–71.

Arendt, Hannah. 1977. *Eichmann in Jerusalem: A Report of the Banality of Evil*. New York: Penguin Books.

Eatherly, Claude, and Günther Anders. 1962. *Burning Conscience*. New York: Monthly Review Press.

Fromm, Erich. 1942/2001. *The Fear of Freedom*. Abingdon: Routledge.

Fuchs, Christian. 2015a. "Martin-Heidegger's Anti-Semitism: Philosophy of Technology and the Media in the Light of the "Black Notebooks"." *Implications for the Reception of Heidegger in Media and Communication Studies. tripleC: Communication, Capitalism & Critique* 13 (1): 55–78.

Fuchs, Christian. 2015b. "Anti-Semitism, Anti-Marxism, and Technophobia: The Fourth Volume of Martin Heidegger's *Black Notebooks* (1942–1948)." *tripleC: Communication, Capitalism & Critique* 13 (1): 93–100.

Fuchs, Christian. 2002. "Zu einigen Parallelen und Differenzen im Denken von Günther Anders und Herbert Macuse." In *Geheimagent der Masseneremiten – Günther Anders*, edited by Dirk Röpcke and Raimund Bahr, 113–27. St. Wolfgang: Edition Art & Science.

Heidegger, Martin. 2015. *Anmerkungen I-V (Schwarze Hefte 1942–1948). Gesamtausgabe, Band 97*. Frankfurt am Main: Klostermann.

Heidegger, Martin. 2014a. *Gesamtausgabe, Band 94: Überlegungen II-VI (1931–1938)*. Frankfurt am Main: Klostermann.

Heidegger, Martin. 2014b. *Gesamtausgabe, Band 95: Überlegungen VII-XI (1938/1939)*. Frankfurt am Main: Klostermann.

Heidegger, Martin. 2014c. *Gesamtausgabe, Band 96: Überlegungen XII-XV (1939–1941)*. Frankfurt am Main: Klostermann.

Heidegger, Martin. 1996. *Being and Time*. Albany, NY: State University of New York Press.

Horkheimer, Max and Theodor W. Adorno. 1947/2002. *Dialectic of Enlightenment. Philosophical Fragments*. Stanford, CA: Stanford University Press.

Kershner, Isabel. 2016. Pardon Plea by Adolf Eichmann, Nazi War Criminal, Is Made Public. New York Times Online, January 27, 2016.

Liessmann, Konrad Paul. 2014. "Between the Chairs: Günther Anders – Philosophy's Outsider." In *The Life and Work of Günther Anders: Émigré, Iconoclast, Philosopher, Man of Letters*, edited by Günter Bischof, Jason Dawsey, and Bernhard Fetz, 73–82. Innsbruck: Studienverlag.

Liessmann, Konrad Paul. 2002. *Günther Anders: Philosophieren im Zeitalter der technologischen Revolutionen*. Munich: C. H. Beck.

Marcuse, Herbert. 1964. *One-Dimensional Man*. London: Routledge.

Molden, Berthold. 2014. "Günther Anders as a Transnational Intellectual in the 1960s." In *The Life and Work of Günther Anders: Émigré, Iconoclast, Philosopher, Man of Letters*, edited by Günter Bischof, Jason Dawsey, and Bernhard Fetz, 59–69. Innsbruck: Studienverlag.

Norris, Robert S., and Hans M. Kristensen. 2010. Global Nuclear Weapons Inventories, 1945–2010. *Bulletin of the Atomic Scientists* 66 (4): 77–83.

Stockholm International Peace Research Institute (SIPRI). 2016. *Global Nuclear Weapons: Downsizing But Modernizing*. https://www.sipri.org/media/press-release/2016/global-nuclear-weapons-downsizing-modernizing.

Trawny, Peter. 2016. *Heidegger & the Myth of A Jewish World Conspiracy*. Chicago, IL: University of Chicago Press.

References

Chapter Four
M. N. Roy's Critique of Ideology, Fascism, and Nationalism

4.1 Introduction

This chapter asks: how can M. N. Roy's radical, Marxist humanism inform the critical study of ideology, fascism, and nationalism? What commonalities are there between Roy's approach and Frankfurt School critical theory?

Manabendra Nath (M. N.) Roy (1887–1954) was a Marxist-humanist thinker and politician. As humanist he opposed Stalinism, Gandhism, and the Indian National Congress' and its leader Subhas Chandra Bose's political position towards Hitler and the Nazis, which placed him outside of the mainstream of both the communist and the anti-colonial movement, which contributed to "the forgetting of M. N. Roy" him being "lost to the historical record" (Manjapra 2010, xiv). He experienced turmoil, wars, and transitions in the 20th century and was a contemporary of Frankfurt School thinkers such as Theodor W. Adorno, Max Horkheimer, and Herbert Marcuse. Coming from India and spending 16 years (1915–1931) in countries such as the USA, Mexico, Germany, Tashkent, France, Luxembourg, and China (see Ray 2016a), he experienced capitalism and colonialism in various parts of the world.

Both Roy and the Frankfurt School were inspired by Marx and humanism and were interested in similar topics such as the human being, technology, culture, communication, ideology, liberalism, fascism, authoritarianism, and nationalism. Roy wrote his book *Revolution and Counter-Revolution in China* in the late 1920s while being connected to the Frankfurt Institute for School Research (Manjapra 2010, xiii, 70, 84, 91 [footnote 27]). In Germany, August Thalheimer became a close friend of Roy and Roy

DOI: 10.4324/9781003256090-4

conversed in communist circles with the likes of Karl Korsch, Georg Lukács, Eduard Fuchs, Willi Münzberg, Franz Mehring, or Felix Weil (Manjapra 2010, 39–40, 67–70). The latter funded the Institute for Social Research.

Subhrajit Bhattacharya (2016, 1432) points out that Roy and Horkheimer at the same time in the 1930s "sought to understand the regression of 'civilisation' in the light of philosophy, one in an Indian prison, another in his exile years in America". Both Roy and the Frankfurt School took a critical interdisciplinary approach that combined political economy, philosophy, sociology, psychoanalysis, and cultural criticism. It is interesting to compare the approaches of Roy and the first generation of the Frankfurt School in respect to the themes of the human being, technology, culture/communication, ideology, liberalism, fascism, authoritarianism, and nationalism.

As introduction, some aspects of Roy's biography will now be discussed (for details see Manjapra 2010, Roy, 1997, Tarkunde 1982). Roy came from a Brahmin family in Bengal. He became a "full-blooded [Indian] nationalist" (Roy 1942, iii) who was convinced that Indian culture was superior to Western culture and determined to organise an armed revolution against the British rule of India. Observers identify three stages in Roy's political development: he "started as an ardent nationalist, became an equally ardent communist and ended as a creatively active Radical Humanist" (Tarkunde 1982, v).

After the first phase in his political development Roy in the second stage became a communist at the time when he was going abroad during the First World War. Roy was a founder of the Mexican Communist Party in 1917 and the Communist Party of India in the 1920s. While staying abroad in the USA and Mexico he gave up the belief that there was a progressive element in nationalism and embraced aspects of Western culture (Roy 1987, 1–13). In the 1920s, he was a member of the Communist International (Comintern)'s Presidium.

At the Second Congress of the Comintern in 1920, Lenin (1920) presented *Theses on the National and Colonial Questions*. Lenin argued that the "entire [communist] policy on the national and the colonial questions should rest primarily on a closer union of the proletarians and the working masses of all nations and countries for a joint revolutionary struggle to overthrow the landowners and the bourgeoisie" (Lenin 1920, 146). Roy (1920) presented *Supplementary Theses on the National and Colonial Question* that were more detailed than Lenin's theses and resulted in Lenin taking up Roy's inputs and agreeing with Roy. In his theses, Roy (1920) argued that European capitalism "depends on control of extensive colonial markets and a broad field of opportunities for exploitation" in order to counter overproduction, that the "super-profits made in the colonies form one of the main sources of the resources of contemporary capitalism", and that therefore the "Communist International must enter into much closer connection with the revolutionary forces that are at present participating in the overthrow of imperialism in the politically and economically oppressed countries".

Roy was expelled from the Comintern in 1929. He was close to Bukharin, whom Stalin wanted to get rid of, and supported anti-Stalinist Marxist movements such as the Communist Party of Germany (Opposition) (KPO), whose leader August Thalheimer was a friend and ally of Roy, and was part of the International Communist Opposition. Communists around Thalheimer and Heinrich Brandler opposed the Stalinist position that the social democrats were the main enemy of the working class. Stalinists described social democrats as "social fascists", and did not enough focus on the critique of Nazi-fascism. Members of the Communist opposition movement such as Thalheimer argued for a united front of social democrats and communists against Nazi-fascism. Roy wrote for the KPO's publications and found the notion of the united front of the exploited and oppressed feasible for struggles in the colonies (see Roy 1929a, 1929b). As a result, Stalinists started to oppose him, which resulted in his expulsion from the Comintern (see Ray 2016b). The Stalinists accused the likes of Thalheimer, Brandler, and Roy of "Luxemburgism" (Manjapra 2010, 43–44, 70–71, 86–87, which, given Rosa Luxemburg's fusion of socialism, Marxism, and humanism, Roy and his comrades did not take as an insult but as the confirmation that they were true communists.

In his third, humanist phase, Roy combined Marxism and humanism. In the 1930s, he joined the Congress Party, where he was active in the socialist faction. He broke with Congress during the Second World World over the question of how Congress should position itself towards Nazi-fascism and the Allied powers. Roy argued that fascism was the world's greatest danger and for the support of the Allies. Others in Congress, such as Gandhi, said that there should only be support on the condition of Indian independence. Gandhi saw Roy as his "enemy number one" (Roy, 1987, 17), whereas Roy characterised Gandhi as "the patron saint of [Indian] nationalism" (Roy, 1987, 67; Roy 1968, 29).

In 1932, Roy was sentenced to 12 years in prison for having conspired to the Kind Emperor of his sovereignty in India in the 1920s. The time he served was reduced so that he was released in late 1936. He was a vocal critic and opponent of Italian and

Introduction

German fascism. Roy founded the League of Radical Congressmen in 1938, the Radical Democratic Party in 1940, and the Radical Humanist Movement in 1948. The Radical Humanist Movement in 1952 together with other humanist movements founded the International Humanist and Ethical Union that is today known as Humanists International.

Whereas Roy (1922) during his communist phase argued for "[r]evolutionary nationalism" (1922, 177) that he distinguished from "reactionary nationalism" (1922, 166, 216; see the same phrases in Roy 1923, 42, 44), during his humanist phase he opposed "capitalist as well as socialist Nationalism" (Roy 1947/1960, 102) and argued that any nationalism is "a totalitarian cult" (1947/1960, 84) that needs to be replaced by the universal "brotherhood of free individuals" (1947/1960, 102) and the "cosmopolitan commonwealth of free men and women" that is "not compatible with the continuation of National States" (Roy 1953, 35).

Although some attention has been given to Roy's work in India, his philosophy and theory is widely forgotten. Roy's magnus opus *Reason, Romanticism and Revolution* that has a great deal in common with Horkheimer and Adorno's *Dialectic of Enlightenment* is a forgotten and undiscovered work. In September 2019, Roy's main book that was published in two volumes in 1952 (volume 1) and 1955 (volume 2) had only 23 citations on Google Scholar.[1] One of the purposes of this chapter is therefore to point critical scholars in the social sciences, humanities, communication and cultural studies towards Roy's works by introducing some important aspects of it.

In order to answer the research question that this chapter poses, it discusses four aspects of Roy's works and assesses their relevance for a critical theory of communication and culture. These themes are ideology (Section 4.2), liberalism as ideology (Section 4.3), nationalism (Section 4.4), and fascism (Section 4.4). Section 4.5 draws some conclusions.

4.2 Ideology

"An ideology is a system of ideas; in other words, an ideology is the ideal sanction for social and political practices" (Roy 1947/1960, 67). Roy has a general understanding of ideology and differs in this respect from thinkers such as Georg Lukács (1971, 66), who sees ideology as reified consciousness that legitimates the interest of the ruling class by trying to "deceive the other classes and to ensure that their class consciousness remains amorphous" or Theodor W. Adorno, who understands ideology as "a consciousness which is objectively necessary and yet at the same time false, as the intertwining of truth and falsehood" (Adorno 1954, 189).

Such critical concepts of ideology stress the illusionary and manufactured character of ideas that make up an ideology and their legitimating role in the class structure. Roy speaks of an "ideal sanction for social and political practices", which can in one sense be understood as legitimation of class relations but is on the other hand formulated in a very general manner, which makes it sound like for Roy ideology exists in all society and not just, as for Lukács, in class societies.

Leaving aside problems of definitions, Roy in his works analyses the ideological structure of some of the main ideologies of the capitalist age, namely liberalism (Section 4.3), nationalism (Section 4.4), and fascism (Section 4.4).

4.3 Liberalism and the Dialectic of Enlightenment

The Enlightenment was a movement against the power of the church, the monarch, and the aristocracy. In the 19th century, liberalism started taking on the form of utilitarianism. Thinkers such as David Hume (1711–1776), Jeremy Bentham (1748–1832), James Mill (1773–1836), and John Stuart Mill (1806–1873) influenced utilitarian thought. "[T]he liberal doctrine of *laisser faire* served the purpose of rising Capitalism; and the rule of law came to be the rule of a minority which under the given circumstances had the power to make laws. Liberalism appeared to provide a moral justification of the economic exploitation of man by man and a philosophical sanction for the modern political theories which subordinated the individual to the State" (1989, 330). Liberal practice has in capitalism undermined the principle of freedom and liberties for all.

Utilitarianism's principle of maximising the individual utility and happiness as much as possible and doing so for the greatest number of individuals is for Roy based on a "clash of two categorial imperatives" (1989, 340), an individualistic and a collectivistic one. The one side of this antagonism bears a potential for the advancement of economic individualism in the form of laissez faire-style capitalism that postulates profit maximisation with no government intervention into the economy (342). The other side of the antagonism fetishises collectivism (happiness of the largest number of people) at the expense of universal rights of all individuals. "The orthodox utilitarian dictum logically justifies suppression of a minority even of forty-nine (because fifty-one is a greater number)" (347). It therefore has the potential to provide "a moral sanction for the various totalitarian cults" (340), to undermine "the equality of men", to advance the "negation of Democracy", and to herald "the advent of dictatorship" (345).

An example of utilitarian logic can be found in debates on the British referendum to leave the European Union. Prime Minister Boris Johnson has repeatedly used utilitarian arguments for justifying the need for a "hard Brexit" without an agreement between the EU and the UK. Johnson identifies "the people" as those who support Brexit. Here are two examples of this demagogic logic of reducing "the people" to those who support Brexit:

BORIS JOHNSON: "What I think people want us to do is to leave the European Union on October 31st"

(BBC 2019)

BORIS JOHNSON: "But the way to unite the country, I am afraid, is to get this thing done. [...] What people want to see is a resolution and they want to see us get this thing done. And that's what we gonna do"

(Johnson 2019)

In the 2016 referendum, 51.9% of the voters opted for Brexit and 48.1% against it. This means there is a very large minority that Johnson excludes from his notion of the people. He speaks in favour of the majority and argues for the interest of the largest group of voters while disregarding the interests of the minority. The result is that he advances the political polarisation of the country into two hostile camps.

The basic problem of utilitarianism is that its ethical foundations deny "the permanence of moral values" (Roy 1989, 340). Utilitarian ethics is a "relativist morality" and "ethical nihilism" (341). The result is that utilitarianism has both potentials for the fetishisation of individual interests (capitalism's individualism without socialism) and the fetishisation of (partial) social interests (collectivism without individuality such as in fascism and Stalinism). It lacks a commitment to universalism (universal rights) and an ethical and political dialectic of individual and social rights.

Roy (1989) argues that positivism and empiricism fetishise scientific knowledge as "a mathematical god" and is a "neo-mysticism" (456, see also 457). Positivism is one aspect of utilitarian liberalism. The logic of calculability supports the accumulation of capital and power because it allows to reduce society to the instrumental logic of costs and benefits.

The Frankfurt School stresses the instrumental character of positivism. Pollock and Adorno, two key members of the Frankfurt School, argue that the rise of mathematics in the social sciences means the "convergence of social-scientific methods toward those of the natural sciences" and is "the child of a society that reifies people" (Pollock and Adorno 2011, 20). For Horkheimer (1947/2004, 41), "[p]ositivism is philosophical technocracy". Habermas (1971, 67) warns that positivism is the "immunization of the sciences against philosophy". Horkheimer and Adorno (1947/2002, 25) argue that the logic of calculation is the foundation of barbarism: "With the spread of the bourgeois commodity economy the dark horizon of myth is illuminated by the sun of calculating reason, beneath whose icy rays the seeds of the new barbarism are germinating".

Alfred Sohn-Rethel was not a member of the Frankfurt School but was in contact with Adorno with whom he shared the critique of positivism. Sohn-Rethel (1978) argues that class society's division of labour includes the separation between head and hand. Positivism is the fetishism of mechanistic, quantifying, mathematical reasoning. It is an expression and result of the division of labour. Georg Lukács (1971) points out that positivism is anti-dialectical: "The methodology of the natural sciences which forms the methodological ideal of every fetishistic science and every kind of Revisionism reject the idea of contradiction and antagonism in its subject matter" (10). Mathematics does not see "the whole system at once" (117). The logic of quantification reduces explanations to basic principles (reductionism) and believes in the exact predictability and calculability of the world (determinism) (117).

In the contemporary social sciences and humanities, digital positivism has emerged as a new form of positivism. It propagates quantitative digital methods, namely big data analytics. The social sciences are thereby re-envisioned as turning into computational social science, a paradigm focused on large datasets, quantification, mathematics, and calculation. Such approaches set out to explain the world based on the analysis of big stocks and flows of data. The problem is that the analysis of big data does not tell us everything that matters. It cannot properly study human motivations, feelings, experiences, norms, morals, values, interpretations, concerns, fears, hopes, etc. It lacks a focus on society's qualities.

Roy (1953, 8) argues that there is a contradiction between "the philosophy and the political practice of Liberalism". Capitalism's "cut-throat competition" undermined democracy and resulted in "the stormy rise of Fascism" (9). Roy observed how the failures of liberalism resulted on the one hand in fascism and on the other hand in Stalinism, the fetishisation of the collectives of the nation and the working class.

"A political system and an economic experiment which subordinate the man of flesh and blood and to an imaginary collective ego, be it the nation or a class, cannot possibly be the suitable means for the attainment of the goal of freedom" (Roy 1953, 53–54).

Roy describes and analyses a *negative dialectic of the liberal Enlightenment* whereby the alienation caused by liberalism let liberalism turn against itself and its own political and moral values, which called forth terror and violence. According to Roy, 19th-century liberalism's utilitarianism, its "law of the jungle" (Roy 1989, 428), and its atomising individualism called forth "the superman cult" (428), cults of collectivism (427), irrationalism (428, 445), "the cult of leadership" (445), dictatorship (445). The result was "the mystic collectivist cult" (436) of fascism and Stalinism. "In modern Liberalism, the individual became the economic man. [...] But in the context of the capitalist society, the economic man could exist either as a slave or as a slaveowner. That debasement of the individual discredited the liberal democratic doctrine of individual freedom. [...] Ultimately, democracy was destroyed in a fierce clash of totalitarian dictatorships" (Roy 1989, 464), namely fascism and Stalinism. Roy says that humans created a machine that now enslaves them (477) so that the "struggle for freedom [...] ultimately" deprives humans of freedom (477). The "creations of man have reduced man to nothingness", which means the "complete subordination of the creator to his creation". Marx (1844) termed this process alienation.

The rise of fascism in Europe was one of the consequencess of the Enlightenment's negative dialectic: "In Europe, Fascism represents a reaction to the negative features of the capitalist civilisation, namely, lonesomeness and helplessness of the individual, resulting from his atomisation. These features are accentuated in the period where the progressive potentialities of capitalist economy are exhausted, and monopolist capitalism increases the degree of social insecurity, particularly for the middle and lower classes. In that period, the reaction becomes more violent, and the cultural sanctions of the capitalist civilisation – humanism, rationalism and liberalism – are assaulted" (Roy 1945/2006, 22).

Liberal individualism and atomism that expresses itself as the exploitation of wage-workers, the fetishisation of private property, capital accumulation, cut-throat competition, and the logic of the accumulation of capital in the economy and of power in the state-system backfired. The social void it created has been filled with movements for repressive collectivism. Whereas liberal individualism fetishises the individual at the expense of social freedom, fascism and Stalinism fetishise the collectives of the nation and the state at the expense of individual freedom. Roy (1989, 477) argues that in contrast, a radical humanist democracy has to "reconcile individual freedom with social organisation". In respect to liberalism's self-contradiction, we find parallels between Roy's work and Horkheimer and Adorno's (1947/2002) *Dialectic of Enlightenment.* Horkheimer and Adorno (1947/2002, xvi) argue that capitalism entails the tendency of the "self-destruction of enlightenment" (Horkheimer and Adorno 1947/2002, xvi) that results in "the reversion of enlightened civilization to barbarism" (xix). Capitalism's structures of exploitation and domination turned against liberalism's Enlightenment values and in the last instance resulted in Auschwitz. "After the brief interlude of liberalism in which the bourgeois kept one another in check, power is revealing itself as archaic terror in a fascistically rationalized form" (68). Horkheimer (1947/2004, v) points out that in capitalism, the Enlightenment tends to nullify itself and turn into its opposite, namely dehumanisation: "Advance in technical facilities for enlightenment is accompanied by a process of dehumanization. Thus progress threatens to nullify the very goal it is supposed to realize – the idea of man". Like Roy, Horkheimer points out the Enlightenment reason emerged as protest against religion. But in capitalism, reason turned into an instrument of domination and exploitation. "Having given up autonomy, reason has become an instrument. [...] Reason has become completely harnessed to the social process. Its operational value, its role in the domination of men and nature, has been made the sole criterion" (14–15). As a result, "the advance of enlightenment tends at certain points to revert to superstition and paranoia" (21). "Less and less is anything done for its own sake. [...] In the view of formalized reason, an activity is reasonable only if it serves another purpose [...] In other words, the activity is merely a tool, for it derives its meaning only through its connection with other ends" (25). The reduction of reason to a mere instrument neutralises reason and calls forth irrationalism. "At the moment of consummation, reason has become irrational and stultified" (87). Liberalism turns into authoritarianism. "[L]iberalism and authoritarianism tend to interact in a way that helps to vest an ever more rigid rational control in the institutions of an irrational world" (49). With the rise of fascism in Europe, "[r]eason [...] ultimately destroyed itself" (Horkheimer 1941, 367). Fascism is an irrational rationality: "The new order of Fascism is Reason revealing itself as unreason" (Horkheimer 1941, 387). Horkheimer and Adorno's argument is that when reason becomes instrumental reason it not just undermines critique but also calls forth irrational forces that advance terroristic systems such as fascism and Stalinism. "Technological rationality" is Herbert Marcuse's term for what Horkheimer calls "instrumental reason": "Rationality is being transformed from a critical force into one of adjustment and compliance. Autonomy of reason loses its meaning in the same measure as the thoughts, feelings and actions of men are shaped by the technical

Liberalism and the Dialectic of Enlightenment

requirements of the apparatus which they have themselves created" (Marcuse 1941/ 1998, 49). Marcuse (1965/1988) argues that technological rationality results in rational irrationality. "In the unfolding of capitalist rationality, *irrationality* becomes *reason*" (207), "bourgeois reason negates itself in its consummation" (221). Comparable to Horkheimer and Marcuse, Roy (1947/1960, 94) argues that fascism makes "man only an automation, a robot, a small wheel in a gigantic social machinery" (Roy 1947/1960, 94). The notions of technological rationality and instrumental reason express several dimensions of capitalism and class society:

- *Technology as an instrument of domination*: Technology is under the conditions of domination and capitalism dominant groups' instrument for the exploitation, control, and surveillance of others.

- *Capitalism as social technology.* Capitalism is a type of social technology that reduces humans to the status of workers and consumers and treats them as instrument, thing, and resource for achieving the goal of capital accumulation. Capitalism is a machine that accumulates capital and produces commodities. It alienates humans from their humanness.

- *Ideology as the instrumentalization of consciousness*: In order to reproduce itself, domination requires ideologies that make structures of domination appear as natural, without alternative, and good. Such ideologies are for example consumerism, fascism, nationalism, racism, technocracy, technological determinism, neoliberalism, conservatism, militarism, etc. Ideology is a particular form of technological rationality that tries to eliminate critical and dialectical thought in order to instil blind, uncritical faith to ruling ideas into humans. It involves the attempt to reduce human consciousness to the status of machines. Attempts to reify and manipulate consciousness try to manipulate humans' consciousness.

- *Technological determinism:* Technological determinism is a specific form of ideology that sees technology as being autonomous from society, as the cause of society's changes, problems or advances.

Since 2008, many societies have experienced profound economic, political, and ideological crises that together resulted in a surge of new nationalisms and new authoritarianism (Fuchs 2018, 2020). Neoliberal capitalism has experienced a new negative dialectic of the Enlightenment. New nationalisms and authoritarianisms are the result of the negative dialectic of neoliberal capitalism and the new imperialism. The commodification of everything, entrepreneurialism, privatisation, deregulation, financialisation, globalisation, deindustrialisation, outsourcing, precarisation, and the new individualism have backfired, extended, and intensified inequalities and crisis tendencies, which created a futile ground for new nationalisms, right-wing extremism, and new fascism.

4.4 Nationalism and Fascism

Roy gives particular attention to the analysis and critique of nationalism and fascism. He argues that fascism is a militant and terroristic form of capitalism. The bourgeoisie is defending its "waning power with the bloody instruments of Fascist dictatorship" (Roy 1938, 6), its members throw off "the mask of parliamentarism and wield their dictatorship openly" (38). Roy argues that fascism cannot be reduced to monopoly capitalism because there are forms of monopoly capitalism without a terroristic state. He rather argues that in phases of crisis where fascist movements rise the capitalist class may find fascist rule a means suited for fostering exploitation and capital accumulation and might therefore support such movements:

> "Fascism is the most outstanding phenomenon of contemporary history. It has to be explained. It is not enough to call it monopoly capitalism or Hitler Imperialism, whatever that curious phrase might mean. It is not historically correct to identify Fascism with monopoly capitalism. The latter had been in operation in other countries years before Fascism rose in Germany. In those countries, Fascists could not capture power. On the other hand, Italy, where Fascism first succeeded, was an economically backward country. Fascism cannot be explained unless ideological antecedents, the cultural atmosphere, are taken into account. The doctrines with which Fascism swept to power in Germany can be traced in the ideological and cultural history of that country. Fascism also was a result of the dynamics of ideas. Monopoly capitalism, more correctly, capitalism in decay, found that those ideas could serve its purpose very well."
>
> (Roy 1947/1960, 68)

Roy (1989) argues that the dialectic of the Enlightenment's weakening of reason results "in the storm of emotions running wild" so that it "is easier to sway the people by appeals to their emotions and prejudices than to their reason. [...] Therefore, democracy has everywhere degenerated into demagogy" (468).

The rise of new authoritarianism has been accompanied by a mass of public discourses that are driven by emotions and ideology. Authoritarians often do not believe in anything that can be reasonably explained and proofed but believe only what they want to believe and fits into their ideology. They distrust experts and academia.

During the campaigns for the 2016 Brexit referendum, Michael Gove, who was back then the British Secretary of State for Justice, declared in a television interview that citizens should not and do not trust experts: "I think that people in this country have had enough of experts [...] from organisations with acronyms, saying that they know what is best and get it consistently wrong"[2]. Some speak of the rise of an era of post-truth politics. Post-truth is, however, a rather unspecific and polite term that misses to point out that the questioning of expertise aims at the advancement of lies and far-right ideology. Donald Trump has perfected the practice of declaring any expertise that questions him as invalid and false. Here is an example:

Donald J. Trump: "The FAKE NEWS media (failing @nytimes, @NBCNews, @ABC, @CBS, @CNN) is not my enemy, it is the enemy of the American People!"

(Twitter, @realdonaldtrump, 17 February 2017)

In this tweet, Donald Trump characterises mainstream media that often report critical about him as "the fake news media". He thereby identifies himself as the ultimate speaker and representative of the American people and implies that criticism of him is anti-American and directed against the Americans. Critics of Trump presented as "the enemy of the American people". Driven by ideology, irrationality, and emotions, Trump and his followers imagine any criticism and facts not fitting their ideology as inventions. They only believe that something that fits into their ideology to be true. Such a demagogic politics aims at radicalising followers and their hatred of identified enemies. It has dangerous, anti-democratic potentials because stoking hatred can easily spill over into violence.

A comparison of critical theories of fascism and authoritarianism shows that there are four elements of right-wing authoritarian ideology, practices, and movements (Fuchs 2018, 2020): authoritarian leadership, nationalism, the friend/enemy-scheme, and militant patriarchy. Figure 4.1 visualises the interaction of these four dimensions. Right-wing authoritarianism has an ideological role. By fetishising the illusionary collective of the nation, right-wing authoritarianism distracts attention from actual class conflicts and class structures. Fascism is a movement that uses terror as its means for advancing capitalism, authoritarianism, nationalism, division, militancy, and patriarchy.

Roy identifies all four features of this model as key dimensions of fascism.

Right-Wing Authoritarianism (RWA)

Individual ⇔ Group ⇔ Institution ⇔ Society

RWA's social role: Deflection of attention from structures
of class, capitalism and domination

Authoritarian Leadership
(in economic, political and cultural systems)

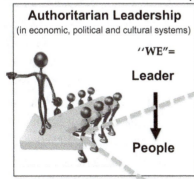

"WE"=

Leader

↓

People

Nationalism
(political fetishism, constructs fictive ethnicity)

"WE"

Friend/Enemy-Scheme

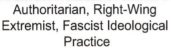

"THEY"

Authoritarian, Right-Wing
Extremist, Fascist Ideological
Practice

Patriarchy & Militarism

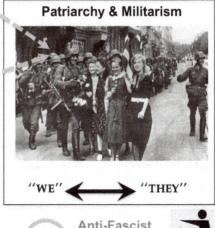

"WE" ⟵⟶ "THEY"

Anti-Fascist,
Socialist
Praxis
Communication

Nationalism and Fascism

FIGURE 4.1 A model of right-wing authoritarianism.

Authoritarian Leadership

The "cult of Superman" is a central feature of fascism (1Roy 938, 40). "A Mussolini or Hitler is the personification of the cult of superman" (53). In fascism, "the State is everything and the individual citizen has no right to exist except as pawn of the absolute power which may gamble away his life whenever it pleases" (53).

Authoritarianism uses a "mass psychology dominated by the fear of freedom" (1945/2006, 13). "The fear of freedom created Fascism in Europe" (1945/2006, 15). The "flight from freedom [...] is the basic social and cultural asset of Fascism" (1945/2006, 23). This flight favours the belief in the need of top-down leadership and a Führer. When speaking of the flight from freedom it is evident that Roy (1945) was influenced by Erich Fromm's (1941/1969) book *Escape from Freedom* that was published in 1941. Fromm in this book analyses the rise of fascism in Europe: "The giant forces in society and the danger for man's survival have increased [...], and hence man's tendency to escape from freedom" (Fromm 1941/1969, xiii). Roy does not explicitly acknowledge the connection to Fromm's works. He does not cite or mention *Escape from Freedom* or Fromm. Fromm himself became also aware of Roy's work. In his book *The Sane Society*, Fromm (1956/2002, 55) describes Roy's book *Reason, Romanticism and Revolution* as "thorough and brilliant analysis". Roy's journal *The Radical Humanist* published articles by Erich Fromm (Manjapra 2010, 160–161).

Nationalism

For Roy, nationalism is an ideology that fetishises the nation. He therefore speaks of "national jingoism" (1938, 89). As a humanist, he politically despised any form of nationalism and argued that nationalism is an element of fascism. "Fascism is nationalism inspired by revivalist ideals" (1938, 40), "The essence of nationalism is to place the interests of one's own country above the interests of the world" (1942, 7). "There is a spiritual affinity between nationalism and Fascism, the latter being only the most extravagant and aggressive form of the former" (1942, 22–23). Roy argues that Marxism is interested in social problems and conflicts, while nationalism "has no reference to social problems" (1945/2006, 85). Nationalism demands the sacrifice of the individual to the nation. "The essence of Nationalism, the denial of the very existence of the individual, manifests itself fully in Fascism" (1945/2006, 29). Roy sees nationalism as a metaphysical and irrational ideology that fetishises the nation:

> "Nazism and Fascism are condemned as totalitarian because they deny the sovereignty of the individual; they do not give the individual any place in society except as a cog in a vast machinery with a collective ego. [...] Nationalism, by its internal logic, cannot but be totalitarian, because it also postulates a collective ego – the nation. It is a metaphysical concept; yet, human beings, of flesh and blood, must sacrifice everything to make the nation great and glorious. That is the essence of Nationalism. That is, to sacrifice a reality at the altar of a fiction, of an illusion."
>
> (Roy 1960/1947, 110–111)

There are parallels of Roy's critical theories of nationalism to the works of Rosa Luxemburg and Eric J. Hobsbawm (see Fuchs 2020). Luxemburg and Hobsbawm, like Roy, stress the illusionary and fictive character of nationalist ideology. Luxemburg (1909/1976, 135) writes that nationalists see the nation as "a homogeneous social and political entity" and that the nation is "misty veil" concealing the "definite historical content" of class society (135). For Hobsbawm (1983a, 1983b, 1992), nationalism is an invented, which means fabricated and therefore illusionary tradition that serves the interests of the capitalist class.

Roy (1945/2006, 85) argues that anti-colonial and anti-imperialist struggles that are nationalist in character are "pseudo-Marxist":

> "The pseudo-Marxist theory of anti-Imperialism [...] panders to the base sentiment of race hatred, and consequently plays into the hands of social reaction. The doctrine of united anti-Imperialist Front divorces political practice from the context of social conflicts, and making it an expression of racial animosity, helps the upper-class minority to use the people as a pawn in the game of power-politics. Providing nationalist power-politics with a pseudo-theoretical foundation, anti-Imperialism helps Nationalism to hide its reactionary social purpose. The misalliance with Nationalism compels Marxism to betray itself."
>
> (1945/2006, 84–85)

The Friend/Enemy-Scheme

The friend/enemy-scheme is the ideological construction of enemies who are blamed for society's problems. Racism, anti-Semitism, anti-socialism, and anti-Marxism are typical enemy constructions that can be found in fascist ideology. Roy (1938) argues that fascism is driven by "fanatical race hatred" (143) and "unscrupulous slander against the opponents, [...] fanning of race prejudice" (1938, 89). Fascism wants to destroy Marxism (93). The "object of Fascism is the destruction of the weak and the triumph of the strong" (133).

Militarism

Capitalism is a "violent form of capitalist domination" (1938, 38). Fascism implements "arbitrary power and unbounded will" (53). "The Fascist state is the instrument of the dictatorship of the bourgeoisie divested of the deceit of parliamentary democracy" (87).

Fascism is a capitalist system that is based on rule of terror. Fascism is "avowedly imperialist" (148), which implies the use of violence and terror for the expansion of capitalist influence.

Roy's understanding of fascism resonates with the one of the Frankfurt School (Jani 2017). Like Roy, Adorno and Horkheimer also identify four dimensions of fascism.

In respect to *authoritarian leadership*, Adorno argues that the fascist leader presents himself as great little man, "a person who suggests both omnipotence and the idea that he is just one of the folks" (Adorno 1951, 142). Collective narcissism is a psychological dimension of authoritarianism. Because it results in the psychological "enlargement of the subject: by making the leader his ideal he loves himself, as it were, but gets rid of the stains of frustration and discontent which mar his picture of his own empirical self" (Adorno 1951, 140).

In the context of *nationalism*, Adorno argues that fascists need forms of repressive egalitarianism – fascist demagogues make use of the logic of repressive egalitarianism: "They emphasize their being different from the outsider but play down such differences within their own group and tend to level out distinctive qualities among themselves with the exception of the hierarchical one" (Adorno 1991, 146). Nationalism is a form of repressive egalitarianism.

Adorno argues that fascists think and act based on the logic of the *friend/enemy-scheme*. The right-wing demagogue "cannot help feeling surrounded by traitors, and so continuously threatens to exterminate them" (Adorno 1975, 78). According to Adorno, identification with the leader and hatred against the out-group allow emotional release (Adorno 1975, 16–20). Such a release of aggression encourages "excess and violence" (1975, 17).

Adorno stresses that fascists see the *military as the model for politics and society* and soldiers as ideal individuals. They consider war, violence, weapons and guns as the best means of handling conflicts. The "model of the military officer" is "transferred to the realm of politics" (Adorno 1975, 49). Love to the leader is an "emotional compensation for the cold, self-alienated life of most people" (Adorno 1975, 37). For fascists, survival, toughness, strength, and the willingness to fight, lead, and compete are moral norms. Any "reference to love is almost completely excluded", and the "traditional role of the loving father" is replaced "by the negative one of threatening authority" (Adorno 1991, 137). Horkheimer (1947/2004, 14) points out that nationalism ends in terror: "The idea of the national community (*Volksgemeinschaft*) first, first set up as an idol, can eventually only be maintained by terror".

4.5 Conclusions

This chapter has engaged with foundations of M. N. Roy's theory and has compared his approach to the Frankfurt School. The first question it asked was: how can M. N. Roy's radical, Marxist humanism inform the critical study of ideology, fascism, and nationalism? We can summarise the main findings in respect to the themes of humanism, technology, culture/communication, and ideology:

Humanism

- Roy argues that utilitarian liberalism created a negative dialectic of the Enlightenment. Liberal individualism and atomism that expresses itself as the exploitation of wage-workers, the fetishisation of private property, capital accumulation, cut-throat competition, and the logic of the accumulation of capital in the economy and of power in the state-system backfired. The social void it created has been filled with movements for repressive collectivism, namely fascism and Stalinism. Whereas liberal individualism fetishises the individual at the expense of social freedom, fascism and Stalinism fetishise the collectives of the nation and the state at the expense of individual freedom.

- Roy identifies four key elements of fascism: authoritarian leadership, nationalism, the friend/enemy-scheme, and militarism. He opposes any form of nationalism because he sees nationalism as the irrational ideological foundation of fascism. Roy stresses that fascism is a violent and terroristic form of capitalism.

- There are strong parallels between Roy's and Herbert Marcuse's analysis of modern technology. Like Roy, Marcuse rejects anti-technological ideology that celebrates toil: Marcuse just like Roy identifies both emancipatory and repressive potentials of modern technology and argues that the actual character and impact of technology depend on broader societal contexts, interests, and struggles. Marcuse like Roy argues for a socialist modernity where technology is shaped and used in manners that overcome toil and advance freedom, and technology is governed in a democratic manner.

- Roy was critical of positivism. His critique of the fetishism of mathematics and calculation resonates with the approaches of Georg Lukács, Theodor W. Adorno, Max Horkheimer, Friedrich Pollock, Alfred Sohn-Rethel, or Jürgen Habermas, who criticised that positivism lacks an understanding of the qualitative and dialectical character of the world.

- There are parallels between Roy's analysis of how liberalism turned against itself into fascism and Stalinism and Horkheimer/Adorno's *Dialectic of Enlightenment*. Roy's analysis of fascism is influenced by Erich Fromm's hypothesis of the escape from freedom. Roy just like the Frankfurt School sees authoritarian leadership, nationalism, the friend/enemy-scheme, and militarism as key features of fascist ideology and movements.

- Roy just like Horkheimer, Adorno, and Marcuse argues that Stalinism and fascism are expressions of how the reason of Enlightenment and liberalism that questioned religious and feudal rule turned against Enlightenment values. Capitalism individualises and instrumentalises humans, which undermines social cohesion and especially in crisis times calls forth reactionary forces that fetishise false and imaginary collectives such as the nation, race, and the absolute state.

- Like Marcuse, Horkheimer, and Adorno, Roy stresses that authoritarianism and fascism try to treat humans like robots. This is the phenomenon of instrumental reason and technological rationality. Instrumental reason/technological rationality has four dimensions: technology as an instrument of domination, capitalism as social technology, ideology as the instrumentalisation of consciousness, and technological determinism.

Both Roy and first-generation Frankfurt School authors such as Max Horkheimer, Theodor W. Adorno, Herbert Marcuse, and Erich Fromm were inspired by Marx and humanist philosophy. The major difference between Roy and the Frankfurt School is that Roy analysed both Western and non-Western society, including India and China, based on Marxist humanism, whereas the Frankfurt School had to limit its analysis to Europe, the United States, and Russia. Marxist humanism is a universal approach that is suited for the analysis of domination, exploitation, ideology, and social struggles in different parts of the world.

Roy's approach shows that the claim that Marxian theory, socialism, and humanism are Western- or Euro-centric and therefore cultural imperialist approaches is erroneous. Whereas Dipesh Chakrabarty (2008, 4) argues that Roy was one of the "illustrious members" of the "modern Bengali educated middle classes" that "warmly embraced the themes of rationalism, science, equality, and human rights that the European Enlightenment promulgated", Kris Manjapra (2010) argues in his book about Roy that the latter was not "entrapped in the ideologies attendant to global capital" (xviii), but a "anti-colonial cosmopolitanism thinker" (xxi). Robert Spencer (2017) argues that post-colonial scholars often tar "all humanisms with the same brush" (121) and "champion difference at the expense of equality" and identity politics over class politics so that to "be a postcolonialist, it seems, is to leave one's humanism at the door" (124). Spencer argues for a humanist postcolonialism that is "exercised above all not by crimes against hybridity but by crimes against humanity" (122), stresses the human "capacity for self-creation" (128), and speaks "the language of rights [...] animated by the conviction that there *are* irreducible features of human life" (128) because "it is convinced that only by eradicating the most devastating forms of in-humanity will the human, with all its variability and unpredictableness, come into its own" (129). Humanism means "critical thinking + the ideal of solidarity" (152).

Marxist/socialist humanism allows us to approach the global world as a unity of diverse tendencies. It is an approach that enables the analysis of society in different contexts based on what Vivek Chibber calls the two universalisms, "the universal logic of capital (suitably defined) and social agents' universal interest in their well-being, which impels them to resist capital's expansionary drive" (Chibber 2013, 291). The first universalism foregrounds the accumulation of economic, political, and cultural power that in different contexts and on different organisation levels of global society creates various inequalities. The second universalism calls for solidarity of the world's oppressed and exploited in their struggles for a better world. One of the "recurring themes" in Roy's works and thought is "the reading of underling unity out of apparent difference" (Manjapra 2010, 168).

Both in the West and the Global South, we today experience a surge of new nationalisms and new authoritarianisms. Far-right movements and new nationalisms are the "cicatrices and scars of a democracy [...] that until today has still not lived up to its own concept" (Adorno 1968/2019, 18). They are the result of the negative dialectic of neoliberal ca-pitalism and the new imperialism. The commodification of everything, entrepreneurialism, privatisation, deregulation, financialisation, capitalist globalisation, the new imperialism, deindustrialisation, outsourcing, precarisation, and the new individualism have backfired, and extended and intensified inequalities and crisis tendencies, which created a futile ground for new nationalisms, right-wing extremism, and new fascism.

Three of the main challenges and global problems that humanity faces today are (a) the threats of exploding inequalities, accelerating and deepening political-economic crises, fascism, war, violence, and genocide posed by the rise of authoritarian capitalism and new nationalisms, (b) the threat posed to human and the environment by natural disasters, climate change, and the global environmental crisis, (c) new forms of control and exploitation in the context of capitalist digital technologies, AI-based automation, and algorithmic politics.

The political-economic crisis, the environmental crisis, and the digital crisis have in common that they are crises of humanity that threaten fundamental aspects of human life, namely democracy, survival of the species and the planet, and self-fulfilment. They are crises of humanity. The three crises together radicalise the alienation of humans from nature, the economy, the political system, and culture to the point that the interaction of these crises can in the future result in a breakdown of humanity and the livelihood for future generations. We need radical alternatives. "The Left [...] requires a compelling vision of the future as *more* just, democratic, ecologically sustainable and subjectively satisfying around which it will be possible to construct a viable counter-hegemony" (Alderson and Spencer 2017, 218). Radical humanism is important today because it advances the counter-vision of a humane society to the dystopias the three crises can result in. Radical humanism can thereby inform social struggles. Radical humanism struggles for the strengthening of the political-economic commons (common control of political and economic organisations), the natural commons (common survival in a natural environment that interacts with humans in sustainable manners), and the knowledge and digital commons (knowledge, culture, and digital resources as common goods).

In the age of new nationalisms and authoritarian capitalism, global environmental crises, capitalist crisis, and the digital crisis, socialist-humanist theories such as the one by M. N. Roy can inspire struggles for a humanist and socialist society as antidotes to the acceleration and deepening of the three crises. In his *Principles of Radical Democracy*, Roy (1953, 52–62) formulates 22 theses. The final one should be seen as the starting point for contemporary socialist, anti-fascist, and anti-nationalist struggles:

"Radicalism starts from the dictum that "man is the measure of everything" (Protagoras) or "man is the root of mankind" (Marx), and advocates reconstruction of the world as a commonwealth and fraternity of free [...] [humans], by the collective endeavour of spiritually emancipated moral [...] [humans]."

(Roy 1953, 62)

Notes

1 Data source: https://scholar.google.com/, accessed on 12 September 2019.
2 https://www.youtube.com/watch?v=GGgiGtJk7MA, accessed on 13 September 2019.

References

Adorno, Theodor W. 1991. *The Culture Industry.* Abingdon: Routledge.

Adorno, Theodor W. 1975. "The Psychological Technique of Martin Luther Thomas' Radio Addresses." In *Soziologische Schriften II.1*, 11–141. Frankfurt am Main: Suhrkamp.

Adorno, Theodor W. 1968/2019. *Aspekte des neuen Rechtsradikalismus.* Frankfurt am Main: Suhrkamp.

Adorno, Theodor W. 1954. "Ideology." In *Aspects of Sociology, ed. Frankfurt Institute for Social Research*, 182–205. Boston: Beacon Press.

Adorno, Theodor W. 1951. "Freudian Theory and the Pattern of Fascist Propaganda." In *The Culture Industry*, 132–57. Abingdon: Routledge.

Alderson, David and Robert Spencer. 2017. "Conclusion." In *For Humanism: Explorations in Theory and Politics*, edited by David Alderson and Robert Spencer, 210–24. London: Pluto Press.

Bhattacharya, Subhrajit. 2016. "Perspectives on Fascism: M. N. Roy, Horkheimer and Adorno." In *M. N. Roy Reader: Essential Writings Volume 3*, edited by Bhaskar Sur and R. M. Pal, 1431–8. Delhi: Aakar Books.

Chakrabarty, Dipesh. 2008. *Provincialzing Europe: Postcolonial Thought and Historical Difference.* Princeton, NJ: Princeton University Press.

Chibber, Vivek. 2013. *Postcolonial Theory and the Specter of Capital.* London: Verso.

Fromm, Erich. 1956/2002. *The Sane Society.* Abingdon: Routledge.

Fromm, Erich. 1941/1969. *Escape From Freedom.* New York: Avon Books.

Fuchs, Christian. 2020. *Nationalism on the Internet: Critical Theory and Ideology in the Age of Social Media and Fake News.* New York: Routledge.

Fuchs, Christian. 2018. *Digital Demagogue: Authoritarian Capitalism in the Age of Trump and Twitter.* London: Pluto Press.

Gandhi, Mohandas Karamchand. 1997. *"Hind Swaraj" and Other Writings.* Edited by Anthony J. Parel. Cambridge: Cambridge University Press.

Gandhi, Mohandas Karamchand. 1948/1983. *Autobiography: The Story of My Experiments with Truth.* Mineola, NY: Dover Publications.

Habermas, Jürgen. 1971. *Knowledge and Human Interest.* Boston: Beacon Press.

Hobsbawm, Eric J. 1992. *Nations and Nationalism since 1780. Programme, Myth, Reality.* Cambridge: Cambridge University Press. 2nd edition.

Hobsbawm, Eric J. 1983a. "Introduction: Inventing Traditions." In *The Invention of Tradition*, edited by Eric J. Hobsbawm and Terence Ranger, 1–14. Cambridge: Cambridge University Press.

Hobsbawm, Eric J. 1983b. "Mass-Producing Traditions: Europe, 1870–1914." In *The Invention of Tradition*, edited by Eric J. Hobsbawm and Terence Ranger, 263–307. Cambridge: Cambridge University Press.

Horkheimer, Max. 1947/2004. *Eclipse of Reason.* London: Continuum.

Horkheimer, Max. 1942/1982. "The Authoritarian State." In *The Essential Frankfurt School Reader*, edited by Andrew Arato and Eike Gebhardt, 95–117. New York: Continuum.

Horkheimer, Max. 1941. "The End of Reason." *Studies in Philosophy and Social Science* 9 (3): 366–88.

Horkheimer, Max and Theodor W. Adorno. 1947/2002. *Dialectic of Enlightenment. Philosophical Fragments*. Stanford, CA: Stanford University Press.

Jani, Disha Karnad. 2017. "The Concept of Fascism in Colonial India: M. N. Roy and *The Problem of Freedom*." *Global Histories* 3 (2): 121–38.

Lenin, Vladimir I. 1920. "Preliminary Draft Theses on the National and the Colonial Questions. For the Second Congress of the Communist International." In *Lenin Collected Works Volume 31*, 144–51. Moscow: Progress Publishers.

Lukács, Georg. 1971. *History and Class Consciousness*. London: Merlin.

Luxemburg, Rosa. 1909/1976. *The National Question: Selected Writings*. New York: Monthly Review Press.

Manjapra, Kris. 2010. *M. N. Roy: Marxism and Colonial Cosmopolitanism*. New Delhi: Routledge.

Marcuse, Herbert. 1965/1988. "Industrialization and Capitalism in the Work of Max Weber." In *Herbert Marcuse: Negations: Essays in Critical Theory*, 201–26. London: Free Association.

Marcuse, Herbert. 1941/1998. "Some Social Implications of Modern Technology." In *Herbert Marcuse: Collected Papers of Herbert Marcuse Volume One: Technology, War and Fascism*, edited by Douglas Kellner, 41–65. London: Routledge.

Marx, Karl. 1844. "Economic and Philosophic Manuscripts of 1844." In *Marx & Engels Collected Works (MECW) Volume 3*, 229–346. London: Lawrence & Wishart.

Pollock, Friedrich and Theodor W. Adorno. 2011. *Group Experiment and Other Writings*. Cambridge, MA: Harvard University Press.

Ray, Sibnarayan. 2016a. "M. N. Roy: A Biographical Chronology." In *M. N. Roy Reader: Essential Writings Volume 3*, edited by Bhaskar Sur and R. M. Pal, 1439–62. Delhi: Aakar Books.

Ray, Sibnarayan. 2016b. "M. N. Roy in Communist Opposition." In *M. N. Roy Reader: Essential Writings Volume 3*, edited by Bhaskar Sur and R. M. Pal, 1289–302. Delhi: Aakar Books.

Roy, M. N. 1989. *Reason, Romanticism and Revolution*. Delhi: Ajanta Publications.

Roy, M. N. 1968. *Men I Met*. Bombay: Lalvani Publishing House.

Roy, M. N. 1953. *New Humanism: A Manifesto*. Calcutta: Renaissance Publishers. 2nd edition.

Roy, M. N. 1950a. "Cultural Requisites of Freedom." In *Modern Age & India*, edited by Atindranath Bose, 177–92. Calcutta: Left Book Club.

Roy, M. N. 1950b. *Fragments of a Prisoner's Diary Volume Two: India's Message*. Calcutta: Renaissance Publishers.

Roy, M. N. 1949. "A Politics for Our Time." In *M. N. Roy Reader: Essential Writings Volume 2*, edited by Bhaskar Sur and R. M. Pal, 927–41. Delhi: Aakar Books.

Roy, M. N. 1947a. *Science and Philosophy*. Calcutta: Renaissance Publishers.

Roy, M. N. 1947b. "Since the *Communist Manifesto.*" In *M. N. Roy Reader: Essential Writings Volume 2,* edited by Bhaskar Sur and R. M. Pal, 890–913. Delhi: Aakar Books.

Roy, M. N. 1947/1960. *Beyond Communism.* Delhi: Ajanta Books.

Roy, M. N. 1945/2006. *Problem of Freedom.* Calcutta: Renaissance Publishers.

Roy, M. N. 1942. *Nationalism: An Antiquated Cult.* Bombay: Radical Democratic Party

Roy, M. N. 1940. *Materialism: An Outline of the History of Scientific Thought.* Dehra Dun: Renaissance Publication.

Roy, M. N. 1938. *Fascism: Its Philosophy, Professions and Practice.* Calcutta: D.M. Library.

Roy, M. N. 1930/1946. *Revolution and Counter-Revolution in China.* Calcutta: Renaissance Publishers.

Roy, M. N. 1929a. "Meine Vebrechen: Offener Brief an die Mitglieder der Kommunistischen Internationale." *Gegen den Strom* 37: 9–11.

Roy, M. N. 1929b. "My Crime. In *M. N. Roy. 2016. M. N. Roy Reader: Essential Writings Volume 1,* edited by Bhaskar Sur and R. M. Pal, 188–95. Delhi: Aakar Books.

Roy, M. N. 1923. *India's Problem and its Solution.* Charleston: Nabu Press. Reprint.

Roy, M. N. 1922. *India in Transition.* Geneva: Edition de la Librairie J.B. Target.

Roy, M. N. 1920. *Supplementary Theses on the National and Colonial Question.* Presented at the Fourth Session of the Second Congress of the Communist International, July 25, 1920. https://www.marxists.org/history/international/comintern/2nd-congress/ch04.htm.

Roy, Samaren. 1997. *M. N. Roy: A Political Biography.* London: Sangam Books.

Roy, Samaren. 1987. *M. N. Roy and Mahatma Gandhi.* Columbia, MO: South Asia Books.

Sohn-Rethel, Alfred. 1978. *Intellectual and Manual Labour: A Critique of Epistemology.* London: Macmillan.

Spencer, Robert. 2017. Postcolonialism is a Humanism. In *For Humanism: Explorations in Theory and Politics,* edited by David Alderson and Robert Spencer, 120–62. London: Pluto Press.

Tarkunde, Vithal Mahaedo 1982. Introduction to the Author. In M. N. Roy. 1946/1982. In *M. N. Roy. 1946/1982. New Orientation,* v–x. Delhi: Ajanta Publications.

References

Chapter Five
Martin Heidegger's Anti-Semitism: Philosophy of Technology and the Media in the Light of the Black Notebooks. Implications for the Reception of Heidegger in Media and Communication Studies

5.1 Introduction

In spring 2014, three volumes of the *Schwarze Hefte* (*Black Notebooks*), Heidegger's philosophical notebooks, were published in the German edition of his collected works (Heidegger 2014a, 2014b, 2014c). They contain notes taken in the years 1931–1941 and have resulted in public debates about the role of anti-Semitism in Heidegger's thought. Especially, the publication of the book *Heidegger und der Mythos der jüdischen Weltverschwörung* (*Heidegger and the Myth of Jewish World Conspiracy*) by Peter Trawny (2014), who edited the *Black Notebooks*, has encouraged this public debate. Most people agree that such public debates about the role of Nazi ideology and anti-Semitism in Heidegger's thought are of crucial importance. They are not just discussions about Heidegger, but at the same time debates about philosophical, ideological, and political thought in Nazi Germany and its legacy.

In the spirit of such debates, this chapter asks: what are and should be the implications of the publication of the *Black Notebooks* for the reception of Heidegger in the study, theory, and philosophy of media, communication, and technology? In the introductory section, I give a brief overview of some of the previous debates about Heidegger and National Socialism. Section 5.2 introduces Theodor W. Adorno and Moishe Postone's contributions to the critical theory of anti-Semitism that are applied in Section 5.3 to passages in Heidegger's *Black Notebooks* that mention Jews. The analysis will show that the logic of modern technology plays an important role in the *Black Notebooks*.

DOI: 10.4324/9781003256090-5

Section 5.4 therefore re-visits some of Heidegger's writings on technology in light of the *Black Notebooks*. In Section 5.5, I draw some conclusions about what proper reactions to the publication of the *Black Notebooks* could be in the interdisciplinary field of media and communication studies.

One of the first works focusing on Heidegger and Nazism was Karl Löwith's article *The Political Implications of Heidegger's Existentialism* (1946). Löwith, one of Heidegger's students, argues in this paper that there is an inherent connection between Heidegger's philosophy and Nazi ideology. Victor Farías (1989) focuses in his book *Heidegger and Nazism* on Heidegger's early career and his role as the University of Freiburg's vice-chancellor. Tom Rockmore (1997) in his book *On Heidegger's Nazism and Philosophy* discusses Heidegger's rectoral address, the *Beiträge zur Philosophie* (1936–1938), and the works on Nietzsche and Hölderlin. He also discusses in one chapter the connection of Nazism and technology in Heidegger's works. Emmanuel Faye's book (2009) *Heidegger: The Introduction of Nazism into Philosophy* predominantly focuses on Heidegger's writings, speeches, lectures, and seminars during the Nazi time. Tom Rockmore (2009) argues that Farías and Faye's books both grounded important phases in the discussion of Heidegger and Nazism.

Victor Farías (1989) concludes that "Heidegger always remained faithful to a whole spate of doctrines characteristic of National Socialism" (7), which would be evidenced by "his radically discriminatory attitude regarding the intellectual superiority of the Germans, rooted in their language and their destiny; in his belief in the primacy of his own thought, much like Hölderlin's, taken as a paradigm and guide for the spiritual development of humanity itself; in his radical opposition to any form of democracy" (7–8).

Tom Rockmore (1997, 5) argues that "Heidegger's philosophical thought and his Nazism are interdependent and cannot be separated", "that he turned to National Socialism on the basis of his philosophy and that his later evolution is largely determined by his continuing concern with Nazism". In Heidegger's works, one finds according to Rockmore (1997, 9) a "constant presence of a metaphysical commitment to the German *Volk* as a central historical goal in his thought, a commitment which, like the theme of a fugue, is consistently renewed at regular intervals beginning in 1933. It is, I believe, this concern – in conjunction with Heidegger's underlying interest in Being – which drew him to National Socialism. This concern remains constant throughout his career and determines the later development of his position, the evolution of which cannot otherwise be grasped".

Tom Rockmore writes: "I am convinced that Heidegger's theory reflects a variety of contemporary influences, some of which he may not have been fully aware of, such as the role of a conservative, nationalistic form of Roman Catholicism in southwestern Germany in his youth, stressed by Ott, Farias, and most recently Thomä; the widespread concern, which he seems to have shared, for Germany, the defeated party in the First World War, to recover as a nation and to assume what many thought was the manifest German destiny; the reintroduction of destiny as an explanatory factor of historical change by Spengler; the interest in the concept of the *Volk* as it was developed in nineteenth-century Germany; and Heidegger's own desire to assume an ever-greater role in the German university system as the central thinker of his day, even to reform the university system according to his own view of higher education. These and other factors are ingredient in Heidegger's theory" (Rockmore 1997, 8).

Emmanuel Faye is the author who expresses most forcefully the idea that Heidegger's philosophy is Nazi ideology. "By its very content, it disseminates within philosophy the explicit and remorseless legitimation of the guiding principles of the Nazi movement" (Faye 2009, 246). "With the work of Heidegger, it is the principles of Hitlerism and Nazism that have been introduced into the philosophy libraries of the planet. [...] In order to preserve the future of philosophical thought, it is equally indispensable for us to inquire into the true nature of Heidegger's *Gesamtausgabe*, a collection of texts containing principles that are racist, eugenic, and radically deleterious to the existence of human reason. Such a work cannot continue to be placed in the philosophy section of libraries; its place is rather in the historical archives of Nazism and Hitlerism" (Faye 2009, 318–319).

Some reviews of the book, such as the one in the German newspaper *Die Zeit*, remark that Faye's arguments are too speculative and indirect, when he for example speculates that Heidegger may have written a speech for Hitler or argues that Heidegger is guilty by association because some of his formulations would sound similar to the ones made by Nazi ideologues (Meyer 2005). Faye (2005) responded to such criticism with quotes from Heidegger's works, such as from his lectures in the years 1933/1934, where Heidegger had said for example:

- "Wenn heute der Führer immer wieder spricht von der Umerziehung zur national-sozialistischen Weltanschauung, heißt das nicht: irgendwelche Schlagworte beibringen, sondern einen *Gesamtwandel* hervorbringen, einen *Weltentwurf* aus dessen Grund heraus er das ganze Volk erzieht. Der Nationalsozialismus ist nicht irgendwelche Lehre, sondern der Wandel von Grund aus der deutschen und, wie wir glauben, auch der europäischen Welt" (Heidegger 2001, 225)

Introduction

My translation: "When the Führer speaks continually of the re-education in the direction of the National Socialist *Weltanschauung*, then this does not mean to inculcate some slogans, but rather to bring about a *total change*, a *plan of the world* (Weltentwurf) out of whose ground he educates the entire people. National Socialism is not any doctrine, but rather the fundamental transformation of the German and, as we think, also the European world." (Heidegger 2001, 225)

• "Der Feind kann in der innersten Wurzel des Daseins eines Volkes sich festgesetzt haben und dessen eigenem Wesen sich entgegenstellen und zuwiderhandeln. Um so schärfer und härter und schwerer ist der Kampf, denn dieser besteht ja nur zum geringsten Teil im Gegeneinanderschlagen; oft weit schwieriger und langwieriger ist es, den Feind als solchen zu erspähen, ihn zur Entfaltung zu bringen, ihm gegenüber sich nichts vorzumachen, sich angriffsfertig zu halten, die ständige Bereitschaft zu pflegen und zu steigern und den Angriff auf weite Sicht mit dem Ziel der völligen Vernichtung anzusetzen" (Heidegger 2001, 91)

Translation: "The enemy may have grafted himself onto the innermost root of the existence [Dasein] of a people, and oppose the latter's ownmost essence, acting contrary to it. All the keener and harsher and more difficult it is than the struggle, for only a very small part of the struggle consists in mutual blows; it is often much harder and more exhausting to seek out the enemy as such, and to lead him to reveal himself, to avoid nurturing illusions about him, to remain ready to attack, to cultivate and increase constant preparedness and to initiate the attack on a long-term basis, with the goal of total extermination." (Faye 2009, 168)

On 2 October 1929, Heidegger wrote in a letter to Viktor Schwoerer that either "we restore genuine forces and educators emanating from the native soil to our German spiritual life, or we abandon it definitely to the growing Jewification (*Verjudung*)" (cited in: Faye 2009, 34; see also Sieg 1989). Richard Hönigswald, who came from a Jewish family, was professor of philosophy at the University of Munich. He lost his professorship in September 1933 as a consequence of Nazi legislation passed in April of the same year that banned Jews from universities and other public services (Gesetz zur Wiederherstellung des Berufsbeamtentums = Law for the Restoration the Professional Civil Service). The Bavarian Ministry of Culture asked Heidegger to comment on Hönigswald's works. Heidegger in a letter responded that he considered "the appointment of this man to the University of Munich to be a scandal, the only explanation for which is the fact that the Catholic system prefers such individuals who are apparently indifferent to any vision of the world, because they are without danger to its own efforts and because they are, in a well-known sense, 'objective-liberal'. [...] Heil Hitler!" (cited in: Faye 2009, 37).

In a lecture from 1935 that after its republication in 1953 resulted in public debates, Heidegger (2000, 213) spoke in the context of National Socialism of the "inner truth and greatness of this movement (namely the encounter between global technology and modern man)"[1]. Jürgen Habermas (1953, 197) drew the German public's attention to his discovery that Heidegger in 1953 "publishes his words, in the meantime eighteen years old, about the greatness and inner truth of National Socialism" and that it was therefore "time to think with Heidegger against Heidegger". Christian E. Lewalter, a journalist writing for *Die Zeit*, as well as Heidegger himself argued that "movement" referred to the passage in parenthesis (Wolin 1993, 187–188). Other people however said that the original did not contain the parenthesised passage (see: Wolin 1993, 188; Pöggeler 1987, 276–278). The original manuscript page containing this passage is missing in Heidegger's estate of works (Heidegger 1983, 234). Petra Jaeger, the editor of some of the volumes of Heidegger's collected works, writes in the postface to the volume that contains this lecture that she has a grounded suspicion (based on a proof sheet from 1953) that Heidegger inserted the parenthesised passage to the 1953 correction (Heidegger 1983, 233–234). Silvio Vietta (1989, 31) has tried to argue that this passage is anti-fascist by claiming that Heidegger by "greatness" means the monstrosity of instrumental reason, "the domination by calculating reason itself"[2] (translation from German). However, we today know from the *Black Notebooks* that Heidegger tended to see calculating reason as Jewish, which shows the absurdity of Vietta's argument.

In a letter to Herbert Marcuse, Heidegger wrote in January 1948 that Marcuse's previous letter, in which he had inquired why Heidegger did not denounce the Nazis publicly, "shows me precisely how difficult it is to converse with persons who have not been living in Germany since 1933 and who judge the beginning of the National Socialist movement from its end" (Wolin 1993, 162) and that there was not just a "regime that murdered millions of Jews", but also one that murdered millions of "East Germans" (Wolin 1993, 163). Marcuse, who coming from a Jewish family and being a Marxist had to flee from Nazi Germany, answered in May 1948 that Heidegger tried "to relativize [...] a crime by saying that other would have done the same thing. Even further: how is it possible to equate the torture, the maiming, and the annihilations of millions of men with the forcible relocation of population groups who suffered none of these outrages" (Wolin 1993, 164).

Introduction

Thousands of pages have been written about Heidegger and Nazi ideology. My short introduction to this issue will suffice to give readers unfamiliar with the issue some basic ideas about this controversy. Of course much more could be said about it. To better contextualise the quotes about Jews that can be found in the *Black Notebooks*, I next want to discuss Theodor W. Adorno's and Moishe Postone's contributions to the critical theory of anti-Semitism.

5.2 The Critical Theory of Anti-Semitism

Theodor W. Adorno (2002) identifies seven elements of anti-Semitism:

- *I. Jews are considered to be a race:*
  "For the fascists the Jews are not a minority but the antirace, the negative principle as such; on their extermination the world's happiness depends" (137).

- *II. Jews are said to be greedy, oriented on monetary interests and power, and to be representatives of financial capital:*
  "The fantasy of the conspiracy of lascivious Jewish bankers who finance Bolshevism is a sign of innate powerlessness, the good life an emblem of happiness. These are joined by the image of the intellectual, who appears to enjoy in thought what the others deny themselves and is spared the sweat of toil and bodily strength. The banker and the intellectual, money and mind, the exponents of circulation, are the disowned wishful image of those mutilated by power, an image which power uses to perpetuate itself " (141).

- *III. Jews are in a fetishist manner blamed for the abstract problems of capitalism:*
  "Bourgeois anti-Semitism has a specific economic purpose: to conceal domination in production" (142).
  "The productive work of the capitalist, whether he justified his profit as the reward of enterprise, as under liberalism, or as the director's salary, as today, was the ideology which concealed the nature of the labor contract and the rapacity of the economic system in general. That is why people shout: 'Stop thief!'-and point at the Jew. He is indeed the scapegoat, not only for individual maneuvers and machinations but in the wider sense that the economic injustice of the whole class is attributed to him" (142).
  "That the circulation sphere is responsible for exploitation is a socially necessary illusion. The Jews had not been the only people active in the circulation sphere. But they had been locked up in it too long not to reflect in their makeup something of

the hatred so long directed at that sphere. Unlike their Aryan colleagues, they were largely denied access to the source of added value" (143)

- *IV. There is hatred against Jewish religious beliefs:*

  "To accuse the Jews of being obdurate unbelievers is no longer enough to incite the masses. But the religious hostility which motivated the persecution of the Jews for two millennia is far from completely extinguished. [...] The others, who repressed that knowledge and with bad conscience convinced themselves of Christianity as a secure possession, were obliged to confirm their eternal salvation by the worldly ruin of those who refused to make the murky sacrifice of reason. That is the religious origin of anti-Semitism. The adherents of the religion of the Son hated the supporters of the religion of the Father as one hates those who know better. This is the hostility of spirit hardened as faith in salvation for spirit as mind" (144, 147).

- *V. The imitation of asserted natural characteristics of Jews is a psychological expression of the human domination of nature and humans and an imitation of magic practices:*

  "There is no anti-Semite who does not feel an instinctive urge to ape what he rakes to be Jewishness. The same mimetic codes are constantly used: the argumentative jerking of the hands, the singing tone of voice, which vividly animates a situation or a feeling independently of judgment, and the nose, that physiognomic *principium individuationis*, which writes the individual's peculiarity on his face. In the ambiguous partialities of the sense of smell the old nostalgia for what is lower lives on, the longing for immediate union with surrounding nature, with earth and slime" (151). "The purpose of the fascist cult of formulae, the ritualized discipline, the uniforms, and the whole allegedly irrational apparatus, is to make possible mimetic behavior. The elaborate symbols proper to every counterrevolutionary movement, the death's heads and masquerades, the barbaric drumming, the monotonous repetition of words and gestures, are so many organized imitations of magical practices, the mimesis of mimesis" (152). "The Jews as a whole are charged with practicing forbidden magic and bloody rituals. [...] They are pronounced guilty of what, as the first citizens, they were the first to subdue in themselves: the susceptibility to the lure of base instincts, the urge toward the beast and the earth, the worship of images. Because they invented the concept of the kosher, they are persecuted as swine. The antiSemites appoint themselves executors of the Old

The Critical Theory of Anti-Semitism

Testament: they see to it that the Jews, having eaten of the Tree of Knowledge, unto dust shall return" (153).

- *VI. Features of a subject, such as domination within society, are projected onto Jews as an object. They are based on this logic said to be e.g. especially powerful:*

  "Anti-Semitism is based on false projection. [...] Impulses which are not acknowledged by the subject and yet are his, are attributed to the object: the prospective victim. [...] Those impelled by blind murderous lust have always seen in the victim the pursuer who has driven them to desperate self-defense" (154). "Instead of the voice of conscience, it [the subject of anti-Semitism] hears voices; instead of inwardly examining itself in order to draw up a protocol of its own lust for power, it attributes to others the Protocol of the Elders of Zion" (156). "No matter what the makeup of the Jews may be in reality, their image, that of the defeated, has characteristics which must make totalitarian rule their mortal enemy: happiness without power, reward without work, a homeland without frontiers, religion without myth" (164–165).

- *VII. Anti-Semitism is based on pure irrational stereotypes, blanket generalisations and judgments, the most radical form of instrumental reason, ticket thinking that labels individuals as belonging to groups that should be annihilated, and hatred against Otherness:*

  "Anti-Semitic views always reflected stereotyped thinking. Today only that thinking is left. People still vote, but only between totalities" (166). "Judgment is no longer based on a real act of synthesis but on blind subsumption" (166–167).

  "It is not just the anti-Semitic ticket which is anti-Semitic, bur the ticket mentality itself. The rage against difference which is teleologically inherent in that mentality as the rancor of the dominated subjects of the domination of nature is always ready to attack the natural minority, even though it is the social minority which those subjects primarily threaten" (172).

  "The disregard for the subject makes things easy for the administration. Ethnic groups are transported to different latitudes; Individuals labeled 'Jew' are dispatched to the gas chambers" (167).

  "It has been shown, in fact, that anti-Semitism's prospects are no less good in 'Jew-free' areas than in Hollywood itself. Experience is replaced by cliche, the imagination active in experience by diligent acceptance" (166).

  "The more superfluous physical labor is made by the development of technology, the more enthusiastically it is set up as a model for mental work, which must not be tempted, however, to draw any awkward conclusions. That is the secret of advancing stupidity, on which anti-Semitism thrives" (167).

The political theorist and historian Moishe Postone grounds a critical theory of anti-Semitism and ideology in Marx's critique of commodity fetishism and points out the inherent connection of anti-Semitism and capitalism. Capitalism is grounded in an antagonism between the commodity's value and exchange-value on the one side and value and use-value on the other side. Postone says that in capitalism, value is "abstract, general, homogeneous", whereas use-value is "concrete, particular, material" (Postone 2003, 90). The commodity logic fetishises the concrete and veils the value as abstract social relation that underlies the commodity. In commodity fetishism, the abstract dimension appears as natural and endless, the concrete dimension as thing without social relations (Postone 2003, 91).

Postone (1980, 109) argues that in the value form, capitalism's "dialectical tension between value and use-value" is doubled in the appearance of money as abstract and the commodity as concrete. Capitalism requires for its existence both money and commodities, value and use-value, abstract and concrete labour. Money mediates commodity-exchange, so money cannot exist without the logic of commodities. Commodities are made for being exchanged. Money is the general equivalent of this exchange of commodities. So commodities cannot exist without exchange-value and a general equivalent. Another way of expressing the dialectic of commodity and money is to say that the sphere of commodity production exists in relation to the sphere of circulation and vice versa. Commodity fetishism is a form of appearance in which the abstract sociality of commodities is split off from its concreteness: only the immediate concrete (the good one consumes, the money one holds in the hand) is taken as reality. This immediate concrete obscures the existence of the more abstract, not directly visible social relations behind the immediate phenomena.

Postone says that in the anti-Semitic ideology, the dual character of the commodity of use-value and value is "'doubled' in the form of money (the manifest form of value) and of the commodity (the manifest form of use-value). Although the commodity as a social form embodies both value and use-value, the effect of this externalization is that the commodity appears only as its use-value dimension, as purely material. Money, on the other hand, appears as the sole repository of value, as the source and locus of the purely abstract, rather than as the externalized manifest form of the value dimension of the commodity form itself" (Postone 2003, 91).

The Critical Theory of Anti-Semitism

Postone argues that modern anti-Semitism is a biologisation and naturalisation of the commodity fetish. It would be based on the "notion that the concrete is 'natural'" and that the "natural" is "more 'essential' and closer to origins" (Postone 1980, 111). "Industrial capital then appears as the linear descendent of 'natural' artisanal labor", "industrial production" appears as "a purely material, creative process" (Postone 1980, 110). Ideology separates industrial capital and industrial labour from the sphere of circulation, exchange, and money that is seen as "parasitic" (Postone 1980, 110). In Nazi ideology, the "manifest abstract dimension is also biologized – as the Jews. The opposition of the concrete material and the abstract becomes the racial opposition of the Arians and the Jews" (Postone 1980, 112). Modern anti-Semitism is a one-sided "critique" of capitalism that sees the sphere of circulation as totality of capitalism, biologistically inscribes Jewishness into circulation and into capitalism, and excludes technology and industry – that are perceived as being productive and Aryan – from capitalism. In Nazi ideology, capitalism "appeared to be only its manifest abstract dimension, which was in turn held responsible for the economic social, and cultural changes associated with the rapid development of modern industrial capitalism" (Postone 2003, 93).

Anti-Semitism identifies the negative changes, dislocations, and deterritorialisations associated with capitalism, such as urbanisation, proletarianisation, individualisation, technification, and detraditionalisation, with the abstract side of capitalism that is perceived as the powerful universality of capitalism, socialism, or some other phenomenon. "Capitalism appeared to be only in its manifest abstract dimension which, in turn, was responsible for the whole range of concrete social and cultural changes associated with the rapid development of modern industrial capitalism" (Postone 1980, 112).

5.3 The *Black Notebooks*

In Heidegger's *Schwarze Hefte* (*Black Notebooks*) one can find passages where he talks about Jews:

- (a) "Die zeitweilige Machtsteigerung des Judentums aber hat darin ihren Grund, daß die Metaphysik des Abendlandes, zumal in ihrer neuzeitlichen Entfaltung, die Ansatzstelle bot für das Sichbreitmachen einer sonst leeren Rationalität und Rechenfähigkeit, die sich auf solchem Wege eine Unterkunft im ‚Geist' verschaffte, ohne die verborgenen Entscheidungsbezirke von sich aus je fassen zu können.

Je ursprünglicher und anfänglicher die künftigen Entscheidungen und Fragen werden, um so unzugänglicher bleiben sie dieser ‚Rasse'" (Heidegger 2014c, 46 [XII, 67–68])

"Jewry's temporary increase in power is, however, grounded in the fact that Western metaphysics, especially in its modern development, furnishes the starting point for the diffusion of a generally empty rationality and calculative ability, which in this way provides a refuge in 'spirit', without being able grasp the hidden decision regions on their own. The more originary and primordial the prospective decisions and questions, the more they remain inaccessible to this 'race'"[3].

- (b) "Die Juden ‚leben' *bei ihrer betont rechnerischen Begabung* am längsten schon nach dem Rasseprinzip, weshalb sie sich auch am heftigsten gegen die uneingeschränkte Anwendung zur Wehr setzen. Die Einrichtung der rassischen Aufzucht entstammt nicht dem ‚Leben' selbst, sondern der Übermächtigung des Lebens durch die Machenschaft. Was diese mit solcher Planung betreibt, ist eine *vollständige Entrassung* der Völker durch die Einspannung derselben in die gleichgebaute und gleichschnittige Einrichtung alles Seienden. Mit der Entrassung geht eine Selbstentfremdung der Völker in eines – der Verlust der Geschichte – d.h. der Entscheidungsbezirke zum Seyn" (Heidegger 2014c, 56 [XII, 82–83]).

"The Jews "live" by their marked talent for calculation second only to the principle of race, which is why they are resisting its consistent application with utmost violence. The establishment [Einrichtung] of racial breeding [eugenics] does not stem from "life" itself, but from the overpowering of life through machination [technology]. What they push forward with such a plan is the complete deracialization of all peoples by clamping them into a uniformly constructed and tailored establishment [Einrichtung] of all beings. At one with de-racialization is the self-alienation of peoples – the loss of history – i.e., the decision regions of Be-ing".

- (c) "Auch der Gedanke einer Verständigung mit England im Sinne einer Verteilung der ‚Gerechtsamen' der Imperialismen trifft nicht ins Wesen des geschichtlichen Vorgangs, den England jetzt innerhalb des Amerikanismus und des Bolschewismus und d. h. zugleich auch des Weltjudentums zu Ende spielt. Die Frage nach der Rolle des *Weltjudentums* ist keine rassische, sondern die metaphysische Frage nach der Art von Menschentümlichkeit, die *schlechthin ungebunden* die Entwurzelung alles Seienden aus dem Sein als weltgeschichtliche, Aufgabe' übernehmen kann" (Heidegger 2014c, 243 [XIV, 121])

The Black Notebooks

"The idea of an understanding with England in terms of a distribution of imperialist 'prerogatives' misses the essence of the historical process, in which England plays along with Americanism and Bolshevism and at the same time world Jewry to an end. The question of the role of world Jewry is not racial, but the metaphysical question of the type of humanity that can accept from Being the world-historical 'task' of uprooting all beings".

- (d) "Das Weltjudentum, aufgestachelt durch die aus Deutschland herausgelassenen Emigranten, ist überall unfaßbar und braucht sich bei aller Machtentfaltung nirgends an kriegerischen Handlungen zu beteiligen, wogegen uns nur bleibt, das beste Blut der Besten des eigenen Volkes zu opfern" (Heidegger 2014c, 262 [XV, 17])

"World Jewry, spurred on by emigrants allowed to leave Germany, is pervasive and impalpable, using all its powers to avoid participating in military actions, whereas all that remains to us is to sacrifice the best blood of the best of our own people".

Peter Trawny (2014, 11) argues in his book *Heidegger und der Mythos der jüdischen Weltverschwörung* (*Heidegger and the Myth of Jewish World Conspiracy*) that such quotes are characteristic for Heidegger's onto-historical anti-Semitism (seins-geschichtlicher Antisemitismus). The question arises how one can interpret these passages with the help of Adorno's elements of anti-Semitism. Heidegger advised the *Black Notebooks* should be published as the final part of his *Collected Works* (see: Heidegger 2014c, 279), which may be an indication that they have a special role, constitute his legacy (Trawny 2014, 12), or the ground of his thought.

Richard Wolin (2014), who had expressed scepticism about Emmanuel Faye's (2009) book *Heidegger: The Introduction of Nazism into Philosophy* (see Cohen 2009), argued after the publication of the *Black Notebooks*: "Heidegger's philosophical partisanship for National Socialism was not a series of contingent errors or odd misjudgements. It was a betrayal of philosophy, of reasoning and thinking, in the most profound sense. [...] Given the disturbing revelations contained in the *Black Notebooks*, any discussion of Heidegger's legacy that downplays or diminishes the extent of his political folly stands guilty, by extension, of perpetuating the philosophical betrayal initiated by the Master himself".

Tom Rockmore, author of *On Heidegger's Nazism and Philosophy* (Rockmore 1997), welcomes Trawny's book, but somewhat disagrees with its conclusions: Trawny "thinks Heidegger had a kind of private anti-Semitism, which was only revealed in the second half of the 1930s in his seinsgeschichtlicher Antisemitismus [onto-historical anti-Semitism], whereas I think that the anti-Semitism was there all the time and was visible for anyone who wanted to look" (Rockmore 2014).

I want to now relate the quotes from the *Black Notebooks* to Adorno's elements of anti-Semitism.

In quote (a), Heidegger sees Jews as a powerful group, which plays with the myth of a Jewish world conspiracy (VI). He furthermore argues that this group has a specific quality, namely a calculative rationality that is grounded in Western metaphysics. He does not argue that this is a biological characteristic, but a socio-natural one, i.e. he constructs "the Jews" as a homogenous collective (VII), attributes to them and blames them for qualities of capitalism (III). The identification of Jews with instrumental rationality has a double feature: instrumental rationality on the one hand is an expression of the drive to accumulate capital and power and on the other hand the operating principle of modern technology. Heidegger blames Jews both for the logic of capitalism and industrialism (II, VII).

Quote (b) implies that Heidegger blames Jews for what he calls "deracialisation" (*Entrassung*). He accuses them here for impurifying blood that he considers pure and original. They would however oppose the application of the principle of race to themselves. What can he mean when he speaks of such an application? The Nazis introduced in 1935 the Nuremberg Racial Laws that classified people with three or four Jewish grandparents as "Jews", those with one or two Jewish grandparents as "crossbreed" (*Mischling*), and those without Jewish grandparents as "Aryans". The preface to the law said that it is "pervaded by the insight that the purity of German blood is the precondition for the survival of the German people" and "ensouled by the unfaltering will to protect the German nation for all future"[4]. It prohibited sex and marriage between what it considered to be Aryans and non-Aryans. Heidegger in this passage seems to allude to these Laws and blame Jews for their own persecution by the Nazis. Heidegger here makes a racist argument (I) that constructs Jews as a general collective (VII) to whom he ascribed biological features (I). He blames the victims for their oppression (VI). Jürgen Habermas (1983, 184) stresses in a different context that Heidegger after 1945 did not publicly condemn the Nazis and his role in the Nazi regime, but blamed the victims. The principle of race would be the consequence of machinations, a concept by which Heidegger means modern technology (Trawny 2014, 22, 34). So Heidegger blames Jews both for the negative features of modern technology as well as for their racist oppression. Heidegger (1989, 1999) also uses the notion of machination (M*achenschaften*) in his *Beiträge zur Philosophie* (*Contributions to Philosophie*, 1936–1938), where he says that the "dominance of reason as equalization of all people is merely the consequence of Christianity and Christianity is fundamentally of Jewish origin"[5] (Heidegger 1999, 38).

In quote (c), Heidegger uses the term "world Jewry" (Weltjudentum), which constructs Jews as a homogenous collective (VII) that rules the world (VI). It would not be a biological, but a social and political feature of Jews that they are "uprooted", by which he means an opposition to what he sees as the German's rootedness in soil, nation, and nature. Heidegger implies that Jews are cosmopolitan and international, which he sees as negative features of modernity that destroy an original organicity that he identifies with the Germans. Heidegger here identifies Jews with modernity (VI, III) and longs for a pre-modern society that he associates with the Germans. He also alludes to traditions, mystic and magic origins that he considers to be lost because of the influence of modernity that he sees as being Jewish in character (V).

In quote (d), Heidegger blames Jews indirectly for the war against Germany by implying that they have influence on the Allied forces (II, VI). He in a racist (I) manner argues that the Germans are victims who have to defend themselves (VI: the actual offenders are interpreted as being victims and victims blamed as being culprits). The formulation "the best blood of the best" in a racist manner assumes that the Germans are a biologically superior race (I).

Heidegger in these quotes employs six of the seven elements of anti-Semitism that Adorno identified: he sees Jews and Germans as forming two races (I), identifies Jews with modernity, capitalism, and modern technology (II, III), makes use of mystical and naturalistic logic by arguing that Jews are uprooted and threaten the Germans' rootedness (V), and describes Jews as a powerful "world Jewry" that rules the world (VI) as well as a homogenous collective to which he ascribes negative biological, social, and political characteristics (VII). The only feature of anti-Semitism that is not present is the religious element (IV), which can be explained by the circumstance that Christian religion does not play a role in Nazi ideology.

All four quotes were written in 1939–1941, which shows that Heidegger after he had stepped down as vice-chancellor of the University of Freiburg in 1934 remained a committed Nazi and anti-Semite at least until 1941. The *Black Notebooks* deconstructs the myth that Heidegger stepped down as vice-chancellor because he was opposed to Nazi ideology. Peter Trawny (2014, 28) argues that Heidegger was disappointed by the

Nazi's modernism and their use of modern technology and that he had a specific version of Nazi ideology in mind that he termed "spiritual National Socialism"[6] (Heidegger 2014a, 135 [Überlegungen und Winke III, §72]). This version of Nazi ideology is, as the quotes show, definitely based on anti-Semitism. In notes made in the *Black Notebooks* in autumn 1932, Heidegger saw Nazism as barbaric and identified this barbarity its greatness: "National Socialism is a barbaric principle. This is its essence and its possible greatness"[7].

Martin Heidegger's son Hermann, who is in charge of the publication of his father's collected works, argues that the comments about Jews are only present on "a total of three out of the *Black Notebook's* 1 250 pages"[8]. He says about the accusation that his father and his philosophy were anti-Semitic: "It is true that he was critical of World-Jewry, but he definitely was not an anti-Semite"[9]. The term World-Jewry (*Weltjudentum*) is in itself problematic because it constructs Jews as homogenous worldwide collective power. It is a dangerous argument to argue that Heidegger was no Nazi and anti-Semite because his anti-Semitic arguments are limited to some quotes. The critique of modernity and modern technology is crucial for Heidegger's work, but his critique remains in most of his works phenomenological without ana-lysing the actual causes. The discussed quotes are so important because they show that Heidegger's critique of modernity was short-circuited and in a manner typical for anti-Semitic ideology blames Jews for phenomena that are characteristic for and have their roots in capitalism as a whole. National Socialism is, as Moishe Postone (1980, 2003) has shown, a short-circuited critique of capitalism that does not question ca-pitalism as totality, but inscribes its negative features into Jews.

Strategies commonly used to defend Heidegger include attempts to argue that the "uninitiated" do not understand the full significance and meaning of his works[10], that Heidegger's political and philosophical positions are non-overlapping (Heidegger the man and Heidegger the thinker), that Heidegger only adhered to Nazi ideology during a short period while he was the University of Freiburg's rector in 1933/34, that he defended Jews, and that he conceptually opposed Nazism (for an overview of such arguments see: Rockmore and Margolis 1989, x; Rockmore, 1997, 3–7). Some of the books on the topic of Heidegger and Nazism, such as the ones by Farías (1989), Rockmore (1997), and Faye (2009), have deconstructed these myths. It is not unlikely that Heideggerians even after the publication of the *Black Notebooks* will come up with defensive arguments similar to the ones made earlier or will extend such lines of thought. They could for example argue that the anti-Semitic passages are limited to single pages, that Heidegger did not publish them during his lifetime, and that his views therefore remained private. Such arguments are now however even harder to make than before publication of the *Black Notebooks*. It is a fact that Heidegger himself instructed that the *Black Notebooks* should be published as part of his collected works' final volumes (Trawny 2014; Heidegger 2014c, 279). Given that his philosophical notes are now public knowledge and Heidegger considered their publication important, it is crucial to engage with them and to discuss their impacts and implications.

It is unlikely that Heidegger's anti-Semitism was restricted to the time of National Socialism (1933–1945). In a letter to his wife, Heidegger in 1920 wrote that villages were "flooded with Jews and racketeers"[11] (Heidegger 2007, 112). The fact that Heidegger treated his Jewish students and his Jewish lover Hannah Arendt with respect, an argument that those who want to defend Heidegger tend to use, does not stand in opposition to his anti-Semitism; it rather may be characteristic for the anti-Semitic acceptance of what Hannah Arendt (1958, 56) in her characterisation of anti-Semitic ideology termed "exceptional Jews"[12]. Victor Farías (1989, 4) argues that when "Heidegger decided to join the National Socialist Party, he was following an already-prepared path" and that Heidegger's thoughts were "nourished in traditions of authoritarianism, anti-semitism, and ultranationalism that sanctified the homeland in its most local sense".

Theodor W. Adorno argues that Nazi ideology also is immanent in *Sein und Zeit* that was published in 1926 (Heidegger 1926). Adorno writes in his analysis that Heidegger's "metaphysics of death" cultivates "the heroic possibilities of death" and is "a propaganda for death" (Adorno 1965/2001, 131; see also Löwith 1946). Heidegger's combination of philosophy and poetry is for Adorno (1960/1961) "provincial kitsch" (229) that uses "archaic language" (230) [translation from German]. For Adorno, Heidegger's fetishism of the origin is a form of mysticism (Adorno 1960/1961, 32–34). The "cult of origin and renewal" would "not by accident and not externally have sympathy with the barbarism that took shape in his [Heidegger's] political history"[13] so that foundations of "National-Socialist ideology" [translation from German] would be contained in *Sein und Zeit* (241). "Heidegger's agreement with fascism and the ideology of the conservative revolution, the more elegant version of fascist ideology, was not a lack of character of the philosopher, but lay in the content of his doctrine"[14] (287).

Farías' (1989) interpretation of *Sein und Zeit* is that it contains "philosophical beliefs that foreshadow Heidegger's later convictions" (60) and that there is an "inner continuity of Heidegger's thinking between 1927 and 1933" (62). Farías (1989, 4) especially stresses in this context Heidegger's concepts of "'authentic' being-in-community, and his own links with the people, the hero, and the struggle (§74) – and his rejection of democratic forms of social life, a rejection inspired by the ideas of Paul Yorck von Wartenburg and Wilhelm Dilthey (§77)".

For the philosophy and study of technology and the media, it is of particular importance that Heidegger in the *Black Notebooks* blames Jews for modern technology's instrumental reason.

5.4 Heidegger, the Media, and Technology

Peter Trawny (2014, 43) points out the importance of the role of technology in Heidegger's anti-Semitic thoughts: "When Heidegger regards the 'skill of calculation' as Jewish and typically modern, then all of this is altogether declared as an epiphenomenon of modern technology" (translation from German). "But the character of the technical, that which is like 'machinations', was the 'groundless' (das Bodenlose) and the 'worldlessness' (das Weltlose) that the philosopher ascribed to Jews" (Trawny 2014, 55; translation from German). Trawny (2014, 79) argues that Heidegger saw modern technology as the enemy of the Germans and therefore asked himself: "Was the triumph of technology not at last the victory of 'world Jewry'?" (translation from German).

Heidegger's technophobic conservative opposition to modern technology was already present in *Sein und Zeit*, where he introduced the concept of das Man (the they) and das Zeug (the equipment). "We shall call the beings encountered in taking care *useful things* [das Zeug]. In our dealings we find utensils for writing, utensils for sewing, utsensils for working, driving, measuring. We must elucidate the kind of being of useful things. This can be done following the guideline of the previous definition of what makes useful thing a useful thing: its utility [Zeughaftigkeit]"[15] (Heidegger 2010, 68).

Technology for Heidegger involves a means-end relationship: "A useful thing is essentially 'something in order to [...]'. The different kinds of 'in order to' such as serviceability, helpfulness, usability, handiness, constitute a totality of useful things. The structure of 'in order to' ['um-zu'] contains a *reference [Verweisung]* of something to something"[16] (Heidegger 2010, 68). "We shall call the useful thing's kind of being in which it reveals itself by itself *handiness* [Zuhandenheit]"[17] (Heidegger 2010, 69).

Heidegger hints at the fact that with the modernisation of society, the use of technologies was no longer limited to the household economy, but was extended to the creation of a public infrastructure: "The work taken care of in each case is not only at hand in the domestic world of the workshop, but rather in the *public world*. Along with the public world, the *surrounding world of nature* is discovered and accessible to everyone. In taking care of things, nature is discovered as having some definite direction on paths, streets, bridges, and buildings"[18] (Heidegger 2010, 70).

There are however problems that technology faces that Heidegger terms das Unzuhandene (the unhandy) (Heidegger 1926, 98–99; Heidegger 2010, 72–73): things that are unusable, missing, obstacles, unsuited, damaged. The unhandy means "conspicuousness, obtrusiveness, and obstinacy"[19] (Heidegger 2010, 73). "Unhandy things are disturbing and make evident the *obstinacy* of what is initially to be taken care of before anything else"[20] (Heidegger 2010, 73).

Heidegger introduces these problems and disturbances caused by technology in §16, which is soon thereafter followed by a section that discusses Descartes' rational ontology of the world that Heidegger sees as opposed to his phenomenology (§§19–21). In the chapter that follows (chapter 4), Heidegger introduces the concept of das Man (the they), a world-less form of being that, given the examples used, stands for modernity and thereby also for modern technology and modern media.

When introducing the they, Heidegger explicitly refers (besides for example public transport) to newspaper and entertainment and argues that the these media bring about massification, anonymity, manipulation, and dictatorship that alienate humans from each other, i.e. from sociality:

> "We have shown earlier how the public 'surrounding world' is always already at hand and taken care of in the surrounding world nearest to us. In utilizing public transportation, in the use of information services such as the newspaper, every other is like the next. This being-with-one-another dissolves one's own Da-sein completely into the kind of being of 'the others' in such a way that the others, as distinguishable and explicit, disappear more and more. In this inconspicuousness and unascertainability, the they unfolds its true dictatorship. We enjoy ourselves and have fun the way *they* enjoy themselves. We read, see, and judge literature and art the way *they* see and judge. But we also withdraw from the 'great mass' the way *they* withdraw, we find 'shocking' what *they* find shocking. The they, which is nothing definite

and which all are, though not as a sum, prescribes the kind of being of everydayness."[21]

(Heidegger 2010, 123)

It here becomes evident that Heidegger advances a conservative critique that sees modern technology as such a problem. The problem is formulated abstractly as das Man (the they), but its causes and context remain unclear in the phenomenology that Heidegger formulated in *Sein und Zeit*. It is for Heidegger certainly not the capitalist use and design of and bureaucratic shaping of technology that form this context because class, the state, and capitalism are categories that are absent from the analysis. Heidegger does not argue for a re-design of modern technology and modern society, but for their abolishment. Tom Rockmore (1997, 215) argues that Heidegger's conservative anti-technologism was influenced by the works of Friedrich Nietzsche, Oswald Spengler, and Ernst Jünger. Were one to put "Heidegger's technological vision [...] into practice, modern life as we know it would have to be abandoned" (Rockmore 1997, 233).

David J. Gunkel and Taylor (2014) argue that the "ceaseless noise of public chit-chat" is a form of das Man (41) and that this concept is of special relevance in the time of social media: "Heidegger's concept of idle talk is particularly prescient, given the advent of narrowcasting applications like Facebook and Twitter" (39). Both platforms are certainly predominantly platforms of mundane everyday information and commu-nication, a lot of which is advertising, entertainment, self-presentation, and reputation management transmitted at high speed, which reflects the instrumental logic of ca-pitalism, neoliberalism, and individualism. Gunkel and Taylor do not discuss in further detail if this feature is in their view immanent in social media as such or if it has not rather to do with the capitalist design and use of these platforms that reflect the very patterns of capitalism. The second assumption also implies the potential for social media's non-capitalist use and re-design that are focused on communicative action, slow politics, political discussion, and political organisation.

For Heidegger (1929), all metaphysics is forgetful of being (Seinsvergessenheit), it equates being (Sein) with bei-ings (Seiendes), forgets and does not ask the question about the truth of being. In the postscript to his 1929 professorial inaugural lecture *Was ist Metaphysik?* (*What is Metaphysics?*) at the University of Freiburg, Heidegger argues that modern science is the dominant form of metaphysics in modern society, "a means of the calculating reification of be-ing"[22] (Heidegger 1929, 43), which shows the inherent connection that Heidegger saw between metaphysics, modern science, and technology. He here again brings up the notion of calculating reason.

Heidegger, the Media, and Technology

In 1935/1936, Heidegger held a lecture titled *Basic Questions of Metaphysics* that was published under the name *What is a Thing?* (Heidegger 1935/1936): he characterises modern science as "a factual, experimental, measuring science" whose "fundamental characteristic is the manner of working with the things and the metaphysical projection of the thingness of the things" (68). So for Heidegger, mathematics is at the core of modern science and technology and its main feature is thingification. He confirms in this lecture that he sees mathematics, technology, and science, and modern metaphysics as inherently connected: "[M]odern natural science, modern mathematics, and modern metaphysics sprang from the same root of the mathematical in the wider sense" (97).

The question *What is a Thing?* brings up the question of reification/thingification. It is evident in *Sein und Zeit* that Heidegger (1926) must have read Lukács (1923) when he asks: "But what does reifying mean? Where does it arise from? Why is being 'initially' 'conceived' in terms of what is objectively present, *and not* in terms of things at hand that do, after all, lie *still nearer* to us? *Why* does this reification come to dominate again and again? How is the being of 'consciousness' *positively* structured so that reification remains inappropriate to it? Is the 'distinction' between 'consciousness' and 'thing' sufficient at all for a primordial unfolding of the ontological problematic?"[23] (Heidegger 2010, 414). Yet, as the *Black Notebooks* shows, the contexts of the thing and of the process of turning the social into things (Verdinglichung, reification, thingification) are very different in Lukács and Heidegger's works. Like in *Sein und Zeit*, also the 1935/1936 lectures connect the critique of calculating reason with a critique of Descartes. Heidegger (1935/1936) makes clear that the question *What is a Thing?* is for him the question concerning technology: "on this [modern] physics are founded all our giant power stations, our airplanes, radio and television, the whole technology which has altered the earth and man with it more than he suspects. These are realities, not viewpoints which some investigators 'distant from life' defend. Does one want science even 'closer to life'? I think that it is already so close that it suffocates us. Rather, we need the right distance from life in order to attain a perspective in which we measure what is going on with us human beings. No one knows this today" (13–14). The longing for origin, pre-modernity, and moving away from technology is evident here and is another dimension that distinguishes Heidegger from Lukács.

In a passage titled *Technology and Uprooting* (Technik und Entwurzelung) Heidegger (2014a, 364 [Überlegungen V, §87]) expresses in the *Black Notebooks* his opposition to technology and argues that the "radio and all kinds of organisation [...] destroy"[24] the village. He sees technology and organisation as "the opposite to all that is 'organic'"[25] (ibid.). The discussion of technology in the *Black Notebooks* shows that Heidegger considered the Nazis to be too modern in that they introduced modern technologies such as the radio that they used for ideological purposes. Heidegger seems to have had a pre-modern version of National Socialism in mind. He leaves no doubt that he not only opposes the Nazis' table-top radio (Volksempfänger) that allowed the audience to just listen to one station controlled by Nazi propaganda, but all forms of the radio and modern communication technology.

Heidegger therefore writes: "From this essential context follows that 'technology' can never be mastered by the völkisch-political worldview [the Nazi ideology]. What is already in essence a slave, can never become a master"[26] (Heidegger 2014a, 472 [Ueberlegungen VI, 87]). He speaks of National Socialism that is influenced by journalism and culture as "vulgar National Socialism"[27] (Heidegger 2014a, 142 [Überlegungen und Winke III, 81]), which makes once more clear that he hoped for the creation of a "spiritual National Socialism"[28] (Heidegger 2014a, 135 [Überlegungen und Winke III, §72]) without modern technology.

Heidegger's most important works on technology are the two essays *The Question Concerning Technology* and *The Turning* that go back to a series of lectures that he gave in the years 1949, 1950, and 1955 in Bremen and Munich. They were together published as the book *Die Technik und die Kehre* (Heidegger 1962) in German and *The Question Concerning Technology and Other Essays* (Heidegger 1977) in English.

When starting to talk about technology in *The Question Concerning Technology*, Heidegger (1962, 6) uses the term Zeug, which can be seen as a reference back to *Sein und Zeit*. For Heidegger, technology in essence is "a way of revealing" (Heidegger 1977, 12). It "has to do with the presencing [*Anwesen*] of that which at any given time comes to appearance in bringing-forth. Bringing-forth brings hither out of concealment forth into unconcealment" (11).

Heidegger (1977, 6) argues that Aristotle identified four important causes (causa materialis, cause formalis, causa finalis, causa efficiens), but modern technology is driven by the causa efficiens that is all about "means to obtain results, effects" (7). Modern technology would be a specific form of revealing, "a challenging [*Herausfordern*]" (14). Such challenging would challenge, i.e. dominate, nature and humans. It would therefore be "the monstrousness" [das Ungeheure] (16), the "*danger*" (26) and have "the character of a setting-upon" (16). Heidegger terms modern technology das *Ge-stell* (the Enframing), by which he means "that challenging claim which gathers man thither to order" (19). The Ge-stell is an instrumental form of revealing. "Enframing means the gathering together of that setting-upon which sets upon man, i.e., challenges him forth, to reveal the real, in the mode of ordering, as standing-reserve" (20). Modern technology as the Ge-stell would be associated with the exact sciences, mathematics, and modern physics (21) that have an instrumentalist worldview and believe in the calculability of the world.

The Ge-stell would result in the alienation of humans; man would have become "the order of the standing-reserve" [Besteller des Bestandes] (27). The Ge-stell endangers "man in his relationship to himself and to everything that is" (27). Heidegger takes newspapers and illustrated magazines as one of the examples for the Ge-stell and says that they "set public opinion to swallowing what is printed, so that a set configuration of opinion becomes available on demand" (18).

The power of capitalism and the modern state, or what Habermas (1984, 1987) terms the systems of modern society that colonise the lifeworld, are absent both in *Being and Time* and *The Question Concerning Technology*, which is idiosyncratic given that modern society is based on the accumulation of capital and bureaucratic power, two structures that frame the development and use of modern technology. So a major problem of Heidegger's approach is that it is not a political economy, but merely a phenomenology of technology. He describes attributes of modern technology, such as instrumental logic, calculation, physics, the exact sciences, mathematics, in both books, but leaves open the question, what the structural context of modern technology is? Heidegger's phenomenology in both books does not give an answer to the question what the causes of the problems he ascertains are. But he makes clear that the problem is not technology itself: "What is dangerous is not technology. There is no demonry of technology" (28). The danger would rather be the Ge-stell (28). The Ge-stell is however not an explanation in-itself, but an attribute of modern society. Heidegger neglects the analysis of capital and state power, two main features of modern society. So the two books leave open the question of the contexts of modernity's problems.

The *Black Notebooks* is, as we have seen in Section 5.3, a work, in which Heidegger tried to provided an answer to the question of what the structural contexts of modernity and modern technology are. And his answer is that the logic of calculability is Jewish. Heidegger identifies instrumental reason with Jews. So for him the cause and context of modernity and modern technology's problems – the rise of worldlessness and alienation – are seen in Jews.

There is a logical link between the *Black Notebooks*, *Being and Time*, and *The Question Concerning Technology*. The first provides the missing link and grounding for the second and the third. The *Black Notebooks* helps explain a theoretical void in the other two books. Das Man (the they) and das Ge-stell (the enframing) have in the *Black Notebooks* a grounding for Heidegger, namely what he and others term "world Jewry", i.e. the myth of a Jewish world conspiracy.

Only the full, unshortened, and uncensored publication of the *Black Notebooks* that Heidegger wrote after 1945 and public access to the Heidegger archive can show if he also wrote anti-Semitic philosophical notes after the Second World War ended and at the time when he wrote *The Question Concerning Technology* and later works.[29]

Heidegger also thought in *The Question Concerning Technology* about how humanity can be saved from the logic of modern technology. Technology could see "the possible arising of the saving power" (32). Heidegger associates such a salvation with "human reflection" (33), art as an alternative form of revealing, "the fine arts" (33), "poetry" (33), "everything poetical" (33), "the arrival of another destining" (39), "truth" (40), a focus on language and thinking (40), "the lightning-flash of the truth of Being" (45), "insight" (47) – what he all together calls the turning (die Kehre). Heidegger finally invokes the notion of the homeland in a mystical manner by asking: "Will we dwell as those at home in nearness, so that we will belong primarily within the fourfold of sky and earth, mortals and divinities?" (49). These thoughts are extremely abstract and idealist.

Heidegger imagines a new language and thinking that is at home in poetry as a form of rescue from modern technology. The only form of concreteness that Heidegger mentions when discussing the turning are poems by Hölderlin, Goethe, and Meister Eckehardt, from which he quotes. He exclusively alludes to non-Jewish German poets, which may be an indication that the turning and rescue also in *The Question Concerning Technology* remained what he in the *Black Notebooks* termed a spiritual National Socialism (see Section 5.3). The new language he imagines is definitely German in character. *Deutschtümelei* (German jingoism) remained an element of Heidegger's philosophy of technology after 1945.

Tom Rockmore (1997, 241, 242–243) concludes his analysis of Heidegger's philosophy of technology by pointing out the role of Nazi ideology in it:

> "Heidegger's failure to denounce, or even to acknowledge, Nazi practice can
> be interpreted as an oblique resistance to the practical consequences of his
> theoretical commitment. He was obviously unwilling to acknowledge the

Heidegger, the Media, and Technology

failure of his turn to Nazism, not for mere psychological reasons, but on good philosophical grounds; for his turn to Nazism was grounded in his own theory of Being, which he never abandoned. For the same reason, he was also unwilling to abandon National Socialism, or at least an ideal form of it, because of his continued interest in certain points where his thought converged with Nazism, including the coming to be of the Germans as German and the confrontation with technology. Heidegger's insensitivity to the effects of Nazism in practice is coupled, then, with a residual theoretical enthusiasm for a form of Nazism in theory. [...] Heidegger's supporters have suggested that Heidegger confronted Nazism through his theory of technology, or even that his theory of technology arises out of his confrontation with Nazism. Study of Heidegger's texts presents a different, darker picture of Heidegger, a thinker stubbornly committed to the metaphysical racism he shared with Nazism and to a revised version of the supposed Nazi effort to oppose technology. Heidegger's theory of technology is, then, not a confrontation with Nazism but a confrontation with technology from a Nazi perspective. Heidegger's theory of technology only extends, but does not free him from, his concern with National Socialism."

Rockmore (2009) also argues that Heidegger's philosophy of technology shares "the insistence on the authentic gathering of the *Volk*. Like his theory of Being, the theory of technology which derives from the theory of Being is intrinsically political, where politics is directed toward the authenticity of the Germans and beyond the Germans, toward knowledge of Being" (207).

Heidegger, in a 1949 lecture in Bremen that focused on the Ge-stell, Heidegger's concept of modern technology, argued: "Agriculture is now a motorized (*motorisierte*) food industry, in essence the same as the manufacturing of corpses in the gas chambers and extermination camps, the same as the blockade and starvation of the countryside, the same as the production of the hydrogen bombs"[30] (cited in: Farías 1989, 287). This talk was one of the events that prepared the publication of *The Question Concerning Technology*. In the published text, the quote was abridged: "Agriculture is now the mechanized food industry" (Heidegger 1977, 15).

Mahon O'Brien (2010) interprets this passage in a way that tries to turn Heidegger into a critical analyst of Nazism by arguing that he does not compare agricultural technologies to gas chambers because the formulation "in essence" would imply a more foundational level of analysis:

"Heidegger believes that the motorized food industry, the Holocaust, the splitting of the atom, nuclear bombs, have as their common feature a technological backdrop. That is, regardless of the moral status of what happens or is done in each, they involve a *technological way of revealing* the world, or people or energy or animals. That is not to say that Heidegger is morally equating the consumption of animals with genocide. What he is saying, I would submit, is that the essence of technology, *Gestell*, holds sway as what is common in their approach to situations which we would *never* have conceived of in that way before. They indicate a mode of revealing the world or people or animals hitherto unimaginable. The fact that we were able to 'reveal' a *people*, in this instance "The Jews", in such a way, might well be more morally repugnant than any of the other examples mentioned. But there is also something terribly sinister in looking for solutions to military problems through the unleashing of nature's stored up and harnessed power and thereby eradicating entire cities. The mass production of meat itself represents a change in the way we look at animals and their habitats. The point is that all of them have at their core a way of revealing the world which Heidegger is trying to call attention to. It is not a moral judgment to the effect that there are no qualitative differences. He is drawing attention to the fact that each of them involves a very specific and disturbing way of *revealing*."

(O'Brien 2010, 13)

Gunkel and Taylor (2014, ix) make a comparable defensive argument: "It is critically important to note here that Heidegger is *not* saying that the mechanization of agriculture and the extermination camps are equivalent phenomena. Instead, the similarity being alluded to is one of *essence*, and it is this conceptualization that has profound implications for our understanding of media as an integral part of a diverse technological environment that shares certain *essential* features". They argue that Heidegger wants to point towards the "wider and more generalizable significance of the uniquely industrial nature of the Holocaust" (x).

Both O'Brien and Gunkel/Taylor try to defend Heidegger by setting up an implicit comparison to Horkheimer and Adorno's (2002) argument in the *Dialectic of the Enlightenment* that instrumental reason results in the Enlightenment's values turning against themselves so that forms of barbarism that enable Auschwitz emerge. Instrumental reason carried to the end enables Auschwitz, but such a development requires a political context, capitalism, and fascism, about which Heidegger tends to be silent in his writings. Moishe Postone (1980, 2003) has built on Horkheimer and Adorno's argument and argues that Auschwitz was a negative factory, by which he means a factory for the annihilation of perceived enemies, absolute negativity.

National Socialism was the ultimate realisation of capitalism's fascist tendencies. It was a political project that tried to destroy Jews, the working class and its political representatives, and other groups with utmost violence, including forced labour and extermination camps. It was not simply an extension or the highest form of capitalism, Fordism, or the capitalist factory system, but rather a negative factory for the extermination of Jews, political opponents, and others whom the Nazis considered as enemies. Moishe Postone describes this system the following way:

> "A capitalist factory is a place where value is produced, which "unfortunately" has to take the form of the production of goods, of use-values. The concrete is produced as the necessary carrier of the abstract. The extermination camps were not a terrible version of such a factory but, rather, should be seen as its grotesque, Aryan, "anticapitalist" negation. Auschwitz was a factory to "destroy value", that is, to destroy the personifications of the abstract. Its organization was that of a fiendish industrial process, the aim of which was to "liberate" the concrete from the abstract. The first step was to dehumanize, that is, to rip away the "mask" of humanity, of qualitative specificity, and reveal the Jews for what "they really are" – shadows, ciphers, numbered abstractions. The second step was to then eradicate that abstractness, to transform it into smoke, trying in the process to wrest away the last remnants of the concrete material "use-value": clothes, gold, hair, soap."
>
> (Postone 1980, 114)

The Nazis fully turned labour into a killing and extermination device. Forced labour forces had to work in the arms industry and other industries that were privately run and required workforces. Auschwitz and other extermination camps were to a large degree negative factories – factories that aimed at the killing of Jews and other groups and individuals whom the Nazis considered as their enemies.

Heidegger only stresses the continuities of instrumental reason and disregards the contexts that make a qualitative difference, namely that Auschwitz does not produce use-values, but annihilate humans, which is captured by the category of the negative factory. This disregard and the context of Heidegger's own political history makes his remark so problematic. Neither O'Brien nor Gunkel/Taylor engage with the critical theory of anti-Semitism when discussing Heidegger's comment. The "care structure" of their arguments seems to be all about defending Heidegger against any criticism that argues that he was a Nazi and that his ideology was reflected in his work. One wonders if the publication of the *Black Notebooks* can challenges such beliefs in and defence of Heidegger or not. Emmanuel Faye (2009, 272) concludes about the passage in the Bremen lecture that it "tends to exonerate National Socialism from its radical responsibility in the annihilation of the Jewish people and the destruction of the human being to which the industry of Nazism was committed".

The Frankfurt School's works form a critique of instrumental reason, a critique of capitalism's reduction of humans to instruments whose labour serves capital accumulation, a critique of domination questioning the instrumentalisation of humans for fostering the rule and power of the few, and a critique of ideology questioning the instrumentalisation of human thinking. Frankfurt School critique of instrumental reason is however fundamentally different from Heidegger's analysis. Whereas Critical Theory's context is political economy, Heidegger's phenomenology is short-circuited and therefore prone to turn into an instrumental ideology itself. Stanley Aronowitz summarises the Frankfurt School's critique of instrumental reason in the introduction to a collection of Horkheimer's essays:

> "The bourgeoisie tolerated critical reason during its revolutionary rise to power against the restrictions imposed by feudal social relations. Once victorious, however, reason could only be tolerated in its quantitative forms – mathematics and science, which became instruments of bourgeois rule insofar as it required the expansion of capital to maintain its hegemony over society. In capitalist society, science was useful to the extent that it was trans-formed into industrial technique. But empiricism had gone too far. It left thought a slave to the given reality. The bourgeoisie systematically demythologized thought of its feudal inheritance, but it created new myths shrouded in the new absolutism of science.
>
> The two sides of bourgeois thought, positivism and metaphysics, are the unified world view of the bourgeoisie, split according to the prevailing division of labor between science, which serves industry, and religions and secular spiritual ideologies, which serve social domination."
>
> (in: Horkheimer 2002, XV)

Horkheimer for example explains the background of instrumental reason the following way:

> "Thus, in Europe, in the last decades before the outbreak of the present war, we find the chaotic growth of individual elements of social life: giant economic enterprises, crushing taxes, an enormous increase in armies and armaments, coercive discipline, one-sided cultivation of the natural sciences, and so on. Instead of rational organization of domestic and international relations, there was the rapid spread of certain portions of civilization at the expense of the whole. One stood against the other, and mankind as a whole was destroyed thereby. [...] In business life, the *Fachgeist,* the spirit of the specialist, knows only profit, in military life power, and even in science only success in a special discipline. When this spirit is left unchecked, it typifies an anarchic state of society."
>
> (Horkheimer 2002, 266)

If one wants to ground a critique of modern technology and media, then approaches are available that are much better grounded in the analysis of society and political economy than Heidegger's phenomenology. Frankfurt School critique is one of them, although certainly not the only one.

5.5 Conclusion

I have in this chapter asked the question: what are and should be the implications of the publication of the *Black Notebooks* for the reception of Heidegger in the study, theory, and philosophy of media, communication, and technology?

The analysis showed that Heidegger's *Black Notebooks* uses most of the elements of anti-Semitism that Adorno identifies: Heidegger sees Jews and Germans as forming two races, identifies Jews with modernity, capitalism, and modern technology, makes use of mystical and naturalistic logic by arguing that Jews are uprooted and threaten the Germans' proclaimed rootedness, and considers Jews as a powerful "world Jewry" that rules the world as well as a homogenous collective to which he ascribes negative biological, social, and political characteristics. He ascribes to Jews a specific feature of capitalism, namely instrumental reason, by saying that they have a talent for calculation, and thereby conducts a National Socialist short-circuited critique of capitalism that ascribes capitalism and its ills to Jews.

Given that Heidegger identifies instrumental reason with Jews, his anti-Semitism has larger implications for his philosophy of technology and the media. There is a logical link between the *Black Notebooks'* anti-Semitism and the analysis of technology in *Being and Time* and *The Question Concerning Technology*. The first provides the missing link and grounding for the second and the third. The *Black Notebooks* helps explaining a theoretical void in these other two books. Das Man (the they) and das Ge-stell (the enframing) have a grounding for Heidegger in the *Black Notebooks*, namely what he and others term "world Jewry", i.e. the myth of Jewish world conspiracy. *Deutschtümelei* (=German jingoism) remained an element of Heidegger's philosophy of technology after 1945.

What can and should the implications of the Black Notebooks' anti-Semitism and their grounding character for other of Heidegger's works be for the field of media and communication studies?

Heidegger's works have had a significant influence on contemporary media and communication studies, as evidenced by works that make him the or a central philosophical influence and focus on issues such as television and broadcasting (Scannell 2014, 1996), information ethics (Capurro 2003; Capurro, Eldred and Nagel 2013), the general philosophy of technology (Stiegler 1998, 2009, 2011; Ihde 2010), the theory of media and digital media (Gunkel and Taylor 2014), robotics and Artificial Intelligence (Gunkel 2012), the Internet (Dreyfus 2009), the philosophy of information (Borgmann 2000), digital culture (Miller 2012), digital media surveillance (Herzogenrath-Amelung 2013), digital media and transport (Herzogenrath-Amelung, Troullinou and Thomopoulos 2015), interaction studies (Dourish 2004), the philosophy of virtual reality (Heim 1993, 1998).

The works of these scholars tend to be interesting and critical. I do not see why they need Heidegger and cannot express the things they want to articulate without Heidegger and by making use of alternative, critical traditions. It rather seems to me that Heidegger fetishism is often l'art pour l'art, Heidegger pour Heidegger, a tactic that aims at creating an aura of complexity by evoking Heidegger although the same content could be expressed without him. Most of these scholars see themselves as political progressives. Often they are also vocal in voicing dissent with the opinion that Heidegger's philosophy is a form of Nazism. So for example Gunkel and Taylor argue that Heidegger's philosophy is a good way for critically understanding technology in Nazism and Nazi ideology:

"There is nothing in Heidegger's philosophy that is innately fascistic. In fact, his critique of technology explored in this book raises profound issues about technology's role in dehumanizing people, of which the Nazi death camps were the darkest historical manifestation. In this case, unalloyed censure of Heidegger's thought based upon his deeply flawed political affiliation is not only an inadequate response – it misses an opportunity to understand better the role technology played in facilitating Nazi ideology."

(Gunkel and Taylor 2014, viii)

At the same time, to my knowledge none of the mentioned scholars has thus far (until March 2015) commented publicly whether or not the anti-Semitism evidenced in the *Black Notebooks* that was published in spring 2014 has to lead to changes in the reception of Heidegger in media and communication studies. The judgement of Tom Rockmore (1997, 2) in his study *On Heidegger's Nazism and Philosophy* is also valid for the reception of the *Black Notebooks*: "To 'bracket' this issue, simply to turn away from the problem, to refuse to confront it, is silently to accept what a number have seen as the totalitarian dimension in one of the most important theories of this century". This non-reaction constitutes a strange asymmetry in the way Heideggerians deal with their philosophical guru's relationship to Nazism.

To be fair, one must say that one can and should not demand from those who are experts on Heidegger to understand German. One can be a perfect expert of a philosopher's works without having read the originals. To claim otherwise is a strange form of jingoism. Neither the *Black Notebooks* nor Peter Trawny's (2014) thoughtful analysis have been translated from German to English, which makes it difficult for scholars who do not read German to comment. Hopefully an English translation of Trawny's analysis will be available soon. In the meantime, also recordings of interesting English talks and discussions about the *Black Notebooks* involving Peter Trawny, Tom Rockmore, and others are available online: Peter Trawny's talks "Philosophy and Anti-Semitism: The Heidegger Case"[31] and "Heidegger, 'World-Judaism', and Modernity"[32], Tom Rockmore's talk "Heidegger's Anti-Semitism: Philosophy or Worldview?"[33], the talks given at the 2014 conference "Heidegger's *Black Notebooks*: Philosophy, Politics, Anti-Semitism"[34], a panel discussion with Emmanuel Faye, Jeffrey van Davis, Karsten Harries, Richard Wolin, and Thomas Sheehan[35], or a panel discussion with Peter Trawny and Babette Babich[36]. Such materials allow and have allowed academics and others to form an opinion on the issue.

So my argument is that there are no good grounds for silence. A good example of a concrete reaction to the publication of the *Black Notebooks* is the anti-fascist practice of

Günter Figal, professor of philosophy at the University of Freiburg, who in early 2015 stepped down from his position as president of the Heidegger Society. He argued that the *Black Notebooks* contain "anti-Semitic sentences" and that it would be difficult for him to "stand for a person, who has made such comments and who has made comments that I can only find detestable [abscheulich]"[37] (translation from German). He says that he thinks the philosophical future is "the end of Heideggerianism"[38] (translation from German).

Peter Trawny (2014), who is editor of the *Black Notebooks* and some other volumes of Heidegger's Collected Works as well as director of the University of Wuppertal's Martin-Heidegger-Institute, argues that given that Heidegger's anti-Semitism was formulated in a philosophical context (120), it is a fact that Heidegger wrote these philosophical comments at a time when Synagogues were burning in Germany (122), and that in them he formulated a lot of sorrow about what he considered to be the Germans' suffering but none about Jewish suffering (122); the *Black Notebooks* will result in a "crisis of the reception of his thought" (114) and require a "revision of the engagement with Heidegger's thinking" (117) [translation from German].

How can and will such an engagement with Heidegger's anti-Semitism look like and which form will it take in the field of media and communication studies, where Heidegger's general philosophy and his philosophy of technology have played an in-fluential role? This chapter is my contribution and an attempt to start such a debate. My personal view is that the most appropriate reaction is that scholars distance themselves from Heidegger's works and stop giving prominence to them within media and communication studies (and other fields). It is time that Heideggerians abandon Heidegger and instead focus on alternative traditions of thought.

The French philosopher Emmanuel Faye (2009, 319) argues that Heidegger, "who has espoused the foundations of Nazism cannot be considered a philosopher" and that the "moment has come to resist the ill-advised opinion that Heidegger was a 'great philosopher'". The publication of the *Black Notebooks* has made this judgement even more topical. It is now also the moment where scholars should consider stopping to eulogise and reference Heidegger when theorising and analysing the media, com-munication, culture, technology, digital media, and the Internet.

Conclusion

Notes

1 German original: "Was heute vollends als Philosophie des Nationalsozialismus her-umgeboten wird, aber mit der inneren Wahrheit und Größe dieser Bewegung (nämlich mit

der Begegnung der planetarisch bestimmten Technik und des neuzeitlichen Menschen) nicht das Geringste zu tun hat, das macht seine Fischzüge in diesen trüben Gewässern der "Werte' und der "Ganzheiten'" (Heidegger 1983, 208).

2 German original: "die Herrschaft des rechnenden Denkens selbst".

3 Source of this and the following translations from the *Black Notebooks*: http://www. counter-currents.com/2014/03/heidegger-on-world-jewry-in-the-black-notebooks/

4 Translation from German: "Durchdrungen von der Erkenntnis, daß die Reinheit des deutschen Blutes die Voraussetzung für den Fortbestand des Deutschen Volkes ist, und beseelt von dem unbeugsamen Willen, die Deutsche Nation für alle Zukunft zu sichern, hat der Reichstag einstimmig das folgende Gesetz beschlossen, das hiermit verkündet wird", http://www.documentarchiv.de/ns/nbgesetze01.html, accessed on February 23, 2015.

5 In German: "sofern aber die Vernunftherrschaft als Gleichsetzung aller nur die Folge des Christentums ist und dieses im Grunde jüdischen Ursprungs" (Heidegger 1989, 54).

6 Translation from German: "Geistiger Nationalsozialismus".

7 Translation from German: "Der Nationalsozialismus ist ein *barbarisches Prinzip*. Das ist sein Wesentliches und seine mögliche Größe" (Heidegger 2014a, 194 [Überlegungen und Winke III, §206]).

8 Translation from German, Interview in: *Junge Freiheit* 40/2014, September 26, 2014.

9 German original: "Es stimmt, daß er kritisch gegenüber dem Weltjudentum war, aber er war auf keinen Fall ein Antisemit". Interview in: *Junge Freiheit* 40/2014, September 26, 2014.

10 Rockmore (1997, 5) argues that this strategy takes on the form that some Heideggerians say that those who are not "able to quote chapter and verse at the drop of a manuscript" and are not "capable on demand of adducing unpublished material in support of an argument" cannot understand Heidegger. Such arguments are typical for the sectarian Heidegger cult. "Heideggerians have tended to seize on the difficulties of Heidegger's thought in order to make of its interpretation an almost mystical, hieratic process. The result, in imitation of Heidegger's own strategy, is to shield Heidegger's thought from any attempt at criticism. [...] The obvious fact that Heidegger experts inevitably have a heavy professional investment in the importance, even the correctness, of his position explains their widespread reluctance to call it in question in any but the most timid manner" (22). "A particularly uncompromising form of this tactic consists in the denial that an outsider either does or possibly could understand the Heideggerian position. Examples include De Waehlens's assertion that Löwith, Heidegger's former student and later colleague, was not sufficiently versed in the thought of the master to criticize it, and Derrida's claim that Farías, who spent a dozen years writing a book about Heidegger's Nazism, could not possibly have spent more than an hour studying Heidegger's thought. A more general form of this tactic is to characterize whatever one says about the master thinker as metaphysics on the theory that Heidegger has somehow gone beyond it. This is tantamount to claiming that, as Ryle used to say, there is a category mistake since a metaphysical statement cannot possibly apply to

Heidegger's view. The tendency to limit the Heideggerian discussion to Heidegger scholars works to preserve the Heideggerian view from prying eyes by rendering it invisible to any but the orthodox believer" (23–24).

11 Translation from German: "überschwemmt von Juden u. Schiebern".

12 "Society, confronted with political, economic, and legal equality for Jews, made it quite clear that none of its classes was prepared to grant them social equality, and that only exceptions from the Jewish people would be received. Jews who heard the strange compliment that they were exceptions, exceptional Jews, knew quite well that it was this very ambiguity – that they were Jews and yet presumably not *like* Jews – which opened the doors of society to them" (Arendt 1958, 56).

13 Translation from German: "Es kommt indessen bei ihm so zu einem Kult von Ursprung oder Erneuerung, dem die Sympathie mit der Barbarei, die in seiner politischen Geschichte sich ausgeprägt hat, nicht zufällig und nicht äußerlich ist" (240).

14 Translation from German: "Heideggers Einverständnis mit dem Faschismus und der Ideologie der konservativen Revolution, der eleganteren Version der faschistischen Ideologie, war keine Gesinnungslosigkeit des Philosophen, sondern lag im Gehalt seiner Doktrin".

15 In German: "Wir nennen das im Besorgen begegnende Seiende das Zeug. Im Umgang sind vorfindlich Schreibzeug, Nähzeug, Werk-, Fahr-, Meßzeug. Die Seinsart von Zeug ist herauszustellen. Das geschieht am Leitfaden der vorherigen Umgrenzung dessen, was ein Zeug zu Zeug macht, der Zeughaftigkeit" (Heidegger 1926, 92).

16 In German: "Zeug ist wesenhaft »etwas, um zu… «. Die verschiedenen Weisen des »Um-zu« wie Dienlichkeit, Beiträglichkeit, Verwendbarkeit, Handlichkeit konstituieren eine Zeugganzheit. In der Struktur »Um-zu« liegt eine Verweisung von etwas auf etwas" (Heidegger 1926, 92).

17 "Die Seinsart von Zeug, in der es sich von ihm selbst her offenbart, nennen wir die Zuhandenheit" (Heidegger 1926, 93).

18 In German: "Das je besorgte Werk ist nicht nur in der häuslichen Welt der Werkstatt etwa zuhanden, sondern in der öffentlichen Welt. Mit dieser ist die Umweltnatur entdeckt und jedem zugänglich. In den Wegen, Straßen, Brücken, Gebäuden ist durch das Besorgen die Natur in bestimmter Richtung entdeckt" (Heidegger 1926, 66).

19 In German: "Auffälligkeit, Aufdringlichkeit und Aufsässigkeit" (Heidegger 1926, 99).

20 In German: "Dieses Unzuhandene stört und macht die Aufsässigkeit des zunächst und zuvor zu Besorgenden sichtbar" (Heidegger 1926, 99).

21 Translation from German: "Früher wurde gezeigt, wie je schon in der nächsten Umwelt die öffentliche »Umwelt« zuhanden und mitbesorgt ist. In der Benutzung öffentlicher Verkehrsmittel, in der Verwendung des Nachrichtenwesens (Zeitung) ist jeder Andere wie der Andere. Dieses Miteinandersein löst das eigene Dasein völlig in die Seinsart »der Anderen« auf, so zwar, daß die Anderen in ihrer Unterschiedlichkeit und Ausdrücklichkeit

noch mehr verschwinden. In dieser Unauffälligkeit und Nichtfeststellbarkeit entfaltet das Man seine eigentliche Diktatur. Wir genießen und vergnügen uns, wie man genießt; wir lesen, sehen und urteilen über Literatur und Kunst, wie man sieht und urteilt; wir ziehen uns aber auch vom »großen Haufen« zurück, wie man sich zurückzieht; wir finden »empörend«, was man empörend findet. Das Man, das kein bestimmtes ist und das Alle, obzwar nicht als Summe, sind, schreibt die Seinsart der Alltäglichkeit vor" (Heidegger 1926, 169).

22 Translation from German: "Weise der rechnenden Vergegenständlichung des Seienden".

23 "Allein was bedeutet Verdinglichung? Woraus entspringt sie? Warum wird das Sein gerade »zunächst« aus dem Vorhandenen »begriffen« und nicht aus dem Zuhandenen, das doch noch näher liegt? Warum kommt diese Verdinglichung immer wieder zur Herrschaft? Wie ist das Sein des »Bewußtseins« positiv strukturiert, so daß Verdinglichung ihm unangemessen bleibt? Genügt überhaupt der »Unterschied« von »Bewußtsein« und »Ding« für eine ursprüngliche Aufrollung der ontologischen Problematik?" (Heidegger 1926, 576).

24 Translation from German: "Während Radio und allerlei Organisation das innere Wachsen und d.h. ständige Zurückwachsen in die Überlieferung im Dorf und damit dieses selbst zerstören, errichtet man Professuren für 'Soziologie' des Bauerntums und schreibt haufenweise Bücher über das Volkstum".

25 Translation from German: "Die Technik und ihre Zwillingsschwester – die *Organisation* – beide das Gegenläufige zu allem *Organischen* – treiben ihrem Wesen nach auf ihr eigenes Ende, die Aushöhlung durch sich selbst, zu".

26 Translation from German: "Aus diesem Wesenszusammenhang ergibt sich, daß die »Technik« niemals durch die völkisch-politische Weltanschauung gemeistert werden kann. Was im Wesen schon Knecht ist, kann nie Herr werden".

27 Translation from German: "Vulgärnationalsozialismus".

28 Translation from German: "Geistiger Nationalsozialismus".

29 See: http://www.hoheluft-magazin.de/2015/02/heidegger-enthuellung/ (accessed on March 1, 2015). Di Cesare, Donatella. Heidegger – "Jews Self-Destructed". New Black Notebooks Reveal Philosopher's Shocking Take on Shoah. Corriere della Sera, February 9, 2015. http://www.corriere.it/english/15_febbraio_09/heidegger-jews-self-destructed-47cd3930-b03b-11e4-8615-d0fd07eabd28.shtml (accessed on March 1, 2015).

30 German original: "Ackerbau ist jetzt motorisierte Ernährungsindustrie, im Wesen das Selbe wie die Fabrikation von Leichen in Gaskammern und Vernichtungslagern, das Selbe wie die Blockade und Aushungerung von Ländern, das Selbe wie die Fabrikation von Wasserstoffbomben" (Heidegger 1994, 27).

31 https://www.youtube.com/watch?v=LwNiMl1g9us, accessed on February 27, 2015.

32 https://www.youtube.com/watch?v=zzLMdQh9iTA, accessed on February 27, 2015.

33 https://www.youtube.com/watch?v=loj5dQr_lJk, accessed on February 27, 2015.

34 https://www.youtube.com/playlist?list=PLgEhVQ4kQGSpaE84Ha2Zec5t7b8c_8CKP, accessed on February 27, 2015.

35 https://www.youtube.com/watch?v=hMizd8GpIEA, accessed on February 27, 2015.
36 https://vimeo.com/93782805, accessed on February 27, 2015.
37 "So denkt man nicht, wenn man Philosophie treibt". Günter Figal: Interview mit *Radio Dreyeckland*, January 9, 2015, https://rdl.de/beitrag/so-denkt-man-nicht-wenn-man-philosophie-betreibt, accessed on March 1, 2015.
38 German original: "Das Ende des Heideggerianertums". In: Interview mit Günter Figal. *Badische Zeitung*, January 23, 2015. http://www.badische-zeitung.de/literatur-und-vortraege/das-ende-des-heideggerianertums, accessed on March 1, 2015.

References

Adorno, Theodor W. 2002. "Elements of Anti-Semitism: Limits of Enlightenment." In *Dialectic of Enlightenment: Philosophical Fragments*, edited by Max Horkheimer and Theodor W. Adorno, 137–72. Stanford, CA: Stanford University Press.

Adorno, Theodor W. 1965/2001. *Metaphysics. Concept and Problems*. Stanford, CA: Stanford University Press.

Adorno, Theodor W. 1960/1961. *Ontologie und Dialektik*. Frankfurt am Main: Suhrkamp.

Arendt, Hannah. 1958. *The Origins of Totalitarianism*. Orlando, FL: Harcourt Brace. New edition.

Borgmann, Albert. 2000. *Holding on to Reality: The Nature of Information at the Turn of the Millennium*. Chicago, IL: University of Chicago Press.

Capurro, Rafael. 2003. *Ethik im Netz*. Stuttgart: Franz Steiner Verlag.

Capurro, Rafael, Michael Eldred and Daniel Nagel. 2013. *Digital Whoness: Identity, Privacy and Freedom in the Cyberworld*. Frankfurt am Main: Ontos.

Cohen, Patricia. 2009. "An Ethical Question: Does a Nazi Deserve a Place Among Philosophers?" *New York Times Online*, November 8, 2009. http://www.nytimes.com/2009/11/09/books/09philosophy.html.

Dourish, Paul. 2004. *Where the Action is: The Foundations of Embodied Interaction*. Cambridge, MA: MIT Press.

Dreyfus, Hubert. 2009. *On the Internet*. Abingdon: Routledge. 2nd edition.

Farías, Victor. 1989. *Heidegger and Nazism*. Philadelphia, PA: Temple University Press.

Faye, Emmanuel. 2009. *Heidegger: The Introduction of Nazism into Philosophy*. New Haven, CT: Yale University Press.

Faye, Emmanuel 2005. "Wie die Nazi-Ideologie in die Philosophie einzog." *Die Zeit Online* August 18, 2005. http://www.zeit.de/2005/34/AntwortHeidegger.

Gunkel, David. 2012. *The Machine Question: Critical Perspectives on AI, Robots, and Ethics*. Cambridge, MA: MIT Press.

Gunkel, David and Paul A. Taylor. 2014. *Heidegger and the Media*. Cambridge: Polity.

Habermas, Jürgen. 1987. *The Theory of Communicative Action. Volume 2*. Boston, MA: Beacon Press.

Habermas, Jürgen. 1984. *The Theory of Communicative Action. Volume 1.* Boston, MA: Beacon Press.

Habermas, Jürgen. 1983. *Der Philosophische Diskurs der Moderne. Zwölf Vorlesungen.* Frankfurt am Main: Suhrkamp.

Habermas, Jürgen. 1953. "Martin Heidegger: On the Publication of the Lectures of 1935." In *The Heidegger Controversy,* edited by Richard Wolin, 186–97. Cambridge, MA: MIT Press.

Heidegger, Gertrud, ed. 2007. *Mein liebes Seelchen! Briefe Martin Heideggers an seine Frau Elfride 1915–1970.* München: btb.

Heidegger, Martin. 2014a. *Gesamtausgabe, Band 94: Überlegungen II-VI (1931–1938).* Frankfurt am Main: Klostermann.

Heidegger, Martin. 2014b. *Gesamtausgabe, Band 95: Überlegungen VII-XI (1938/1939).* Frankfurt am Main: Klostermann.

Heidegger, Martin. 2014c. *Gesamtausgabe, Band 96: Überlegungen XII-XV (1939–1941).* Frankfurt am Main: Klostermann.

Heidegger, Martin. 2010. *Being and Time.* Translated by Joan Stambaugh. Albany, NY: State University of New York Press. Revised edition.

Heidegger, Martin. 2001. *Gesamtausgabe, Band 36/37: Sein und Wahrheit. Freiburger Vorlesungen Sommersemester 1933 und Wintersemester 1933/1934.* Frankfurt am Main: Klostermann.

Heidegger, Martin. 2000. *Introduction to Metaphysics.* New Haven, CT: Yale University Press.

Heidegger, Martin. 1999. *Contributions to Philosophy.* Indianapolis, IN: Indiana University Press.

Heidegger, Martin. 1994. *Gesamtausgabe, Band 79: Bremer und Freiburger Vorträge.* Frankfurt am Main: Klostermann.

Heidegger, Martin. 1989. *Gesamtausgabe, Band 65: Beiträge zur Philosophie.* Frankfurt am Main: Klostermann.

Heidegger, Martin. 1983. *Gesamtausgabe, Band 40: Einführung in die Metaphysik.* Frankfurt am Main: Klostermann.

Heidegger, Martin. 1977. *The Question Concerning Technology and Other Essays.* New York: Harper.

Heidegger, Martin. 1962. *Die Technik und die Kehre.* Stuttgart: Klett-Cotta.

Heidegger, Martin. 1935/1936. *What is a Thing?* South Bend, IN: Gateway Editions.

Heidegger, Marin. 1929. *Was ist Metaphysik?* Frankfurt am Main: Klostermann. Siebente Auflage.

Heidegger, Martin. 1926. *Sein und Zeit. Gesamtausgabe Band 2.* Frankfurt am Main: Klostermann.

Heim, Michael. 1998. *Virtual Realism.* Oxford: Oxford University Press.

Heim, Michael. 1993. *The Metaphysics of Virtual Reality.* Oxford: Oxford University Press.

Herzogenrath-Amelung, Heidi. 2013. "Ideology, Critique and Surveillance." *tripleC: Communication, Capitalism & Critique* 11 (2): 521–34.

Herzogenrath-Amelung, Heidi, Pinelopi Troullinou and Nikolas Thomopoulos. 2015. "Reversing the Order: Towards a Philosophically Informed Debate on ICT for Transport." In *ICT for Transport: Opportunities and Threats*, edited by Nikolas Thomopoulos, Moshe Givoni, and Piet Rietveld. Cheltenham: Edward Elgar.

Horkheimer, Max. 2002. *Critical Theory. Selected Essays.* New York: Continuum.

Horkheimer, Max and Theodor W. Adorno. 2002. *Dialectic of Enlightenment. Philosophical Fragments.* Stanford, CA: Stanford University Press.

Ihde, Don. 2010. *Heidegger's Technologies: Postphenomenological Perspectives.* New York: Fordham University Press.

Löwith, Karl. 1946. "The Political Implications of Heidegger's Existentialism." In *The Heidegger Controversy*, edited by Richard Wolin, 167–85. Cambridge, MA: MIT Press.

Lukács, Georg. 1923. "History and Class Consciousness." *Studies in Marxist Dialectics.* Cambridge, MA: The MIT Press.

Meyer, Thomas. 2005. "Denker für Hitler." *Die Zeit Online* July 21, 2005. http://www.zeit.de/2005/30/Heidegger.

Miller, Vincent. 2012. "A Crisis of Presence: On-Line Culture and Being in the World." *Space and Polity* 16 (3): 265–85.

O'Brien, Mahon. 2010. "Re-assessing the 'Affair': The Heidegger Controversy Revisited." *Social Science Journal* 47 (1): 1–20.

Pöggeler, Otto. 1987. *Martin Heidegger's Path of Thinking.* Atlantic Highlands, NJ: Humanities Press International.

Postone, Moishe. 2003. "The Holocaust and the Trajectory of the Twentieth Century." In *Catastrophe and Meaning. The Holocaust and the Twentieth Century*, edited by Moishe Postone and Eric Santner, 81–114. Chicago, IL: University of Chicago Press.

Postone, Moishe. 1980. "Anti-Semitism and National Socialism: Notes on the German reaction to "Holocaust"." *New German Critique* 19 (1): 97–115.

Rockmore, Tom. 2014. Heidegger's Anti-Semitism: Philosophy or Worldview? Contribution at the Conference Heidegger's Black Notebooks: Philosophy. Politics. Anti-Semitism. September 5–6, 2014. Emory University. Accessed on February 27, 2015. Audio recording: https://www.youtube.com/watch?v=Ioj5dQr_IJk.

Rockmore, Tom. 2009. "Foreword to the English Edition." In *Heidegger: The Introduction of Nazism into Philosophy*, edited by Emmanuel Faye, vii–xxi. New Haven, CT: Yale University Press.

Rockmore, Tom. 1997. *On Heidegger's Nazism and Philosophy.* Berkeley, CA: University of California Press.

Rockmore, Tom and Joseph Margolis. 1989. "Foreword." In *Heidegger and Nazism*, edited by Victor Farías. ix–xxi. Philadelphia, PA: Temple University Press.

Scannell, Paddy. 2014. *Television and the Meaning of "Live": An Enquiry into the Human Situation.* Cambridge: Polity.

Scannell, Paddy. 1996. *Radio, Television and Modern Life*. Oxford: Blackwell.

Sieg, Ulrich. 1989. "Die Verjudung des deutschen Geistes". *Die Zeit*, December 22, 1989. Accessed on February 27, 2015. http://www.zeit.de/1989/52/die-verjudung-des-deutschen-geistes.

Stiegler, Bernard. 2011. *Technics and Time 3: Cinematic Time and the Question of Malaise*. Stanford, CA: Stanford University Press.

Stiegler, Bernard. 2009. *Technics and Time 2: Disorientation*. Stanford, CA: Stanford University Press.

Stiegler, Bernard. 1998. *Technics and Time 1: The Fault of Epimetheus*. Stanford, CA: Stanford University Press.

Trawny, Peter. 2014. *Heidegger und der Mythos der jüdischen Weltverschwörung*. Frankfurt am Main: Klostermann.

Vietta, Silvio. 1989. *Heideggers Kritik am Nationalsozialismus und an der Technik*. Tübingen: Max Niemeyer.

Wolin, Richard. 2014. "National Socialism, World Jewry, and the History of Being: Heidegger's Black Notebooks." *Jewish Review of Books* Summer 2014, http://jewishreviewofbooks.com/articles/993/national-socialism-world-jewry-and-the-history-of-being-heideggers-black-notebooks/.

Wolin, Richard, ed. 1993. *The Heidegger Controversy*. Cambridge, MA: The MIT Press.

Chapter Six

Anti-Semitism, Anti-Marxism, and Technophobia: The Fourth Volume of Martin Heidegger's Black Notebooks *(1942–1948)*

6.1 Introduction

The fourth volume of Martin Heidegger's (2015) *Schwarze Hefte* (*Black Notebooks*) was published in March 2015. It contains philosophical notes written in the years 1942–1948. In 2014, the first three volumes, covering the years 1931–1941, were released. Their anti-Semitic passages have resulted in a sustained public debate. Heidegger in them wrote, for example, that Jews have a marked talent for calculation or that "world Jewry" means the uprooting of all being. The editor of the *Black Notebooks* Peter Trawny (2014, 11) says in his book *Heidegger und der Mythos der jüdischen Weltverschwörung* (*Heidegger and the Myth of Jewish World Conspiracy*) that such quotes are characteristic for Heidegger's onto-historical anti-Semitism and his imagination of a Jewish world conspiracy.

According to Trawny (2014, 43), Heidegger in the *Black Notebooks* makes a connection between modern technology, calculating reason, and Jews. Trawny calls for a "revision of the engagement with Heidegger's thinking" (117). Such a revision has already started: in light of the *Black Notebooks*, Günter Figal stepped down from his position as president of the Heidegger Society. He says that he thinks the philosophical future is "the end of Heideggerianism"[1]. The University of Freiburg has considered abolishing Heidegger's former chair by rededicating from a full professorship in phenomenology to a junior professorship in logic and linguistic analysis.[2] Is the fourth volume a continuation of or a break with the thinking that can be found in the first three books?

DOI: 10.4324/9781003256090-6

Heidegger starts one of the now published notebooks (Anmerkungen V) with a quote by Leibniz: "Qui me non nisi editis novit, non novit" (325) – "He who knows me by my published works alone does not know me at all". The *Black Notebooks* is not a regular publication, but contains private philosophical notes that Heidegger wanted to have released as the final volumes of his collected works. The quote is an indication that he thought that one cannot know his thought without knowledge of the *Notebooks* and that he therefore considered its publication as important in order to give a more complete picture of his thought.

6.2 Deutschtümelei

The book shows Heidegger's deep disappointment by University of Freiburg's decision in January 1946 to revoke his licence to teach. He saw this verdict as a betrayal of philosophy and thinking as such, and a betrayal of the German people (see: Heidegger 2015, 71, 79–80, 83–85, 87, 96–97).

All of the following are among the phenomena that Heidegger in the *Black Notebooks'* fourth volume sees negatively and as expression of what he called the machinations (Machenschaften) and the forgetfulness of being (Seinsvergessenheit): abstract art, America, anthropology, anti-fascism, Asia, Christianity, cultural philosophers, democracy, directors, existentialism, film, Georges Braques, Great Britain, historians, Jean-Paul Sartre, journalism, Juan Gris, Jews, Karl Jaspers, Karl Marx, magazines, mathematics, modern technology, museums, news, novels, Pablo Picasso, philology, psychology, radio, records, researchers, Russia, socialism, surrealism, television, tractors.

The few phenomena that he, in contrast, discusses positively taken together are an expression of Deutschtümelei (German jingoist ideology): Adalbert Stifter, Bauer (=farmer, but also builder/creator in German), customs, Ernst Jünger, fatherland, forests, Friedrich Hölderlin, Friedrich Nietzsche, German language, handwriting, heroism, homeland, hut, keeping silent, Meister Eckhart, Oswald Spengler, peasantry, poetry, South West Germany, teachers.

6.3 Anti-Semitism and the Hatred of Modernity, Technology, and Socialism

Heidegger says that Jewry is the principle of destruction, means self-destruction of history, that Marx is an expression of this principle because he saw spirit and culture as superstructure, and that it is bidden to combat the Jewish:

"The anti-Christ must like every anti-stem from the same essential ground like that against which it is anti- – hence like "the Christ". It stems from Jewry that in the age of the Christian Occident, i.e. the age of metaphysics, is the principle of destruction. The destructive lies in the reversal of the completion of metaphysics – i.e. in the reversal of Hegel by Marx. Spirit and culture become the superstructure of "life" – i.e. the economy, i.e. the organisation – i.e. the biological – i.e. the "Volk". If only the by essence "Jewish" fights in the metaphysical sense against the Jewish, the peak of history's self-destruction is reached; given that the "Jewish" has everywhere seized domination completely, so the combat against "the Jewish" becomes above all bidden in it"[3] (20).

This anti-Semitism and anti-socialism that oppose and equate Marx, materialism, and Jewry are substantiated by an anti-socialist remark noted in 1946/1947: "*Socialism is the peacelessness of humanity arranged as society in modernity, created by the technological civilisation*"[4] (238). Heidegger here further adds technology as a negatively perceived force and equates modern technology and socialism.

6.4 The Belittlement of the Nazi System

Heidegger belittles the Nazi system by arguing that the allied forces' occupation, collaboration of the Germans with the allied forces after 1945, or what he describes as modernity's nihilism would be worse than the horrors of the Nazi regime:

- He argues against an abstract nihilism that would be worse than concentration camps: "The terror of the ultimate nihilism is still scarier than all massiveness of the hangman's assistants and the concentration camps"[5] (59). With the term nihilism Heidegger refers to the "momentarily political world constellation"[6] (59).
- "The Germans now stand in the shadowing (Beschattung) by its own betrayal of its own essence directed against themselves – a process that must not refer to the inevitable consequences of the disappeared system's terror regiment – rather a behaviour that is blinder with rage (blindwütiger) and more destructive than the widely visible devastation and the horrors depicted on posters"[7] (84–85). The editor remarks in a footnote that Heidegger likely here refers to posters the allied forces put up in Germany after the end of the war that showed images from the Nazi extermination camps with the headline: "These infamous actions: Your fault!"[8] (84, footnote 45).

- "How miserable this helpless truckling to the shadowing by the planetary terror of the world public is, compared to which the massive brutality of the historyless 'National Socialism' is the pure harmlessness – despite the highly visible palpability of the havoc that it *co*-wreaked"[9] (87). "Wouldn't for example the *misjudgement* of this Geschick[10] – that did not belong to ourselves, wouldn't the suppression of the *world's want* (*Weltwollen*) – be an even more substantial 'guilt' and a 'collective guilt', whose extent could not even in essence be measured in the horrors auf the 'gas chambers' – more sinister than all publicly 'denounced' 'crimes' – that of course in the future nobody may excuse. Does 'one' have an idea that already now the German people and country are a single *concentration camp* – one that 'the world' certainly has never 'seen' before and that 'the world' also does not *want* to see – *this* not-wanting is even more *wanting* than our *absence of will* (*Willenlosigkeit*) against *National Socialism*"[11] (99–100).

Heidegger in 1946 criticised that the Nazi regime despised the spirit (209), but in the same year says that 1933, the year Hitler came to power, was the attempt of "overcoming metaphysics"[12] (147) and the "opportunity for a possible total consciousness (Gesamtbesinnung) of the Occident"[13] (174). He also writes that one "everywhere only sees 'victims', although maybe the preconditions of victims may have been missing"[14] (136).

Heidegger relativises and denies the singularity of the Nazi systems' horrors by drawing comparisons and arguing that after 1945 something even more horrific was happening in Germany. He argues that the German collaboration with the allied forces after the end of the war, the world public's denunciation of the Germans, and the allied forces' occupation after their liberation of Germany from the Nazi system are worse than the Nazi system and its crimes.

In the so-called 1986 "Historians' Dispute" (Historikerstreit), German intellectuals discussed the question of the singularity or non-singularity of the Nazi systems' crime. It among others involved contributions by the German philosopher and historian Ernst Nolte, who during the Nazi time was a student of Heidegger, and the philosopher Jürgen Habermas. Nolte argued for a revised historical account of Nazi Germany, including that one should consider the thesis for discussion that the president of the Zionist Organization Chaim Weizmann's 1939 statement that the "Jews in around the world fight in this war on England's side"[15] may substantiate the hypothesis that "Hitler was allowed to treat the German Jews as prisoners of war and to detain them"[16] (in: Augstein et al. 1987, 24). He also formulated that Auschwitz was not primarily driven by anti-Semitism, but was a reaction to the Russian Revolution: "Auschwitz does not primarily result from a traditional anti-Semitism and was at its core not a pure 'genocide', but it was first and foremost a fear-born reaction to the Russian Revolution's extermination processes"[17] (in: Augstein et al. 1987, 32). "Wasn't the Bolshevists' 'class murder' the logical and factual prius of the Nazis' 'racial murder'?"[18] (in: Augstein et al. 1987, 45).

Jürgen Habermas argued that Nolte belittled the Nazis' crimes and that he "denies the Nazi crimes' singularity"[19] (in: Augstein et al., 1987, 97). "The Nazi crimes lose their singularity when they are at least vulgarised as response to (today enduring) Bolshevist extermination threats. Auschwitz shrinks then to the format of a techno-logical innovation and is explained by the 'Asian' threat posed by an enemy that still stands in front of our doors"[20] (71).

Assuming a singularity of Auschwitz and the Nazi system stresses the moral and political guilt of the Nazis and the Nazi system. Comparing this system, trying to causally explain it as a reaction to something external, or arguing that something much more horrific happened before or after in history therefore excuses the Nazi system. According to Habermas, Nolte justified the Nazi system and its crimes by denying their singularity and causally reducing it to a reaction to Bolshevism. Both Nolte's as-sumptions and some of Heidegger's arguments in the *Black Notebooks*' fourth volume share the denial of the singularity of the Nazi system and of the immanent causes of this system of extermination. Heidegger relativises the Nazi system by expressing the opinion that after 1945 something much more horrible took place in Germany.

Nolte was not just a student of Heidegger during the Nazi time, but also defends him against the criticism that his works reflect Nazi ideology. Nolte (1988), for example, stands up for Heidegger in a review of Victor Fárias' (1989) book *Heidegger and Nazism*. Fárias convincingly argues that Heidegger's thoughts were "nourished in traditions of authoritarianism, anti-semitism, and ultranationalism" (Farías, 1989, 4). Nolte (1988) says Farías' book is "only a symptomatic product of that denunciation literature that at the present time booms in many fields"[21] (108) and that it opposes "the whole German and European tradition in so far as it is not 'enlightened' in the author's understanding"[22] (113). Heidegger and Nolte are both not just representatives of right-wing ideology in politics and philosophy, but also seem to share the view that the Germans are the true victims in the 20th century's history.

Heidegger in the *Black Notebooks*' fourth volume shows little sympathy for the Nazis' victims, but a lot of mourning about what he describes as the attempted destruction of

The Belittlement of the Nazi System

the Germans and their culture. He, in 1946, speaks of "a *world shame* (W*eltschande*) that threatens the German *people*"[23] (146), of a "*killing machinery* that has now been set in motion in Germany"[24] (148), that the logic of the atom bomb has the same logic as a "killing machinery that is set on the Germans"[25] (151). In 1948, he voiced the same view by saying that there is a project "*to wipe out the Germans spiritually and historically.* One should not fool oneself. An old spirit of revenge goes round the Earth"[26] (444–445). Heidegger's ideology is clearly anti-democratic when he writes for example in 1946/1947: "The anti-fascists are the lowest slaves of the coming great fascism (Großfaschismus) that is called democracy in America and Russia"[27] (249).

6.5 Media and Technology

Heidegger sees a world conspiracy at play. He asks in 1946: "How much long may the haste of calculation (Verrechnen) dominate? Or is it even still in the process of arranging itself as the law of machination (Machenschaft)?"[28] (142). In 1948, Heidegger specifies the character of this machination as involving culture, technology, and Jewish religion: "Also culture is like the cultural consciousness that is given by it part of history, i.e. of subjectivity. It, culture namely, is grounded in the essence of technology as the instituting machination of squalidness (Verwahrlosung). The modern systems of total dictatorship originate from Jewish-Christian monotheism"[29] (438). This passage is a form of religiously motivated anti-Semitism: Heidegger blames the Jews for what he sees as the decline he associates with modern technology and culture. One can find such an anti-Semitic passage in Heidegger's notes in 1948 just like in a letter from 1916, when the 27-year-old wrote to his wife Elfride: "Our culture and universities' Jewification (Verjudung) is certainly frightening and I think the German race should still put about so much inner strength to lift itself up"[30] (Heidegger 2005, 51). There are continuities in Heidegger's thought.

When speaking of domination or dictatorship in the years after the end of the Second World War covered in the *Black Notebooks'* fourth volume, Heidegger typically means modern media and modern technology. So in 1946 he for example wrote about "the public's dictatorship by the domination of the 'newspaper'"[31]. In 1946/1947 he said that technology has since 350 years meant the "destruction of being and human essence"[32] (251). In 1948, Heidegger wrote that "the domination by public opinion is already so dictatorial"[33] (460) and he spoke of "the technical organisation of the public's Total Domination"[34] (460), "the public's dictatorship today and its instruments"[35] (509). Such passages give an idea of what he most likely meant when describing modern systems of total dictatorship that originated from Jewish-Christian monotheism.

The *Black Notebooks'* fourth volume shows that Heidegger in the years 1942–1948 saw a world conspiracy at play that he identified with Jews, modern technology, modern media, socialism, and democracy. He wrote down such thoughts also in 1948, just one year before he gave some of the talks that prepared his second most widely read book *The Question Concerning Technology and Other Essays* (Heidegger 1977), which was published in German in 1953 as *Die Technik und die Kehre* (Heidegger 1953).

In one of these preparatory talks that Heidegger held on 1 December 1949, in Bremen (Heidegger 1953, 3), he made the infamous remark that agriculture "is now a motorized (*motorisierte*) food industry, in essence the same as the manufacturing of corpses in the gas chambers and extermination camps, the same as the blockade and star-vation of the countryside, the same as the production of the hydrogen bombs"[36] (translation cited in: Farías 1989, 287) (for a discussion see Fuchs 2015, 71–73).

In *The Question Concerning Technology*, Heidegger (1977) terms modern technology das *Ge-stell* (the Enframing), by which he means "that challenging claim which gathers man thither to order" (19). The Ge-stell is an instrumental form of revealing. Modern technology as the Ge-stell would be associated with the exact sciences, mathematics, and modern physics (21) that have an instrumentalist worldview and believe in the calculability of the world.

The *Black Notebooks'* fourth volume illuminates that in the year before Heidegger gave the first preparatory talks for the *Question Concerning Technology*, he continued to hold a right-wing worldview that associates technology with a world conspiracy. Heidegger's main work on technology just like his other writings lacks an analysis and critique of the modern political economy of capitalism that frames and shapes modern technology's design and use. Heidegger instead believed in a world conspiracy whose main manifestation was for him modern technology. The *Question Concerning Technology* is grounded in Heidegger's right-wing ideology, which makes it in-comprehensible why many analysts and theorists of technology, including many Internet and media scholars, positively reference this work. The right time to say goodbye to Heidegger's works and his analysis of technology has long come. The *Black Notebooks'* fourth volume and the right-wing worldview it reveals for the years

1942–1948 reinforce this judgement. Heidegger and the critical theory of society, the media and technology are irreconcilable. Such a theory can in contrast in a feasible manner be grounded in Karl Marx's dialectic of technology, Georg Lukács' notion of reification, Max Horkheimer and Theodor W. Adorno's concept of instrumental reason, and Herbert Marcuse's category of technological rationality.

Notes

1 German original: "Das Ende des Heideggerianertums". In: Interview mit Günter Figal. *Badische Zeitung*, January 23, 2015. http://www.badische-zeitung.de/literatur-und-vortraege/das-ende-des-heideggerianertums, accessed on March 1, 2015.
2 Streit um Heidegger-Lehrstuhl. Martin? Edmund! *FAZ Online*. February 27, 2015. http://www.faz.net/aktuell/feuilleton/streit-um-heidegger-lehrstuhl-martin-edmund-13452086.html.
3 German original: "Der Anti-christ muß wie jedes Anti-aus dem selben Wesensgrund stammen wie das, wogegen es anti-ist – also wie ‚der Christ'. Dieser stammt aus der Judenschaft. Diese ist im Zeitraum des christlichen Abendlandes, d.h der Metaphysik, das Prinzip der Zerstörung. Das Zerstörerische in der Umkehrung der Vollendung der Metaphysik – d.h. Hegels durch Marx. Der Geist und die Kultur wird zum Überbau des ‚Lebens' – d.h. der Wirtschaft, d.h. der Organisation – d.h. des Biologischen – d.h. des ‚Volkes'. Wenn erst das wesenhaft ‚Jüdische' im metaphysischen Sinne gegen das Jüdische kämpft, ist der Höhepunkt der Selbstvernichtung in der Geschichte erreicht; gesetzt, daß das, Jüdische' überall die Herrschaft vollständig an sich gerissen hat, so daß auch die Bekämpfung, des Jüdischen' und sie zuvörderst in die Botmäßigkeit zu ihm gelangt" (20).
4 "*Sozialismus* ist die durch technische Zivilisation erzeugte Friedlosigkeit des zur Gesellschaft eingerichteten Menschentums der Neuzeit" (238).
5 "Der Terror des endgültigen Nihilismus ist noch unheimlicher als alle Massivität der Henkerknechte und der Kz".
6 "augenblickliche politische Weltkonstellation".
7 "Die Deutschen stehen jetzt in der Beschattung durch die eigene gegen sich selbst betriebene Verräterei am eigenen Wesen – ein Vorgang, der sich nicht auf unvermeidliche Folgen des Terrorregiments des verschwundenen Systems berufen darf – ein Verhalten vielmehr, das blindwütiger ist und zerstörerischer als die weithin sichtbare Verwüstung und die in Plakaten anschaulich zu machenden Greuel" (84–85). Heidegger uses the German term Beschattung (that can best be translated as shadowing) instead of Besatzung (occupation). It has two different connotations: (a) surveillance and (b) casting a shadow on someone. The he employs this word indicates his negative view of Germany's occupation by the Americans, the British, the French, and the Russians, which neglects that it was the necessary consequence of the liberation from the Nazi system that was a German project

oriented on anti-Semitism, fascism, racism, anti-democracy, anti-Marxism, social Darwinism, nationalism, imperialism, and leadership cult.

8 "Diese Schandtaten: Eure Schuld!". For an example, see: http://www.hdg.de/lemo/bestand/objekt/plakat-schande-schuld.html.

9 "Wie erbärmlich ist dies ratlose Kriechen unter der Beschattung durch den planetarischen Terror einer Weltöffentlichkeit, mit dem verglichen die massive Brutalität des geschichtslosen, Nationalsozialismus' die reine Harmlosigkeit ist – trotz der unübersehbaren Handgreiflichkeit der von ihm *mit*angerichteten Verwüstung?" (87).

10 The German term Geschick means skill, but is also related to the terms Schicksal (destiny, fate) and schicken (sending). In *Being and Time*, Heidegger (2010) defines Geschick as "the occurrence of the community of a people (Volk)" (366) and "occurrence of Dasein in being-with-others" (368). He however also speaks of "the vicissitudes" (Geschicke) of questioning (19). Heidegger in *Über den Humanismus* (*Letter on Humanism*) writes: "Das Sein hat sich dem Denken schon zugeschickt. Das Sein ist als das Geschick des Denkens" (Heidegger 1949, 55) – "Being has already sent itself to thinking. Being is as the destiny of thinking". Here Heidegger uses the terms Geschick and schicken/zugeschickt in the same context. Given the polysemy of the word "Geschick", it may be best to leave it untranslated.

11 "Wäre z.B. die *Verkennung* dieses Geschicks – das uns ja nicht selbst gehörte, wäre das Niederhalten im *Weltwollen* – nicht eine noch wesentlichere, Schuld' und eine, Kollektivschuld', deren Größe gar nicht – im Wesen nicht einmal am Greuelhaften der ,Gaskammern' gemessen werden könnte; eine Schuld – unheimlicher denn alle öffentlich ,anprangerbaren', Verbrechen' – die gewiß künftig keiner je entschuldigen dürfte. Ahnt ,man', daß jetzt schon das deutsche Volk und Land ein einziges *Kz* ist – wie es ,die Welt' allerdings noch nie ,gesehen' hat und das ,die Welt' auch nicht sehen *will* – *dieses* Nicht-wollen noch *wollender* als unsere *Willenlosigkeit* gegen die Verwilderung des *Nationalsozialismus*" (99–100).

12 "Überwindung der Metaphysik".

13 "Gelegenheit einer möglichen Gesamtbesinnung des Abendlandes".

14 "überall nur ,Opfer' sieht, wo vielleicht die Voraussetzung zum Opfer fehlte".

15 German original: "nach der die Juden in aller Welt in diesen Krieg auf der Seite Englands kämpfen würden".

16 German original: "daß Hitler die deutschen Juden als als Kriegsgefangene (a) behandeln und d.h. internieren durfte".

17 German original: "Auschwitz resultiert nicht in erster Linie aus einem überlieferten Antisemitismus und war im Kern nicht ein bloßer ,Völkermord', sondern es handelte sich vor allem um die Angst geborene Reaktion auf die Vernichtungsvorgänge der Russischen Revolution".

18 German original: "War nicht der ,Klassenmord' der Bolschewiki das logische und faktische Prius des ,Rassenmords' der Nationalsozialisten?".

19 German original: "Nolte die Singularität der NS-Verbrechen leugnet".

Media and Technology

20 German original: "Die Nazi-Verbrechen verlieren ihre Singularität dadurch, daß sie als Antwort auf (heute fortdauernde) bolschewistische Vernichtungsdrohungen mindestens verständlich gemacht werden. Auschwitz schrumpft auf das Format einer technischen Innovation und erklärt sich aus der ‚asiatischen' Bedrohung durch einen Feind, der immer noch vor unseren Toren steht".

21 German original: "es ist lediglich ein symptomatisches Produkt jener Denunziationsliteratur, die gegenwärtig wieder auf vielen Gebieten Konjunktur hat".

22 German original: "Der eigentliche Zielpunkt der Anklageschrift von Farías ist nicht der Mensch und Philosoph Heidegger, sondern die ganze deutsche und europäische Tradition, soweit sie nicht im Sinne des Verfassers, aufgeklärt' ist".

23 "*Weltschande,* die dem deutschen Volk *droht*".

24 "jetzt in Deutschland […] in Gang gebrachte *Tötungsmaschinerie*".

25 "eine Tötungsmaschinerie an den Deutschen angesetzt ist".

26 "*die Deutschen geistig und geschichtlich auszulöschen.* Man mache sich nichts vor. Ein alter Geist der Rache geht um die Erde".

27 "Die Antifaschisten sind die niedrigsten Sklaven des kommenden Großfaschismus, der sich in Amerika und Rußland Demokratie nennt".

28 "Wie lang noch mag die Hast des Verrechnens herrschen? Oder ist sie gar erst dabei, sich als Gesetz der Machenschaft einzurichten?"

29 "Auch die Kultur gehört, wie das mit ihr gegebene Kulturbewußtsein zur Historie, d.h. zur Subjektivität. Sie gründet, die Kultur nämlich, im Wesen der Technik als der sich einrichtenden Machenschaft der Verwahrlosung. Die modernen Systeme der totalen Diktatur entstammen dem jüdisch-christlichen Monotheismus".

30 German original: "Die Verjudung unserer Kultur u. Universitäten ist allerdings schreckerregend u. ich meine die deutsche Rasse sollte noch soviel innere Kraft aufbringen um in die Höhe zu kommen".

31 "Diktatur der Öffentlichkeit durch die Herrschaft der, Zeitung'".

32 "Zerstörung des Seyns und Menschenwesens".

33 "die Herrschaft der öffentlichen Meinung ist schon so diktatorisch".

34 "technischen Organisation der Totalen Herrschaft der Öffentlichkeit".

35 "die heutige Diktatur der Öffentlichkeit und ihr Instrumentarium".

36 German original: "Ackerbau ist jetzt motorisierte Ernährungsindustrie, im Wesen das Selbe wie die Fabrikation von Leichen in Gaskammern und Vernichtungslagern, das Selbe wie die Blockade und Aushungerung von Ländern, das Selbe wie die Fabrikation von Wasserstoffbomben" (Heidegger 1994, 27).

References

Augstein, Rudolf et al. 1987. *"Historikerstreit": Die Dokumentation der Kontroverse um die Einzigartigkeit der nationalsozialistischen Judenvernichtung.* München: Piper.

Farías, Victor. 1989. *Heidegger and Nazism*. Philadelphia, PA: Temple University Press.

Fuchs, Christian. 2015. "Martin-Heidegger's Anti-Semitism: Philosophy of Technology and the Media in the Light of the "Black Notebooks". Implications for the Reception of Heidegger in Media and Communication Studies." *tripleC: Communication, Capitalism & Critique* 13 (1): 55–78.

Heidegger, Martin. 2015. *Anmerkungen I–V (Schwarze Hefte 1942–1948). Gesamtausgabe, Band 97*. Frankfurt am Main: Klostermann.

Heidegger, Martin. 2010. *Being and Time*. Translated by Joan Stambaugh. Albany, NY: State University of New York Press. Revised edition.

Heidegger, Martin. 2005. *"Mein liebes Seelchen!" Briefe Martin Heideggers an seine Frau Elfride 1915–1970*. München: btb.

Heidegger, Martin. 1994. *Gesamtausgabe, Band 79: Bremer und Freiburger Vorträge*. Frankfurt am Main: Klostermann.

Heidegger, Martin. 1977. *The Question Concerning Technology and Other Essays*. New York: Harper.

Heidegger, Martin. 1953. *Die Technik und die Kehre*. Stuttgart: Klett-Cotta.

Heidegger, Martin. 1949. *Über den Humanismus*. Frankfurt am Main: Klostermann.

Nolte, Ernst. 1988. Eine Höhepunkt der Heidegger-Kritik? Victor Farías' Buch "Heidegger et le Nazisme". *Historische Zeitschrift* 247 (1): 95–114.

Trawny, Peter. 2014. *Heidegger und der Mythos der jüdischen Weltverschwörung*. Frankfurt am Main: Klostermann.

Part II

Applications

Chapter Seven
Fascism 2.0: Hitler on Twitter

7.1 Introduction

Hitler was born on 20 April 1889. In 1939, on Hitler's 50th birthday, the day became a bank holiday in Nazi Germany. After 1945, the day remained of huge symbolic importance for fascist groups and movements. So, for example in 2016, the right-wing group Thügida, a group associated with the German Pegida movement, organised a torch march in the German city of Jena. In 2008, around 1,000 ultra fans of the Austrian football team Rapid Wien gathered in Vienna's city centre to celebrate Hitler's birthday. They had, for example, a banner that read "Happy Birthday 18". "18" stands symbolically for Adolf Hitler's initials AH. German neo-Nazis celebrated Hitler's birthday in 1991 in a Berlin club, arguing: "This is the day, where one can say 'Foreigners out!'. [...] We now go out and when we see some foreigners, then we beat them up! This is our day!"[1]. European neo-Nazis in 1984 founded the Committee for the Preparation of the Festivities for Adolf Hitler's 100th Birthday.

Remembering Hitler on social media also stands in the context of a shift in the memory of Hitler and Nazism in popular culture (see Rosenfeld 2015). Whereas in the decades after the Second World War, serious forms of commemoration such as museums, memorials, ceremonies, and documentaries dominated, since the 1990s a radical shift has occurred: Hitler has now become a source of entertainment in films, novels, short stories, comics, theatre, music culture, satire, fashion, pornography, advertisements, artworks, and on the Internet. Stiglegger (2011) speaks in this context of the emergence of Nazi chic and Nazi trash. For Rosenfeld (2015, 7), these developments are an

DOI: 10.4324/9781003256090-7

expression of the normalisation of the Nazi past which threatens to overturn the "perceived exceptionality of the Nazi era".

The Internet's possibilities for the convergence of production and consumption (user-generated content, "participatory" culture) and the global distribution of information have certainly enhanced the possibilities of Hitler "becoming" popular culture. Online examples include Internet memes (Disco Hitler, Advice Hitler, Hi Hitler, the section Hitler on memegenerator.net, etc.), web sites (hipsterhitler.com, catsthatlooklikehitler.com, thingsthatlooklikehitler.com, etc.), video games (Sim Heil, Six Degrees of Hitler, etc.), YouTube videos (Downfall, Hitler Gets a Report on His Death, Hitler Disco, Hitler is the Scatman, Ich hock' in meinem Boncker, Hitler Sings: Born to Be Alive!, etc.), online language and puns ("lolcaust", "Rebeccacaust", etc.). Difficult questions have emerged: is it morally acceptable to laugh about Hitler? Does popular Hitler culture and Hitler humour automatically turn the Nazi legacy into an "empty signifier" (Rosenfeld 2015, 341) with Hitler turned from a symbol of evil into a symbol of humour? Does Hitler in popular culture deny the singularity of the Shoah and trivialise it? Can there be forms of popular cultural engagement with Nazism that foster anti-fascism? There are no straightforward answers to such questions.

This chapter first outlines the study's methodology, then presents the major results (organised in four sections), and finally draws conclusions.

7.2 Methodology

This study uses an empirical Marxist ideology critique as a method for studying how Twitter users celebrated Hitler's 127th birthday on 20 April 2016. The approach taken stands in the tradition of Karl Marx (Marx and Engels 1845), Georg Lukács (1971), and the Frankfurt School (see Rehmann 2013). What these approaches have in common is that they understand and study ideology as semiotic structures and practices that justify one group's or individual's power, domination, or exploitation of other groups or individuals by misrepresenting, one-dimensionally presenting or distorting reality in symbolic representations (Fuchs 2015, chapter 3).

Marxist ideology critique analyses the text of ideologies in their political-economic context. It wants to understand the semiotic, linguistic, communicative, cultural, and mediated ways used for expressing social reality in manners that justify domination in the light of how capitalism and state power are changing and what political-economic changes those who express such ideologies desire. Ideology critique is therefore not just a critique of ideologies but also a critique of the political and economic interests that ideologies represent.

Marxist ideology critique is related, but not identical, to Critical Discourse Analysis (CDA). CDA is a body of approaches that study discourse, power, language, and ideology (for an overview, see Wodak and Meyer 2009). Marx and Marxist theory have influenced some, but not all CDA approaches (Wodak and Meyer 2009, 20). There is also no common understanding of ideology in CDA.

So, on the one hand, there are approaches in CDA that are sceptical of Marx and Marxism. For example Teun van Dijk argues that the approach "initiated by Marx, focused on the more or less deterministic influence of social class on knowledge and more generally on thoughts or ideas" (van Dijk 2014, 141). However, the claim that Marx had a deterministic understanding of ideology disregards that for Marx, materialism does not mean that thought, ideas, worldviews, and ideologies can be read off the economy. Marx also does not say that ideas are immaterial. For him, materialism means that they are social products, i.e. produced by humans in the social relations taking place in society. This is why he stresses that ideas must be seen in the context of "their real relations and activities, of their production, of their intercourse, of their social and political conduct" (Marx and Engels 1845, 41). Norman Fairclough, in contrast to Teun van Dijk, argues that critical linguistics and CDA "have both been shaped by Marxism" (Fairclough 2010, 304) and reads Marx as being a "critical discourse theorist *avant la lettre*" (Fairclough 2010, 340).

In conducting this study, I *first* gathered relevant data from Twitter. On 23 April 2016, I used hashtagify.me in order to obtain hashtags related to #Hitler, #AdolfHitler, and #HappyBirthdayAdolf. This allowed me to identify the major hashtags having to do with Hitler that were used around the time of his 2016 birthday. I used the tool Texifter in order to obtain all tweets from 20 April 2016 that mentioned any of the following hashtags: #hitler OR #adolfhitler OR #hitlerday OR #1488 OR #AdolfHitlerDay OR #HeilHitler OR #SiegHeil OR #HappyBirthdayAdolf OR #HitlerNation OR #HappyBirthdayHitler OR #HitlersBirthday OR #MakeGermanyGreatAgain OR #WeMissYouHitler. The search resulted in 4,193 tweets that were automatically imported into Discovertext, from where I exported them along with meta-data into a csv file.

Second, I analysed the language and visuals of all tweets by focusing on the way they describe, symbolise, name, and display opponents and what kind of arguments they use.

Methodology

Third, I contextualised the tweets by relating them to elements of a broader worldview, i.e. the question what kind of society they imagine. In this context, the Marxist/critical theory of fascism plays a key role. The contextualisation made use of this theory in order to interpret how language and visuals used on Twitter express elements of fascist ideology.

Fourth, I reflected on the practical consequences for anti-fascist politics.

Social media analysis often ignores questions of research ethics (Zimmer and Proferes 2014). One extreme is that social media researchers ignore ethical questions. Another extreme is a form of Internet research ethics that wants to prescribe obtaining informed consent for every piece of data one collects online, which can censor critical studies. A critical-realist approach is to engage with research ethics and apply its principles to a feasible extent. In the study at hand, I used a recommendation by the British Psychological Society which argues that online observation should only take place when and where users "reasonably expect to be observed by strangers" (British Psychological Society, 2009, 13). The use of a hashtag about Hitler and Hitler's birthday communicates information to the public. Such users therefore expect to be observed by strangers. In such cases, obtaining informed consent is not appropriate. I do not mention any usernames in this chapter.

For the purpose of studying "fascism 2.0", one needs an understanding of what fascism is. Taking a purely historiographical approach in defining fascism that only associates fascism with Hitler and Mussolini risks underestimating the possibility that certain political systems can emerge under different historical contexts. Daniel Woodley (2010) discusses basic elements of a critical theory of fascism. Based on the work of Marx and Moishe Postone (1993), he connects fascism to the fetishism concept. He argues that fascism is "a populist ideology which seeks, through a mythology of unity and identity, to project a 'common instinctual fate' (uniform social status) between bourgeois and proletarianized groups, eliding the reality of social distinction in differentiated class societies" (Woodley 2010, 17).

Fascism is an ideology that not just shapes the worldviews of fascist individuals and movements, but is also a form of political praxis aimed at creating a particular model of society.

> "[F]ascism must *itself* be understood as a political commodity: fascism is not simply a subjectively generated, reactive strategy – a desperate attempt by atomized individuals to overcome the disenchantment and inauthenticity of modernity – but an aesthetic innovation which transcends existing patterns of

differentiation and political subjectification to disrupt established narratives of history and progress. [...] the fetishization of communal identities which conceal the true nature of the commodity as a structured social practice, bridging the gap between the specificity of the nation-state (as the nexus linking culture and power) and the rationalization of circuits of capital."

(Woodley 2010, 17–18)

Based on a critical theory of fascism, one can therefore identify four broad elements of fascism:

1) Authoritarian populism guided by the leadership principle;

2) Nationalism;

3) Friend-enemy scheme;

4) Patriarchy and naturalism.

7.3 Fascism 2.0's First Element: Leadership Ideology and Authoritarian Populism

Charismatic leadership and authoritarian political structures form a first element of fascism. Fascism tends to erode the distinction between the state and society. The state is seen as being everything and everywhere. Fascist ideology penetrates all spheres of life. The state is defined as being coextensive with the political leader. Absolute obedience to the leader is demanded. There is no legal political opposition. Not just political parties and social movements not associated with the leader and his party are banned, but also political organisations of the working class such as trade unions are outlawed.

Theodor W. Adorno (1951, 137) stresses the importance of leadership in fascist ideology. Hitler presented himself as a "threatening authority". Psychology would play an important role in the fascist attempt to make individuals believe in, collectively project their selves into, and follow the Führer. "It is precisely this idealization of himself which the fascist leader tries to promote in his followers, and which is helped by the *Führer* ideology" (Adorno 1951, 140). Collective narcissism would be an underlying psychological process of fascism. The leader image would result in the "enlargement of the subject: by making the leader his ideal he loves himself, as it were, but gets rid of the stains of frustration and discontent which mar his picture of his own empirical self" (Adorno 1951, 140). "The narcissistic *gain* provided by fascist propaganda is obvious" (145). Hitler presented himself at the same time as superman and ordinary, a "great little man" (142). This "unity trick" (146) tries to construct unity within the fascist community in order to preach hatred against out-groups such as Jews and socialists.

The leadership principle was found in the analysed Twitter dataset in five different forms. A *first* way of how admiration for Hitler's leadership was expressed on Twitter was by associating Hitler and Nazi symbols with birthday culture, including coffee, cake, and cookies.

The tweet "Wake and bake #HitlersBirthday #420" (No. 2984) was by far the most liked and re-tweeted post in the analysed dataset. It was posted by a neo-Nazi account devoted to Hitler that has around 408,000 followers[2]. The account describes itself as "Destroyin' pussy and Jews". Figures 7.1–7.3 show three more examples of how Hitler was combined with birthday culture.

FIGURE 7.1 The fascist aesthetic of Hitler birthday culture on Twitter (No. 189).

Happy Birthday to the greatest leader of the 20th Century! #420 #HappyBirthdayHitler

WHERE IS...

MEIN CAKE!

RETWEETS	LIKES
40	66

FIGURE 7.2   The fascist aesthetic of Hitler birthday culture on Twitter (No. 456).

Admiration for Hitler is expressed by the superlative "the greatest leader of the 20th century" and by referring to him by his first name "Adolf": two of the tweets speak of "Happy birthday Adolf" (Figures 7.1 and 7.3). The cake shown in Figure 7.3 says in German "Happy birthday, Adolf" and expresses fascist aesthetic by using the symbols of the SS and the Swastika. The cake's colours furthermore imitate the red, white, and black of the Nazi Party's so-called Blood Flag. The formulation "Hitler was right" expresses agreement with Hitler's politics of annihilation and imperialism. The use of images that show Hitler's image in a cup of coffee's milk froth, Swastika cookies, a Swastika cake, and Hitler demanding like an anxious child "Where is my cake!" downplay and trivialise the horrors of Nazi fascism by visual and linguistic means.

The historian Wolfgang Benz (2000, 264) estimates that the Nazi regime resulted in more than 50 million dead people, including 6 million Jews, who were the victims of a systematic, industrialised extermination campaign. Jonathan Friedman (2011, 1),

Fascism 2.0's First Element: Leadership Ideology and Authoritarian Populism

My mother ███████████ made an awesome cake to celebrate Adolf's birthday, #HappyBirthdayHitler

RETWEETS   LIKES
7   18

FIGURE 7.3 The fascist aesthetic of Hitler birthday culture on Twitter (No. 1605).

professor and director of Holocaust and Genocide Studies at West Chester University, estimates that the Nazi regime also resulted in the killing of "several hundred thousand Roma-Sinti, two million Polish civilians, three million Soviet prisoners of war, several thousand gay men and Jehovah's Witnesses, tens of thousands of political prisoners, and 200,000 persons with disabilities. Never before had a government and its operating ideology grouped these disparate European outcasts together as part of a program of persecution". Estimates of the murdered Roma and Sinti vary between 150,000 and 1.5 million (Friedman 2011, 381).

Hitler's name is intrinsically associated with these victims and the Nazi politics of extermination, war, and enslavement. Birthday cakes and parties imply happiness and are symbols of celebration. Celebrating Hitler's birthday symbolically celebrates the barbarity of his regime and thereby trivialises it.

Figure 7.2 is an Internet meme. Such combinations of text and image can be generated with tools such as Imgur, MemeGenerator, ImgFlip, or LiveMeme. According to Richard Dawkins (1999, 192), a meme is an idea that spreads in culture. It "propagate[s] itself, spreading from brain to brain". Internet memes are a digital subculture associated with sites such as 4chan, Tumblr, and Reddit. Image macros are one genre of Internet meme (Shifman 2014, 118): they combine an image (usually of a person) and some text in order to express a specific cynical, ironic, sarcastic, satirical, or parodistic meaning. Graham Meikle (2016, 55) stresses the practical aspect of sharing memes and defines Internet memes as "shared, rule-based representations of online interactions that are not only adopted, but also adapted by others". For Shifman, Internet memes are connected digital content units that are "circulated, imitated, and/or transformed via the Internet by many users" (Shifman 2014, 177).

The meme that depicts Hitler as a child protesting that he wants to have "mein cake" plays with the public perception of children as innocent, pure, ingenuous, unspoiled, and original. The constructed child-like behaviour makes Hitler look sympathetic and apolitical. Such constructions distract attention from the historical results of Nazism. Shifman argues that Internet memes enable participatory culture and that they "expand the range of participatory options in democracies: citizens can express their political opinions in new and accessible ways, engage in heated debates, and enjoy the process to boot" (Shifman 2014, 144). Often overlooked is the fact that social media is not just a realm of progressive politics but also one of "participatory fascism", in which users generate symbols that depict, propagate, or trivialise fascism. Given that fascism is opposed to participatory democracy, it can in fact never be participatory-democratic. Fascism mobilises the masses by the leadership cult, but leadership as such as opposed to grassroots democracy, in which not leaders but the people take decisions. Fascist mass mobilisations bring together demagogic power from above and hegemonic power from below. Democracy is one of fascism's main enemies. The terms *user-generated fascism* and *fascism 2.0* are more appropriate than participatory fascism. In the tweet shown in Figure 7.1, the fascist message and downplaying of Nazism's horror is underpinned by calling Hitler the "greatest leader of the 20th century".

A *second* way, in which Hitler was presented as leader in the analysed dataset, was by foregrounding the claim that he was a strong political figure. Figures 7.4–7.6 show examples.

Ian Kershaw, author of the most widely read biography of Hitler (Kershaw 2008), argues that the specificity of Nazism was not Hitler's personality, but the form of rule that he and the Nazis embodied (Kershaw 2004). Kershaw based on Max Weber's (1978) theory argues that Nazism's uniqueness is the combination of "Hitler's

FIGURE 7.4 The fascist representation of Hitler as leader on Twitter: "The 127th Anniversary of My Führer" (No. 956).

#HappyBirthDayHitler #fourtwentyproblems =
not enough know how truly amazing He was,
DONT beLIEve the lies!

RETWEETS LIKES
20   26

FIGURE 7.5 The fascist representation of Hitler as leader on Twitter (No. 196).

'charismatic authority'", the Führer cult and myth, "and its promise of national salvation" (Kershaw 2004, 246). It aimed at "racial cleansing and imperialism" (Kershaw
2004, 249), the Shoah, and a world war, and used the most modern state and military
apparatus for executing its ideology. The core points of Hitler's ideology were: "'re-
moval of the Jews' [...]; attaining 'living space' to secure Germany's future (a notion

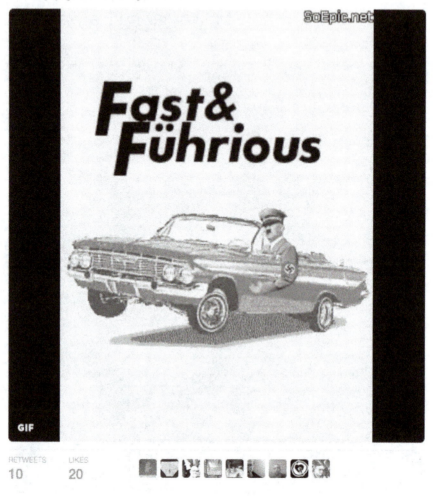

FIGURE 7.6 The fascist representation of Hitler as leader on Twitter (No. 855).

vague enough to encompass different strands of expansionism); race as the explanation of world history, and eternal struggle as the basic law of human existence" (Kershaw 2004, 252). Franz Neumann (2009, 83–97) shares the analysis that Hitler was a charismatic leader, who was seen as possessing "[s]uperhuman qualities" (Neumann 2009, 85). Neumann stresses that top-down leadership was not just a principle of the Nazi state, but of all realms of Nazi society. The "principle of leadership [...] dominates all social and political organizations" (Neumann 2009, 83). Hitler was "the leader of the party, the army, and the people" (Neumann 2009, 84).

The images in Figures 7.4–7.6 evoke the impression of Hitler as God, captain, and driver. Different metaphors are visually employed for stressing Hitler's leadership qualities. Whereas the aura in Figure 7.4 is one of static adoration that has religious undertones of constancy, sacredness, and eternity, Figures 7.5 and 7.6 create the impression of movement and change by using the images of a carriage and a car. The idea that the Führer moves society into the right direction is underpinned in Figure 7.6 by the use of an animated image, in which the car bounces up and down. The tweet in Figure 7.4 plays with the idea of Hitler being superhuman and bringing salvation. He is shown as a God-like figure in the centre of the image, surrounded by the symbol of the Imperial Eagle that communicates loyalty and unity. Figure 7.5 draws a distinction between Stalin as boss and Hitler as leader. It compares Stalinism and Nazism and communicates that Stalin controlled and enslaved wretched masses, whereas it also claims that Hitler was an ordinary German, who was one of the people and worked hard to lead them into the right direction. The tweet also expresses admiration of Hitler by claiming he was "truly amazing". Prefixing the adverb "truly" intensifies the adjective's connotation.

The concept of charismatic leadership does not mean an individualistic analysis of fascism because it implies that citizens follow, legitimate, enable, and support authoritarian rule and in specific social contexts enact its principles and act like small leaders. Max Weber (1978, 243) therefore speaks of the connection of a charismatic leader to a charismatic community that is "based on an emotional form of communal relationship". Figures 7.4 and 7.5 also visualise the relationship between Hitler as leader and his followers: a mass of anonymous followers expresses their loyalty by practising the Nazi salute. We do not see their faces and bodies, but only their hands, which symbolises the fascist demand for collective uniformity determined by dominant principles. The use of the words "Mein Führer" (My Führer) communicates a close relationship between the leader and the followers that is defined by the imaginative bond of race and nation. Fascism requires an internalisation of authority so that the followers not just see the Führer as one of them, but consider him and the principles he stands for as something they would give their lives for.

The tweet shown in Figure 7.6 uses a popular culture reference to the action movie *The Fast and the Furious* that combines with political mythology. The film's plot is about car racing in New York. The first part was released in 2001; a number of sequels followed. The tweet plays with the transformation of the movie title into *Fast & Führious*. By creating the term "Führious", it combines the meanings of the German noun *Führer* (leader) and the verb *führen* (that means to lead, but also to drive) into an adjective.

The image communicates that Hitler not just brought about fast change, but was also highly determined and effective. The car and the motorway play a special role in myths about Nazi Germany: those who say that Nazi fascism also had good sides tend to bring up the building of motorways and the design of the VW Beetle as some of the first examples. In a German survey conducted in 2007, 25% of the participants argued that Nazi Germany also had good sides (Die Welt 2007). The German motorways were a frequently mentioned example. The connection of cars and Hitler in the tweet may not be completely arbitrary, but appeals to the cliché that Hitler created jobs and an efficient and effective economy by building motorways and that he made cars affordable.

Hitler appealed to the car industry by giving the opening address to the 1934 International Automobile and Motor-Cycle Exhibition in Berlin, in which he announced tax relief for the car industry and a road-building programme (Kershaw 2008, 270–272). For Hitler, motorways and the mass production of the VW Beetle were populist ideological symbols that stood for what he saw as the opportunities of the German *Volksgemeinschaft* (community of the German people). Yet the initiative to build a motorway between Hamburg, Frankfurt and Basel (HaFraBa) goes back to 1926 and was not a Nazi idea (Deutsche Welle, 2012). The Nazis first opposed this project, which in 1933 became part of Hitler's plan to build a *Reichsautobahn*. "Between 1941 and 1942, construction almost ground to a halt. From 1943 onwards, the autobahns were opened up to cyclists because of the low volume of vehicle traffic" (Deutsche Welle DW, 2012). Although 336,000 exemplars of Hitler's people car (the VW Beetle) were ordered, none was ever delivered because the car industry produced for military purposes during the Second World War (Kershaw 2008, caption to image 80; Kopper 2013, 174). For the creation of motorways, at the peak level, 124,483 workers were employed in 1936, not 600,000, as initially planned by General Inspector for Road Building Fritz Todt (Oster 1996). It is a myth that Hitler conceptualised the motorway, designed a people's car, created lots of jobs, and that such projects benefited everyone.

A *third* way of how Hitler's leadership was celebrated used music in tweets. Figure 7.7 shows a neo-Nazi example.

The tweet says in German: "We do not let our celebrations today be prohibited, and you? We have planned everything. #Adolf #Hitler #20041889". It links to the rock song "Gemeinsam in den Sieg" (Together into Victory) by Nordsturm. The song's refrain is: "The only real holiday is the one that I am not allowed to mention. Every year in April,

Wir lassen uns heute das Feiern nicht verbieten, und ihr? Bei uns ist alles geplant.
#Adolf #Hitler #20041889

View translation

Nordsturm - Im April
youtube.com

FIGURE 7.7 Music as means for the fascist celebration of Hitler on Twitter (No. 1006).

we get up together: Today is birthday! We drink to it!"[3]. The tweet communicates that prohibition of celebrating Hitler's birthday should be ignored, that one should be proud of Hitler, and therefore drink to him on this day. The tweet wants to appeal to Nazis and young people prone to Nazism. It uses not just rock culture, but also military aesthetic and a reference to drinking culture.

Another tweet (Figure 7.8) uses a rock ballad, namely Bryan Adams' 1991 song "(Everything I Do) I Do It For You". This piece of music is a love song. Its lyrics say: "Yeah, I would fight for you, I'd lie for you. Walk the wire for you, yeah, I'd die for you. You know it's true: Everything I do, oh, I do it for you". Fascism's charismatic authority

Fascism 2.0's First Element: Leadership Ideology and Authoritarian Populism

Happy Birthday Uncle Adolf!
#HappyBirthdayHitler

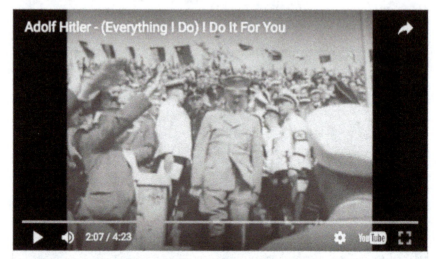

Adolf Hitler - (Everything I Do) I Do It For You
I made my first video exactly 1 year ago, and within 1 year I got this far, but I could...
youtube.com

FIGURE 7.8 The music video as medium for the fascist celebration of Hitler on Twitter and YouTube (No. 296).

is here expressed by de-contextualising a love song and re-contextualising it in the context of fascism: the video shows Hitler surrounded by cheering crowds, including children, women, and soldiers. The message is twofold: it implies on the one hand that Hitler acted out of love for the Germans. And on the other hand it communicates that one should love and identify with Hitler and Nazism. The emotional message of a personal relation to the Führer is further intensified by the tweet's message "Happy Birthday Uncle Adolf!". Both the video and the written text are emotionalisations and personalisations. They create the impression of a family, in which the uncle is the head who can be trusted.

The expression of a personal relation to Hitler is also underpinned by the use of his first name. The personal emotional relation of Germans and Austrians to Hitler was expressed during the Nazi period by the fact that Adolf was one of the most popular first names given to newborn boys.[4] Since the early 1950s, this name

Adolf Hitler - We built this city youtu.be
/IsRXRcAOfcU #HappyBirthdayHitler

FIGURE 7.9 The music video as medium for the fascist celebration of Hitler on Twitter and YouTube (No. 432).

has practically disappeared.[5] Also many of those whose family name was Hitler, changed their surname. Today no Hitler can be found in the Austrian phonebook.[6] There is just one person named Hitler in the German phonebook[7].

Figure 7.9 shows another example that uses Starship's 1985 song "We Built this City". The refrain goes: "We built this city, we built this city on Rock 'n' Roll". The video shows a colourful, youthfully dressed Hitler driving on a Nazi bike through a city. The bike carries a basket that is decorated by a Nazi flag. A cat sits in the basket and sings along with Hitler. Hitler has magic powers that allow him to create and destroy things. Several themes are combined in this video: Hitler as entertainment and popular culture, online culture symbolised by the cat, Hitler as magician, Hitler as builder and creator. The video creates an aura of a popular architect who has magical powers. The idea that a charismatic leader has supernatural and superhuman powers is evoked. The

Fascism 2.0's First Element: Leadership Ideology and Authoritarian Populism

#HappyBirthdayHitler

RETWEETS LIKES
3   10

FIGURE 7.10 Hitler as popular music culture (No. 820).

video trivialises Nazism by distracting attention from the circumstance that Hitler was first and foremost one of the architects of the Shoah and the Second World War.

Figure 7.10 offers another example. It uses an animated gif, in which Hitler is shown dancing in disco lights. The animation is an excerpt from one[8] of several YouTube videos[9] that have become known as Disco Hitler and Dancing Hitler. The animated dancing Hitler is underpinned by techno music. The video's name is "Hitler dance" and its description speaks of "Hitler Guetta", which is a reference to the French house DJ

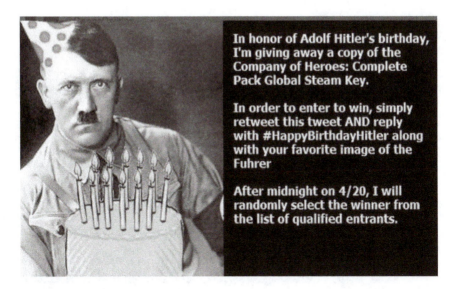

In honor of Adolf Hitler's birthday, I'm giving away a copy of the Company of Heroes: Complete Pack Global Steam Key.

In order to enter to win, simply retweet this tweet AND reply with #HappyBirthdayHitler along with your favorite image of the Fuhrer

After midnight on 4/20, I will randomly select the winner from the list of qualified entrants.

FIGURE 7.11 A fascist tweet using a contest for spreading images of Hitler (No. 409).

and musician David Guetta. Hitler is presented as a symbol of coolness. The focus on the culture of cool renders any historical references to the horrors of the Shoah and German Nazi imperialism invisible.

A *fourth* form of online fascism that is focused on Hitler as person uses games and contests. Figure 7.11 shows a tweet that tried to promote posting images of Hitler and the use of the hashtag #HappyBirthdayHitler by staging a contest, in which users could win a copy of the video game *Company of Heroes* by posting images of Hitler. The tweet trivialised Nazism by showing Hitler in birthday mood. *Company of Heroes* is a war game. Its first part was released in 2006. Relic Entertainment describes its game the following way: "Command the company that changed history: Delivering a visceral WWII gaming experience, Company of Heroes redefines real time strategy gaming by bringing the sacrifice of heroic soldiers, war-ravaged environments, and dynamic battlefields to life. Beginning with the D-Day Invasion of Normandy, players lead squads of Allied soldiers into battle against the German war machine through some of the most pivotal battles of WWII"[10]. The tweet implicitly communicates that Hitler is a military hero who led the German army into battle. It aims at glorifying war and Nazi imperialism.

A *fifth* form of leadership-focused online fascism presents Hitler as a man of the people. The tweet in Figure 7.5 is one example. Figure 7.12 shows another one.

Fascism 2.0's First Element: Leadership Ideology and Authoritarian Populism

Did someone mention #Obama?
Happy Birthday Adolf #Hitler

Adolf Hitler's motorcade

RETWEETS   LIKES
35   63

FIGURE 7.12 Fascist presentation of Hitler as a popular, common person who is close to the people (No. 1169).

The tweet presents Hitler as a common, popular leader, who is of the people and loved by them. It contrasts this image with one that implies that Obama is distant and alienated from citizens. Juxtaposing these two images also communicates that Obama is afraid of the people and therefore protects himself with lots of police. In contrast, the second image implies that Hitler wanted to be as close as possible to the people. There is also a certain racist undertone: it is not an accident that Hitler is juxtaposed to

Obama, whose father was black and was born in Kenya. So implicitly the image also communicates: "White leaders are popular and close to the people, whereas leaders who are black or have a black parent are unpopular and alienated from the people".

Ideologies hold together repressive collectives by providing a collective identity for them. In fascist ideology, Hitler is an important symbol of identification. One ideological strategy is positive self-presentation (van Dijk 1998, 309–311; Reisigl and Wodak 2001, 44–46). Strategies for positive self-presentation in fascism 2.0 that are focused on Hitler, as we have seen in this section, include: the combination of fascist symbols with symbols of harmlessness and happiness such as coffee, cakes, children, biscuits; the claim that Hitler was a strong political leader; the claim that Hitler was a popular, ordinary person who was close to the people; the use of Internet memes, animated gifs, songs, popular culture, entertainment, rock music, or disco music. Harmless symbols and popular symbols usually not associated with Hitler help to draw attention away from Nazism's barbarism.

7.4 Fascism 2.0's Second Element: Nationalism

Fascism appeals to a mythic collective such as the nation and race. It thereby diverts attention from class. "[R]acism and Anti-Semitism are substitutes for the class struggle" (Neumann 200, 125). "[B]lood, community, folk, are devices for hiding the real constellation of power" (Neumann 2009, 464). Such collectivism is often said to be able to overcome the individualisation and atomisation brought about by capitalism, globalisation, and modernity.

Fascist parties are not just, as often wrongly assumed, middle class parties, but have historically also appealed to blue-collar workers and other social groups. Woodley argues in this context that "the social function of fascism is to create a unity of social forces incorporating propertied interests, lower-middle class voters and plebeian elements" (Woodley 2010, 76). The ideological construction of national and/or racial unity deflects attention from class conflicts and aims to appeal with nationalist and racist demagogy to a large part of the population across social strata and classes. Via nationalist and racist ideology, fascism tries to construct a unity that is held together through hatred of an imagined outside so that class structures can be hidden.

We saw that there are tweets that try to define a collective unity and identity around Hitler as leader. There are other tweets that try to define such a unity around an imaginary national collective. A *first* way of doing so is to invoke the racist ideology of the existence of an Aryan race. Here are two examples:

> "We must secure the existence of our race and a future for our progeny. #HappyBirthdayHitler #MAGA" (No. 259).

> "On this day, 20th April of 1889 was born #AdolfHitler, The Führer and the true leader of aryan race. #NAZI #Birthday" (No. 336).

The first of these tweets is white supremacist in nature. It defines a white collective ("our race") that is perceived to be under threat and calls for preserving this collective. It is a reformulation of the white supremacist *Fourteen Word* slogan "We must secure the existence of our people and a future for white children". David Edan Lane coined this slogan. He was one of the founders of the neo-Nazi terror organisation The Order. The formulations "our race", "our progeny", and "Aryan race" are somatonyms and racionyms (Reisigl and Wodak 2001, 48). They try to "racialise" and biologise society, i.e. present society as consisting of races. The use of the possessive pronoun "our" tries to intensify the feeling of belonging to this illusionary collective. The use of the verb "secure" communicates a threat and attack and the urgency that something needs to be done. The first tweet uses the hashtag #MAGMA that stands for "Make America Great Again", the main political slogan used by the 2016 Republican Presidential candidate Donald Trump.

A *second* way of constructing collective unity is to focus on Europe. Figure 7.13 shows an example. On the one hand, a personal, family-like relation to Hitler is expressed by showing someone holding a signed image of Hitler and by the use of the personalising formulation "Onkel Adolf!" (Uncle Adolf). Referring to Hitler as uncle implies that there is a blood relationship between all those who are considered to be part of the imagined collective. In the shown tweet, this collective is presented as Europe. Associating Europe with Hitler and speaking of Hitler as "Europe's greatest Son!" implies that Hitler is a symbol for a European cultural or biological collective.

Yet Hitler defined himself as German. He saw Europe as imperial Lebensraum (living space) for the territorial expansion of Germany, the augmentation of the number of Germans and the expansion of German culture. He called for the "enlargement of our national domain of life [*Lebensraum*] in Europe" (Hitler 1941, 949) and wrote that his party's aim is "to guarantee the German nation the soil and territory to which it is entitled on this earth" (947). "The folkish movement must be not the attorney for other nations, but the vanguard fighter of its own" (950). "Germany will be either a world

Happy 127th Onkel Adolf!
Europe's greatest Son!

#HappyBirthdayHitler

RETWEETS 40   LIKES 49

FIGURE 7.13   Fascist construction of Hitler as great European (No. 673).

power or will not be at all" (950). "Today we are eight million Germans in Europe! That foreign policy will be acknowledged as correct only if, a bare century from now, two hundred and fifty million Germans are living on this continent" (979). Claiming that Hitler was a great European, as the tweet in Figure 7.13 does, lacks any understanding of political history. Hitler defined himself as a German nationalist and racist. He saw Europe merely as potential colonial German territory.

This section showed that in the analysed dataset two nationalist strategies were used for positive identity definition of an imagined white collective: the appeal to either a German, "Aryan" collective or a European collective.

7.5 Fascism 2.0's Third Element: The Friend-Enemy Scheme

Fascist ideology not just works with opportunities for psychological projections "upwards" (into the Führer), but also downwards: it invites individuals to define

Fascism 2.0's Third Element: The Friend-Enemy Scheme

themselves as a national collective that is different from outsiders that are presented as enemies and subhuman beings (*Untermenschen*). The mythic collective is in fascist ideology distinguished from constructed enemies. Fascism argues for terror against as well as the intimidation and annihilation of these illusionary enemies.

Fascism uses ideological forms of national unity. These ideologies define unity against specific opponents: "The demon reappears in all manner of forms, across the whole spectrum of representations of the enemy; the bellicose Communist, the lascivious Jew, or the indolent citizen. [...] Each in his own way threatens to devour the not-yet-fully-born soldier" (Theweleit 1989, 378).

Franz Neumann in his study of Nazi Germany stressed the racist character of German Nazi imperialism ("racial imperialism"). The ideology of the friend-enemy-scheme motivates exterminatory and imperialistic politics. "The essence of the theory is extremely simple. Germany and Italy are proletarian races, surrounded by a world of hostile plutocratic capitalistic-Jewish democracies. [The war is thus a war for] [...] the attainment of a better life for the master race through reducing the vanquished states and their satellites to the level of colonial peoples" (Neumann 2009, 187, 193). Nazi imperialism is based on the ideology of creating "Aryan" living space (Lebensraum) by military means (Neumann 2009, 130). Nazi imperialism according to Neumann constructs the "Aryans" as proletarian have-nots who are threatened by Jews, democracy, and socialism (Neumann 2009, 221).

"Positive self-presentation and negative other-presentation seems to be a fundamental property of ideologies" (van Dijk 1998, 69). We saw in previous sections ways of how fascism 2.0 uses positive presentations of Hitler and collectives. Fascism always defines itself against imagined enemies. So negative other-presentation is also a key feature of fascism 2.0.

A *first* strategy of the use of the friend-enemy-scheme in the analysed dataset was the general praise of the Shoah. Some examples follow.

> "#HappyBirthdayHitler thanks for killing the jews" (No. 644)

> "I hear April showers bring Mayflowers. This is due to post-gas Jews providing excellent fertilizer. #HappyBirthdayHitler" (No. 752)

The first tweet expresses agreement to the Shoah by thanking Hitler for Nazism's exterminatory anti-Semitic politics. The second tweet expresses such approval by an

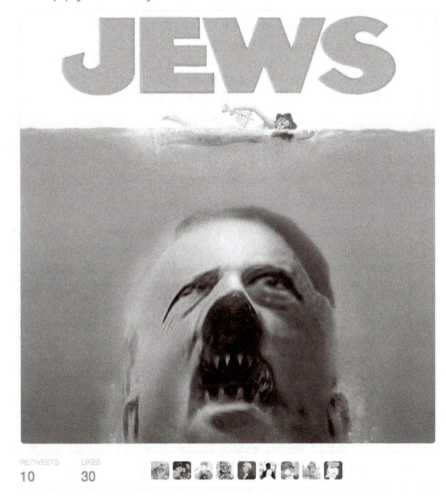

He could have saved us all.
#HappyBirthdayHitler

RETWEETS   LIKES
10   30

FIGURE 7.14   Anti-Semitic tweet (No. 573).

inhumane joke that suggests that gassed Jews should be used as fertiliser. Figure 7.14 shows an anti-Semitic tweet that visualises Hitler as a shark that is about to attack a swimmer who is depicted as being Jewish. The tweet text "He could have saved us all" expresses that in the opinion of this Twitter user, Nazism's exterminatory politics that killed six million Jews did not go far enough and that it should have exterminated all Jews in the world.

Fascism is often thought of as being humourless. Empirical studies have in contrast shown that humour is often deliberately used as fascist strategy. Michael Billig (2002) analysed racist joke sites linked to the Ku Klux Klan. His study illustrates connections between humour and hatred. Humour "can provide a means for expressing hatred and, thus, bigotry can bring its own pleasures to the bigot [...]. The KKK jokes [...] treat humans as non-human" (Billig 2001, 285, 279).

Simon Weaver (2011) analysed racist jokes on five websites. He found that "humour can act as a form of racist rhetoric and thus should not always be seen as 'just a joke' or fundamentally harmless" (Weaver 2011, 431). He identifies two basic ideal-types of racist jokes, one operating through "the inclusion of the 'other' through inferiorization", the other using "the exclusion of the 'other'" (Weaver 2011, 431). The first type justifies discrimination and exploitation. The second type legitimates segregation, deportation and annihilation.

Hitler jokes on social media show fascist online joy in torment and fascist pleasure in exclusion, stereotyping, humiliation, and hatred and its expression in the online world as user-generated content. They confirm that fascism and humour are compatible – also in the online world.

A *second* friend-enemy-strategy that could be found in the dataset was the identification of Jews with finance capital. An example:

> "Philosopher. Hero. Genius. Liberator. He fought for freedom & against the tyranny of international finance. #Hitler" (No. 3403)

This anti-Semitic tweet received a particularly high approval of 86 re-tweets and 144 likes. It presents Hitler as a heroic liberator and the Shoah as a form of freedom. It identifies Jews with "international finance", which expresses several anti-Semitic prejudices, namely that "Jews are criminal world conspirators", "Jews are business-minded, tricky and fraudulent; they are the prototypical capitalists", "Jews are social parasites" (Reisigl and Wodak 2001, 56). Hitler constantly expressed such anti-Semitic stereotypes. He for example spoke of the "despotism of international world finance, Jewry!" and of "international world finance Judaism"'s (Hitler 1941, 674) goal of enslaving the world.

A *third* friend-enemy strategy that was present in the dataset was the association of Hitler with contemporary political opposition to migrants, refugees, and people of colour (Figure 7.15):

And then a holy war began
Happy #AdolfHitlerDay
#holocaust #refugeesarewelcome in my shower

FIGURE 7.15   Fascist tweet calling for a "Holocaust against refugees" (No. 2455).

> "The agenda for tonight is to send the Negroes back to Africa. #HappyBirthdayHitler" (No. 3513)

The first tweet uses the racionym "Negroes" for characterising black people in a derogatory manner. Blacks are presented as being inherently non-Western and to belong to Africa. The second tweet calls for the killing of refugees. It expresses approval of the Shoah and calls for a systematic, industrial mass extermination of refugees. The impression of the demand of a "Holocaust against refugees" is achieved by combing the two hashtags #Holocaust and #RefugeesAreWelcome and adding that refugees are welcome "in my shower". This formulation plays with the fact that in the Nazi extermination camps gas chambers were often presented to victims as showers. Calling mass extermination a "holy war" plays with the anti-Semitic and anti-Muslim prejudices that Jews and Muslims are different in culture and religion from Europeans, therefore do not belong to the West, and that the "Jews are the murderers of Christ, [...] desecrators of hosts, ritual murderers and well-poisoners" (Reisigl and Wodak 2001, 56).

Such tweets transfer Hitler's barbaric politics to contemporary times and call for deporting or killing black people and refugees.

A *fourth* friend-enemy strategy used in the analysed tweets focused on conspiracy theories.

Fascism 2.0's Third Element: The Friend-Enemy Scheme

"#Hitler started WWII. Oh really? I think not. https://t.co/ngz7pkVJDL#tcot#ccot3altright#wr#WWII#israel#jews" (No. 3734)

This tweet links to an article titled "Hitler Was a War Monger! He Started WWII... Oh Really???". It links to various quotes and documents that together want to suggest that it was not Nazi Germany that started the Second World War. The claim is that Jewish organisations declared war on Germany after Hitler rose to power in 1933. It shows an excerpt from a *Daily Mail* article from 24 March 1933, titled "Judea Declares War on Germany". Vladimir Zhabotinsky, who established militant Jewish self-defence groups, is quoted as saying in 1934: "Our Jewish interests demand the final destruction of Germany". It also shows a *Daily Express* article from 24 March 1933, which reported that 14 million Jews "declare war on the German persecutors of their co-religionists". The implication that the article wants to make is that it was not Hitler and Nazism, but Jewry that caused the Second World War.

The conspiracy theory that Jews were responsible for the Second World War uses single quotes from single persons and media sources. It ignores that Hitler's eliminationist anti-Semitism was evident much earlier to everyone who read what he wrote or listened to him. In *Mein Kampf*'s Volume 1 that was published in 1925, he wrote that the Jew is "always only a *parasite* in the body of other peoples" (Hitler 1941, 419). "But this spreading is the typical symptom of all parasites; he always looks for a new feeding soil for his race. [...] He is and remains the typical parasite, a sponger who, like a harmful bacillus, spreads out more and more if only a favorable medium invites him to do so" (Hitler 1941, 420). The biologistic description of Jews as parasites, spongers, and bacillus implies a danger that needs to be eliminated.

Another tweet said "Adolf #Hitler 20th April 1889–30th April 1945 We celebrate because we know the #truth" (#1346) and linked to the apologetic and revisionist documentary *Adolf Hitler: The Greatest Story Never Told*. The tweet achieved a fairly large attention of 86 re-tweets and 120 likes. The reference to the "truth" and a "story never told" as well as the use of the hashtag #truth imply the claim that there is a hidden reality of Nazism that has been kept secret and that the documentary reveals this to the public. Conspiracy theories always work with the claim that they make hidden secrets visible and public. Among other things, the video questions the existence of the Holocaust, documenting voices that claim that there is no proof that gas chambers existed. It says for example: "Only in Eastern European camps, where no investigations ever occurred or were allowed, it is still claimed that millions of Jews entered the gas chambers". The movie's end titles thank the white supremacist, neo-Nazi Internet forum Stormfront "for their help in transcribing the series".

We have in this section seen that the friend-enemy scheme is in fascism 2.0 present as various strategies of negative other-online presentation. Such strategies include for example general praise for the Shoah and other fascist crimes; the identification of Jews with finance capital; the visual and textual association of Hitler with contemporary political opposition to migrants, refugees and people of colour; or the spread of conspiracy theories.

7.6 Fascism 2.0's Fourth Element: Patriarchy and Naturalism

In relation to nature, biology, and the social construction of gender, fascism tends to idealise the body, nature, male supremacy, fitness and health of the population, physical labour and toil, the soldier and the army, and the importance of procreation. It tends to define the sphere of production as a masculine and reproduction as a feminine/private sphere. At the same time, the private becomes militarised, statised, and subordinated to nationalism and racism. Procreation is defined as a national duty. The model of the soldier defines images and practices of health, sports, fitness and the body. Also the motive of the competitive, physically strong male soldier can be found in fascist culture. An example is Leni Riefenstahl's movie *Olympia*. Not just the body, but also nature is part of fascist ideology that often presents blood, soil, and love of nature as part of the homeland.

Fascism tends to view homosexuality "as a threat to the integrity of the race-nation" (Woodley 2010, 228). Klaus Theweleit argues that fascism is sexually schizophrenic because it is based on the double bind "thou shall love men" (Theweleit 1989, 339), which includes the contradictory principles of "love for the leader" (Theweleit 1989, 60) and "thou shall not be homosexual" (Theweleit 1989, 339). Theweleit sees a connection between fascism's "male bonding and the white terror – a connection that provides the pleasure of power" (Theweleit, 1989, 325).

In the analysed dataset, a *first* form of fascist patriarchy 2.0 focused on the claim that Hitler was the heartthrob of all women, cared about families, and loved children. Figure 7.16 shows an example.

The tweet links to a video that shows children, pregnant women, a mother with her child, happy couples, interlaced with sound and text from a Hitler speech: "The most precious possession you have in the world, is your own people! And for this people and

#HappybirthdayHitler
#Hitler The man who the fought the jews
#nationalsocialism

FIGURE 7.16 An example of fascist patriarchy 2.0 (No. 346).

for the sake of this people, we will struggle and fight! And never slacken! And never tire! And never lose courage! And never despair!". The tweet adds the message "The man who fought the Jews". The combination of the video and the tweet text glorifies the Nazis' racist population policies that according to Franz Neumann focused on a double goal, namely (a) the commandment of women to "produce children" and (b) the S.S.'s "commandment to kill those who are not fit to live" (Neumann 2009, 112). The Nazis' maxim was: "Produce as many children as possible so that the earth can be ruled by the master race; kill the unhealthy so that the masters need not be burdened by the care of the weak" (Neumann 2009, 112).

Second, there were tweets in the dataset that suggested that Hitler had been a lover of nature and animals. Figures 7.17 and 7.18 show two examples.

Showing Hitler as loving animals (dogs, roe deer, etc.) suggests that he was a loving and caring leader. The German shepherd dog often symbolises loyalty and bravery.

#HappyBirthday #Hitler #HappyBirthDayHitler!
#AdolfHitler Loved& cherished animals!
Nat.Soc. = 1st environmentallist

RETWEETS   LIKES
19   31

FIGURE 7.17 An example of fascist naturalism 2.0 (No. 231).

Hitler was often portrayed with his female shepherdess Blondi and other dogs. Such images, as also used in the tweet shown in Figure 7.18, communicate that Hitler found the qualities ascribed to the shepherd as important and that the German people should practise loyalty to the Führer and bravery. The German shepherd stands in Nazism for the militarisation of society that sees society as constant warfare and citizens as warriors for "Aryanism".

The tweet in Figure 7.17 claims that Hitler "loved & cherished animals" and that he was the first environmentalist. The roe deer is a symbol of beauty, grace, peace, innocence, or benevolence. Portraying Hitler as a lover of animals and naturalist tries to justify Nazism by presenting positive claims about Hitler that distract attention from the barbarity of the Nazis' politics. It is an attempt at impression management by inverting the association of Nazism with terrorism, imperialism, racism, and extermination by advancing symbols that stand for opposed properties such as care, peace, tolerance and love.

Fascism 2.0's Fourth Element: Patriarchy and Naturalism

#HappyBirthdayHitler
#NationalSocialism

RETWEETS   LIKES
23   24

FIGURE 7.18 An example of fascist naturalism 2.0 (No. 1146).

The tweet in Figure 7.18 contrasts images of Hitler with women and Hitler with German shepherds. It communicates fascisms' patriarchal dualism that draws a strict ideological separation between men/women, society/nature, body/mind, rational/irrational, production/reproduction, war/peace, public/private, intellectual/emotional, aggression/love, active/passive, etc. Fascism's model and vision of society is an extremely hierarchical and militarised form of patriarchy, in which there is a strict gender division of labour and the male soldier is the ideal citizen.

Hitler's patriarchal model of society becomes evident in *Mein Kampf*, where he writes that in marriage, "the woman is here only the passive part, anyhow" (Hitler 1941, 342). He also says that the "*goal* of female education has invariably to be the future mother" (Hitler 1941, 621). Education would have to focus on physical education, military discipline, authoritarianism, and nationalism in order to make children and youth respect authority, prepare the boys for the military and to instil in them enthusiasm for soldierdom: "His entire education and development has to be directed at giving him the conviction of being absolutely superior to the others. With his physical force and skill he has again to win the belief in the invincibility of his entire nationality. For what once led the German army to victory was the sum of the confidence which the individual and all in common had in their leaders" (Hitler 1941, 618). "In the folkish State, therefore, the army [...] has to be looked upon as the ultimate and highest school of patriotic education" (Hitler 1941, 620). Exercise would be important to create what Hitler considered to be beautiful German bodies. The "most beautiful bodies find one another and thus help in giving the nation new beauty" (Hitler 1941, 619).

This section has shown how fascism 2.0 expresses elements of patriarchy on Twitter: the focus on German women's love to Hitler, Hitler's relation to animals and nature, distracts attention from the horrors of Nazism and presents fascism in a positive light. It also expresses a highly militaristic and patriarchal model of society that is modelled on the male soldier and grounded in a repressive ideological dualism.

7.7 Conclusion

This chapter has with the example case of Hitler's birthday on Twitter contributed to the analysis of how fascism 2.0 works. It identified four elements of fascism 2.0: online authoritarianism, online nationalism, the friend-enemy scheme online, and online patriarchy and naturalism. These elements are ideal types that can be found partly separately and partly interacting.

Fascism 2.0 both has form and ideological content. Its form includes the use of text, hashtags, links to online materials, images, animated pictures, jokes, satire, cartoons, movies, the de- and re-contextualisation and combination of symbols, entertainment, popular culture, songs, music videos, memes, etc.

At the content level, we saw that fascism 2.0 strategies can for example include positive self-presentation by the use of harmless symbols (cake, coffee, cookies, etc.); the presentation of Hitler as strong political leader and ordinary person; the appeal to a unitary national, racial, or cultural collective; the association of fascism with the love for families, children, nature, and animals; or the idealisation of militarism, patriarchy, and authoritarianism. Another strategy of fascism 2.0 is negative other-presentation that tries to deride fascism's enemies by presenting them as inferior and parasitic, celebrating and rationalising their extermination, the denial of extermination and other fascist crimes, the association of Hitler and fascism with contemporary scapegoats, or the use of conspiracy theories.

Why does a significant number of Twitter users find it appealing to celebrate Hitler on social media? *On the one hand,* there are straightforward ideological reasons: the ongoing economic, political, and social crisis of capitalism is a fascism-producing crisis that has in many parts of the world resulted in an expansion of authoritarian populist, far-right, right-wing populist, fascist, and neo-Nazi expressions, groups, movements, and parties and in a significant level of support for such tendencies among citizens. Geoff Eley (2015) compares the far-right then and now. He says that in the age of the Golden Dawn, Jobbik, the Front National, the Austrian Freedom Party, the Belgian Flemish Block, the Danish People's Party, the Norwegian Progress Party, the Swiss People's Party, or the Dutch Party for Freedom,

> [f]ar-right advocacy has increasingly regrouped around the programmatic defense of the distinctiveness of national culture and its threatened integrity. In the language deployed by right-wing populists, cultural identity has become key to how the alienness of "iimmigrants" can be publicly rationalized; such intruders are people who share neither a national heritage nor "European civilization" as historically transmitted, who do not belong, who are foreign to the way "we" live, who lack "our" cultural and moral values.
>
> (Eley 2015, 109)

Today, one would find a "culturalized racism" (Eley 2015, 109). The danger is for Eley that a crisis of society is often a "fascism-producing crisis" (Eley 2015, 112). Given that the contemporary age of crisis is also an age of social media, it is self-evident that the mediation of fascism also takes place online on platforms such as Twitter, Facebook, YouTube, Instagram, and Pinterest.

On the other hand, in a culture of neoliberalism, competitive individualism and mediated spectacles, where the commodity form has colonised large parts of life in society and ever more social relations not just become competitive, but also realms of advertising and promotional culture, cool capitalism as a specific form of capitalism has emerged (McGuigan 2012, 2009). Cool capitalism has the capacity "to repackage virtually anything for mass distribution" so that even the "most brutal, misogynistic and homophobic features" of society can become "another consumer item, to be tasted and discarded at will" (McGuigan 2009, 98). In cool capitalism, even war and fascism's most horrendous crimes can turn into entertainment and popular culture. Fascism 2.0 is to a specific degree a popular cultural spectacle that works with re-contextualisation, culture jamming, symbols and practices of Internet subculture (such as Internet memes), and popular cultural expressions. To a specific degree the motivation of popular cultural fascism is certainly ideologically motivated fascism. In others, it is the drive to shock in order to impress, create public attention, and define a particular identity. It can also be the combination of both motivations.

It is interesting to observe that whereas offline fascism tends to attract anti-fascist protests, anti-fascism can to a much lesser degree be found in online spaces where fascism 2.0 exists. When the right-wing Thügida group organised a torch march on Hitler's 2016 birthday in the German city of Jena, it had to face several thousand anti-fascist protestors. On social media, protests against the online celebration of Hitler's birthday were in contrast rare.

One user spoke of a "bunch of drug/Hitler loving idiots" (No. 2137) using the hashtag #Happy420. Others posted: "All y'all people saying #happybirthdayhitler deserve to go to hell he killed innocent civilian lives and y'all applaud him wtf" (No. 657); "Grund zum feiern gibt es in zehn Tagen: 30.04.45 – Todestag des Massenmörders #AdolfHitler" (No. 1138) ["There will be reason to celebrate in ten days: 30.04.45 – the day of death of the mass murderer #AdolfHitler"]. Such expressions of disagreement were, however, single in character. To be effective, anti-fascism needs to challenge fascism wherever it occurs, including on social media.

The question arises what could be done against fascism 2.0. A significant share of its expressions violates Twitter's (and other platforms') terms of service. The Twitter Rules prohibit abusive behavior and hateful conduct: "we do not tolerate behavior that crosses the line into abuse, including behavior that harasses, intimidates, or uses fear to silence another user's voice. [...] Hateful conduct: You may not promote violence against or directly attack or threaten other people on the basis of race, ethnicity, national origin, sexual orientation, gender, gender identity, religious affiliation, age, disability, or disease. We also do not allow accounts whose primary purpose is inciting harm towards others on the basis of these categories".[11]

Twitter has a report button that allows users to directly report a displayed tweet as being spam, abusive, or harmful. And it also has a report form that allows reporting

Conclusion

abusive, harassing, violent, and offensive behaviour as well as spam and privacy violations. The problem is that in order to always respond accordingly and in a timely manner to fascism 2.0, enough well-trained and fairly paid employees are needed. If precarious workers who hardly have enough time available to deal with a single tweets in detail, then an effective response becomes impossible. Online culture is often fairly complex, is not always straightforward, and therefore it takes time to understand what particular tweets are about. A possibility that could be further explored is to introduce a fascism-report button on Twitter and other social media platforms and to train and employ anti-fascist social media experts specialised in responding to online fascism.

Given the complexity of online communication systems, it will never be possible to perfectly control online expressions of fascism. Fascism 2.0 is a societal problem, so there is no technical fix to it. Theodor W. Adorno stresses in this context: "The past will have been worked through only when the causes of what happened then have been eliminated. Only because the causes continue to exist does the captivating spell of the past remain to this day unbroken" (Adorno 1959, 103). Deletion can spur the incentive to multiply fascism 2.0's efforts and the development of sophisticated camouflage strategies.

The question is then how popular culture could be used on social media in order to create and diffuse intelligent, enlightening, critical engagements with the history and reality of fascism. On the one hand, official commemorations often do not reach broad parts of the public. Popular culture is in contrast a mass phenomenon. But on the other hand, Hitler as popular culture risks that the Shoah and fascism are trivialised and questions of historical guilt are not asked. Popular culture and humour in the context of fascism and fascism 2.0 should invite historical engagement, offer critical knowledge, and provide a critique of the history and reality of fascism. It should be an offer for deeper discussions and enlightening engagement among users. At the same time such serious popular anti-fascist culture cannot replace the need for in-depth documentary films, exhibitions, public events, and memorials.

Horkheimer and Adorno acknowledged the "ambiguity of laughter" (Horkheimer and Adorno 2002, 60): "If laughter up to now has been a sign of violence, an outbreak of blind, obdurate nature, it nevertheless contains the opposite element, in that through laughter blind nature becomes aware of itself as such and thus abjures its destructive violence". Humour may be a way of how the oppressed try to cope with their oppression or may be part of challenging oppression. It is possible that anti-fascist online videos are enlightening, humorous and serious at the same time. The problem is that this genre hardly exists and that there is a dominance of superficial and often problematic content about Hitler and fascism in Internet culture. Charlie Chaplin's film *The Great Dictator* is both a parody and enlightening. Anti-fascism 2.0 requires equivalents to *The Great Dictator* in the social media age. Chaplin commented on his movie: "Pessimists say I may fail – that dictators aren't funny any more, that the evil is too serious. That is wrong. If there is one thing I know it is that power can always be made ridiculous. The bigger that fellow gets the harder my laughter will hit him" (van Gelder 1940). Even Adorno was a Chaplin fan. Intelligent, critical, enlightening popular culture about Hitler could be spread on 20 April and on other symbolic fascist occasions on social media. Anti-fascism 2.0 requires a multidimensional political strategy and is in the end a matter of the time, people, praxis, institutions, and resources needed for challenging fascist narratives and telling anti-fascist counter-narratives online.

Adorno argues: "That fascism lives on [...] is due to the fact that the objective conditions of society that engendered fascism continue to exist" (Adorno 1959, 98). In this situation, "only exaggeration per se today can be the medium of truth" (Adorno 1959, 99). This assumption seems to imply that exaggeration not just of content, but also of the form of memory, is not per-se affirmative, but can also take on critical form. Adorno stressed that education is an important mechanism for remembering the past and the causes of fascism and working towards not repeating it. The question that arises today is how the educational memory of Nazism and Hitler can take on such a critical form on the Internet.

Notes

1 http://www.spiegel.de/video/vor-20-jahren-rechte-feiern-hitlers-geburtstag-video-1106162.html, accessed on May 2, 2016.

2 Accessed on May 3, 2016.

3 Translation from German: "Der einzig wahre Feiertag, ist der, den ich nicht nennen darf. Jedes Jahr im April stehen wir zusammen auf: Heute ist Geburtstag! Wir trinken darauf!".

4 http://www.beliebte-vornamen.de/4501-adolf.htm

5 Ibid.

6 http://www.herold.at, accessed on May 4, 2016.

7 http://www.dastelefonbuch.de, accessed on May 4, 2016.

8 https://www.youtube.com/watch?v=OoV_gsbYcxI (accessed on March 4, 2016).

9 Other examples include (accessed on March 4, 2016): https://www.youtube.com/watch?v=pg6duaXzKBo, https://www.youtube.com/watch?v=6_PtfImONc4.

10 http://www.companyofheroes.com/games/company-of-heroes, accessed on May 5, 2016.
11 Twitter Rules, https://support.twitter.com/articles/18311, accessed on May 6, 2016.

References

Adorno, Theodor W. 1959. "The Meaning of Working Through the Past." In *Critical Models: Interventions and Catchwords*, 89–103. New York: Columbia University Press.

Adorno, Theodor. 1951. "Freudian Theory and the Pattern of Fascist Propaganda." In *The Culture Industry*, 132–57. Abingdon: Routledge.

Benz, Wolfgang. 2000. *Geschichte des Dritten Reiches*. München: Beck.

Billig, Michael. 2001. "Humour and Hatred: The Racist Jokes of the Ku Klux Klan." *Discourse & Society* 12 (3): 267–89.

British Psychological Society (BPS). 2009. *Code of Ethics and Conduct*. Leicester: BPS.

Brustein, William. 2003. *Roots of Hate: Anti-Semitism in Europe Before the Holocaust*. Cambridge: Cambridge University Press.

Courtois, Stéphane, et al. 1999. *The Black Book of Communism*. Cambridge, MA: Harvard University Press.

Dawkins, Richard. 1999. *The Selfish Gene*. Oxford: Oxford University Press. New edition.

Deutsche Welle (DW). 2012. The Myth of Hitler's Role in Building the Autobahn. http://www.dw.com/en/the-myth-of-hitlers-role-in-building-the-autobahn/a-16144981.

Die Welt. 2007. "Viele Deutsche sehen Nazi-Zeit teils positiv." *Die Welt Online*, 17 October 2007. https://www.welt.de/politik/article1272668/Viele-Deutsche-sehen-Nazi-Zeit-teils-positiv.html.

Eley, Geoff. 2015. "Fascism Then and Now." *Socialist Register* 52: 91–117.

Encke, Julia. 2015. "High Hitler." *FAZ Online*, September 13, 2015.

Erk, Daniel. 2012. *So viel Hitler war selten*. München: Heyne.

Fairclough, Norman. 2015. *Language and Power*. New York: Routledge. 3rd edition.

Fairclough, Norman. 2010. *Critical Discourse Analysis. The Critical Study of Language*. Harlow: Longman.

Falter, Jürgen W. 1987. "Warum die deutschen Arbeiter während des „Dritten Reiches" zu Hitler standen." *Geschichte und Gesellschaft* 13 (2): 217–31.

Friedman, Jonathan, ed. 2011. *The Routlege History of the Holocaust*. Abingdon: Routledge.

Fuchs, Christian. 2015. *Culture and Economy in the Age of Social Media*. New York: Routledge.

Habermas, Jürgen. 1989. *The New Conservatism*. Cambridge: Polity.

Hitler, Adolf. 1941 [1925/26]. *Mein Kampf. Volume 1 and 2*. New York: Reynal & Hitchcock.

Horkheimer, Max and Theodor W. Adorno. 2002. *Dialectic of Enlightenment*. Stanford, CA: Stanford University Press.

Kershaw, Ian. 2008. *Hitler: A Biography*. New York: W.W. Norton & Company.

Kershaw, Ian. 2004. "Hitler and the Uniqueness of Nazism." *Journal of Contemporary History* 39 (2): 239–54.

Kopper, Christopher. 2013. "Germany's National Socialist Transport Policy and the Claim of Modernity: Reality or Fake?" *The Journal of Transport History* 34 (2): 162–76.

Lukács, Georg. 1971 [1923]. *History and Class Consciousness*. London: Merlin.

Marx, Karl and Friedrich Engels. 1845. *The German Ideology*. Amherst, NY: Prometheus.

McGuigan, Jim. 2012. "The Coolness of Capitalism Today." *tripleC: Communication, Capitalism & Critique* 10 (2): 425–38.

McGuigan, Jim. 2009. *Cool Capitalism*. London: Pluto.

Meikle, Graham. 2016. *Social Media. Communication, Sharing and Visibility*. New York: Routledge

Neumann, Franz. 2009 [1944]. *Behemoth: The Structure and Practice of National Socialism, 1933–1944*. Chicago, IL: Ivan R. Dee.

Oster, Uwe. 1996. "The Autobahn Myth." *History Today* 46 (11): 39–41.

Postone, Moishe. 1993. *Time, Labor, and Social Domination. A Reinterpretation of Marx's Critical Theory*. Cambridge: Cambridge University Press.

Rehmann, Jan. 2013. *Theories of Ideology*. Leiden: Brill.

Reisigl, Martin and Ruth Wodak. 2001. *Discourse and Discrimination: Rhetorics of Racism and Antisemitism*. London: Routledge.

Rosenfeld, Gavriel D. 2015. *Hi Hitler! How the Nazi Past is Being Normalized in Contemporary Culture*. Cambridge: Cambridge University Press.

Shifman, Limor. 2014. *Memes in Digital Culture*. Cambridge, MA: The MIT Press.

Stiglegger, Marcus. 2011. *Nazi-Chic und Nazi-Trash: Faschistische Ästhetik in der populären Kultur*. Berlin: Bertz + Fischer.

Theweleit, Klaus. 1989. *Male Fantasies. Volume 2: Male Bodies: Psychologyzing the White Terror*. Minneapolis, MN: University of Minnesota Press.

Theweleit, Klaus. 1987. *Male Fantasies. Volume 1: Women, Floods, Bodies, History*. Minneapolis, MN: University of Minnesota Press.

van Dijk, Teun. 2014. *Discourse and Knowledge. A Sociocognitive Approach*. Cambridge: Cambridge University Press.

van Dijk, Teun. 1998. *Ideology: A Multidisciplinary Approach*. London: Sage.

van Gelder, Robert. 1940. "Chaplin Draws a Keen Weapon." *New York Times*, September 8, 1940.

Weaver, Simon. 2011. "Jokes, Rhetoric and Embodied Racism: A Rhetorical Discourse Analysis of the Logics of Racist Jokes on the Internet." *Ethnicities* 11 (4): 413–35.

Weber, Max. 1978. *Economy and Society*. Berkeley, CA: University of California Press.

Wodak, Ruth. 2015. *The Politics of Fear: What Right-Wing Populist Discourses Mean*. London: Sage.

References

Wodak, Ruth and Michael Meyer, eds. 2009. *Methods of Critical Discourse Analysis*. London: Sage. 2nd edition.

Woodley, Daniel. 2010. *Fascism and Political Theory: Critical Perspectives on Fascist Ideology*. Abingdon: Routledge.

Zimmer, Michael and Nicholas John Proferes. 2014. "A Topology of Twitter Research: Disciplines, Methods, and Ethics." *Aslib Journal of Information Management* 66 (3): 250–61.

Chapter Eight

Red Scare 2.0: User-Generated Ideology in the Age of Jeremy Corbyn and Social Media

8.1 Introduction

8.2 Theoretical Foundations: Ideology Critique or Ideology Theory?

8.3 Methodology

8.4 Context: Anti-Socialist Ideology

8.5 Analysis

8.6 Conclusion

References

8.1 Introduction

This chapter asks: how was Jeremy Corbyn during the Labour Leadership Election framed in discourses on Twitter in an ideological manner? How have such ideological discourses been challenged? It uses ideology critique for the investigation of 32,298 tweets mentioning Jeremy Corbyn that were collected in the time period from 22 August until 13 September 2015.

Jeremy Corbyn, Andy Burnham, Yvette Cooper, and Liz Kendall were the four candidates for the leadership of the Labour Party after Ed Miliband had stepped down in light of Labour's fruitless attempt to beat the Conservatives in the British 2015 general election. The Labour Party in 2014 changed its electoral process from a system, in which Labour parliamentarians, members, and trade unions/affiliated organisations had equal weight to one, in which members and affiliated supporters elect the Labour Party's leader. Candidates need to be nominated by 15% of Labour's MPs, which meant 35 parliamentarians in 2015. Jeremy Corbyn made it with 36 nominations only closely to the list of candidates, whereas Burnham achieved 68 nominations, Cooper 59, and Kendall 41. Most of the hustings and rallies with Corbyn were overcrowded, opinion polls predicted his victory, and a movement that especially attracted young people rallied behind him. With more than 550,000 members and supporters, the number of people supporting Labour almost tripled since 2014.

The chapter first engages with the concept of ideology that forms the theoretical foundation of the analysis (Section 8.2). It then describes the methodology of Twitter

DOI: 10.4324/9781003256090-8

ideology critique adopted in this chapter (Section 8.3), sets out some aspects of the history of anti-socialist ideology (Section 8.4), provides an analysis of anti-socialist Twitter ideology in the context of the Jeremy Corbyn leadership campaign (Section 8.5), and finally draws some conclusions (Section 8.6).

8.2 Theoretical Foundations: Ideology Critique or Ideology Theory?

There are different traditions in ideology critique and theory (Eagleton 1991, Rehmann 2013, Žižek 1994). There is no general agreement among these approaches on how to define ideology. A general distinction is between the line of thought that goes back to Gramsci and the one that goes back to Lukács. It allows us to discern between ideology theory and ideology critique (Fuchs 2015, chapter 3).

Terry Eagleton (1991, chapter 1) maps distinction between general ideology theory and ideology critique clearly by distinguishing six understandings of ideology that range from general meanings on the one end to specific ones on the other: (1) ideology as the "production of ideas, beliefs and values in social life" (28) (=ideology as culture) (28), (2) ideas and beliefs of "a specific, socially significant group or class" (29) (=ideology as worldview), (3) "the *promotion* and *legitimation* of the interests" of a group "in the face of opposing interests" (29), (4) "the promotion and legitimation of sectoral interests" in the "activities of a dominant social power" (29) (=ideology as dominant worldviews), (5) "ideas and beliefs which help to legitimate the interests of a ruling group or class specifically by distortion and dissimulation" (30), (6) "false or deceptive beliefs [...] arising not from the interests of a dominant class but from the material structure of society as a whole" (30).

Marx, Lukács, and the Frankfurt School have inspired my understanding of ideology (Fuchs 2015, Fuchs 2016a,b). It is therefore close to the fifth and sixth meanings in Eagleton's classification. By ideology I understand thoughts, practices, ideas, words, concepts, phrases, sentences, texts, belief systems, meanings, representations, artefacts, institutions, systems, or combinations thereof that represent and justify one group's or individual's power, domination, or exploitation of other groups or individuals by misrepresenting, one-dimensionally presenting, or distorting reality in symbolic representations (Fuchs 2015). What is often overlooked is that ideology is not an abstract structure, but that there is ideological labour that produces and reproduces ideologies (Fuchs 2015, chapter 3). Marx speaks of such ideology-producing labour as "the thinkers of the [ruling] class", its "active, conceptive ideologists", who based on a division of labour within the ruling class "make the formation of the illusions of the class abut itself their chief source of livelihood" (Marx and Engels 1845, 68).

My definition presupposes moral realism and socialist praxis: it is assumed that humans have the capacity to understand how the world really looks like, what the complex causes of societal problems are, and to deconstruct misrepresentations of these causes. And it is based on the grounded judgement that societies structured by domination and exploitation are politically unacceptable, do not accord to general human interests, should be abolished and replaced by a society that guarantees wealth for all and that benefits all. Such a society is commonly called socialism. Eagleton's fifth and sixth understanding are based on a distinction between socialism and class societies and the judgement that ideologies want to justify class and dominative societies.

8.3 Methodology

This chapter uses ideology critique for studying Twitter. As argued in the previous section, we can generally understand ideology as semiotic structures that justify domination. It often reifies domination by describing it as unchangeable, natural, or best possible state of affairs. It either does not discuss alternatives or declares them to be impossible, utopian, undesirable, or having negative impacts. The method used here is certainly related to critical discourse analysis (CDA) that studies how discourses establish, reproduce, and change asymmetric power relations (compare the methods discussed in Wodak and Meyer 2009), but it does not consider itself as a strict application of any form of CDA, but rather as a Marxist ideology critique. Social media such as Twitter are still relatively new, which is one of the reasons why also research about ideologies on social media has remained thus far limited (see: Khosravinik 2013). The mainstream in social media research is quantitative big data analysis (for a discussion of this dominant paradigm, see Fuchs 2017, chapter 2), an approach that is very different from ideology critique that wants to understand the structure, context, and implications of ideologies. The dominant paradigm of social media positivism has also posed limits for critical research.

The approach of ideology critique I advocate for critical social media analysis follows the following steps:

1) Identify ideological macro-topics;

2) Search for tweets that represent these macro-topics;

3) Analyse for each macro-topic the structure of ideology;

4) In this search, watch out for additional macro-topics and associated tweets;

5) Analyse how online ideology is related to the broader societal context, i.e. the relations of the online-semiotic elements to the broader societal context;

6) Identify ways how ideology is or can be challenged on Twitter.

The methodology follows a general two-step approach for semiotic, discursive, and ideological critique, in which first a general thematic macro-analysis is conducted that is followed by an in-depth analysis (see Krzyżanowski 2010, 81–89). As *first, preliminary and preparatory step*, I tried to identify ideological macro-discourse topics by analysing the news coverage on Corbyn in the major British national newspapers during the final phase of the Labour leadership election (August 23–September 13, 2015). The analysis focused on digital and online versions of the following newspapers: *Daily Express, Daily Mail, Daily Mirror, Daily Star, Daily Telegraph, Financial Times, The Guardian, The Independent, The Sun, The Times*. These are the major national British newspapers. All articles that mentioned Corbyn in their headline were read daily at around 09:00 a.m. BST. 1,681 articles mentioning Corbyn were identified. The task was to identify if discourses were present that tried to negatively frame Jeremy Corbyn. If a discourse-topic was present multiple times (in at least three articles), then it was formulated in the form of an ideal-type statement. Overall, the analysis identified four recurrent ideological discourse topics.

Table 8.1 identifies one economic, two political, and one cultural context of the ideological discourse about Jeremy Corbyn. Also asserted negative consequences of a Corbyn leadership were noted if they were recurring at least three times (see Table 8.2). Very frequently it was noted that Corbyn belongs to the "hard-left", which was considered as the cause of his left-wing policy suggestions (see also Table 8.2).

The connection between Tables 8.1 and 8.2 is that Table 8.1 specifies how Jeremy Corbyn is characterised in anti-socialist ideology, whereas Table 8.2 outlines the consequences and implications that representatives of anti-socialist ideology suggest to draw based on certain conditions. In the discourse-historical approach of Critical Discourse Analysis (CDA, see Reisigl and Wodak 2001, 2009), the characterisation of conditions is called in linguistic terms nomination and predication: specific identities are constructed by (positive or negative) self-presentation and (positive or negative) other-presentation.

TABLE 8.1 Ideological topics in the public discourse about Jeremy Corbyn

Dimension	Ideological discourse topics
Economic ideology: command economy	"Jeremy Corbyn wants to create a centralised, state-bureaucratic economy. Such policies are backwards-oriented and do not work".
Political ideology of security: enemy-loving politics	"Jeremy Corbyn is a sympathiser of extremists, dictators, terrorists, racists, Islamists, anti-Semites, and communists".
Political ideology: politics of disloyalty	"Jeremy Corbyn is disloyal and a rebel; he has defied the whip more than 500 times".
Cultural ideology: loony-left hippie-culture, lifestyle and personality	"Jeremy Corbyn is a vegetarian hippie, eco-zealot and clown, who dresses badly, is the worst dressed politician, has no style, hates cars, celebrates immigration and multiculturalism. A guy with such a lifestyle is not a proper politician. He enjoyed a privileged life as child and now with his politics of envy wants to deny others wealth and a good life".

TABLE 8.2 Asserted causes and consequences of Jeremy Corbyn's politics in ideological Corbyn discourses

Conditions and causes	Implications
"Jeremy Corbyn is a radical, Marxist, socialist, communist, militant, revolutionary left-wing extremist whose politics are outdated and old-fashioned"	"One should hinder Corbyn from becoming Prime Minster"; "One must stop Jeremy Corbyn's threat to Britain's national security"; "Jeremy Corbyn will destroy the Labour Party"; "Jeremy Corbyn will be considered unelectable, which will result in an everlasting Tory rule"; "Jeremy Corbyn will destroy the British economy and society"; "Corbyn's victory will result in a state of violence and chaos"

Teun van Dijk (2011) has proposed a scheme called the *Ideological Square* for the analysis of ideologies. He argues that there are four common ideological argumentation strategies:

- To emphasize positive things about Us (=the in-group);
- To emphasize negative things about Them (=the out-group);
- To de-emphasize negative things about Us;
- To de-emphasize positive things about Them.

"The complex meta-strategy of the ideological square tells us that group members will tend to speak or write positively about their own group, and negatively about those out-groups they define as opponents, competitors or enemies" (van Dijk 2011, 397). Reisigl and Wodak (2009) call the discourse strategy of setting up a Us/Them difference "predication". Predication is the "discursive qualification of social actors,

Methodology

objects, phenomena, events/processes and actions" as "more or less positively or negatively" (Reisigl and Wodak 2009, 94).

Arguments can have certain fallacies, whereas the implications are termed topoi. Topoi are "conclusion rules" that "connect the argument of arguments with the conclusion, the claim. As such, they justify the transition from the argument or arguments to the conclusion" (Reisigl and Wodak 2001, 75). In our study, this distinction means that we can distinguish between the ideological characterisations and the implications and conclusions that are drawn and suggested for specific practices. Anti-socialist ideology characterises Corbyn in specific ideological ways and then draws conclusions about what should practically be done against him.

The discourse topics, causes, and implications were used as foundation for the Twitter discourse analysis. I did not assume that these are the only possible discourses that can be found in the tweets, but was rather actively searching for additional ideological discourse topics.

The British press is traditionally fairly right-wing. A poll conducted by YouGov in the UK, Denmark, Finland, Germany, France, Norway, and Sweden confirms that the British to a larger degree perceive their national newspapers as right-wing than citizens in the other six countries (YouGov 2016). The British press described Jeremy Corbyn for example as "the bearded leftie" (*Sun*, 6 September 2015), someone who "can hardly see a terrorist without wanting to kiss their butt" (*Sun*, 6 September 2015), "Bennism with a beard" (*Times*, 6 September 2015), "left-wing nutter" (*Sun*, 7 September 2015), "a danger to national security" (*Times*, 7 September 2015), "a gormless Marxist who delights in describing as 'friends' every possible enemy of this country" (*Sun*, 9 September 2015), "a vegetarian" who "looks halfdead" (*Sun*, 11 September 2015), "Casual Corbyn" (*Daily Mail*, 11 September 2015), looking like "a grandfather popping down to the local garden centre for some extra compost" (*Daily Mail*, 11 September 2015), "Jez What Do You Look Like Corbyn" (*Sun*, 12 September 2015), "Jezbollah" (*Daily Mirror*, 12 September 2015), "Jeremy Cor bin-Laden" (*Times*, 13 September 2015), "the left's Duracell Bunny" (*Times*, 13 September 2015), "several times winner of the Worst Dressed MP award" (*Independent*, 4 September 2015), "malevolent clown" (*Daily Telegraph*, 1 September 2015), "Marxist ideologue" (*Daily Telegraph*, 1 September 2015), "Deserter rat Jez" (*The Sun*, 2 September 2015), "Labour loon" (*Sun*, 2 September 2015), "Loony byn" (*Sun*, 31 August 2015), someone having "Barmy surplus" (*Sun*, 3 September 2015), "Comrade Corbyn" (*Daily Mail*, 5 September 2015), "Hard Left class warrior" (*Daily Mail*, 5 September 2015), "Sexpot Trot" (*Daily Mail*, 5 September 2015), or "vegetarian, eco-zealot" (*Daily Mail*, 5 September 2015).

The *second, main and most time-consuming step* in the research process was the collection and analysis of tweets. I collected data from Twitter with Discovertext during the final phase of the Labour leadership contest. The data gathering was active for 23 days, from 22 August (23:25 BST) until 13 September 2015 (12:35 BST). Corbyn was announced as the winner on 12 September (11:45 BST). Based on the historical examples presented in Section 8.2 and newspaper articles, I identified smear keywords used in anti-socialist discourses. In the data search, I combined the keyword "Corbyn" with such smear words. I collected all tweets during the search period that satisfied the following logical condition: Corbyn AND (anti-Semite OR anti-Semitic OR chaos OR clown OR commy OR communism OR communist OR loony OR Marx OR Marxist OR pinko OR red OR reds OR socialism OR socialist OR Stalin OR Stalinist OR terrorist OR violent OR violence). These keywords were identified based on smear words used against Tony Benn and Ken Livingstone in the 1980s (Curran, Gaber and Petley 2005; Hollingsworth 1986). The data collection resulted in a total of 32,298 tweets that were exported into a xls-file.

When doing Internet research, it is important to reflect on research ethics. Internet research faces the problem that from an ethical perspective it should not harm users by its analyses. The danger of overdoing Internet research ethics is that it results in a de-facto censorship and ethical prohibition of the critical investigation of ideologies. The British Psychological Society argues that online observation should only take place when and where users "reasonably expect to be observed by strangers" (BPS, 2009, 13). It is reasonable to assume that users, who tweet about a political issue such as Jeremy Corbyn during a time of general public attention to Corbyn direct their messages at the public for discussion and therefore also reasonably expect to be observed by strangers such as journalists and researchers. Not revealing the profile names of everyday users, but instead using pseudonyms, seems in this context to therefore be a sufficient ethical measure that I take in this chapter.

Table 8.3 shows the most active and most mentioned users in our dataset. I have anonymised users who use a combination of first and family names as Twitter user names, whereas I indicate the names of general accounts that do not mention specific individuals operating them. 17,954 of the 32,298 tweets (55.6%) were re-tweets, which indicates that because of its 140-character limit, Twitter is not a medium for discussion, but for sharing information.

The most active users were robots (redscarebot, mywoodthorpe), news accounts (ncolewilliams, houseoftwits, houseoftwitscon, anotao_news, anotao_nouvelle), right wing lobby-accounts (gcinews, friedrichhayek, sunnyherring1), and a private Corbyn

Methodology

TABLE 8.3 The most active and the most mentioned users in the Corbyn-dataset

Users with largest no. of tweets	Frequency	Most mentioned users	Frequency
redscarebot	322	anonymous2 (UKIP supporter)	723
mywoodthorpe	241	ggreenwald	689
ncolewilliams	237	independent	552
houseoftwits	51	davidschneider	324
houseoftwitscon	43	rupertmurdoch	323
gcinews	38	jeremycorbyn	311
anotao_news, anotao_nouvelle	37	telegraph	284
sunnyherring1	34	RT_com	221
anonymous1 (Corbyn-supporter)	32	edsbrown	215
friedrichhayek	32	uklabour	212

supporter (anonymous1). The most mentioned users (mainly in re-tweets) were a UKIP supporter, accounts of well-known journalists (Glenn Greenwald, the leading journalist in the Snowden-revelations, BBC Newsnight's Ed Brown), news media accounts (The Independent, The Daily Telegraph, Russia Today, News Corporation's CEO Rupert Murdoch), and the profiles of comedian David Schneider and politicians (Jeremy Corbyn, Labour Party).

Social media and traditional mass media are not two separate media domains, but are dialectically articulated with each other: journalists use social media for reaching a broader audience and social media users refer to traditional news media articles. There is intertextuality: social media texts and traditional news media texts are interconnected. New media dialectically sublate old media: the continued importance of old media shapes newer media. At the same time, new media shape old media. The ten most mentioned accounts had on average 600,000 followers[1]. The average Twitter user had in 2015 around 200 followers[2]. The reputation of the mass media, politicians and celebrities allows them to accumulate followers on Twitter and gain high online visibility. Visibility on social media is asymmetrically distributed. In political Twitter discourse, politicians, traditional news media and celebrities have significant influence.

8.4 Context: Anti-Socialist Ideology

Anti-socalism is not new, but has accompanied the history of socialist thought and politics. They already existed at the time of Karl Marx: on 2 January 1873, *The*

Times published an article in which it portrayed Marx as a totalitarian "autocrat of the [communist] movement". After Marx's death, British right-wing media described *Das Kapital* as being "repellent in its cold formalism" and called Marx the "cold and methodical organiser of the International Association of Workers" (*The Morning Post*, 19 March 1883). So anti-socialist ideology here evoked the images of socialism as cold and repellent. *The Times* (18 January 1919) wrote three days after Rosa Luxemburg and Karl Liebknecht had been assassinated about Luxemburg: "Had power in Germany fallen into her hands, she would have surpassed the reign of terror of the Russian Bolshevists". This statement indirectly welcomes her murder.

The so-called Red Scare entailed the public stoking of fears about communism in the United States and attempts to curtail communist activities, especially of the Communist Party of the USA (CPUSA). There were two phases, one after the October Revolution and one (also known as the "McCarthy era") in the late 1940s and the 1950s. The Conservative Senator Joseph McCarthy, FBI Director J. Edgar Hoover and the House Un-American Activities Committee played important roles in the second phase. Suspected members of the CPUSA were prosecuted and jailed for planning to overthrow the US government (Fariello 1995). The trials were often based on mere suspicion (Schrecker 1998).

In the 1980s, right-wing British news media characterised the Labour Party-left and especially the Greater London Council, local London councils, Ken Livingstone and Tony Benn, as the "Loony Left". The term "Loony Left" "combines two concepts, insanity and left-wing politics, with a subtext that suggests irrational authoritarianism" (Curran, Gaber and Petley 2005, 229; see also Hollingsworth 1986). Also New Labour under Tony Blair took up the discourse of the "old" loony Labour for promoting itself as "new" alternative (Curran, Gaber and Petley 2005, chapter 7). The right-wing press again used the Loony Left-ideology for characterising Ken Livingstone's London mayoralty in the years 2000–2008. The logical implication of such smear campaigns against those who argue for fairness and equality is the demand for an unfair, unjust, classist, racist, patriarchal society that privileges the rich and powerful. In 2015, *The Sun* characterised Ed Miliband's father Ralph as Jewish, immigrant Marxist, who hated Britain, in order to try to discredit the son (Stoegner and Wodak 2016). Anti-socialism is an ideology because it tries to ridicule and misrepresent practices and ideas that aim to establish a society that benefits all in order to implement right-wing politics. Anti-socialist ideology has also played a role in the context of Jeremy Corbyn becoming the leader of the Labour Party.

Context: Anti-Socialist Ideology

8.5 Analysis

The analysis of the collected tweets showed that five discourse topics could be identified.

8.5.1 Anti-Corbyn Hatred: "Jeremy Corbyn is a Lunatic Socialist Pig"

A first category of tweets characterised Jeremy Corbyn negatively in more general terms without drawing conclusions for the economy, politics or culture from such characterisations. Such tweets are pure hatred without any explicitly communicated implications.

RedScareBot is a robot that automatically re-tweets postings that contain keywords such as socialism or communism and inserts short comments. Mywoodthorpe seems to be a robot that re-tweets some of RedScareBot's postings. RedScareBot says on its Twitter-profile that its name is Robot J. McCarthy. It describes itself the following way: "Joseph McCarthy claimed there were large numbers of Communists and Soviet spies and sympathizers inside the United States federal government and elsewhere". RedScareBot seems to understand re-tweeting and commenting on left-wing tweets as a form of 21st-century McCarthyism that uncovers online communism. The robot for example tweeted:

> "Muppet brainwashed RT @anonymous #Corbyn: radical socialist or closet conservative? http://t.co/0fB6Cgy5ANhttp://t.co/VIFTifMRcC" (No. 1860)

No. 1860 shows Twitter's intertextuality. It contains links to the Economist article "Jeremy Corbyn: Closet Conservative". Nomination, referencing and predication are discursive strategies for characterising persons or phenomena in specific ways (Reisigl and Wodak 2001, 44-56). The cited tweet is a politonym (Reisigl and Wodak 2001, 51): it polarises by characterising Corbyn simultaneously as socialist and conservative.

The discourse topos of disloyalty that had been identified in the news coverage could not be found in the Twitter dataset. Twitter users did not at all mention that Corbyn defied the whip more than 500 times. This fact does not seem to be relevant for their opinions of Jeremy Corbyn. **General opinions** presented without arguments formed an important discourse topic in the dataset. One general bias that was frequently encountered in this respect was that Corbyn is a "loony" left-winger:

"Corbyn is wholly unelectable (as head of Lab in a UK Gen Election). Always will be. Policies are loony." (No. 5)

"the radical extreme left wing lunacy of Jeremy left wing lunacy left wing loony lefty extreme radical Corbyn" (No. 438)

"Jeremy extreme left wing lunacy loony idealist Corbyn" (No. 439)
"Who is this marxist spouting idiot?" (No. 1046)

"a wet handwringing leftie terrorist supporting anti Semite for Prime Minister Corbyn will Drive Brit off a cliff" (No. 242)

"have you seen this loony Marxist nutter?" (No. 3373)

"Labor party should now be referred to as the New Monster Raving Loony Party as Corbyn is an absolute NUTTER." http://t.co/meNPXTmWns (No. 7319)

"He is the epitomy of a socialist nutjob." (No. 10493)

"Corbyn is a radical left wing idiot" (No. 17528)

"Corbyn is a left wing socialist scumbag" (No. 20456)

"My concern over #Corbyn is that militant wing of the loony left will start believing it has mandate for civil disobedience #JezWeDid" (No. 25729)

Anthroponyms give specific names to humans. Somatisation is a strategy that constructs anthroponyms that characterise humans in terms of their body. One subtype are somatonyms that make references "in terms of the state of health" (Reisigl and Wodak 2001, 49). The cited examples are somatonyms that characterise Corbyn as mentally ill. Such characterisations not just concern the mental state as part of the human body, but are also pathologonyms (Reisigl and Wodak 2001, 52) that try to pathologise Corbyn. All of these characterisations are also an argument ad hominem, i.e. "a verbal attack on the antagonist's personality and character (of her or his credibility, integrity, honest, expertise, competence and so on) instead of argumentatively trying to refute the antagonist's arguments" (Reisigl and Wodak 2001, 72).

Another ideological strategy found in the dataset was the construction of politonyms (=political characterisations; Reisigl and Wodak 2001, 50) that characterised Corbyn by alarmism ("dangerous"), swearing ("bloody", "satan", "screwed", "fraud", "bastard", "fuck"), or biologism ("toxic", "bloody", "pig"):

"Dangerous communist" (No. 1228)

"Bloody pinko" (No. 1287)

"Corbyn is no threat to Tories as unelectably toxic extremist socialist peacenik" (No. 1593)

"Corbyn is satan" (No. 4927)

"Roses are red Violets are blue Corbyn is red Labour are screwed" (No. 12328)

"socialist pig" (No. 12741)

"Jeremy Corbyn ... A communist fraud ...... hope he goes the way of Trotsky #Mexico1941 #NeverForget" (No. 15440)

"When will everyone realise that #Corbyn is a communist bastard? He's gonna fuck this country up if he gets in power #Labour" (No. 17405)

Many of these tweets follow the logic that Corbyn is dangerous, lunatic, a scumbag, an idiot, a bastard, a nutjob, a nutter, Satan, a toxic extremist, a radical, a terrorist, or an anti-Semite because he is left-wing. Some tweets simply presented these descriptions of Corbyn as a matter of fact: "Corbyn is satan", "Corbyn is an absolute NUTTER", "the New Monster Raving Loony Party". Others only foreground that he is left-wing and intensify this assessment with negatively connoted adjectives or nouns such as bloody or pig: "Bloody pinko", "socialist pig". Other tweets linguistically combined the characterisation of Corbyn as left-wing with the predication that he is crazy or dangerous: "a wet handwringing leftie terrorist supporting anti Semite", "the radical extreme left wing lunacy of Jeremy left wing lunacy left wing loony lefty extreme radical Corbyn", "Jeremy extreme left wing lunacy loony idealist Corbyn", "marxist spouting idiot", "Dangerous communist, toxic extremist socialist peacenik", "loony Marxist nutter", "a socialist nutjob", "A communist fraud", "a communist bastard", "a radical left wing idiot", "left wing socialist scumbag".

Such tweets imply that because Corbyn is left-wing, it follows that he is a terrorist, anti-Semite, radical, extreme, a loony, an idiot, dangerous, toxic, a fraud, a bastard, and a scumbag. The linguistic strategy of such posts is to combine a series of negative terms with the fact that someone is politically left-wing.

In the examples set out here, right-wing Twitter users try to strengthen their own identity and its representation by emphasising negative aspects about their enemy, namely the Left symbolised by Jeremy Corbyn. They discursively qualify Corbyn in particular and socialism in general in negative terms by using negative predicates in order to justify right-wing ideology. It is likely that those making such attacks on Corbyn want to imply that being conservative, right-wing, and right-wing extremist is natural, appropriate and the right-thing-to-do, whereas questioning and opposing these ideologies is seen as crazy. Such discursive strategies are ideological because they aim to distort the public's perception of socialism by not characterising its actual contents, but ridiculing, negatively framing and swearing at it.

Some postings went one step further and made statements about the assumed implications of Corbyn's leadership. The argument was that if Britain were ruled by Corbyn, this would result in violence and a breakdown: "civil disobedience", "He's gonna fuck this country up", "Corbyn will Drive Brit off a cliff". A statement comparable to the latter formulation could around the same time also be found in a = article written by Tony Blair (2015) in the *Guardian* about Corbyn: "The party is walking eyes shut, arms outstretched, over the cliff's edge to the jagged rocks below".

Other tweets said that with a left-wing leader, the Labour Party would be unelectable and destroy itself: "red Labour are screwed", "unelectable as PM; just look @ Foot, Kinnock, Ed Miliband". Such statements imply that Britons are naturally conservative, despise the idea of a socialist democracy, and love to live in a society with high levels of inequality. They assume that socialism is naturally bad and capitalism naturally good. Single tweets even expressed the wish that Corbyn is killed because he is left-wing: "hope he goes the way of Trotsky #Mexico1941". The Stalinist agent Ramón Mercader assassinated Leon Trotsky on August 20, 1940. Although the tweet indicates the wrong year, it is clear that it refers to Trotsky's assassination and thereby indirectly calls for killing Jeremy Corbyn. Another user linked to the fiction story "Prime Minster Corbyn ... and the 1,000 days that destroyed Britain" (*Daily Mail*, 22 August 2015) and commented: "Loony leftie, he should be arrested" (No. 638). Calls for direct violence were not limited to Twitter. The *Independent* reported that a senior British Army general said that the Army "would not allow a prime minister to jeopardise the security of this country and I think people would use whatever means possible, fair or foul to prevent that" (Mortimer 2015).

Some of these tweets were intertextual in nature. One included for example a link to the Daily Express-article "Jeremy Corbyn 'to BLOCK Britain from attacking Islamic State if he becomes Labour leader'" (5 September 2015). 371 of the dataset's tweets contained links to the press agency Reuters' online article "Karl Marx admirer Corbyn rides socialist wave to lead Britain's Labour Party" (12 September 2015). Most of them only contained a link and the article-title. The headline itself communicates nothing about Corbyn's policies, but foregrounds that he is a Marxist. Similarly the article does not discuss any of Corbyn's policy suggestions in detail, but stresses he is a vegetarian, an admirer of Marx, Chavez, that he is "hard-left", etc. The popularity of this headline on Twitter shows that general, sensationalist statements well suit right-wing online discourse that is expressed in 140 characters.

The sensationalist right-wing anti-Corbyn Twitter-discourse was not simply accepted, but contested. There were various strategies that Corbyn supporters have used for challenged anti-socialist ideology online. One is that they associated Corbyn with positive general characteristics: "What's weird is I don't find #Corbyn at all 'radical' or 'hard left'. He seems to be about common sense and decency and so very normal/nice" (No. 422), "he is sensible, clear, knowledgeable & decent" (No. 606), "In my view he just preaches common sense" (No. 22591), "Just normal" (No. 28373). The negative scapegoating of Corbyn is opposed by associating positive terms with him and presenting him as someone who understands everyday people's concerns and is one of them. A second strategy was to use the strategy of discursive dialectical reversal (see Žižek 2014 and Fuchs 2014 for a discussion of this concept): "Surely extremism is: -Welfare cuts -Bedroom tax -Iraq war -Trident -Zero hours contracts" (No. 1175), "Iain Duncan Smith schemes to force one million more on sickness benefits into work. But Jeremy Corbyn is the extremist" (No. 1620), "Jeremy Corbyn: Saving us from the loony right!" (No. 3772), "If Corbyn is a communist then you and Cameron are Nazis" (No. 216).

The argument made in this strategy is that not Corbyn, but the Tories are extremist, radical, violent, hard-right, and dangerous. Along with this argumentative strategy came the argument that the dominant political discourse in Britain had shifted so far to the right that humanism could be branded as left-wing extremism. If right-wing extremism is hegemonic, then everything questioning it can more easily be presented as extremist: "Crazy that somebody as moderate as Corbyn is seen as some kind of radical revolutionary. Is that how far politics has shifted in the UK?" (No. 756), "The Conservative Party have moved so far to the right that a moderately left wing Labour leader is considered a Trot or Marxist" (No. 14239), "anyone who shows humanity in this country is instantly a communist" (No. 14971).

A third strategy was to use satire and humour to ridicule anti-socialist ideology. It is based on the insight that ideologies are often irrational and emotional. They are difficult to challenge by rational arguments. The hashtag #suggestacorbynsmear that emerged on Twitter on August 31, 2015, and was used within 24 hours more than 11,000 times

What's your Jeremy Corbyn smear campaign headline?

Jeremy Corbyn + the day you were born + the month you were born.

1ˢᵗ	likes the same flavour crisps as	17ᵗʰ	gave 20p to
2ⁿᵈ	smiled at	18ᵗʰ	received a leaflet from
3ʳᵈ	stood in front of	19ᵗʰ	picked up litter dropped by
4ᵗʰ	shared a bus with	20ᵗʰ	shared the same love for corduroy trousers as
5ᵗʰ	had a friend who knew a guy who knew	21ˢᵗ	used the same reusable shopping bag as
6ᵗʰ	has a cat who looks like	22ⁿᵈ	returned a wallet dropped by
7ᵗʰ	ate a muffin with a face like	23ʳᵈ	was born in the same decade as
8ᵗʰ	joked at a party about	24ᵗʰ	stopped a childhood friend from bullying
9ᵗʰ	uses the same mobile phone network as	25ᵗʰ	woke his wife talking in his sleep about
10ᵗʰ	likes the same music as	26ᵗʰ	"ironically" retweeted
11ᵗʰ	used deodorant endorsed by	27ᵗʰ	actually is the reincarnation of
12ᵗʰ	wrote an essay quoting	28ᵗʰ	momentarily thought about
13ᵗʰ	fell over a wall belonging to	29ᵗʰ	is the great grand-cousin (twice removed) of
14ᵗʰ	drew a picture as an infant that resembled	30ᵗʰ	has central heating, just like
15ᵗʰ	has the same blood type as	31ˢᵗ	had a facebook friend request from
16ᵗʰ	has a mole in exactly the same place as		

January	Stalin's dog	July	a holocaust denier
February	Robert Mugabe's ex wife	August	David Icke
March	Trotsky	September	a 9/11 conspirator
April	a statue of Lenin	October	the ghost of Marx
May	Rolf Harris	November	North Korea
June	Tony Benn	December	Hiter's cat

FIGURE 8.1 Instructions for #suggestacorbynsmear circulated on Twitter.

(Wilkinson 2015) is an example. It was a satirical reaction to the right-wing smear attacks against Corbyn that could be found online and in right-wing papers such as *The Sun*, *The Daily Mail*, the *Daily Telegraph*, the *Daily Express*, and the *Times*. Instructions how to generate ridiculously sounding smears circulated on Twitter (see Figure 8.1). #suggestacorbynsmear used overemphasis as political strategy: it radicalised the absurdity and irrationality of the Corbyn-smears so that this over-affirmation turned into a critique of right-wing scapegoating. Examples in the analysed dataset included: "Jeremy Corbyn shares the letter 'n' with Stalin and Satan, and the letters 'e' and 'r' with Hitler! #suggestacorbynsmear" (No. 5229), "Jeremy Corbyn was born in 1949. Stalin was alive in 1949. Coincidence? I think not. #suggestacorbynsmear" (No. 5251).

A fourth strategy was that Corbyn supporters denounced specific discourses as biased and sensationalist. A large number of viewers complained about the BBC Panorama documentary "Jeremy Corbyn: Labour's Earthquake" (7 September 2015, 20:30), arguing that it violated the BBC's legal commitment to impartiality. Labour MP Diane Abbott argued that the BBC conducted a "hatchet job" (Dathan 2015). Tweets in our dataset criticised BBC Panorma for example in the following way (see also Figure 8.2

#Panorama cheap smear campaign against Corbyn tonight trying to link him to terrorist group short memory of this

RETWEETS FAVOURITES
116   52

FIGURE 8.2 A Twitter-critique of the BBC Panorma documentary on Corbyn that uses visual dialectical reversals by showing images of Gordon Brown and Tony Blair with Gaddafi, Blair with Assad, and Thatcher with Pinochet.

for a critique that uses the strategy of argumentative dialectical reversal): "Why are BBC 1 trying to portray Jeremy Corbyn as some kind of left wing socialist Nazi without mentioning another of his actual policies?" (No. 8405), "hardly objective" (No. 8409), "BBC broadcasts a documentary about the Queen straight after a Corbyn documentary, which comments on how scary socialism is; coincidence?" (No. 8418), "WHY DOES THE BBC BETRAY J CORBYN AS A COMMUNIST DICTATOR USING WORDS LIKE: COMRADE, LEFTIE AND CONSTANTLY SUGGESTING HE'S UNELECTABLE" (No. 31151).

8.5.2 Security Policy: "Corbyn is a Friend of Britain's Enemies"

The **security policy discourse topic that Corbyn loves Britain's enemies** played a major role in the analysed dataset. Some tweets swear at Corbyn by claiming he loves and supports terrorists:

"#Corbyn your a Terrorist loving Cunt." (No. 1591)

"Fuck off Corbyn you terrorist loving twat!" (No. 14612)

Such characterisations are at the same time nominations and predications (Reisigl and Wodak 2009, 94): they construct social actors discursively by qualifying them in specific manners. In the security policy discourse, these characterisations are relational: Corbyn is characterised negatively by the claim that he loves terrorists.

Others made a direct link between Marxism and sympathies for Britain's enemies by combining anti-socialist and nationalist ideology:

"Corbyn is Marxist, he hates Britain" (No. 1145)

"Corbyn this filthy Marxist enemy of Britain" (No. 9088)

In these examples, the politonym "Marxist" is used for making a specific logical conclusion in the form of the topos of danger and threat (Reisigl and Wodak 2001, 77): being a Marxist is presented as a danger to Britain's national security.

One tweet by the most re-tweeted user in the dataset added to this combination the claim that Corbyn is pro-immigration. The implication is that Corbyn will open British borders, invite terrorists to the country, and thereby destroy Britain.

"RT if you will never vote for the Labour Party led by anti British, pro immigration pro terrorist traitor Corbyn" (No. 20162).

This tweet included an image of Corbyn saying "Share if you will never vote for the Labour Party led by this anti-British traitor", which increased its effectiveness. It had 482 re-tweets in the dataset. In this tweet, there is a combination of a negative political collectivisation ("anti-British"), a politicised xenonym (political friend of immigrants), and a relational securitisation (friend of terrorists) that is used as logical foundation for the conclusion that one cannot vote for Corbyn. It is argued Corbyn is unelectable by evoking the logic of numbers ("nobody will vote for such a guy").

Some tweets discussed implications of Corbyn's alleged terrorist links, suggesting that he is a national security risk, should be locked up or put on a list of terrorists:

"Jeremy Corbyn's #IRA links make him 'national security risk' [+link to Daily Mail article Corbyn's #IRA links make him 'national security risk', 23 August 2015]" (No. 163)

"@jeremycorbyn is a security risk to this country." (No. 14758)

"It is clear that commie Corbyn is a terrorist and should be locked up as soon as possible! [+link to Daily Telegraph article "Jeremy Corbyn calls death of Osama bin Laden a "tragedy", 31 August 2015]" (No. 4983)

"Hope Cameron puts #Corbyn on terrorist watch list" (No. 26059).

These tweets use the relational predication of Corbyn as a friend of Britain's enemies and of terrorists as foundation of the argument. These are politonyms that combine a nationym ("We Britis") with a militaronym ("These enemy terrorists want to attack us Brits") (see Reisigl and Wodak 2001, 50–51). This construction is used for a arguing with the help of the topoi of danger and threat that Corbyn should be jailed, repressed, or (in some versions) killed.

Links in tweets that used the enemy of Britain discourse particularly were to online articles in the Daily Mail and the Daily Telegraph, two right-wing tabloids that took a leading role in the anti-Corbyn campaign.

Corbyn has frequently stressed that one does not create peace by bombs, but by political solutions that bring together those who oppose each other in peace talks. "To bring about a peace process, you have to talk to people with whom you may profoundly disagree. There's not gonna be any peace process unless there are talks" (Channel 4 News, 13 July 2015). So anti-socialist Twitter ideology directed against Corbyn neglects presenting what he actually says about security and how to achieve it, but instead characterises socialists who argue for peace, peace talks and against an escalating spiral of violence as being themselves violent. Such a negative predication is used for trying to distort the public perception of Corbyn's position on security.

Corbyn supporters questioned this ideological discourse. They for example pointed out that Jews and Israelis defended Corbyn against the claim he was anti-Semitic and his positive relations to the Jewish community:

"An 89 year old Jewish friend finds anti-Semitic attacks on #Corbyn ludicrous." (No. 208)

Also the strategy of the argumentative dialectical reversal was used: some users made the point that not Corbyn, but his opponents have extremist links:

"Tony Blair calls Corbyn a terrorist sympathizer whilst Blair helped create ISIS and is currently supporting terrorist dictators worldwide." (No. 8299)

"Is Corbyn part of an EU grouping that includes documented anti-semitic parties? Cameron is" (No. 13)

"In an era when Thatcher was calling Mandela a terrorist, Jeremy Corbyn was protesting against apartheid." (No. 873)

"Young Cameron was on all expenses trips 2 S Africa & Thatcher was calling Nelson Mandela a terrorist." (No. 699).

"Corbyn supported Mandela when Thatcher branded him a terrorist. Opposed Saddam when your lot were selling him weapons." (No. 12059).

As part of the strategy of discursive dialectical reversal, some users pointed out that it is a perverse right-wing logic that those arguing for peace not bombs are called terrorist allies:

"Corbyn suggests peaceful & non-violent solutions and he's a terrorist ally? Is war the only way we communicate?" (No. 11183)

"World according to UK right wing media fascists is black/white upside/down. War Criminal #Blair is moderate. #Corbyn is dangerous extremist." (No. 18502)

In right-wing ideology, pacifists and humanists are branded as terrorists and violent and warlords seen as freedom fighters. War is peace. Peace is war: a truly Orwellian logic. When Corbyn was labelled terrorist-sympathiser by the right-wing media after he called Osama Bin Laden's assassination a tragedy, Glenn Greenwald in a post that was re-tweeted 588 times alluded to the fact that it is a strange reversal the main Nazis criminals were put on trial in Nüremberg, while today those calling for trials are called extremists: "Capturing & giving trials before killing people is now considered extremist & embarrassing? Like at Nuremberg?" (No. 4375).

It can also happen that limited skills and capacities result in self-defeating tweets. Former Tory MP and columnist Louise Mensch, who with around 100,000 Twitter followers reaches high attention on this medium, created the hashtag #ToriesForCorbyn in order to encourage Tories to sign up as affiliated supporters to the Labour Party and vote for Corbyn because she believed that thereby the Tory's rule could be strengthened. She tweeted on 21 August that Corbyn's supporters tend to be anti-Semitic:

LOUISE MENSCH: "Twitter's autocomplete on Liz Kendall MP. This is the sewer that is Jeremy Corbyn's support. pic.twitter.com/H7gAQWkfGa"[Image that shows Louise Mensch's Twitter account where she tips @lizforleader

> into te search box and a drop-down menu shows the following items: "@lizforleader zionist", "@lizforleader nazi", "@lizforleader Jewish", "@lizforleader Jews"
>
> (Twitter: @louisemensch, 21 August 2015)

She did not realise that Twitter's autocomplete search suggestions are based on previous searches. Corbyn supporters commented: "HUMILIATED: Louise Mensch Tweets Her Own Twitter Searches, Claims Corbyn Supporters Are Anti-Semitic As a Result http://t.co/XmXfp67dml (No. 440; 46 re-tweets)".

8.5.3 Economy: "Corbyn Wants a Stalin-Like Command Economy and Hates the Free Market"

Also the **command economy-discourse** topic could be found on Twitter. Some examples:

> "Waiting for #Corbyn to come out with a Stalin-esque 5 year plan for the economy, collective farms? #LabourDebate" (No. 6807)

> "Jeremy Corbyn economics died in USSR. His views on terrorism and dictator-ships ended when the Gulags closed. He is Stalin resurrected." (No. 11261)

> "#corbyn communist policies if brought in would lead to mass starvation like in China." (No. 12287)

> "Hold on to your wallets people … Corbyn is out and about with his socialist loony toons! #bbc #Panorama" (No. 8397)

> "You're not having any of my money Corbyn, you bloody communist!" (No. 23575)

These tweets use politonyms (communist, friend of terrorists), pathologynyms, and somatonyms (loony) as foundation for arguing with the topos of history and the topos of reality (Reisigl and Wodak 2001, 79–80) that if elected, Corbyn would shipwreck the British economy. The argument goes that the history of the Soviet Union and of social-democratic welfare states has shown that communists and socialists mismanage economies. Corbyn would be "one of them" and would therefore have no economic competence.

This economic discourse is based on two related claims: "Corbyn will implement a command economy like Stalin in Russia and Mao in China". "The result will be starvation, poverty for all, and Gulags". A third claim is that Corbyn will take away individuals' hard-earned income and implement tax and spend-policies that will bankrupt Britain. This claim has historical parallels in Margaret Thatcher's neoliberal ideology. She argued: "Socialist governments traditionally do make a financial mess. They always run out of other people's money" (Thatcher 1976). "It's the Labour Government that have brought us record peace-time taxation. They've got the usual Socialist disease – they've run out of other people's money. And it's the Labour Government that have pushed public spending to record levels. And how've they done it? By borrowing, and borrowing and borrowing" (Thatcher 1975). The Thatcher quote about running out of other people's money was twice mentioned in our dataset (No. 18768, No. 18729). The formulation "running out of other people's money" assumes that the rich have created their wealth themselves and therefore have a natural right to own it. It also implies that taxation is theft. This possessive-individualist claim overlooks that not capital, but labour creates wealth that it does not own, and that a lot of wealth is inherited.

Corbyn supporters also contested the command economy ideology on Twitter. They used the strategies of positive connotation and dialectical reversal ("Jeremy Corbyn's anti-austerity plans are sound & the austerity agenda is extremist" [No. 726], "The Tories Have Done More Damage Through Austerity Then Jeremy Corbyn Ever Could With Socialism" [No. 26643]). They also stressed that Corbyn's economic policies stand for social justice ("remember that Britain is the most unequal society in the EU", [No. 995], "Congratulations to Corbyn. Unity, equality, social justice" [No. 20752]). And they referred to authorities by e.g. arguing that economists support Corbyn's plans (No. 1, No. 32, No. 28927) or characterising Corbyn's economic strategy as Keynesian (e.g. No. 350, No. 28117). Some tweets made intertextual reference to a support letter of 42 economists published in the Observer and to the accompanying front-page headline "Corbyn wins economists' backing for radical plan" (23 August 2015).

8.5.4 Culture: "Corbyn is a Loony-Left Hippie"

Raymond Williams argues that "culture is not only a body of intellectual and imaginative work; it is also and essentially a whole way of life" (Williams 1958, 325). Culture as everyday life is for Williams about people's ordinary daily routine activities. In the analysed tweets, one could also find postings about Corbyn's lifestyle. So also the **cultural discourse topic that Corbyn is a loony-left hippie** with an odd lifestyle was present in the dataset. Some users pointed out that Corbyn is bearded, old, rides a bike, is a vegetarian, and does not dress appropriately for a party leader:

> "Never trust a vegetarian with a beard and terrorist friends" (No. 17197).
>
> "Corbyn is grumpy old man on bike" (No. 12090).
>
> "Can't this Marxist dinosaur afford socks?" (No. 1811).
>
> "Jeremy Corbyn plots his first days as Labour leader in shorts and t-shirt" (No. 11671).

These are ad hominem attacks on Corbyn's look and lifestyle, namely on his style of dressing, going to work, and his eating habits. There is also a somatisation (focus on his beard) and a gerontonym (Reisigl and Wodak 2001, 49) that characterises him as old (dinosaur, old man). All of these attacks are personalisations, blunt personal attacks without any political arguments.

Some of these posts linked to newspapers, such as the Daily Mail-article "Corbyn shows some leg" (11 September 2015) that argued that Corbyn is looking "more like a pensioner popping out for a pint of milk than someone who is about to take charge of one of the world's best-known political parties". Other tweets linked to images of Corbyn's birth house and tabloid articles about it (e.g. "Jeremy Corbyn, the boy to the manor born", Daily Telegraph, 22 August 2015) and argued for example: "Welcome to the seven-bedroom home where Jeremy Corbyn set out on his radical path" (No. 77). The implication expressed is that Corbyn had a privileged upbringing and today wants to deny the rich the same privileges. Others argued that Corbyn's idea of women-only carriages for safer transport is "crazy, extremist" (No. 2021) and "Sharia compliant" (No. 2701), or that Corbyn after his victory went to "a packed pub", "singing the Red Flag" (BBC political editor Laura Kuenssberg, No. 18847).

Corbyn supporters contested such personal attacks on his look, lifestyle, manners and family by pointing out that his cultural policy ideas are nuanced. One user posted that Corbyn argued that he "would consult with women" on women-only carriages (No. 2021). Another strategy was to link to Corbyn's arts and culture policy strategy document ("Jeremy Corbyn: My radical plan for the arts will make Britain happier", No. 5598)). Users pointed out that "The Red Flag is the @UKLabour anthem". "It's therefore no surprise that people, including #Corbyn, are singing it" (No. 20967). The comedian David Schneider used sarcasm as strategy (see the tweet example below). The post was re-tweeted 245 times in the dataset.

DAVID SCHNEIDER: "Corbyn to consult women on train harassment => extremist loon.
Workers may not even get 1% pay rise => not a problem".
(Twitter: @davidschneider, 26 August 2015, https://twitter.com/
davidschneider/status/636441456555761664)

8.5.5 Politics: "Jeremy Corbyn just like Stalin and Mao Wants a Totalitarian State"

A discourse topic that was hardly present in the news media, but could be found on Twitter was the one of **authoritarian and totalitarian politics**: "Jeremy Corbyn just like Stalin and Mao wants a totalitarian state". Some examples:

"Corbyn, Stalin, Mao all ingredients in same pie!" (No. 4277)

"Lenin Stalin Mao Kim Corbyn #CultOfPersonality" (No. 6922)

"Mao, Stalin, Pol Pot, Hitler and now Corbyn" (No. 21039)

"BREAKING NEWS: THE UNITED KINGDOM LITERALLY JUST BECAME A PROLETARIAN DICTATORSHIP! JEREMY 'STALIN II' CORBYN HAS BEEN ELECTED LABOUR LEADER" (No. 23872)

"freedom of the press? For how much longer under a communist corbyn" (No. 14247)

"CORBYN. communism is back baby! prepare the gulags." (No. 13357)

The linguistic strategy of these tweets is to mention Corbyn in a row with dictators, to reason that he is like them, and that the result of it will therefore be dictatorship, the end of civil liberties, and mass killings. These tweets use historicising politonyms: Corbyn is characterised as communist and communism is put into the historical context of dictators like Stalin, Mao, Pol Pot, Kim Il-sung. The hashtag #CultOfPersonality and the references to freedom of the press, proletarian dictatorship and the Gulag use the topos of history in order to imply that given the predicated parallels to historical dictators, it is likely that if Corbyn comes to power, he will implement a totalitarian political system.

Another user combined the authoritarianism topos with the cultural topos, describing Corbyn as "Stalin dressed as Santa Claus" (No. 11924). Some users in this context agued that Corbyn's ideas are totalitarian because communism failed historically: "I refer you to 1970/80s East Europe" (No. 17233). "Estimated 85–100 million killed – particularly by starvation by #communism. #corbyn supporters forget history"

Analysis

(No. 12412). Such tweets imply that given the violent history of Stalinism and Maoism, any left-wing idea is corrupted and must fail.

For questioning that Corbyn is totalitarian, his supporters pointed out that he is a defender of human rights and believes in democracy: "Jeremy Corbyn is a democratic socialist" (No. 29769), "SHOCK, HORROR! Corbyn would respect international human rights law" (No. 2954). Others argued that Corbyn is a decent person: "Corbyn sure seems like a decent fella" (No. 17315). One strategy was to use an argumentative dialectical reversal to stress that not Corbyn, but the Tories support human rights abuses: "David Cameron is also a supporter of human rights abuses in Saudi Arabia " (No. 3614). In reference to the creation of a British surveillance state and GCHQ's mass surveillance of communications, Glenn Grenwald in a satirical manner also used the argumentative strategy of dialectical reversal (see Žižek 2014 and Fuchs 2014 for a discussion of this concept), implying that the surveillance state is extremist and Corbyn opposes it: "After exposing him for advocating trials, what extremist ideas will UK media next reveal Corbyn favors? Spying warrants?" (No. 5529). This posting resulted in 136 re-tweets.

8.6 Conclusion

Anti-socialist ideology that redbaits the Left is not new. It already existed at the time of Marx and found one of its culminations in McCarthyism. In Britain, there were previous campaigns against the Labour Left that portrayed politicians such as Tony Benn or Ken Livingstone and their ideas as "loony left". The argumentative core of anti-socialist ideology has remained the same in the age of social media, but the forms and means of ideological expression and its contestation have changed.

Ideologies are semiotic structures that justify domination. Twitter limits linguistic expression to 140 characters. User-generated ideology such as online redbaiting therefore has to compress ideology. User-generated ideology is the use of digital media for producing and spreading semiotic structures that justify domination by distorting reality, misrepresenting it, or inventing false representations of reality. By making claims, insults and personal attacks without underlying arguments and justifications, users compress ideology on Twitter into 140 characters. A feature of many anti-socialist tweets was that they made claims about Corbyn without arguments and proof. They never or only in single cases referred to Corbyn's extended arguments, interviews with him or to his team's strategy and policy documents.

Anti-socialist ideology often uses the strategy of ridiculing individuals (by for example calling Corbyn and Labour Depty Leader Tom Watson "the Tom and Jerry show" [No. 13358]), associating them with violence, dictatorship and terrorism; and describing them by negatively connoted terms ("loony", "terrorist", "extremist", "radical", "dangerous", "enemy") that can easily stir up negative emotions. Twitter's speed, ephemerality and brevity can intensify the compression-tendency of ideologies that neglects profound arguments, advances claims without proofs and claims that are inconsistent with reality. One Corbyn-supporter noted this tendency: "Have u noticed that Tories never provide intelligent arguments opposing J Corbyn? They just comment things like 'LEFT LOONY' 'FKN COMMUNIST'" (No. 23376). During the Labour leadership election, Jeremy Corbyn's team published 12 policy strategy documents on arts, housing, railways, the economy, small businesses, the environment, education, Britain's North, young people, gender equality, peace & defence, and mental health. Not a single one of the analysed ideological tweets mentioned or linked to any of these policy documents.

In the analysed dataset, users for example argued that because of being left-wing, Corbyn is loony, an extremist and dangerous (compressed general ideology), is a friend of terrorists, radicals and dictators and thereby supports Britain's enemies (foreign policy discourse topic), wants to create a state-controlled economy that will result in poverty and deprivation for all (command economy-discourse topic), wants to create a totalitarian state like Stalin or Mao did (authoritarian and totalitarian politics discourse politics), and is an old, badly dressed, vegetarian, bike-riding loony-left hippie with a beard (culture and lifestyle discourse topic). The foreign policy, command economy, and lifestyle-discourse topics were also prominently featured in the right-wing media. User-generated ideology on Twitter in these cases is closely related to ideologies spread by the mass media. It copies the latter's contents by linking to articles, using certain headlines or biased phrases such as "the Loony Left" and at the same times feeds these media by showing that there is an interest in and positive response to stories that scapegoat the Left. There were also ideological discourse topics in the dataset that were not prominently featured in the mass media. This included especially the assumption that Corbyn stands for authoritarian state politics and wants to create a dictatorship. Import was also general scapegoating that drew biased claims about Corbyn without making further arguments for grounding or justifying them.

Twitter is a new medium, but anti-socialism is an ideology that has a history. Anti-socialism on Twitter is an old ideology expressed in new ways (140 characters) in

Conclusion

a new medium. It is a re-contextualisation of ideological discourse. The content of user-generated ideologies is to a specific degree originally created by users and to a specific degree a reflection of exiting ideologies. Ideological topics and texts created online tend to interact with other texts. In the analysed Twitter dataset this became evident by tweets that refer to mainstream newspaper articles. Ideological tweets especially referred to articles about Corbyn in the Daily Mail, the Daily Telegraph, the Daily Express, the Sun and the Times, which are Britain's key nation-wide right-wing newspapers. The ideological topos that Corbyn is disloyal and defied the whip more than 500 times did not at all play a role on Twitter, but was more important in the mainstream news media. This circumstance shows that ideologies online and offline stand in specific relations of dialectical articulation to each other, but also have relative autonomy. Offline ideologies can reach into online space, online ideologies into offline spaces. But there can also be ideologies that play a more important role in specific mediated spaces than in others.

Basil Bernstein (1990, 11) defines a code as a selection and integration of meanings, which implies that each code evokes certain contexts. A specific instance of a code, such as the expression of an anti-socialist ideology, stands in a primary context (Bernstein, 1990, 52), the original context of production. Recontextualisation means that a discourse is relocated from one context to another one (Bernstein, 1990; Krzyżanowski 2010, 78; Krzyżanowski 2016, 314).

Section 8.4 has shown with various examples that socialism has in its history been accompanied by anti-socialist ideology. This can be explained by the fact that socialism challenges class society and that representatives of class orders resist such challenges in various forms, including discursively. Recontextualisation of anti-socialist ideologies involves the embedding of anti-socialism into specific political contexts such as Marx's death, the murder of Rosa Luxemburg, the McCarty era in the USA, Thatcherism in the UK, and in the case studied in this chapter, the contemporary British political context of Thatcher-inspired neoliberalism and its challenge by Jeremy Corbyn's version of socialism. Recontextualisation also means that anti-socialism can be embedded into various media formats and technologies that have specific affordances that shape the way this ideology is expressed. The analysis in this chapter has shown that in the case of Twitter, anti-socialist ideology must be compressed into 140 characters, which often results in ad hominem attacks and the use of slur words without any underlying arguments.

In the case of anti-socialist ideology on Twitter, it is a common strategy that users post links to online articles in right-wing mainstream tabloids. As the URLs are often too long, short tiny URLs tend to be generated and posted. The URL is a reference that connects the Twitter text to the newspaper text. It helps to delocate the primary context and to transfer it into a different context that allows the use of hashtags and the networking with other users via re-tweets and comments. So the transformation that the ideology undergoes when relocated into Twitter is that it is embedded into a more social and networked environment, where anti-socialist ideology is communicated in compressed form at high speed. The necessary compression to 140 characters results in the fact that anti-socialist ideology expressed in sensationalist terms in tabloids is further simplified and even more tabloidised on Twitter so that anti-socialist ideology on Twitter tends to be mere hatred, empty negative claims without any underpinning arguments.

Ideologies are not static and fixed, but change dynamically. Because humans are reflective, active, social beings, they have the capacity to challenge, contest and "see through" ideologies. Social struggle therefore can also take place in the ideological realm. In the analysed dataset, users challenged ideological anti-Corbyn discourse topics in various ways. Users are not the helpless victims of anti-socialist and other ideologies, but can contest, oppose and struggle against ideologies. Online technologies such as Twitter, Facebook and other social media platforms not just allow to express, but also to challenge ideologies in linguistic, visual and audio-visual ways.

Strategies that Corbyn-supporters used for challenging anti-Corbyn ideologies on Twitter included the foregrounding of Corbyn's characteristics in positive terms (decent, honest, humanist, gives hope, democrat, defends human rights, cares for everyday people, etc.); using satire, sarcasm, cynicism, and humour (e.g. the #suggestacorbynsmear-hashtag); reference to authorities supporting Corbyn; providing links to what Corbyn really says and thinks and to his real political ideas and policy documents; the strategy of argumentative dialectical reversal ("Not Corbyn, but the Tories and right-wing media are extremists, radical, fundamentalist, supporters of human rights abuses because they do this and that …"); pointing out anti-socialist ideology's hypocrisy and contradictions; or spreading information about some of Corbyn's opponents' self-defeating silliness (e.g. the example of Louise Mensch' anti-Semitism tweet). In general the responses to anti-socialist ideology tend to be smart, complex, dialectical, reflective, and argumentative,

Conclusion

whereas ideologies tend to be rather irrational, one-dimensional, unreflected, and to make claims without proofs and arguments. Anti-socialism's non-dialecticity aims at what Herbert Marcuse (1964) terms the "liquidation of two-dimensional culture" (60), of dialectical language and of "two-dimensional, dialectical modes of thought" (88).

Social media is a communication space where ideologies are expressed and challenged. Studying user-generated ideologies online therefore allows identifying and analysing the structure of anti-socialist and anti-Corbyn ideologies and how they can best be challenged. Ideologies tend to be irrational, emotional, affective, personalising, scandalising, and to creative discursive divisions between in- and outgroups (van Dijk 2011, 397–398; van Dijk 1998, 267). It is in general difficult to challenge them. Jeremy Corbyn argues it is best to ignore smear campaigns. Often it may indeed be good to not immediately react to ideological scapegoating, but to retreat and not start a discursive offensive. Generally neglecting to react to and contest ideology can however also be a disadvantage because discourses can have real impact on how citizens judge and relate to politicians, how they vote, etc. The question and difficulty is how to respond in a smart tactical manner. The analysis shows that promising strategies for Jeremy Corbyn's team could be to use satire and humour, use the strategy of argumentative dialectical reversals for responding to ideological attacks, and to point out the contradictions and limits of ideological claims. Left-wing social media users have developed smart, complex, dialectical strategies of how to react to ideological smear campaigns. Studying counter-discourses to anti-socialist ideology can inform political campaigns at a time when redbaiting is again omnipresent in politics. There is no guarantee that attempted counter-campaigns can be successful because the opponents are powerful. The only thing that remains is to attempt to develop intelligent forms of struggle that challenge anti-socialism.

Notes

1 The numbers of followers for the ten accounts were accessed on September 27, 2015, 18:21 BST.

2 http://www.digitalinformationworld.com/2015/01/twitter-marketing-stats-and-facts-you-should-know.html, accessed on September 27, 2015.

References

Bernstein, Basil. 1990. *Class, Codes and Control. Volume IV: The Structuring of Pedagogic Discourse*. London: Routledge.

Blair, Tony. 2015. "Even If You Hate Me, Please Don't Take Labour Over the Cliff Edge." *The Guardian Online*, 13 August 2015.

British Psychological Society (BPS). 2009. *Code of Ethics and Conduct*. Leicester: BPS.

Curran, James, Ivor Gaber, and Julian Petley. 2005. *Culture Wars. The Media & the British Left*. Edinburgh: Edinburgh University Press.

Dathan, Matt. 2015. "Jeremy Corbyn's Team Send a Complaint to the BBC Over Its "Hatchet Job" Panorama Programme." *The Independent Online*, 11 September 2015

Eagleton, Terry. 1991. *Ideology: An Introduction*. London: Verso.

Fariello, Griffin, ed. 1995. *Red Scare. Memories of the American Inquisition. An Oral History*. New York: W.W. Norton & Company.

Fuchs, Christian. 2017. *Social Media: A Critical Introduction*. London: Sage. 2nd edition.

Fuchs, Christian. 2016a. *Critical Theory of Communication: Lukács, Adorno, Marcuse, Honneth and Habermas in the Age of the Internet and Social Media*. London: University of Westminster Press.

Fuchs, Christian. 2016b. *Reading Marx in the Information Age: A Media and Communication Studies Perspective on "Capital Volume 1"*. New York: Routledge.

Fuchs, Christian. 2015. *Culture and Economy in the Age of Social Media*. New York: Routledge.

Fuchs, Christian. 2014. "The Dialectic: Not Just the Absolute Recoil, but the World's Living Fire That Extinguishes and Kindles Itself. Reflections on Slavoj Žižek's Version of Dialectical Philosophy in "Absolute Recoil: Towards a New Foundation of Dialectical Materialism"." *tripleC: Communication, Capitalism & Critique* 12 (2): 848–75.

Hollingsworth, Mark. 1986. *The Press and Political Dissent*. London: Pluto.

Khosravinik, Majid. 2013. "Critical Discourse Analysis, Power, and New Media Discourse." In *Why Discourse Matters: Negotiating Identity in the Mediatized World*, edited by Yusuf Kalyango Jr. and Monika Weronika Kopytowska, 287–305. New York: Peter Lang.

Krzyżanowski, Michał. 2016. "Recontextualisation of Neoliberalism and the Increasingly Conceptual Nature of Discourse: Challenges for Critical Discourse Studies." *Discourse & Society 27 (3)*: 308–21.

Krzyżanowski, Michał. 2010. *The Discursive Construction of European Identities*. Frankfurt am Main: Peter Lang.

Marcuse, Herbert. 1964. *One-Dimensional Man*. Boston, MA: Beacon Press.

Marx, Karl and Friedrich Engels. 1845/1998. *The German Ideology*. Amherst, NY: Prometheus Books.

Mortimer, Caroline. 2015. "British Army Could "Stage Mutiny Under Corbyn", Says Senior Serving General." *The Independent Online*, 20 September 2015.

Rehmann, Jan. 2013. *Theories of Ideology*. Leiden: Brill.

Reisigl, Martin and Ruth Wodak. 2009. "The Discourse-Historical Approach." In *Methods of Critical Discourse Analysis*, edited by Ruth Wodak and Michael Meyer, 87–121. London: Sage.

Reisigl, Martin and Ruth Wodak. 2001. "Discourse and Discrimination." *Rhetorics of Racism and Antisemitism*. London: Routledge.

Schrecker, Ellen. 1998. *Many are the Crimes: McCarthyism in America*. Boston, MA: Little, Brown and Company.

Stoegner, Karin and Ruth Wodak. 2016. ""The Man Who Hated Britain" – the Discursive Construction of "National Unity" in the Daily Mail." *Critical Discourse Studies 13* (*2*): 193–209.

Thatcher, Margaret. 1976. "TV Interview with Margaret Thatcher." *Thames TV: This Week*. February 5, 1976. http://www.margaretthatcher.org/document/102953.

Thatcher, Margaret. 1975. *Speech to Conservative Party Conference*. October 10, 1975. http://www.margaretthatcher.org/document/102777.

van Dijk, Teun. 2011. "Discourse and Ideology." In *Discourse Studies. A Multidisciplinary Introduction*, edited by Teun van Dijk, 379–407. London: Sage.

van Dijk, Teun. 1998. *Ideology. A Multidisciplinary Approach*. London: Sage.

Wilkinson, Michael. 2015. "Twitter's Funniest Smear Attacks on Jeremy Corbyn as #suggestacorbynsmear Goes Viral." *Telegraph Online*, 1 September 2015.

Williams, Raymond. 1958. *Culture & Society, 1780–1950*. New York: Columbia University Press.

Wodak, Ruth and Michael Meyer, eds. 2009. *Methods of Critical Discourse Analysis*. London: Sage. 2nd edition.

YouGov. 2016. *British Press "Most Right-Wing" in Europe*. https://yougov.co.uk/news/2016/02/07/british-press-most-right-wing-europe/.

Žižek, Slavoj. 2014. *Absolute Recoil. Towards a New Foundation of Dialectical Materialism*. London: Verso.

Žižek, Slavoj, ed. 1994. *Mapping Ideology*. London: Verso.

Chapter Nine

Racism, Nationalism, and Right-Wing Extremism Online: The 2016 Austrian Presidential Election on Facebook

9.1 Introduction

Norbert Hofer was the Freedom Party of Austria's (FPÖ) candidate in the 2016 Austrian presidential election. In the first round, he achieved 35.05% of the votes cast and became the strongest candidate. The second round took place on 23 May and saw a run-off between Hofer and Alexander Van der Bellen. Hofer's share of the vote was 49.64%. Van der Bellen, who was the Austrian Green Party's leader from 1997 until 2008, won with a voting share of 50.35% in the second round and a lead of just a bit more than 30,000 votes. The Austrian presidential election received lots of international interest and people were asking themselves how it was possible that a far-right candidate achieved almost half of the vote. The FPÖ filed a complaint to the Constitutional Court of Austria that resulted in a re-run of the run-off.

This chapter asks: how did voters of Hofer express their support on Facebook? It applies critical discourse analysis to data collected from postings on two public Facebook pages (Norbert Hofer, Heinz-Christian Strache). The analysis situates Hofer supporters' ideological discourse in Austria's political context and history.

DOI: 10.4324/9781003256090-9

Section 9.2 engages with theoretical foundations by discussing the notion of ideology. Section 9.3 focuses on the theoretical clarification of nationalist and new racist ideology. Section 9.4 provides an overview of the Freedom Party's ideology. Section 9.5 explains the methodology. Section 9.6 presents the analysis and interpretation. Section 9.7 draws some conclusions.

9.2 Theoretical Foundations: What is Ideology?

This work studies online nationalism and online xenophobia. It is a contribution to empirical ideology critique. An underlying theoretical question that arises in this context is how one should best understand the notion of ideology. There are different traditions of how to define and study ideology. Approaches include for example Marx's theory of commodity fetishism, Lukács theory of reification, Gramsci's theory of hegemony, the Frankfurt School, Hallian Cultural Studies, various forms and schools of Critical Discourse Analysis, Foucauldian discourse analysis, Althusserian ideology theory (Eagleton 1991; Rehmann 2013; Žižek 1994). These theories do not have a consensus on what ideology is and how it should be defined. Two major schools in the critical study of ideology go back to Antonio Gramsci and Georg Lukács.

Whereas Gramsci's approach can be characterised as ideology theory, the one by Lukács can be seen as ideology critique (Fuchs 2015, chapter 3). Gramsci understands ideology as worldviews, the "superstructure of a particular structure" (Gramsci 1988, 199) and a "conception of the world" (Gramsci 1988, 343). Lukács, based on Marx's theory of commodity fetishism, sees ideology as reified thought emerging in reified societies. He therefore argues that the "emergence and diffusion of ideologies appears as the general characteristic of class societies" (Lukács 1986, 405).

Terry Eagleton (1991, chapter 1) discerns various understandings of ideology by identifying six theoretical approaches:

- 1) Ideology as the "production of ideas, beliefs and values in social life" (28) (=ideology as culture) (28);
- 2) Ideas and beliefs of "a specific, socially significant group or class" (29) (=ideology as worldview);
- 3) The "*promotion* and *legitimation* of the interests" of a group "in the face of opposing interests" (29);

- 4) The "promotion and legitimation of sectoral interests" in the "activities of a dominant social power" (29) (=ideology as dominant worldviews);
- 5) "[I]deas and beliefs which help to legitimate the interests of a ruling group or class specifically by distortion and dissimulation" (30);
- 6) "[F]alse or deceptive beliefs [...] arising not from the interests of a dominant class but from the material structure of society as a whole" (30).

Especially Marx, Lukács, and the Frankfurt School have influenced the theoretical concept of ideology used in this chapter and the Marxian theory approach that underlies it (Fuchs 2015, 2016b,c). The notion of ideology employed relates to Eagleton's fifth and sixth meanings of ideology. By ideology, I understand thoughts, practices, ideas, words, concepts, phrases, sentences, texts, belief systems, meanings, representations, artefacts, institutions, systems or combinations thereof that represent and justify one group's or individual's power, domination, or exploitation of other groups or individuals by misrepresenting, one-dimensionally presenting or distorting reality in symbolic representations (Fuchs 2015). Ideology is not simply an abstract structure, but has a concrete, lived reality: ideological workers produce and reproduce ideologies (Fuchs 2015, chapter 3). Marx characterises the producers of ideology as "the thinkers of the [ruling] class", its "active, conceptive ideologists", who based on a division of labour within the ruling class "make the formation of the illusions of the class abut itself their chief source of livelihood" (Marx and Engels 1845, 68).

The definition taken in the theory approach underlying this work implies moral realism and socialist praxis: humans can analyse and understand the world's reality and complex problem's real causes. Ideology critique is the deconstruction of falsehood, of knowledge that is presented as truth, but is deceptive. Socialist moral realism implies that dominative and exploitative societies negate humans' general interests. They therefore should from a political point of view be abolished and replaced by a societal formation that benefits all economically, socially, politically and culturally. Such a society of the commons is a socialist society. Eagleton's fifth and sixth meanings of ideology are based on a dialectical contradiction of class societies and socialism. These are critical-political understandings that imply political praxis and the transcendence of class, capitalism, and domination.

Not everyone agrees with such a definition of ideology. Theories of ideology generally disagree. For Louis Althusser (2005), ideology is an "*organic part of every social totality*" (232). "Ideology is a system (with its own logic and rigour) of representations (images, myths, ideas or concepts, depending on the case) endowed with a historical existence and role within a given society" (231). Althusserian ideology theory has been influential.

Stuart Hall (1986/1996, 26) defines ideology as "the mental frameworks – the languages, the concepts, categories, imagery of thought, and the systems of representations – which different classes and social groups deploy in order to make sense of, define, figure out and render intelligible the way society works". Hall (1982) identifies the critical paradigm in media studies with the study of ideology. The origin would have been the Frankfurt School's challenge of behaviourist media effects research. Hall's notion of ideology is grounded in structural linguistics and the works of Gramsci, Althusser, and Laclau.

The problems of Hall's understanding are twofold. First, humans are denied subject positions. Discourse and ideological structures are turned into a subject. Such structuralism becomes evident when structures are presented as actively doing something and humans are seen as structure's objects. Hall for example writes that humans are positioned and languaged (80), ideological discourses win their way (80), discourse speaks itself through him/her (88). It is then not humans who communicate ideology and discourse through language, but ideology that languages, speaks, communicates, etc. Ideology is in this approach an articulation of linguistic elements, of rules, codes, linguistic systems, classificatory systems, matrixes, and sets of elements. Missing is the insight that ideology is an active communicative process and a social relation, in which humans, groups, and classes produce and reproduce power relations. Production and reproduction of power entails the possibilities to undo, perturb, challenge, and oppose existing power relations just like it entails possibilities to take over, justify, sustain, and legitimate such relations.

The second problem is associated with the first: social struggle becomes in a structuralist approach a struggle between ideologies. It is not seen as a power relation between humans, in which they actively produce and reproduce discourses and ideologies. Not ideologies struggle with each other, but humans, human groups and classes struggle against each other with various means, including the means of communication, and with specific capacities to mobilise power. Such resources in ideological and other struggles have specific distributions that enable various degrees of power. Hall's approach is a relativistic determinism, in which ideological struggles and alternative interpretations emerge with necessity. He therefore speaks of ideology as a "site of struggle" (between competing definitions) (70) and of significations as "controversial and conflicting" (70). There is certainly always the possibility for contestation, but no necessity for it. Asymmetric power relations can equip humans, groups and classes to different degrees with capacities to speak, communicate, be heard, visible and listened to, and to get information across to others.

General understandings of ideology represent the first and second meanings identified by Eagleton. The problem is that such a generalist understanding is morally and politically relativist. If the views that "Jews are inferior beings, that women are less rational than men, that fornicators will be condemned to perpetual torment" are "not instances of false consciousness, then it is difficult to know what is; and those who dismiss the whole notion of false consciousness must be careful not to appear cavalier about the offensiveness of these opinions" (Eagleton 1991, 15). If democratic socialism and anti-fascism are the dominant paradigms in a society, then in such a societal context, fascism, racism, and capitalism are in a general understanding of ideology forms of ideology critique. Such a generality is a disservice for a critical theory of society. Max Horkheimer (1972, 28) remarks in this respect about Karl Mannheim's general theory of ideology that such general approaches "thoroughly purge from the ideology concept the remains of its accusatory meaning". According to Adorno (1981, 38), generalising theories of ideology employ "the terminology of social criticism while removing its sting". Whereas the critique of ideology is "determinate negation in the Hegelian sense, the confrontation of the ideational with its realization" (Adorno 1972, 466), general theories of ideology replace the determinate negation by the analysis of "general worldviews" (Adorno 1972, 472).

Eagleton's fifth and sixth definition do not imply, as claimed by Stuart Hall (1986/1996, 30), "economic and class reductionism". In the theory of false consciousness and false society, class background and position do not determine, but condition consciousness. A dominant class is often organised in competing class factions that also have competing ideologies. The example of Marx and Engels, who came from quite bourgeois families, shows that individuals are not trapped in certain ideologies because of their background. Consciousness is dynamic and reflects in complex non-linear ways the total of an individual's experiences, social positions, and social relations in society.

Also in the tradition of Critical Discourse Analysis (CDA), there are different understandings of ideology. Norman Fairclough (2010, 73) distinguishes between critical and descriptive concepts of ideology. Teun van Dijk (1998, 8) has a more descriptive approach and defines ideology as a mental framework that is "the *basis of the social representations shared by members of a group*" that allows the organisation of the group members' social beliefs and practices. In contrast to van Dijk, Fairclough defines ideology as "representations which contribute to the constitution, reproduction, and transformation of social relations of power and domination" (Fairclough 2010, 73). His understanding is close to the fourth, fifth, and sixth meanings of ideology identified by Eagleton. Reisigl and Wodak (2009, 88) understand ideology as a "one-sided perspective or world view" of a particular social group that is a means for "establishing and maintaining unequal power relations through discourse". Wodak explicitly acknowledges the influence of Frankfurt School critical theory on the discourse-historical approach of CDA (Wodak 2009, 34–35; Reisigl and Wodak 2001, 32).

Theodor W. Adorno's works show ideology critique in action. The dominant tendency is to reduce Adorno to the critique of the culture industry (Horkheimer and Adorno 2002, 94–136; for a discussion and critique of this tendency, see: Fuchs 2016b, chapter 3). Such readings overlook the wealth of Adorno's ideology critique that includes also for example studies of the ideology of anti-Semitism (Horkheimer and Adorno 2002, 137–172), fascist and authoritarian ideology (Adorno 1955, 1973), ideologies in everyday life (Adorno 1951), astrology, superstition and occultism (Adorno 1955, 1962), ideology and its critique in education (Adorno 1971), etc. Adorno understands ideology in a Lukácsian sense as "a consciousness which is objectively necessary and yet at the same time false, as the intertwining of truth and falsehood" (Adorno 1954, 189). For Adorno (1954, 190), the need for ideology critique follows from the existence of ideology. The understanding of ideology underlying this chapter stands in the tradition of Marx, Lukács and the Frankfurt School. Jürgen Ritsert (1972) has based on the Frankfurt School tradition defined empirical ideology critique as a method of critical social research.

9.3 Nationalism and New Racism

Through ideologies, humans, groups, and classes try to persuade, influence, reify, hide, distort, promote, legitimate, deceive, misrepresent, or justify dominative interests. Karl Marx (1867, section 1.4) saw capitalism's structure as inherently fetishistic: the commodity form hides the social character of capitalism behind things. Fetishism is not just an economic phenomenon, but can in class societies be found in peculiar ways in the realms of politics and ideology. Ideology tries to naturalise domination by hiding its social and historical character and dissimulating attention from the power relations underlying heteronomous societies. An example is the construction of an ideology that claims that "we" national citizens are all together facing society's problems (unemployment, poverty, crime, precariousness, crises, lack of adequate housing, welfare, education, health care, etc.), that "we" have these problems because of foreign influences, and can as a nation fight these dark forces. The ideological trick in such arguments is to disguise that "we" are not a unitary subject in a class society, but have different positions and capacities in power relations. Nationalism ism a particular form of ideology.

It was Rosa Luxemburg (1976), who first used Marx's notion of fetishism as a political concept to question the fetishistic character of the nation and nationalism. She argues that nationalist ideology "ignores completely the fundamental theory of modern socialism – the theory of social classes" (135). Nationalism is a "misty veil" that "conceals in every case a definite historical content" (135). "In a class society, 'the nation' as a homogeneous socio-political entity does not exist. Rather, there exist within each nation, classes with antagonistic interests and 'rights'" (135). Nationalism is an ideology that in a particular manner veils and distracts attention from society's class relations and the role they play in society's problems.

Some common elements of Marxist theories and understandings of nationalism are the following ones (compare: Balibar and Wallerstein 1991; Hall 1993; Hobsbawm 1992; Luxemburg 1976; Özkirimli 2010):

- *Ideology:* nationalism is an ideology that constructs an Us/Them difference, in which the in-group is conceived as a unitary, homogeneous collective defined either by common claims to biology, genealogy, kinship, and family ("race") or by claims to a common culture (commonality of language, communication, upbringing, moral values, traditions, customs, law, religion, emotions, experiences, identity, means of communication), a common state/political system/constitution, or a common economy. Nationalism as ideology makes claims to territorial power for organising a national economic and a national political system. Nationalism constructs/invents/ fabricates the nation and fictive national identity. Nationalist identity stresses fixity and homogeneity, whereas in reality all societies are complex, hybrid and diverse.
- *Dialectic of racism/xenophobia and nationalism:* racism/xenophobia and nationalism are inherently linked. Xenophobia is an ideological construction of the out-group that is not part of the illusionary national collective.
- *Political fetishism:* nationalism, xenophobia, and racism are a form of political fetishism that ideologically distracts from how society's class antagonisms bring about social problems. The distraction from and veiling of class are often achieved by the construction of scapegoats and by steering hatred against them.
- *Forms of nationalism:* nationalism, xenophobia, and racism can be directed

against an inner enemy (migrants, minorities) or an outer enemy (other nations, foreign groups). One can draw a distinction between sociological and institutional racism/nationalism and between inclusive (exploitative) and exclusive (exterminatory) racism/nationalism. Furthermore there are biological and cultural forms of racism/nationalism.

- *Militarism*: nationalism is associated with internal militarism (repression and law-and-order politics directed against immigrants and minorities) and external militarism (imperialist warfare).

Whereas nationalism constitutes an inward-oriented ideology constructing the identity of an invented political and cultural collective, racism and xenophobia define the outside of this collective, those who are considered not to be part of the nation, the nation's outsiders, foreign elements, or enemies. Racism is *"a supplement internal to nationalism"* (Balibar and Wallerstein 1991, 54). "Racism is constantly emerging out of nationalism. [...] And nationalism emerges out of racism" (Balibar and Wallerstein 1991, 53). Classical nationalism often constructed the outsider in biological terms as a "race", whereas today it has become more common to define the outsider in cultural and political terms. Whereas some observers therefore like to distinguish between racism and xenophobia, Étienne Balibar has coined the notion of the new racism to describe ideological continuities and parallels:

> "The new racism is a racism of the era of 'decolonization' [...] [It] fits into the framework of 'racism without races' [...] It is a racism whose dominant theme is not biological heredity but the insurmountability of cultural differences, a racism which, at first sight, does not postulate the superiority of certain groups or peoples in relation to others but 'only' the harmfulness of abolishing frontiers, the incompatibility of life-styles and traditions; in short, it is what P. A. Taguieff has rightly called a *differentialist racism.*"
>
> (Balibar and Wallerstein 1991, 21)

Pierre-André Taguieff, to whom Balibar refers, argues that racism is ideologically naturalising differences, "either by scientist biologization or by ethnicization or 'culturalist' fixing" (Taguieff 2001, 200). He distinguishes between two basic types of racism. Racism type 1 biologises differences and argues that one postulated "race" is superior to another and that such differences are natural and eternal. Racism type 2 culturalises and celebrates differences. It concludes that specific cultures should therefore not mix. "Naturalization is therefore either *biologizing* or *culturalist*" (207). Both versions draw comparable political conclusions that include the erection and defence closure of borders, ending migration, and the opposition to multiculturalism: "Irreducible, incomparable, and unassimilable, the human types that differ (the reasons for difference are infinite), moreover, may not communicate with each other, neither de facto nor de jure. The impossibility of a human community beyond the enclosures is the ultimate conclusion of the thesis of *incommunicability*. Hence the violent denunciations of 'cosmopolitanism' or 'globalism,' processes and ideals that are supposed to destroy singular and closed communities, and, more profoundly and less distinctly, their 'identity.'" (204). Taguieff's key insight, on which Balibar builds, is that there are biologistic and culturalist versions of racism.

Banks and Gingrich (2006, 2) use the term neo-nationalism for the "re-emergence of nationalism under different global and transnational conditions". Parliamentary neo-nationalists in Europe tend to be opposed to immigration and the EU and to argue for differentialist racism. They embrace strong leadership and cultural populism. Much "neo-nationalist rhetoric is sufficiently pragmatic to accept that blood-based homogeneity can never define the boundaries of the national, let alone the sate, and seeks instead to generate an argument based upon historical association. [...] 'cultural fundamentalism' [...] has often come to replace race in the discourse of neo-nationalists. [...] [Neo-nationalism is] an essentialist and seclusive reaction against the current phase of globalisation [...] [that] primarily relates to 'culture'" (Banks and Gingrich 2006, 9, 15, 17).

Ajanovic, Mayer and Sauer (2015, 2016)'s analysis of right-wing extremist discourses in Austria confirms the existence of a neo-racism that takes on a cultural form. Such ideological discourses tend in Austria to have a strong anti-Muslim orientation. A negative difference between Austrians and Muslims is proclaimed. Muslims and immigrants are said to cause social problems and cultural decline. The authors document ideological arguments for keeping social spaces (schools, religious space, public space, kindergartens, transportation, work places, local spaces, etc.) free from what is perceived as foreign influences. Political ethno-pluralism is the political conclusion drawn from such discourses: the implication of this ideology is Austria should close its borders for migrants, oppose a multicultural society, and that, if at all, only assimilated migrants are acceptable.

Immanuel Wallerstein argues that racism and sexism are necessary elements of capitalism. Racism and xenophobia are in capitalism strategies to "minimize the costs of production" and to "minimize the costs of political disruption (hence minimize – not eliminate, because one cannot eliminate – the protests of the labour force)" (Balibar and

Wallerstein 1991, 33). Sexism would invent houseworkers and assert they are "not 'working', merely 'keeping house'" (35). Housework not just reproduced labour-power, but is also an "indirect subsidy to the employers of the wage labourers in these households" (34). The connection of sexism and (new) racism in capitalism is that they are both anti-universalist ideologies that legitimate low- and no-wage labour and discrimination.

Given the concepts of ideology and nationalist ideology, we can next have a short look at how the Freedom Party of Austria (FPÖ) has made and advanced a particular form of Austrian nationalism that has turned it measured in election results into Europe's most successful far-right parliamentary party.

9.4 The Freedom Party of Austria's History and Ideology

The Freedom Party of Austria (Freiheitliche Partei Österreichs, FPÖ) emerged in 1955 from the Association of the Independents (Verband der Unabhängigen) that was founded in 1949 and was the home of many former Austrian members of the Nazi Party. Until 1986, the FPÖ had both a liberal and a German-nationalist wing. In 1983, the FPÖ under the liberal leadership of Norbert Steger entered a coalition government with the Social Democrats. In 1986, Jörg Haider became the FPÖ's new leader. The Social Democrats ended the coalition government because they saw the rise of Haider as a shift of the FPÖ towards the far-right. In 1991, Haider praised Hitler's employment policy by saying: "In the Third Reich, they carried out an orderly employment policy, which is not even accomplished by your government in Vienna"[1]. Haider ignored that Hitler's employment offensive was part of Germany's armament and his plan of starting the Second World War. "This respectable occupation of people, which is described here in such positive terms, served, as we all know, to prepare for a war of extermination" (Wodak 2002, 40). Bailer-Galanda and Neugebauer (1997, 102) write that the "FPÖ represents a successful new adaptation of old right-wing extremism".

Under Haider's right-wing populist leadership, the FPÖ continuously extended its voting share in national elections. Haider used election slogans such as "Stop der Überfremdung!" (*Stop the overforeignisation!*). In 1993, he started the anti-immigration-referendum „Österreich zuerst!" (*Austria first!*). 7.35% of the electorate signed the referendum that called for completely stopping immigration and creating the constitutional provision that "Austria is not an immigration country". In 1999, the FPÖ reached 26.91% in the federal elections, became the second strongest party, and formed a coalition government together with the Conservative Party ÖVP. This right-wing coalition was in power from February 2000 until April 2005. It was isolated in the European Union. The FPÖ split into two parties, which weakened both temporarily.

In 2008, Jörg Haider died in a car accident. Heinz-Christian Strache became the Austrian far-right's new leader. He has been the FPÖ's leader since 2005. Strache used campaign slogans such as "Daham statt Islam. WIR für EUCH" ("Homeland instead of Islam: WE are for YOU"), "Wien darf nicht Istanbul werden" ("Vienna must not turn into Istanbul"), "Mehr Mut für unser ‚Wiener Blut': Zu viel Fremdes tut niemandem gut" ("More courage for our 'Viennese Blood': Too much foreignness is not good for anyone"). In the Austrian federal elections 2013, the FPÖ reached 20.51% of the votes. In national opinion polls on electoral preference, the FPÖ has since 2014 continuously achieved the highest share of potential votes (up to 35%) and has significantly stayed ahead of the Social Democratic Party of Austria (SPÖ) (data source: neuwal.com). Michał Krzyżanowski (2013) argues that the FPÖ has undergone an ideological transition from a focus on general opposition to immigration under Jörg Haider in the years 1986–2005 towards Islamophobia since 2005.

Austria is one of the European countries hit much less by the 2008 economic crisis than others. So for example its unemployment rate stayed relatively constantly around 5% in the years 2008–2015, whereas in Greece it increased from 7.8% in 2008 to 24.9% in 2015 (data source: Eurostat). In Spain, the increase was from 11.3% to 22.1% (data source: Eurostat). But nonetheless one can observe a very significant increase of the far-right's support in Austria, which shows that we cannot simply assume that supporters of the far-right are the losers of modernisation, crisis and globalisation, but project their fears of potential future social decline into foreigners and minorities. Neo-nationalist and new racist campaigns often "address and instrumentalise concerns and fears about downward social mobility" (Gingrich 2006, 47). Heribert Schiedel (2007, 49–50, 59) argues in this context that crises can condition fears of social downfall and that in such situations it is crucial whether citizens find meaningful alternatives to right-wing populism. It is an important factor in such situations, to which degree right-wing populists try to create chauvinist, xenophobic, racist and anti-Semitic fear so that citizens are encouraged to project their aggressions into surrogate objects.

Norbert Hofer was a co-author of the 2011 FPÖ's party programme that defines Austria as being culturally German:

"We are committed to our homeland of Austria as part of the German-

The Freedom Party of Austria's History and Ideology

speaking linguistic and cultural community, to the groups of people native to our country and to a Europe of free peoples and fatherlands. [...] The language, history and culture of Austria are German. The vast majority of Austrians are part of the German peoples', linguistic and cultural community. [...] Austria is not a country of immigration."

(FPÖ, 2011)

The FPÖ defines the nation based on language, history, and culture. It claims that Austrians are part of the German cultural nation and that nations must be kept separate, which is why it opposes multiculturalism. It misses that Austria has since the time of the Austrian empire since a long time been a multicultural society. To define Austria as exclusively German has been the project of the Nazis during the time of Hitler.

The Austrian president has a symbolic role. The major power lies with the government. Hofer in his electoral campaign announced that he would as Austrian president change this division of power and act not just act symbolically, but would dismiss the government if it does not accord to his prospects, for example in respect to refugee and immigration policies. "I have said that I dismiss the government if it breaks laws, breaks the constitution or again and again takes measures that harm the country. And then, the last step, the ultimo ratio, in order to avert damage from the country, can be the government's dissolution"[2] (ATV, May 15, 2016). Green Party candidate Van der Bellen commented: "This would mean that the government acts by order of the President. But it is exactly the other way round: The President has to respect the government's suggestions. If you are elected and you really pursue this style, then we are on the way into an authoritarian republic"[3] (ATV, May 15, 2016).

Who votes for the FPÖ? In the Austrian federal elections 2013, where the FPÖ achieved 20.5% of the vote, it was the strongest party among men (28%), blue-collar workers (33%), those aged 16–29 (22%), and those whose highest educational attainment is a polytechnic school (35%, = a one-year practical education that prepares pupils at the age of 14 for starting an apprenticeship) (SORA 2013). The typical FPÖ voter is a young, male blue-collar worker with a low level of education (Pelinka 2002). In 2014, the EU-wide average share of those who were aged 25 or above and held at least a bachelor's degree, was 22.3% (data source: UNESCO Statistics). Austria had with 12.25% the lowest share of all 22 EU countries, for which data is available (data source: UNESCO Statistics).

Also in the 2016 presidential election, such divisions of the social structure of voters became evident: in the second round, 60% of the male voters cast their ballot for Hofer, but only 40% of the women did the same. 86% of the blue-collar workers supported Hofer, whereas 60% of the white-collar workers voted for the Green party candidate Alexander Van der Bellen. 55% of those who only completed compulsory education cast their vote for Hofer. The same can be said about 67% of those who completed apprenticeships and about 58% of those whose highest educational attainment is the completion of a vocational school (*berufsbildende mittlere Schule*, BMS). In contrast, 73% of those who have passed school leaving examinations (*Matura*) and 81% of the university-educated voters opted for Van der Bellen (source of all data: SORA 2016). Class and education are key influencing factors on voting behaviour in Austria.

We will next discuss the methodology of the empirical research conducted for this chapter.

9.5 Methodology

Netvizz is a software tool that allows extracting data from Facebook groups and pages. I used Netvizz in order to collect comments on postings related to Hofer's presidential candidacy. I accessed Norbert Hofer and Heinz Christian Strache's Facebook pages on 30 May 2016, and used Netvizz for extracting comments to postings made between 25 and 30 May. Given that the collected comments were posted in the days after the presidential election's second round, it is likely that the dataset contains data that refers to the political differences between Hofer and Van der Bellen. I selected postings by Hofer and Strache that were particularly polarising. This selection resulted in a total of 15 postings: ten by Strache, five by Hofer. There were a total of 6,755 comments posted as responses to these 15 Facebook postings. So the analysed dataset consisted of 6,755 items.

I conducted a critical discourse analysis of the dataset. *First*, I identified discourse topics. Discourses are semantic structures that consist of certain topics. A discourse topic is a semantic macro-propositions (van Dijk 1987, 48–50) or an interpretative repertoire that is a bounded linguistic building block for actions and their representations (Potter and Wetherell 1988, 172). *Second*, I searched for typical examples of these discourse topics that were included in further analysis. *Third*, I looked at how the comments constructed an Us/Them-distinction. This included an analysis of how "We" and "They" were characterised. In critical discourse analysis such characterisations are called nominations and predications. These are discursive strategies for characterising persons or phenomena in specific ways (Reisigl and Wodak 2001, 44–56). Predication is the "discursive qualification of social actors, objects, phenomena, events/processes and actions" as "more or less positively or negatively" (Reisigl and Wodak 2009, 94). I tried to identify ideological strategies of positive self-presentation and negative other-presentation that were used for constructing a collective identity.

Teun van Dijk's (2011) *ideological square*-model is based on the assumption that there are four common ideological argumentation strategies:

- To emphasize positive things about Us (=the in-group);
- To emphasize negative things about Them (=the out-group);
- To de-emphasize negative things about Us;
- To de-emphasize positive things about Them.

"The complex meta-strategy of the ideological square tells us that group members will tend to speak or write positively about their own group, and negatively about those out-groups they define as opponents, competitors or enemies" (van Dijk 2011, 397).

When conducting social media analysis, questions of research ethics should be considered. It therefore is feasible to review such questions as far as they are relevant for the study presented in this work. Boellstorff et al. (2012) in their textbook *Ethnography and Virtual World: A Handbook of Methods* argue for an ethics of care position in virtual world research that focuses on obtaining informed consent, avoiding harm, providing benefits to study participants, etc. The online world has moved on from virtual worlds such as Second Life and World of Warcraft to social media such as Facebook and Twitter that are now far more popular. So we today need an Internet ethics focusing on social media that takes the complex relation between public and private on these sites into account.

Janet Salmons (2016) in her textbook Doing Qualitative Research Online distinguishes extant, elicited and enacted online research methods. Extant methods study existing online materials created independently of the researcher's influence. Elicited methods study date that participants elicit in response to the researcher's questions. Enacted methods study data that researchers generate with participants in a study. Each type would have specific ethical requirements. There are different ethical traditions and theories. They have different implications for online research (59–68): deontology focuses on ethical rules and guidelines (such as the guidelines of the Association for Internet Researchers). Consequentialism focuses on research outcomes. Virtue ethics focuses on the researcher's self-defined moral principles. The ethics of care give attention to participants' preferences. Salmons argues for finding a synthesis between such positions in online research. Online platforms are to varying degrees public or private. Salmons identifies a continuum that ranges from public online environments that are openly accessible without barriers to private online environments that only provide access by permission. Salmons argues that many ethical guidelines do not require informed consent for collecting data from public online platforms when the researcher does not influence the creation of the data (85–86). Hewson, Vogel and Laurent (2016, 111) in their textbook *Internet Research Methods* argue that public online data is "perhaps the least contentious in terms of being clearly in the public domain, and thus arguably available for the use as research data" without obtaining informed consent.

The British Psychological Society (BPS) argues in its *Code of Ethics and Conduct* that online observation should only take place when and where users "reasonably expect to be observed by strangers" (BPS, 2009, 13). In its *Ethics Guidelines for Internet-Mediated Research*, the BPS (2013, 6) stresses the blurring between public and private space on the Internet, which complicates research ethics. "Where it is reasonable to argue that there is likely no perception and/or expectation of privacy (or where scientific/social value and/or research validity considerations are deemed to justify undisclosed observation), use of research data without gaining valid consent may be justifiable" (BPS 2013, 7).

The Facebook pages of Norbert Hofer and Heinz Christian Strache are public pages. All postings and comments on them are visible to everyone visiting them, not just to those who like them. One does not have to have a Facebook profile to access the two pages. They can also be viewed without logging into Facebook. All postings and all comments are visible in public. Furthermore, politicians are public figures. Citizens expect them to stand in and be present in the public. This includes that they on social media post in public and offer possibilities for public communication on their profiles. Given the public character of Strache and Hofer's Facebook pages, it is reasonable to assume that someone posting a comment on such a page can reasonably expect to be observed by strangers. In such a case, one does not have to obtain informed consent for analysing and quoting such comments. Given that the users are not public figures themselves, but only make public comments when posting on a politician's public Facebook page, I do not mention the usernames in the analysis. Netvizz does not save the usernames so that the collected dataset does not contain any identifiers. The original comments were posted in German. In this chapter, I only provide English translations of quotes, not the German originals.

9.6 Analysis and Interpretation

Table 9.1 in the annex shows English translations of the postings by Strache and Hofer that were selected as data sources for the empirical analysis. In their Facebook postings, Strache and Hofer try to present the FPÖ as a reliable and responsible centre party that represents, takes care of, and defends Austrian interests. They emotionalise the relationship of Hofer and the Austrians by calling him the "President of Hearts". This formulation implies that Hofer is a true patriot who loves Austria. The implication is that Alexander Van der Bellen is unpatriotic. The FPÖ's patriotic love to Austria is also expressed by formulations such as "our homeland Austria and its people!" ("We are committed to our homeland Austria and its people!") or "our Austria" ("We will in any case continue to take care of our Austria"). So one of the rhetoric strategies is the emotionalisation of Austrian nationalism. Austria is presented is a homogeneous national collective that is under threat. Strache and Hofer identify a negative outside for constructing a nationalistic identity.

Many of these postings contain links to online articles published in newspapers (oe24.at, krone.at, diepresse.com) and blogs (unzensuriert.at). This fact is a manifestation of the intertextuality of online discourse: discourses are not contained in themselves, but take networked forms. In the online world, this means that news media refer to the comments and social media profiles of politicians, whereas politicians link to articles that mention them favourably or attack those that are critical of them. The media have played a particular role in the making of Jörg Haider, HC Strache, and Norbert Hofer. By engaging in helping to perform the right-wing populist spectacle, they hope to gain a larger number of users, readers, viewers and listeners. unzensuriert.at is a blog that has gained particular interest among supporters of Austria's far-right. The media company 1848 Medienvielfalt (1848 Media Plurality) published it. Its managing director Walter Asperl worked for FPÖ MP Martin Graf, while the latter was deputy speaker in the Austrian Parliament.

Chief Editor Alexander Höferl was Graf's press officer. Unzensuriert understands itself as being "committed to the truth" and as fostering media plurality. It also operates a YouTube channel that in August 2016 had around 11,000 subscribers, a Facebook page (around 47,000 likes in August 2016), and a Twitter account. It makes use of a multitude of popular social media formats, in which the FPÖ, Strache, and Hofer are very frequently the main topics. Far-right social media presences, the sensationalist press, and the FPÖ stand in a mutually beneficial relationship.

This perceived threat to Austria is characterised as consisting of social democrats, the Green Party's presidential candidate Alexander Van der Bellen, the Ministry of the Interior, the European Union (in the form of the President of the European Parliament Martin Schulz and the President of the European Commission Jean-Claude Juncker), and the Austrian government. Nationalism is not just constructed by positive self-presentation, but also by negative other-presentation: it works by saying that others have insulted the FPÖ and have characterised the party as far-right, that they divide the country and play with fire, that there were abnormalities, malpractices and illegalities in the counting of the votes in the presidential election, that foreigners try to lecture Austrians, and that there is the destruction of Austria and the centralisation of power. The net effect is the attempt to create the impression that Austria is under attack by a union of foreign powers and left-leaning politicians.

9.6.1 The First Discourse Topic: Charismatic Leadership

In the dataset, a *first discourse strategy* focused on constructing an *in-group* of Hofer and Strache supporters by mentioning positive aspects of both politicians and presenting the two politicians as *charismatic leaders*. Here are some examples:

"7 of 9 federal states have voted for Norbert Hofer. He is the President of Hearts" (No. 1098).

"I find Mr Hofer and Mr Strache very sympathetic and highly competent" (No. 2514).

"An extraordinarily sympathetic person. [...] His statements are communicated in a very comprehensive manner to people who have not studied" (No. 5948)

"Dear Mr Hofer, You can express yourself very elegantly and you are a comforting person" (No. 5988)

"You [Norbert Hofer] are a man of character and it is to wish that you become our real President of Hearts" (No. 5196)

Analysis and Interpretation

"Mr Hofer is a very impressive personality. Thank you that you stood as candidate for Austria" (No. 5493)

"I am proud of politicians like you and it makes hope that not-yet everything is lost in our country as long as we have such great, charismatic, honest politicians" (No. 5879)

These comments have in common that they emotionalise and personalise Hofer and Strache. The commenters do not assess politicians based on their ideas, but on subjective impressions of their personality and the way they present themselves. The attributes of being sympathetic, competent, comforting, charismatic, honest, and having a good character create positive emotional attachments. Hofer presents himself in public as calm, sympathetic and as for a politician relatively young. Personalisation and emotionalisation was part of his electoral campaign. The comments indicate that such emotional politics seem to work among the followers of the FPÖ. The image of Hofer as the President of Hearts goes one step further: it tries to politically utilise feelings of love. Both Strache and Hofer used these politics of love in Facebook postings (see Table 9.1: #1 and #12). Users positively reacted to this discourse topic and called Hofer their President of Hearts. This image not just expresses voters' admiration for Hofer, but also has a nationalist subtext: it expresses that Hofer loves Austria because of his scepticism of immigration and refugees.

The idealisation of Strache and Hofer is also based on the longing for strong leadership figures. The justification of the leadership ideology "is charismatic: it rests on the assertion that the Leader is endowed with qualities lacking in ordinary mortals. Superhuman qualities emanate from him and pervade the state, party, and people" (Neumann 2009, 85). FPÖ supporters in the analysed comments tended to construct Strache and Haider as superhuman leaders.

A somatisation is "the linguistic construction of social actors by synecdochisingly picking out a part or characteristic of their body" (Reisigl and Wodak 2001, 53). On the one hand, users in the dataset used gerontonyms for characterising Hofer: they argued that it is refreshing that he for a politician looks relatively young. On the other hand they also used general positive somatisations, characterising Hofer as good looking:

"One enjoys listening to him and he moreover looks so well-groomed" (No. 5948).

"Oh yes, and when someone looks good, then this is even better ... Beautiful people have it easier than ugly ones ...;-)) See Van der Bellen for example;-((" (No. 5867).

"You two [Strache and Hofer] not just have a great party, but also look damn good" (No. 5124).

The second example shows that somatisations tend to be used ideologically for defining a bodily difference between the in-group and the out-group. The characterisation of beauty comes along with a repressive definition of an outsider as ugly. In this case, Hofer is characterised as beautiful and Van der Bellen as ugly. This is a personalisation that implies that one should vote for those characterised as beautiful and not for those who are presented as being ugly. Personalisation reduces politics to simple bodily, psychological, emotional, and other subjective features of individuals. It empties out political issues from politics and results in superficial discourses focused on lifestyles, gossips, scandals, sensationalism, and celebrification.

Jörg Haider strongly advanced emotionalisation, personalisation, and subjectification as strategies of populist politics in Austria. He appeared as "fashionable, trendy, and entertaining" (Gingrich 2002, 68). This included informality, events, jokes, music; visits of discos, clubs, beer tents, and Sunday morning pints (the so-called *Frühschoppen*); the staging of Haider as sportsman; or the use of different traditional, fashionable, stylish, or casual fashion outfits for the right occasions. "Almost everyone finds popular entertainment, fun, leisure time, sports, relaxation, and dancing to be normal and sympathetic, and a politician who conspicuously and effectively emphasizes such activities looks more like a normal family man than do those others who constantly talk about complicated political, economic, and social matters. Emphasizing the average, the normal, and the popular thus is Haider's access route through mass culture to mainstream voters" (Gingrich 2002, 74).

Right-wing populists tend to make use of celebrity culture and the personalisation and commodification of politics: they "oscillate between self-presentations as *Robin Hood* (i.e. saviour of 'the man and woman in the street') and self-presentations as 'rich, famous and/ or attractive' (i.e. an 'idol'), frequently leading to a 'softer' image" (Wodak 2013, 28). Strache and Hofer in many respects copy Haider's strategies of the personalisation and commodification of politics. They continue the Haiderisation of politics (Wodak 2013).

Other comments personalised politics by arguing that Hofer and Strache were symbols of Austrian national unity:

Analysis and Interpretation

"Mr Strache, Mr Hofer. You two are Austria's guardian angels" (No. 94)

"Yes to Austria and yes to our protector Norbert Hofer. That's the only way it can work" (No. 203)

"Hofer is at least a real Austrian name. :-)" (No. 1804)

"Our president [Hofer] who stands for us Austrians" (No. 6083).

"Norbert Hofer!!!! Austria again and again" (No. 6144)

"Dear HC Strache. To be totally honest!!! You from the FPÖ are the only hope for our beloved homeland Austria!! Please continue this way and keep a very very strict eye on these traitors to the country and the people!!! I wish you all the best on your way forward!!! Comradely greetings from a convinced Austrian patriot!!!;-)" (No. 3422)

These users argue that Hofer has a German name, represents Austria, and that the FPÖ stands for the love of the homeland and patriotism. The use of linguonyms (German family name) and nationyms (nation, homeland, etc.) serves the purpose of describing Austria as a German-speaking cultural nation that should be kept free from immigrants and refugees. Hofer and Strache are seen as the symbols of Austrian nationalism. The reference to Hofer as a "real Austrian name" is an indirect reference to the fact that Van der Bellen is a Dutch name and that Alexander Van der Bellen's ancestors lived in Russia and Estonia. His parents emigrated from Estonia to Austria. The implication of such arguments is that a presidential candidate who was not born in Austria cannot represent Austrian interests and is likely to be immigration-friendly. It is the call that Austrians should prefer xenophobic, racist and nationalist politicians. "Austria again and again" is a reference to a popular chant of Austrian football fans at matches of the Austrian national team.[4] "Immer wieder Österreich" (Austria all over again) is also the title an election song that the FPÖ used in the 2015 Vienna local elections[5]. The description of Strache and Hofer as Austria's guardian angels, of Hofer as protector and as representing "us Austrians" is an expression of the ideological belief in a strong leader who protects the Austrian nation from immigrants and other perceived enemies.

9.6.2 The Second Discourse Topic: Austrian Nationalism

A *second discourse topic* was *Austrian nationalism*. It varies from the first in that it did not identify individual leaders as symbols of Austrian nationalism, but spoke about the importance of unifying the Austrian nation in more general terms.

"But also we are compelled to advocate our homeland and care for a better future" (No. 20)

"Austria must be preserved for us as Austrians" (No. 3526)

"Austria first" (No. 4010)

"Love for the home country is not a crime!!! But to watch how Austria is becoming destroyed is one ..." (No. 5318)

Karl Marx (1867) introduced the concept of commodity fetishism. He describes the commodity as "strange" (163), "metaphysical" (163), "mystical" (164), and "mysterious" (164) entity that "transcends sensuousness" (163). The commodity "stands on its head" so that odd ideas about the nature of the commodity can emerge. As a consequence, the social relations between humans appear not "as direct social relations between persons in their work, but rather as material relations between persons and social relations between things" (166). "Grotesque ideas" (163) that naturalise forms of domination and exploitation are the result. Fetishistic thought is not limited to the economy, where the commodity, class, money, capital, etc. appear as natural, but also extends to the political world.

Nationalism is a form of political fetishism that presents a constructed national community as unitary, naturally grown, necessary, superior, and mythological by focusing on stressing a common culture, history, language, ethnicity, territory, etc. It tries to deflect attention from how class relations and power inequalities shape society. Nationalism tries "through a mythology of unity and identity, to project a 'common instinctual fate' (uniform social status) between bourgeois and proletarianized groups, eliding the reality of social distinction in differentiated class societies" (Woodley 2010, 17). Nationalism is an ideology that a) "divides the world into 'us' and 'them', 'friends' and 'foes', positing a homogeneous and fixed identity on either side and stressing the characteristics that differentiate 'us' from 'them'" (Özkirimli 2010, 208), b) makes temporal claims to an authentic connection of national citizens and their common past as well as c) spatial claims to territory in the form of "the quest for a 'home'" (Özkirimli 2010, 209).

Analysis and Interpretation

In 1993, the FPÖ conducted an anti-immigration referendum that was signed by 7.35% of Austria's eligible voters. The referendum's title was "Austria first". One of its demands was to add a clause to the Austrian constitution stating that "Austria is not a country of immigration". In 2009, HC Strache published a rap song titled "Austria first" (*Österreich zuerst*). In 2011, the FPÖ titled its official party programme "Austria First" (Freiheitliche Partei Österreichs FPÖ, 2011).

Many comments in the analysed dataset propagate Austrian nationalism. They argue that Austria as a homeland should come first and that it faces the threat to be destroyed by immigrants and refugees. The implication is that Austria must be defended against foreign influences and should be a unitary cultural nation. Austrian nationalism constructs the Austrian nation as a homogeneous unit of Austrian-born German-speaking individuals who form a national bond by history, language, traditions, and culture. It sees this unity under attack by immigration, refugees and transnational institutions such as the EU. The consequence of this ideology is a call to defend the Austrian nation. Austrian national unity is just like all nationalism a pure ideological construction. The dialects spoken in Burgenland and Vorarlberg, the easternmost and westernmost Austrian federal states, are so different that citizens living in the two regions often have to resort to standard German in order to understand each other. Burgenland was part of Hungary from 1648 to 1921 and only became part of Austria in 1921. So the joint history of contemporary Austria is historically fairly recent. Gruber is the most common German family name in Austria[6]. In 2016, there were 915 entries for this surname in Vienna's telephone book[7]. Nowak is a very common Czech name. In 2016, there were 301 entries for it in Vienna's phone directory[8]. The prevalence of both German and non-German family names shows Austria's multicultural nature: many Austrian families have immigrant roots that date back to an earlier generation.

9.6.3 The Third Discourse Topic: The Friend-Enemy Scheme

In ideologies, positive self-presentation of the in-group is often accompanied by negative other-presentation of the out-group. In far-right ideology, the out-group is often presented as the enemy who threatens the in-group and should therefore be controlled, excluded or removed. The "friend-enemy distinction implied by Manichean demonization [...] plays a fundamental role in codifying enmity" (Woodley 2010, 9). Manichaeism is a highly polarising worldview that sees the world as constituted by opposing good and evil forces. A *third discourse topic* found in the analysed comments was a Manichean worldview that used the *friend-enemy scheme* for constructing a hostile out-group. Van der Bellen was presented as the leader of the out-group and as its most despicable representative.

Some referred to Van der Bellen as "Woof-Woof" (Wau-Wau):

"We want Norbert Hofer as president and not the Woof-Woof" (No. 338).

"Now the Woof-Woof is the leader of the red-green mafia" (No. 333).

Such statements are a vilification of Van der Bellen's name, playing with the fact that "bellen" means to bark in German. Linguistic animalisation and biologisation is a typical semiotic strategy in far-right ideology. The aim is to dehumanise the enemy and to present him/her as a lower type of being.

Van der Bellen was also presented as being a communist and dictator:

"But let us now be glad and happy that Mr VdB saves us as communist – because communism has of course only always done the best for the people" (No. 564)

"VdB is de-facto the 2nd [Austrian] republic's first dictator, a flawless anti-democrat!!!" (No. 1147)

"Also Stalin ignored the people – Isn't Bello also a communist, right?" (No. 1623)

"A dictator, but one would not have expected anything else from this green liar" (No. 1742)

"The Austrian Stalin" (No. 2237)

"Joseph Stalin and Tito look down to us. You have found a worthy successor in the People's Republic of Austria under the leader VdB" (No. 1846)

A common comment of FPÖ supporters on Facebook was that they described Van der Bellen as a dictator comparable to Stalin and Tito. By calling Van der Bellen a communist, such users lluded to the fact that Van der Bellen at the age of twenty had once voted for the Austrian Communist Party KPÖ. The use of strongly emotionally connoted politonyms such as "communist" and "dictator" aims at communicating political danger and presenting the enemy as dangerous.

Analysis and Interpretation

Most of these postings refer to Alexander Van der Bellen's declaration that as Austrian President he would not provide a mandate to the FPÖ to form a government if the party were the relatively strongest force after elections. On 24 May, the German public service broadcasting channel ARD interviewed Van der Bellen, who said in the news programme *Tagesthemen*: "My concerns are not of a personal nature. I have always stressed this fact. They are a matter of European politics because the FPÖ so to speak plays in various suggestions with fire. It flirts with the re-nationalisation of the European Union"[9]. In another interview, Van der Bellen also commented on this issue: "We are not in favour of the world's LePens governing us"[10]. In Van der Bellen's view, the FPÖ spreads nationalism and xenophobia. His fear is that it has an anti-democratic agenda. This is the reason why he argues against a FPÖ mandate to form the Austrian government. Strache in one of his Facebook postings (see Table 9.1: #5) inverted this logic and asked: "Who splits the country and plays with fire?". He thereby implied that not the FPÖ, but Van der Bellen advanced a dangerous form of politics.

Article 70 of the Austrian Federal Constitution regulates that the "Chancellor and on his/her recommendation the other members of the federal government are appointed by the President"[11]. It does not provide regulations, to which party leader the President gives the mandate to form a government. That the Austrian President chooses not to provide such a mandate to the strongest party after election because s/he is afraid there are anti-democratic tendencies in this party is within the democratic merit of the Austrian constitution. It is by no means anti-democratic or dictatorial. To argue that Van der Bellen is anti-democratic ideologically inverts and distorts political reality.

Other commenters used the somatisation of Van der Bellen as dirty and ill for characterising him:

"Who splits the country and plays with fire? A good question that can be answered quickly: The grotty and geriatric '68 generation" (No. 1886).

"The old, dishevelled man" (No. 1991).

"This train station vagabond should go and shit himself" (No. 2188).

"Unshaved, shabby trench tramp" (No. 2189).

"Allegedly the old one has cancer from smoking" (No. 6356).

In 2016, Van der Bellen was 72 years old and Norbert Hofer 45. Descriptions of Van der Bellen as old, shabby, unshaved, ill, dishevelled, or grotty aim at setting up a dichotomy that aims at delegitimising Van der Bellen and legitimising Hofer by references to bodily appearance and health. Right-wing ideology often codes the Us/Them distinction inherent in the friend-enemy scheme as a series of dualisms: on the one side we find something on the inside that is presented as modern, popular, entertaining, colourful, young, attractive, ordinary, good-looking, or healthy; on the other side, the opposition is presented as outdated, timid, boring, unappealing, old, unattractive, withdrawn, dirty, or ill.

Other enemies mentioned in comments were the European Union, mass media like the Austrian Broadcasting Corporation, social democrats, Greens, migrants, and Islam:

> "[EU Commission President] Juncker must go!!! The Brussels terrorists" (No. 3640)

> "Hopefully this pigsty EU decays soon!" (No. 3659)

> "The lying press says the FPÖ is the problem and not mass immigration, criminality, Islamisation, the EU, the ECB [European Central Bank], bureaucratisation, the loss of prosperity, etc. That's also how the GDR [German Democratic Republic] ended, and the red-green-black [= alliance of Social Democrats-Greens-Conservatives] dictatorship will end exactly the same way!" (No. 4145)

> "The aggressive ORF moderator [Lou Lorenz-Dittlbacher, who conducted a critical TV interview with Strache] is annoying – just like the whole contaminated ORF! [Austrian Broadcasting Corporation = Austria's public service broadcaster] Somehow understandable, they all fear for their jobs. If the FPÖ had to decide on that: No compulsory licence fees any longer → No ORF any longer. Sometime it will happen" (No. 4279).

Jean-Claude Juncker congratulated Van der Bellen on his (preliminary) victory. The president of the European Parliament, Martin Schulz, said that this preliminary win was a "defeat of Eurosceptics"[12]. In the analysed dataset, FPÖ supporters reacted in a very Manichean and defensive manner to any criticism of Hofer, Strache, or the FPÖ. They presented themselves as victims of a conspiracy instigated by a union of green, social democratic and conservative politicians, the media, the EU, immigrants and refugees, communists, Freemasonry, etc. They perceive themselves and the FPÖ to be under constant attack and construct themselves as victims, which disregards that it is the FPÖ and its followers who tend to construct scapegoats, especially migrants, refugees and Islam. The perceived association of enemies is verbally attacked by the use of on the one hand strong political categories (terrorism, dictatorship, etc.) and on the other hand biologistic language (pigsty, contamination, etc.).

Analysis and Interpretation

It is not a surprise that one of the identified enemies is the EU. The FPÖ already under Jörg Haider turned into a Eurosceptic party. Haider for example wrote in 1993: "If this Europe is not to be a cultural and linguistic pabulum coming from the Brussels bureaucrats' meat chopper, then the development into a Europe of peoples and ethnic groups must be enabled" (cited in: Bailer-Galanda and Neugebauer 1997, 192), In 1996, he said: "But our idea of Europe is not a pabulum in Brussels, but our idea is a Europe of home countries" (cited in: Bailer-Galanda and Neugebauer 1997, 193). The FPÖ's (2011) Party Programme is committed to a "Europe of free peoples and fatherlands". It spells out that the EU is questioned because it as seen as a danger to nationalism. "We are committed to a Europe of peoples and autochthonous groups of people which have developed through history, and firmly reject any artificial synchronisation of the diverse European languages and cultures by means of forced multiculturalism, globalisation and mass immigration. Europe shall not be reduced to a political project of the European Union" (Freiheitliche Partei Österreichs FPÖ, 2011). Austrian nationalism that puts "Austria first" was also evident in the analysed comments. Euroscepticism was very present. Hofer argues for an Austrian referendum on leaving the EU (Öxit, Auxit) in case of "Turkey joining – but also if the EU becomes more centralistic"[13].

9.6.4 The Fourth Discourse Topic: New Racism

A *fourth discourse topic* found in the dataset was *new racism and xenophobia*. It is closely related to the friend-enemy scheme. Immigrants and refugees were seen as the main threat to the Austrian nation.

> "For the FPÖ, the Austrian to whom this country belongs first, also when refugees are on the way the Austrian MUST come first!" (No. 3964)

> "The SPÖ and its friends have destroyed, estranged and islamised our country!" (No. 4144)

> "Please do something before Islam swamps us!!!!!!!!" (No. 119)

> "They [those not born in Austria] do not have our roots, not our religion" (No. 205)

> "Austria must first look for its own citizens, in respect to jobs, that they are motivated and have a meaningful life. Only then can we think of asylum seekers!!" (No. 6457)

> "What are the SPÖ [Social Democratic Party of Austria] and the Greens? In

my view they are hostile towards native citizens [inländerfeindlich] ....
Because they allow the mass immigration of criminals .... Rapists, killers etc ...
Where will this end?" (No. 584)

"I do not want that we in Austria give shelter to even more 'refugees' that
are none, on a mandatory basis every year, are you still normal at all? Who
wants that, not me and also not 50%!" (No. 2585)

"I feel sorry for people who for example live in Traiskirchen [Austrian town
with the country's largest refugee camp] or parents in Vienna, Salzburg or
Linz, whose children commute to school per train, subway or bus day by day.
They live in the daily fear whether their children get home safely. [...] For me,
our own country is important, the future as well as safeguards for my children
[...] I am a realist and patriot who loves his country and its population!!!"
(No. 5307).

"The country needs other politicians. Austrians first. These politics suck.
Foreigners receive more than we taxpayers" (No. 64)

"We do not need even more asylum seekers in our beautiful Austria because
we have enough of our own people who are in need of help. In my opinion
one first and foremost has to do something for us Austrians before we always
throw money at others" (No. 5916).

Whereas nationalism defines an illusionary inside of a national community, new racism
is a repressive politics that defines and struggles against the perceived outside and
makes use of racialising ideological practices for defending the inside/outside differentiation with violent means. The defence of boundaries takes not just place outside, but
also inside a nation state. "Racism is constantly emerging out of nationalism, not only
towards the exterior but towards the interior" (Balibar and Wallerstein 1991, 53). New
racism operates "by constructing impassable symbolic boundaries between racially
constituted categories, and its typically binary system of representation constantly
marks and attempts to fix and naturalize the difference between belongingness and
otherness" (Hall 1989/1996, 445). The out-group is often presented in the form of
stereotypes that reduce, essentialise, naturalise, and fix the power differences between the in- and the out-group (Hall 1997, 258). New racism justifies the exploitation,
exclusion, domination, or annihilation of an out-group. One can draw a "distinction
between a racism of extermination or elimination (an 'exclusive' racism) and a racism
of oppression or exploitation (an 'inclusive' racism)" (Balibar and Wallerstein 1991, 39).

The new racism present in the cited comments makes use of a number of classical stereo-types that can be summarised in the following statements (see Reisigl and Wodak 2001, 55):

- Cultural stereotypes: "There are already too many foreigners here and more immigrants and refugees in the country overforeignise our culture and society. Foreigners have a different culture, religion and lifestyle that does not belong into our country";
- Economic stereotypes: "Foreigners take away Austrians' jobs and dump wages";
- Criminal stereotypes: "Foreigners are criminals, violent and aggressive";
- Welfare stereotypes: "Foreigners cost lots of money that we need for our own people. They are socio-parasites who get more out of the welfare and tax system than they pay in";
- Gender stereotypes: "Foreigners are sexists and rapists. They have an inherently repressive patriarchal attitude towards women".

The new racism immanent in the discussed statements constructs Austrians as an in-group who are under attack by foreigners as an out-group who come to Austria as immigrants and refugees. It aims at defending a pure Austrian nation from foreign influences and implicitly argues that only Austrian-born, white, German-speaking Roman-Catholics should be allowed to live in the country. Foreigners are presented as an alien social and cultural out-group that threatens Austria's culture (language, customs, habits, religion, lifestyle), economy (jobs, wages), and the social system (crime and violence, welfare, gender relations). The statements imply an exclusive new racism, i.e. that foreigners should have to leave the country.

9.6.5 The Fifth Discourse Topic: Violence

The *fifth discourse topic* present in the dataset is a radicalisation of the friend/enemy-scheme: the threat or wish to use *violence against the perceived enemies*.

"Only a rebellion of patriots would now help and EVERYONE JOINS IN!" (No. 3163)

"If the EU violently imposes penalties on differing opinions, then this is clearly dictatorship and that's something the majority will not accept. There will then be uprisings and demonstrations with more or less outbursts of violence" (No. 167).

"The time will come where they all fall into the pit … AND WE WILL THEN FILL UP THE PIT!!!!!" (No. 5862)

[Users about the Austrian writer Robert Menasse's voiced opinion that Strache is a Nazi and a local SPÖ-politician's support for Menasse's statement]:

"Such people should be immediately imprisoned" (No. 894)

"I would immediately revoke the Austrian citizenship of SPÖ-local party secretary Reinhard Kadlec and Mr Robert Menasse" (No. 656)

"They all together belong into an internment camp because they are a danger to all citizens" (No. 742)

"For this statement, he deserves to have his face smashed in" (No. 571)

"Aha, this pinko should be blown away" (No. 1426)

[About Alexander Van der Bellen]:

"If the FPÖ would indeed achieve the majority of the votes and Bello carries out this threat, then he should be chased out of office with a wet shred" (No. 1913)

"My partner is already a bit afraid that I throw the next thing into the direction of the TV when I see VdB! I must really restrain myself because this morning I answered to the greetings of a Romanian who lives in my house by saying 'Go and shit yourself' …" (No. 3880)

"And then people wonder if the cold lust to kill comes up in a decent Hofer-voter …" (No. 1945)

[About the journalist Lou Lorenz-Dittlbacher, who conducted a critical interview with Strache]:

"I would have landed the OBNOXIOUS Dittlbacher one in the face. She is even more disgusting than Thurnher [=another ORF television journalist]" (No. 4571)

Some of the comments demanded demonstrations, a rebellion and uprisings in the light of Van der Bellen's preliminary victory in the May 2016 Austrian presidential election. Civil society protests are mostly peaceful and it is politically dangerous to frame them in the context of violence. There were, however, also comments that explicitly demanded demonstrations with "outbursts of violence". Far-right ideology tends to argue for a strong state that enforces law-and-order politics. Some commenters demanded a tota-litarian state that limits freedom of speech by imprisoning, interning and stripping citizenship rights from political opponents of the FPÖ. There were calls to chase Van der Bellen out of office and to kill him. There were calls for physical violence against politicians, writers and journalists. Acts of violence mentioned as means that should be directed at identified enemies included hitting, shooting, and general killing.

Such comments display the inherent violent potentials of far-right ideology. The ideological definition of a unitary nation as in-group and enemy out-groups polarises political relations. Stereotypes aim at ideologically dehumanising the out-groups and at fostering the in-group's aggression and hatred towards the constructed enemies. Right-wing extremism tends to use a "violent linguistic rhetoric", advance the "damaging of the political opponent", and has an inherent "linguistic latency of aggression and defamation" (Holzer 1993, 65). Constant far-right demagoguery against humanists, immigrants, refugees, socialists, etc. can lower the inhibition threshold of citizens who are prone to such ideology and can condition that they voice violent threats against perceived enemies or engage in physical attacks, anonymous online or offline threats, etc.

The German legal theorist Carl Schmitt, who was associated with Nazism, introduced the friend/enemy scheme in his book *The Concept of the Political.* "The specific political distinction to which political actions and motives can be reduced is that between friend and enemy" (Schmitt 1932/1996, 26). War and physical killing are for Schmitt inherent aspects of the very concept of the enemy: "For to the enemy concept belongs the ever present possibility of combat. [...] The friend, enemy, and combat concepts receive their real meaning precisely because they refer to the real possibility of physical killing. War follows from enmity. War is the existential negation of the enemy. It is the most extreme consequence of enmity" (32–33).

The friend/enemy scheme was also at the heart of Nazi fascism. It conceived Germans as a superior race that needs to form a nation and rid itself of what it considered to be its enemies, especially Jews, socialists, the working class movements, and communists. Hitler called for the annihilation of Nazism's enemies. "If the international Jewish financiers in and outside Europe should succeed in plunging the nations once more into a world war, then the result will not be the bolshevization of the earth, and thus the victory of Jewry, but the annihilation of the Jewish race in Europe, for the time when the non-Jewish nations had no propaganda is at an end" (Hitler 1939). A fascist society based on mass extermination is the most devastating potential consequence of nationalism and fascism. Far-right ideology does not see social problems as the result of structural power inequalities and contradictions of society, but it personalises them and inscribes them biologically or/and culturally into individuals and groups. It uses specific naturalised and essentialised characteristics that are assigned to belong to what is conceived of as enemy groups. Fetishistic thought can lead to violence and in the final instance to fascism, Nazism, and politics of mass annihilation.

9.7 Conclusion

The historian Willibald Holzer (1993) lists the following characteristics of right-wing extremism:

- Stress of the existence and importance of a national community;
- Exclusion of the foreign; Social Darwinism; ethnocentrism; ethnic separatism;
- Authoritarianism, anti-pluralism, opposition to democracy;
- Anti-socialism, focus on competition and performance;
- Authoritarian state;
- Scapegoating;
- Orientation on traditions; apologetic concept of history;
- A political style that features demagogy and acceptance of violence.

The core of right-wing extremism can be summarised as consisting in the principles of (1) authoritarian leadership, (2) nationalism, (3) the friend/enemy scheme, and (4) the combination of patriarch and militarism (Fuchs 2018). This chapter analysed how voters of Norbert Hofer expressed their support on Facebook. The analysis showed that all key elements of right-wing extremism could be found in online comments.

The leadership principle online was expressed as admiration for Hofer and Strache. Both were seen as charismatic leaders, to whom voters have an emotional relationship. Supporters projected Austrian nationalism into the image of superhuman leaders. Hofer was described as sympathetic, young, good-looking, which reduced politics to personalisation. Austrian nationalism online was expressed by arguments that claimed that a unitary Austrian nation consisting of a homogeneous Austrian-born linguistic and cultural community exists that is under threat by immigration, refugees, socialists, communists, Greens, critical media and transnational institutions such as the EU.

The friend/enemy scheme online could be found in the analysed dataset in the form of Manichean views of and hatred spread against the Green party presidential candidate Alexander Van der Bellen, journalists, the European Union, the Austrian Broadcasting Corporation ORF, migrants, refugees, Islam, social democrats and the Green party. Van der Bellen was characterised as dictator, communist, animal, dirty, ill, ugly, old, dishevelled, and grotty. Immigrants and refugees were seen as the main threat to the Austrian nation. Users made use of cultural, economic, criminal, and gender stereotypes. Online militarism was present in the form of violent threats to and death wishes for politicians such as Alexander Van der Bellen, writers, and journalists.

The overall result of the analysis is that right-wing extremist ideology was very significantly observable in the comments made on the Facebook pages of the leading FPÖ politicians Heinz-Christian Strache and Norbert Hofer. Online leadership ideology, online nationalism, new racism online and online xenophobia, the friend/enemy scheme online, and online militarism constitute important elements of right-wing extremism online. On the one hand, demagogues exercise far-right ideology "from above". On the other hand such ideology can only persist through hegemony "from below". Social media is an important platform that fosters right-wing extremist responses from below to far-right ideology from above. As a result of violence propagated online, Alexander Van der Bellen was after the May 2016 presidential election put under special police protection. One Facebook posting had published his private address and called for terrorist attacks against him. Let us have a look at some examples of online violence in the context of the Austrian presidential election:

1) Vienna will fall first. And then we'll see further;
2) The chancellery and the Hofburg [office of the Austrian president] ought to be stormed, and the parliament be burnt down;
3) Those who voted for van der Belln ought to be burnt on the stake;
4) The Glock 17 [a type of pistol] is loaded and ready to fire;
5) It will surely be a bombastic atmosphere;
6) The weapon is unpacked!;
7) Onto the streets in order to run riot;
8) What a shame. One really should take to the streets and bring everything to a halt.

Examples of online violence in the context of the 2016 Austrian presidential election (translated from German to English), source: http://www.oe24.at/oesterreich/politik/Mord-Drohung-gegen-Van-der-Bellen/237125974

Answers to the question of how to react to right-wing extremism online are not straightforward. Calls for violence should of course always be reported to the police. At the same time, the Internet will always provide possibilities for anonymity, so there will always be loopholes for militant online fascism. A small number of Van der Bellen supporters posted criticism of far-right ideology on Strache and Hofer's Facebook pages. Two example comments:

> The FPÖ is a "nationalist, xenophobic party under the disguise of love for the homeland" (No. 5619).

> "How violent are you actually? This is simply just brutal! [...] And express your opinions without death threats. I have heard that now even the Cobra [special police unit] must protect Van der Bellen because someone made death threats. You create fear. How do you think that he now feels? Nobody deserves this" (No. 5847)

Hofer and Strache supporters largely ignored such appeals and arguments. They did not react to them. In some cases, they voiced threats against Van der Bellen supporters:

> "What if once something happens to you, when you are the centre of an act of violence, will you then wake up?" (No. 4060)

The crisis of capitalism has resulted in an intensification and extension of right-wing extremism that promises simple xenophobic and new racist solutions to social problems. The intensification of online right-wing extremism is a manifestation of this tendency. There are no easy fixes to this unsettling reality. Only profound social, political, socio-economic, educational, and cultural responses can ground an effective form of contemporary anti-fascism. Slavoj Žižek (2016, 100) argues that what is needed is "a positive universal project shared by all participants", a project for the commons that makes different suffering groups see that they "are parts of one and the same universal struggle" (101). Such a project is commonly called "socialism". Given the inherent connection of capitalism, nationalism and new racism, a fundamental change of power relations, the economy and politics is needed in order to avoid the possibility of a "fascism-producing crisis" (Eley 2015, 112).

Conclusion

The reasons for the rise of the FPÖ in Austria are complex and manifold. They include an incomplete Denazification process, Austrian nationalism, Austrian neoliberalism, the role of right-wing media, the institutional containment of class struggle, weakness of the political Left, a low level of general education, and the patronage system (see Fuchs 2016a for a detailed discussion). The FPÖ's electoral successes are an indication that the "'spectre which is haunting Europe', some 60 years after the end of the Third Reich and its national-socialist ideology, is the 'spectre of radical right-wing populism'" (Wodak 2013, 24). One must certainly add that the spectre of new racism, new nationalism, and the New Right is articulated with capitalist development and class structures – destructive forces that already Marx and Engels criticised when publishing the *Communist Manifesto* in 1848. Right-wing populism combines social issues with nationalism and new racism and pretends to fill the vacuum that has been created by social democracy's move towards embracing neoliberalism and shifting itself towards the right in the political spectrum.

New right populism is "the price the Left pays for renouncing any radical political project, and accepting market capitalism as 'the only game in town'" (Žižek 2000/2006, 41). "The populist Right moves to occupy the terrain evacuated by the Left, as the only 'serious' political force that still employs an anti-capitalist rhetoric – even if thickly coated with a nationalist/racist/religious veneer" (Žižek 2000/2006, 33–34). The only feasible challenge to right-wing populism solution is the re-invention of the Left and the creation of a new socialism for the 21st century. If such a project fails, then we may very well be on the path towards a new fascism in Europe and throughout the world. We are today again at the crossroads that Rosa Luxemburg, citing Friedrich Engels, identified exactly 100 years ago: "Bourgeois society stands at the crossroads, either transition to socialism or regression into barbarism" (Luxemburg 1916, 388).

Notes

1 "Im Dritten Reich haben sie ordentliche Beschäftigungspolitik gemacht. was nicht einmal Ihre Regierung in Wien zusammenbringt" (Protokoll der Sitzung des Kärntner Landtags, June 13, 1991).
2 Original: "Ich habe gesagt, dass ich die Regierung entlasse, wenn die Regierung Gesetze bricht, die Verfassung bricht oder immer wieder Maßnahmen setzt, die dem Land schaden. Dass dann, um Schaden abzuwenden vom Land, der letzte Schritt, die Ultimo Ratio, sein kann, die Regierung zu entlassen".
3 Original: "Das würde ja heißen, die Bundesregierung handelt auf Anordnung des Bundespräsidenten. Es ist aber genau umgekehrt: Der Bundespräsident hat auf Vorschläge der Bundesregierung zu achten. Falls Sie diesen Stil tatsächlich, falls Sie gewählt werden sollten, [...] einschlagen sollten, sind wir auf dem Weg in eine autoritäre Republik"
4 See: https://www.youtube.com/watch?v=wSg6Okplacs&feature=youtu.be, accessed on July 5, 2016.
5 See: https://www.youtube.com/watch?v=xzyUuRXRQfo, accessed on July 5, 2016.
6 http://www.telefonabc.at/haeufigste-nachnamen.aspx, accessed on June 8, 2016.
7 http://www.herold.at/telefonbuch, accessed on June 8, 2016.
8 http://www.herold.at/telefonbuch, accessed on June 8, 2016.

9 "Meine Bedenken sind nicht persönlicher Art, das habe ich immer betont, sondern euro-
papolitischer Art vor allem, weil die FPÖ in verschiedenen Andeutungen sozusagen mit dem
Feuer spielt, mit der Renationalisierung der Europäischen Union liebäugelt" (ARD Tagesthemen,
May 24, 2016).

10 "Wir sind doch nicht dafür, dass die Le Pens dieser Welt uns regieren" (*Die Presse*, May
18, 2016).

11 Bundes-Verfassungsgesetz: German version, accessed on https://www.ris.bka.gv.at (July
6, 2016).

12 Schulz-Kern-Treffen: Hofburg-Ergebnis "Niederlage für Euro-Skeptiker". *Kronen Zeitung*,
May 27, 2016.

13 http://www.ots.at/presseaussendung/OTS_20160702_OTS0027/hofer-in-oesterreich-eu-
austrittsreferendum-wenn-eu-zentralistischer-wird, accessed on July 6, 2016.

References

Adorno, Theodor W. 1981. *Prisms*. Cambridge, MA: MIT Press.

Adorno, Theodor W. 1973. *Studien zum autoritären Charakter*. Frankfurt am Main: Suhrkamp.

Adorno, Theodor W. 1972. *Soziologische Schriften I*. Frankfurt am Main: Suhrkamp.

Adorno, Theodor W. 1971. *Erziehung zur Mündigkeit*. Frankfurt am Main: Suhrkamp.

Adorno, Theodor W. 1962. "Aberglaube aus zweiter Hand." In *Soziologische Schriften I*, 146–76.
Frankfurt am Main: Suhrkamp.

Adorno, Theodor W. 1956. "The Stars Down to Earth." In *Soziologische Schriften II.2*, 7–120.
Frankfurt am Main: Suhrkamp.

Adorno, Theodor W. 1955. "Schuld und Abwehr: Eine qualitative Analyse zum
Gruppenexperiment." In *Soziologische Schriften II.2*, 121–324. Frankfurt am Main: Suhrkamp.

Adorno, Theodor W. 1954. "Ideology." In *Aspects of Sociology*, edited by Frankfurt Institute for
Social Research, 182–205. Boston: Beacon Press.

Adorno, Theodor W. 1951. *Minima Moralia*. Frankfurt am Main: Suhrkamp.

Ajanovic, Edma, Stefanie Mayer and Birgit Sauer. 2016. "Spaces of Right-Wing Populism and
Anti Muslim Racism in Austria." *Czech Journal of Political Science* 23 (2): 131–48.

Ajanovic, Edma, Stefanie Mayer and Birgit Sauer. 2015. "Umkämpfte Räume. Antipluralismus in
rechtsextremen Diskursen in Österreich." *Austrian Journal of Political Science* 44 (2): 75–85.

Althusser, Louis. 2005. *For Marx*. London: Verso.

Bailer-Galanda, Brigitte and Wolfgang Neugebauer. 1997. *Haider und die Freiheitlichen in
Österreich*. Berlin: Elefanten Press.

Balibar, Étienne and Immanuel Wallerstein. 1991. *Race, Nation, Class*. London: Verso.

Banks, Marcus and Andre Gingrich. 2006. "Introduction: Neo-Nationalism in Europe and
Beyond." In *Neo-Nationalism in Europe & Beyond*, edited by Andre Gingrich and Marcus
Banks, 1–26. New York: Berghahn.

Boellstorff, Tom, Bonnie Nardi, Celia Pearace and T.L. Taylor. 2012. *Ethnography and Virtual Worlds: A Handbook of Methods.* Princeton, NJ: Princeton University Press.

British Psychological Society (BPS). 2013. *Ethics Guidelines for Internet-Mediated Research.* Leicester: BPS.

British Psychological Society (BPS). 2009. *Code of Ethics and Conduct.* Leicester: BPS.

Eagleton, Terry. 1991. *Ideology: An Introduction.* London: Verso.

Eley, Geoff. 2015. "Fascism Then and Now." *Socialist Register* 52: 91–117.

Fairclough, Norman. 2010. *Critical Discourse Analysis. The Critical Study of Language.* Harlow: Pearson Education.

Freiheitliche Partei Österreichs (FPÖ). 2011. *Party Programme.* English version. https://www.fpoe.at/fileadmin/user_upload/www.fpoe.at/dokumente/2015/2011_graz_parteiprogramm_englisch_web.pdf (accessed on June5, 2016).

Fuchs, Christian. 2018. *Digital Demagogue: Authoritarian Capitalism in the Age of Trump and Twitter.* London: Pluto Press.

Fuchs, Christian. 2016a. Capitalism Today: The Austrian Presidential Election and the State of the Right and Left in Europe. *LSE Eurocrisis in the Press-blog.* June 16, 2016. http://blogs.lse.ac.uk/eurocrisispress/2016/06/16/capitalism-today-the-austrian-presidential-election-and-the-state-of-the-right-and-the-left-in-europe/.

Fuchs, Christian. 2016b. *Critical Theory of Communication: New Readings of Lukács, Adorno, Marcuse, Honneth and Habermas in the Age of the Internet.* London: University of Westminster Press.

Fuchs, Christian. 2016c. *Reading Marx in the Information Age: A Media and Communication Studies Perspective on "Capital Volume 1".* New York: Routledge.

Fuchs, Christian. 2015. *Culture and Economy in the Age of Social Media.* New York: Routledge.

Gingrich, Andre. 2006. "Nation, Status and Gender in Trouble? Exploring Some Contexts and Characteristics of Neo-Nationalism in Europe." In *Neo-Nationalism in Europe & Beyond,* edited by Andre Gingrich and Marcus Banks, 29–49. New York: Berghahn.

Gingrich, Andre. 2002. "A Man for all Seasons. An Anthropological Perspective on Public Representation and Cultural Politics of the Austrian Freedom Party." In *The Haider Phenomenon in Austria,* edited by Ruth Wodak and Anton Pelinka, 67–91. New Brunswick, NJ: Transaction.

Gramsci, Antonio. 1988. "The Antonio Gramsci Reader." In *Selected Writings 1916–1935,* edited by David Forgacs. London: Lawrence and Wishart.

Hall, Stuart, ed. 1997. *Representation.* London: Sage.

Hall, Stuart. 1993. "Culture, Community, Nation." *Cultural Studies* 7 (3): 349–63.

Hall, Stuart. 1989/1996. "New Ethnicities." In *Stuart Hall: Critical Dialogues in Cultural Studies,* edited by David Morley and Kuan-Hsing Chen, 441–9. London: Routledge.

Hall, Stuart. 1986/1996. "The Problem of Ideology: Marxism without Guarantees." In *Stuart Hall: Critical Dialogues in Cultural Studies,* edited by David Morley and Juan-Hsing Chen, 25–46. London: Routledge.

Hall, Stuart. 1982. "The Rediscovery of "Ideology": Return of the Repressed in Media Studies." In *Culture, Society and the Media*, edited by Michael Gurevitch, Tony Bennett, James Curran and Janet Woollacott, 56–90. London: Methuen.

Hewson, Claire, Carl Vogel and Dianna Laurent. 2016. *Internet Research Methods*. London: Sage. 2nd edition.

Hitler, Adolf. 1939. *Speech Before the German Reichstag*. January 30, 1939. https://archive.org/details/SpeechOfJan.301939.

Hobsbawm, Eric. 1992. *Nations and Nationalism Since 1780: Programme, Myth, Reality*. Cambridge: Cambridge University Press. 2nd edition.

Holzer, Willibald I. 1993. "Rechtsextremismus – Konturen, Definitionsmerkmale und Erklärungsansätze." In *Handbuch des österreichischen Rechtsextremismus*, edited by Dokumentationsarchiv des österreichischen Widerstandes, 11–96. Vienna: Deuticke. 2nd edition.

Horkheimer, Max. 1972. *Sozialphilosophische Studien*. Frankfurt am Main: Fischer.

Horkheimer, Max and Theodor W. Adorno. 2002. *Dialectic of Enlightenment*. Stanford, CA: Stanford University Press.

Krzyżanowski, Michał. 2013. "From Anti-Immigration and Nationalist Revisionism to Islamophobia: Continuities and Shifts in Recent Discourses and Patters of Political Communication of the Freedom Party of Austria (FPÖ)." In *Right-Wing Populism in Europe: Politics and Discourse*, edited by Ruth Wodak, Majid KhosraviNik and Brigitte Mral, 135–48. London: Bloomsbury Academic.

Lukács, Georg. 1986. *Werke. Band 14: Zur Ontologie des gesellschaftlichen Seins. 2. Halbband*. Darmstadt: Luchterhand.

Luxemburg, Rosa. 1916. "The Junius Pamphlet." In *Rosa Luxemburg Speaks*, 371–477. New York: Pathfinder.

Luxemburg, Rosa. 1976. *The National Question: Selected Writings*. New York: Monthly Review Press.

Marx, Karl. 1867. *Capital: A Critique of Political Economy. Volume 1*. London: Penguin.

Marx, Karl and Friedrich Engels. 1845. *The German Ideology*. Amherst, NY: Prometheus Books.

Neumann, Franz. 2009 [1944]. *Behemoth: The Structure and Practice of National Socialism, 1933–1944*. Chicago, IL: Ivan R. Dee.

Özkirimli, Umut. 2010. *Theories of Nationalism: A Critical Introduction*. Basingstoke: Palgrave Macmillan. 2nd edition.

Pelinka, Peter. 2002. "The FPÖ in the European Context." In *The Haider Phenomenon in Austria*, edited by Ruth Wodak and Anton Pelinka, 213–29. New Brunswick, NJ: Transaction.

Potter, Jonathan and Margaret Wetherell. 1988. *Discourse and Social Psychology. Beyond Attitudes and Behaviour*. London: Sage.

Rehmann, Jan. 2013. *Theories of Ideology*. Leiden: Brill.

Reisigl, Martin and Ruth Wodak. 2009. "The Discourse-Historical Approach." In *Methods of Critical Discourse Analysis*, edited by Ruth Wodak and Michael Meyer, 87–121. London: Sage.

References

Reisigl, Martin and Ruth Wodak. 2001. "Discourse and Discrimination." *Rhetorics of Racism and Antisemitism*. London: Routledge.

Salmons, Janet. 2016. *Doing Qualitative Research Online*. London: Sage.

Schiedel, Heribert. 2007. *Der rechte Rand: Extremistische Gesinnungen in unserer Gesellschaft*. Wien: Edition Steinbauer.

Schmitt, Carl. 1932/1996. *The Concept of the Political*. Chicago, IL: University of Chicago Press.

SORA. 2016. *Wahlanalyse Stichwahl Bundespräsidentschaft 2016*. http://www.sora.at/fileadmin/ downloads/wahlen/2016_BP-Stichwahl_Wahlanalyse.pdf (accessed on June7, 2016).

SORA. 2013. *Wahlanalyse Nationalratswahl 2013*. http://www.strategieanalysen.at/bg/isa_ sora_wahlanalyse_nrw_2013.pdf (accessed on June6, 2016).

Taguieff, Pierre-André. 2001. *The Force of Prejudice. On Racism and its Doubles*. Minneaplois, MN: University of Minnesota Press.

van Dijk, Teun. 2011. "Discourse and Ideology." In *Discourse Studies. A Multidisciplinary Introduction*, edited by Teun van Dijk, 379–407. London: Sage.

van Dijk, Teun. 1998. *Ideology. A Multidisciplinary Approach*. London: Sage.

van Dijk, Teun. 1987. *Communicating Racism. Ethnic Prejudice in Thought and Talk*. Newbury Park, CA: Sage.

Wodak, Ruth. 2013. ""Anything Goes!" – The Haiderization of Europe." In *Right-Wing Populism in Europe: Politics and Discourse*, edited by Ruth Wodak, Majid KhosraviNik, and Brigitte Mral, 23–37. London: Bloomsbury Academic.

Wodak, Ruth. 2009. *The Disourse of Politics in Action*. Basingstoke: Palgrave Macmillan.

Wodak, Ruth. 2002. "Discourse and Politics: The Rhetoric of Exclusion." In *The Haider Phenomenon in Austria*, edited by Ruth Wodak and Anton Pelinka, 33–60. New Brunswick, NJ: Transaction.

Woodley, Daniel. 2010. *Fascism and Political Theory: Critical Perspectives on Fascist Ideology*. Abingdon: Routledge.

Žižek, Slavoj. 2016. *Against the Double Blackmail. Refugees, Rerror and Other Troubles with the Neighbours*. London: Allen Lane.

Žižek, Slavoj. 2000/2006. "Why we all Love to Hate Haider." In *The Universal Exception*, 33–41. London: Continuum.

Žižek, Slavoj, ed. 1994. *Mapping Ideology*. London: Verso.

Appendix: Norbert Hofer's and Heinz-Christian Strache's Postings on Facebook

TABLE 9.1 An overview of the Facebook postings by H.C. Strache and Norbert Hofer that formed the basis of the analysis

ID	Source	Date of posting	Text (translated from German)
1	Strache's Facebook page	30 May 2016	"We are committed to our homeland Austria and its people! We continue reliably and consequently on our path! Thank you for your huge support!"
2	Strache's Facebook page	30 May 2016	"Norbert Hofer is and remains the President of Hearts! [Image text: President of Hearts]"
3	Strache's Facebook page	29 May 2016	"That's just primitive and shabby! [Link to an online article titled "SPÖ local party secretary derails completely: Voters of Hofer are 'Nazis, fascists, idiots'"]"
4	Strache's Facebook page	29 May 2016	"Such rants are simply primitive, disgraceful and outrageous! Our FPÖ vice-mayor Michael Schnedlitz (image) has uncovered of a high SPÖ-functionary in Wiener Neustadt [Link to an online article titled "SPÖ politician designates Hofer as a Nazi"]"
5	Strache's Facebook page	28 May 2016	"Who splits the country and plays with fire? [Link to an online article titled "Alexander Van der Bellen plays with fire"]"
6	Strache's Facebook page	28 May 2016	"Miraculous augmentation of the postal voting cards by 60.000! Chief election administrator MA Stein (from the Federal Ministry of the Interior) comes under significant pressure!" "Besides the five districts, in which the votes were counted illegally without election assessors (the Minister of the Interior filed charges), there was a fabulous turnout of 146% in Waidhofen/Ybbs, one double vote thanks to an postal voting card (uncovered by a video-blogger), and many other hints and inconsistencies!" "Furthermore there was the questionable projection by the Federal Ministry of the Interior that showed 56.5% for Norbert Hofer with 65% of ballots counted. Computers usually do not err!"

(Continued)

TABLE 9.1 (Cont.)

ID	Source	Date of posting	Text (translated from German)
			"The Federal Ministry of the Interior had published the result of the postal votes online at the evening of election Sunday before the postal votes were counted on Monday after 9 o'clock. The information was later deleted and dismissed as error and malfunction! Computers usually do not make mistakes, only the people who control and operate them do!!!"
			"Mr Stein spoke in a ZIB2-interview [evening news programme on the public service broadcasting channel ORF 2] of 740,000 postal votes (a projectionist from his ministry spoke of exactly 738,055) that then miraculously and inexplicably further increased significantly (even by about 60,000!)."
			"There was an internationally completely unique, questionably high amount of invalid ballots among the postal voting cards! And much more!"
			"Full transparency, control and elucidation are now the order of the day! It is now a question of democracy and the rule of law! And a question of citizens' trust in this rule of law and its basic democratic rules!"
7	Strache's Facebook page	27 May 2016	"The Austrians surely have waited for Mr Schulz's "good" advice to [the Austrian Chancellor] Kern [Link to the online article "Hofburg election result is 'a defeat of the Euro-sceptics'"]"
8	Strache's Facebook page	27 May 2016	"Junker is happy to be able to construct a centralistic EU-federal state together with Van der Bellen. The truth is that this is about Austria's abolition. We will in any case continue to take care of our Austria! [Link to posting titled "Juncker painted a heart on the letter of congratulation to Van der Bellen"]"
9	Strache's Facebook page	25 May 2016	"Every day we hear about the allegedly deep divide in the population!"
			"The cause is not the division of the country and of the people, but the population's loss of confidence in those up there in the government! This is what infuriates the Austrian population."
			"The FPÖ is not the problem (but rather the solution). The problems are the SPÖ/ÖVP-government's dramatic errors and the politics of sustainable harm caused to the country."
10	Strache's Facebook page	25 May 2016	"My interview in yesterday's ZIB 2 [embedded video]"
11	Hofer's Faebook page	30 May 2016	"Hofer's reposting of Strache's posting no. 1" (#1)
12	Hofer's Faebook page	30 May 2016	"Here is the current issue of the "New Free Newspaper", featuring images of and articles on the presidential

TABLE 9.1 (Cont.)

ID	Source	Date of posting	Text (translated from German)
			election: http://nfz.fpoe.at/s [Image text: Norbert Hofer remains the "President of Hearts"]"
13	Hofer's Faebook page	26 May 2016	"The FPÖ is not a right-wing extremist party. If a right-wing extremist party had run in Austria, it would have received an election result of maybe two percent. The share of fools in Austria is definitely not larger. We are a highly responsible centre-right party. [Link to online article titled "Hofer: 'Share of fools in Austria is at the most two percent'"]"
14	Hofer's Faebook page	25 May 2016	"Here are my statements from yesterday's joint press conference with HC Strache"
15	Hofer's Faebook page	25 May 2016	"My interview with the ORF [Austrian Broadcasting Corporation] from yesterday [embedded video]"

Chapter Ten

A Frankfurt School Perspective on Donald Trump and His Use of Social Media

Christian Fuchs' (2018) book *Digital Demagogue: Authoritarian Capitalism in the Age of Trump and Twitter* analyses economic, political, and ideological dimensions of Donald Trump's power. The study is based on Frankfurt School critical theory and works by some of its representatives such as Theodor W. Adorno, Franz Neumann, and Erich Fromm. The piece published here shows how aspects of Frankfurt School theory allow us to understand Trump's Twitter populism.

Donald Trump won the US presidential election against all expectations. Hillary Clinton organised a big data campaign that did not succeed against Trump's ideological campaign that focused on scapegoating, American nationalism, friend/enemy-logic, political anti-correctness, breaking taboos, and the mobilisation of emotions (Fuchs 2016).

10.1 Twitter and Trump as Culture Industry

A *first aspect of Frankfurt School critique* is that it analyses how culture for the matter of profitability is turned into an industry and a show. In mid-January 2017, Trump had almost 20 million followers on Twitter. The number of his followers increased rapidly after he had won the election. Trump is not just a president, candidate, and capitalist. Trump is a brand and a media spectacle that celebrates itself and thereby accumulates capital, power, and

DOI: 10.4324/9781003256090-10

followers. Trump is also an ideology – Trumpology. Trumpology is Trump-style ideology. It is not the ideology of a single person, but rather a whole way of thought and life that consists of elements such as hyper-individualism, leadership, the friend/enemy-scheme, and Social Darwinism, and the fetishism of hard labour. This became evident in the way Trump acted as host and chief eliminator in *The Apprentice*. As US president, Trump has become the chief-populist-Twitterer, the master of 140-character-politics. The acceleration, compression, superficiality, tabloidisation, and one-dimensionality of politics and ideology have found a new point of culmination in Trump's Twitterverse. Critical theorists Max Horkheimer and Theodor W. Adorno wrote about traditional commercial mass media that "[c]ommunication makes people conform by isolating them". In the world of Twitter and Trumpology, communication makes people conform by networking them as "friends", "followers", "likers", and "re-tweeters" of their leader.

10.2 Authoritarianism Online

A *second aspect of Frankfurt School critique* is the analysis of authoritarianism and the authoritarian personality. The *leadership principle* is an important element of authoritarianism. Theodor W. Adorno writes that an authoritarian leader "characteristically indulges in loquacious statements about himself" (Adorno 1975, 11). Twitter's structure supports me-centredness by its focus on individual profiles, postings, and the accumulation of followers and re-tweets. Trump likes to present himself on Twitter as lone wolf who is a winner and does it all his way:

Donald J. Trump:	"I thought and felt I would win big, easily over the fabled 270 (306). When they cancelled fireworks, they knew, and so did I".
	(Twitter: @realdonaldtrump, 2 January 2017)
Donald J. Trump:	"Various media outlets and pundits say that I thought I was going to lose the election. Wrong, it all came together in the last week and …".
	(Twitter: @realdonaldtrump, 2 January 2017)

Trump's populist, aggressive, attack-oriented, offensive, proletarian language and style make him appear as a great little man, who is on the top, but at the same time an ordinary person. The great little man is according to Adorno "a person who suggests both omnipotence and the idea that he is just one of the folks". The leader often presents himself as a lone wolf fighting against political elites. This comes along with "aversion to the professional politician and perhaps to any kind of expertness". Trump-style politics are "post-truth" politics, where not facts, themes and debate, but ideology, personalities and emotions matter. It turned out that the great little man Trump appointed many representatives of the billionaire class to his cabinet. That a billionaire turns president means a significant change in the relationship between the state and the economy. Big capital has more opportunities to rule directly. Promising to challenge the rule of the political elite, Trump installed the rule of yet another elite – the billionaire class.

10.3 Tweeting Nationalism

Donald J. Trump: "The Establishment and special interests are absolutely killing our country. We must put #AmericaFirst".

(Twitter: @realdonaldtrump, 5 August 2016)

Nationalism is another *feature of authoritarianism*. Trump argues that he will make "America great again". He promises prosperity, wealth, and worldwide recognition to American citizens. By playing with nationalism, Trump detracts attention from the actual class differences within the United States. Twitter's allows the use of pictures and images for visualising ideologies such as nationalism.

Donald J. Trump: "Thank you Florida. My Administration will follow two simple rules: BUY AMERICAN and HIRE AMERICAN! #ICYMI"

(Twitter: @realdonaldtrump, 16 December 2016)

10.4 Online Liking of Friends, Online Hating of Enemies

Another *feature of authoritarianism* is that it makes use of the *friend-enemy scheme*. Authoritarianism has an extremely polarised relationship to the powerful and the weak. Critical theorist Erich Fromm says in this context: "To the one group all good characteristics are ascribed and they are loved, and to the other group all negative characteristics are ascribed and they are hated". Critical theorist Franz L. Neumann argues that in authoritarianism, "[h]atred, resentment, dread, created by great up-heavals, are concentrated on certain persons who are denounced as devilish conspirators" (Neumann 1957, 279). In such situations, the "fear of social degradation [...] creates for itself 'a target for the discharge of the resentments arsing from damaged self-esteem'" (Neumann 1957, 287). Trump constructs out-groups such as illegal immigrants, Mexico, China, Muslims, oppositional politicians, and his critics. They are presented as threatening the greatness of the American nation. The speed and anonymity of social media allows the fast and global spread of rumours, fake news, stereotypes, and prejudices.

Donald J. Trump: "We will stop heroin and other drugs from coming into New Hampshire from our open southern border. We will build a WALL and have security".

(Twitter: @realdonaldtrump, 9 February 2016)

Donald J. Trump: "After today, Crooked Hillary can officially be called Lyin' Crooked Hillary".

(Twitter: @realdonaldtrump, 7 July 2016)

Data scientists conducted a quantitative analysis of Trump's tweets (Tsur, Ognyanova and Lazer 2016). They found that Trump tends to use language that is negative and scapegoats: "But what's truly distinctive is *how* he uses adjectives: He combines an adjective followed by someone's name a stunning 10 times more than any other candidate. This is primarily because of his proclivity for using Twitter to launch personal attacks on specific individuals, like 'lightweight' Megyn Kelly, 'little' Marco Rubio, 'low-energy' Jeb Bush, 'dopey' Bill Kristol, etc. [...] Trump is also distinctive in his use of pronouns ('I,' 'you,' 'he,' 'she,' 'we,' 'us,' etc.). Trump uses pronouns in a very different way than the other candidates. 'I' and 'me' (as well as Trump's own name) are used much more than other candidates. While @realDonaldTrump's use of 'we' is within the range of other candidates', Trump hardly uses the pronoun 'us' – a bit surprising for a presidential candidate who is expected to lead America to a 'great' shared future".

Donald J. Trump: "Chuck Jones, who is President of United Steelworkers 1999, has done a terrible job representing workers. No wonder companies flee country!"

(Twitter: @realdonaldtrump, 7 December 2016)

Donald J. Trump: "Just watched @NBCNightlyNews – So biased, inaccurate and bad, point after point. Just can't get much worse, although @CNN Is right up there!"

(Twitter: @realdonaldtrump, 11 December 2016)

Donald J. Trump:	"The Theater must always be a safe and special place. The cast of Hamilton was very rude last night to a very good man, Mike Pence. Apologize!"

(Twitter: @realdonaldtrump, 19 November 2016)

Trump's Twitter-politics is a politics of 140 characters that consists of a world polarised into friends and enemies. Via Twitter, Trump broadcasts news about how his personal friend/enemy-scheme evolves. There are two sides: the side of the friends, whom he characterises as great, impressive, nice, successful, and talented. And the side of the enemies, whom he characterises as bad, biased, failing, inaccurate, dishonest, nasty, not nice, one-sided, overrated, poor, rude, sad, terrible, untalented, or wrong. Trump's politics is a world of polar opposites, in which representatives of the two sides have completely opposed characteristics.

10.5 Militarism and Patriarchy

Patriarchy plays a peculiar role in authoritarianism. The male warrior, who fights and does not show emotions, is presented as the ideal human being that should be imitated. According to Adorno (1975, 49), in authoritarianism the "model of the military officer" is "transferred to the realm of politics":

Donald J. Trump:	"General James "Mad Dog" Mattis, who is being considered for Secretary of Defence, was very impressive yesterday. A True General's General!"

(Twitter: @realdonaldtrump, 20 November 2016)

For Trump, Twitter is a symbolic and communicative battlefield. Trump calls social media his "method of fighting back": "It's a great form of communication. [...] I think I picked up yesterday 100,000 people. I'm not saying I love it, but it does get the word out. When you give me a bad story or when you give me an inaccurate story or when somebody other than you and another network, or whatever, 'cause of course, CBS would never do a thing like that right? I have a method of fighting back. That's very tough. [...] I really believe that the fact that I have such power in terms of numbers with Facebook, Twitter, Instagram, et cetera, I think it helped me win all of these races where they're spending much more money than I spent".[1]

The other side of militarism in patriarchal ideology is the disrespect towards women.

Donald J. Trump: "Did Crooked Hillary help disgusting (check out sex tape and past) Alicia M become a U.S. citizen so she could use her in the debate?"

(Twitter: @realdonaldtrump, 29 September 2016)

10.6 Tweeting Emotions, Tweeting Ideology

Critical theorist Wilhelm Reich argued that authoritarian politicians are convinced that one cannot "get at the masses with arguments, proofs, and knowledge, but only with feelings and beliefs" (Reich 1972, 83). Twitter is a medium that supports politics that are based on feelings, beliefs and irrationality instead of arguments, proofs and knowledge. Donald Trump has made emotionally laden ideological Twitter politics a key element of his political strategy. He uses Twitter's brevity of 140 characters for a politics that does not rely on arguments, but on negative emotions that he communicates and tries to stir among his followers. Twitter is the best-suited medium for the emotional and ideological politics of outrage, scapegoating, hatred, and attack because its ephemerality, brevity, and speed support spectacles and sensationalism. It leaves no time and no space for substantial debates. The custom of liking and re-tweeting on Twitter appeals to Trump's narcissistic side so that he enjoys his status as a celebrity, brand and political leader. Trump makes use of Twitter for broadcasting 140-character sound bites about what he likes and dislikes.

10.7 Twitter Diplomacy

Donald J. Trump: "The United States must greatly strengthen and expand its nuclear capability until such time as the world comes to its senses regarding nukes"

(Twitter: @realdonaldtrump, 22 December 2016)

Donald J. Trump: "China is not our friend. They are not our ally. They want to overtake us, and if we don't get smart and tough soon, they will".

(Twitter: @realdonaldtrump, 21 February 2013)

Donald J. Trump: "Do you think Putin will be going to The Miss Universe Pageant in November in Moscow – if so, will he become my new best friend?"

(Twitter: @realdonaldtrump, 18 June 2013)

Diplomacy is a form of political communication that requires direct communication, listening, empathy, compromise, and agreement. In a world in crisis, diplomacy is of tremendous importance in order to prevent new wars. Trump's 140 character-"Twitter diplomacy" operates by offense, unpredictability, provocation, attack, and disagreement. What lots of people fear is that Trump's personality is too uncontrolled and too revengeful, which could be dangerous in a ticklish political situation. China's Xinhua news agency, a mouthpiece of the Chinese government, commented that Trump's "obsession with 'Twitter diplomacy' is undesirable" (Hunt 2017).

10.8 Liberal Media = Trump's Political-Economic Allies

The *New York Times* saw its paid subscriptions increasing by 132,000 during a three-week period in November 2016, a growth rate ten times higher than during the same period in 2015 (Belvedere and Newberg 2016). The first television debate between Trump and Clinton reached a total of 84 million US viewers, the largest audience ever in 60 years of televised US presidential debates (Stelter 2016). In the world of the capitalist spectacle, the capitalist media need Trump just like Trump needs the media.

"How to deal with Trump's tweets" (*CNN*, 12 December 2016, https://edition.cnn.com/2016/12/12/opinions/using-trump-tweets-ben-ghiat/index.html).

"Can Reporters Keep up With Trump's Tweets?" (*CNN*, 12 December 2016, https://edition.cnn.com/2016/12/12/opinions/using-trump-tweets-ben-ghiat/index.html)

"What Trump got wrong on Twitter this week" (*Washington Post*, 6 January 2017, https://www.washingtonpost.com/news/fact-checker/wp/2017/01/06/what-trump-got-wrong-on-twitter-this-week/),

"If Trump Tweets It, Is It News? A Quandary for the News Media" (*New York Times*, 29 November 2016, https://www.nytimes.com/2016/11/29/business/media/if-trump-tweets-it-is-it-news-a-quandary-for-the-news-media.html)

The mainstream media's Trump spectacle also continues after the election. It has now become common that they devote front pages and entire articles and reports to Trump tweets. Either they report what Trump tweets or in a Kafkaesque manner discuss whether it is good or not that the media report about Trump's tweets. The point is that they give constant attention to Trump and provide free Trump brand propaganda. The continued attention for Trump is itself the message. Trump makes strategic use of the fact that he sells attention. Trump: "The cost of a full-page ad in the New York Times can be more than $100,000. But when they write a story about one of my deals, it doesn't cost me a cent, and I get more important publicity. I have a mutually profitable two-way relationship with the media – we give each other what we need. And now I am using that relationship to talk about the future of America. [...] These media types sell more magazines when my face is on the cover, or when I bring a bigger audience to their television show than they normally attract, and by far. And what's funny is that it turns out the best way for them to get that attention is to criticize me" (Trump 2015).

A truly critical strategy would be to provide no free promotion to Trump by ignoring him. To say nothing, report nothing, and comment on nothing that is right-wing populist in character has to be part of breaking the right-wing spectacle's spell. According to a report, NBC, CBS, and ABC gave 23.4 times more coverage to Trump than to Sanders (Boehlert 2015). An alternative strategy also requires changing the balance of forces in media coverage.

Trump's tweets are the ultimate expression of populist and ideological communication in a capitalism that is based on high velocity, high one-dimensionality, and high superficiality. The only practical hope for political communication is the struggle for dialectical forms of political communication that provides space and time for reporting and debating the world's complexity.

Note

1 https://www.scribd.com/document/330970776/Trump-60-Minutes-2#download&from_embed, accessed on 1 December 2016.

References

Adorno, Theodor W. 1975. "The Psychological Technique of Martin Luther Thomas' Radio Adresses." In *Soziologische Schriften II.1*, 11–141. Frankfurt am Main: Suhrkamp.

Belvedere, Matthew J. and Michael Newberg. 2016. "New York Time Subscription Growth Soars Tenfold, Adding 132,000, After Trump's Win." *CNBC*, 29 November 2016. https://www.cnbc.com/2016/11/29/new-york-times-subscriptions-soar-tenfold-after-donald-trump-wins-presidency.html.

Boehlert, Eric. 2015. "ABC World News Tonight Has Devoted Less Than One Minute To Bernie

Sanders' Campaign This Year." *MediaMatters*, December 11, 2015. http://mediamatters.org/blog/2015/12/11/abc-world-news-tonight-has-devoted-less-than-on/207428.

Fuchs, Christian. 2018. *Digital Demagogue: Authoritarian Capitalism in the Age of Trump and Twitter*. London: Pluto Press.

Fuchs, Christian. 2016. "What The US Presidential Election Result Tells Us About the Failures Of Big Data Analytics And Neoliberalism As Big Data Capitalism." *Huffington Post*, 16 November 2016, https://www.huffingtonpost.co.uk/christian-fuchs1/what-the-us-presidential-_b_12948356.html.

Hunt, Katie. 2017. "China Tells Donald Trump to Lay Off Twitter." *CNN*, 5 January 2017, https://edition.cnn.com/2017/01/04/politics/china-trump-twitter/index.html.

Neumann, Franz. 1957. *The Democratic and the Authoritarian State*. Glencoe, IL: The Free Press.

Reich, Wilhelm. 1972. *The Mass Psychology of Fascism*. London: Souvenir Press.

Stelter, Brian. 2016. "Debate Breaks Record as Most-Watched in U.S. History." *CNN*, 27 September 2016. https://money.cnn.com/2016/09/27/media/debate-ratings-record-viewership/.

Trump, Donald. 2015. *Crippled America: How To Make America Great Again*. New York: Threshold Editions

Tsur, Oren, Katherine Ognyanova and David Lazer. 2016. "The Data Behind Trump's Twitter Takeover." *Politico Magazine*, April 29, 2016. http://www.politico.com/magazine/story/2016/04/donald-trump-2016-twitter-takeover-213861.

Chapter Eleven
Donald Trump and Neoliberal Fascism

11.1 Fascism

There is an intellectual debate on whether or not the power of the likes of Trump, Farage, Le Pen, Orbán, or Salvini constitutes fascism. Analysts such as Noam Chomsky, Neil Faulkner, John Bellamy Foster, Robert Kagan, Gáspar Miklós Tamás, or Enzo Traverso speak of creeping fascism, new fascism, or post-fascism. They signal that there are both continuities and discontinuities between classical and contemporary forms of fascism. Representatives of this position hold that Trump is not Hitler, but stress certain similarities between the two. In contrast, intellectuals such as Wendy Brown, Nancy Fraser, Chantal Mouffe, Roger Griffin, Cas Mudde, Robert Paxton, David Renton, or Slavoj Žižek argue that it is an exaggeration to characterise Trump and other contemporary demagogues as fascists. Representatives of this position prefer terms such as new authoritarianism, libertarian authoritarianism, reactionary neoliberalism, right-wing populism, the populist radical right, or demagoguery on behalf of oligarchy. They see Trump as dangerous, but stress that he is quite different from Hitler.

In this debate, Giroux tends to take the first position. He speaks of "the new form of fascism updated under the Trump administration" (58) and "an updated American version of fascism of which Trump is both symptom and endpoint" (54). He argues that Trump does not use storm troopers and concentration camps, but divisive language that is a form of violent action. Fascism is not uniform, but dynamic and therefore takes on variegated forms in different historical and societal contexts. For Giroux, Trump constitutes the rise of neoliberal fascism and the culmination of a long history of authoritarianism in US capitalism that includes historical moments such as the oppression of native Americans, slavery, US imperialism, torture, or extrajudicial

DOI: 10.4324/9781003256090-11

detention and imprisonment (Guantánamo). The background to Trump's rise is the culture of fear since 9/11 and neoliberalism's dismantling of public education, critical reason, and radical imagination that is a "full-scale attack on thoughtful reasoning" (12).

In debates about fascism, it is important to specify the level of analysis. Fascism can exist on the levels of an individual's character, individual action, ideology, the collective consciousness, and practices of movements/groups/organisations/parties, structures and institutions, or society as a whole. Fascism on one level is a necessary foundation but not a sufficient condition for fascism on the next level. Erich Fromm and Theodor W. Adorno characterised the authoritarian, sadomasochistic, necrophilic personality as the psychological foundation of fascism. For a fascist society to come into existence, particular political, economic, and ideological conditions of capitalist development need to call forth collective political practices of authoritarian personalities that result in the institutionalisation of authoritarianism at the level of society and are enacted by authoritarian movements conducted by a fascist leader.

In the essay *Anxiety and Politics*, Frankfurt School critical theorist Franz L. Neumann (1957/2017) specifies conditions necessary for the emergence of a fascist society. They include crises, the alienation of labor, destructive competition, or social alienation that threatens certain social groups' prestige, income, and existence; political alienation, the institutionalisation of collective political anxiety in the form of a fascist movement, fascist practices, fascist institutions, propaganda, and terror; and persecutory anxiety expressed in the form of nationalism, political scapegoating, xenophobia, etc. A condition that needs to be added to Neumann's list is the weakness of the political left, for example in the form of rivalries, internal trench wars that lead to fractioning, splintering and isolation, or orthodoxy that miscalculates the actual dangers of the political situation. In the Weimar Republic, the Communist Party of Germany did not consider the Nazis, but the Social Democrats as their main enemy. Stalinist communists characterised the Social Democratic Party as social fascism and believed German capitalism would automatically collapse after Hitler's rise to power.

In the debate on fascism, many observers agree that we today find leaders with an authoritarian personality and ideology in a significant number of countries and that there are conditions that can lead to fascist regimes. But does the claim that countries such as the USA have become fascist societies go too far? One must be careful not to mix up the different levels of fascism. In a fully fascist society, there is no rule of law and the political opposition and other identified enemies are imprisoned or killed by the exercise of terror. A fascist society is a political Behemoth. Trumpism poses a very negative development potential that could fully develop into a Trumpian political economic system if the opposition to Trump cannot establish an alternative. But there is a still a difference between Trump's character structure and the total character of US society today.

Giroux (2019) uses the category of "neoliberal fascism" for characterising the contemporary negativity of politics. But he also uses terms such as "populist authoritarianism" (13), "American authoritarianism" (32), "authoritarian populism" (10, 48), "right wing populism" (46), or "inverted totalitarianism" (64). The term populism is vague and creates more confusion than elucidation. Both the notions of totalitarianism and populism are often used for arguing that socialism and the far-right are dangers to democracy. For example, Jan-Werner Müller writes in his book *What is Populism?* that populism is "a danger to democracy" and that Trump and Sanders are "both populists, with one on the right and the other on the left" (Müller 2017, 9). Such theorisations often end up in the legitimation of what Tariq Ali (2018) calls the "extreme centre" of neoliberal ideology.

Right-wing authoritarianism is a more general formation that includes fascism but also less directly violent movements such as Conservatism, the radical right, and right-wing extremism. Fascism is the most extreme version of right-wing authoritarianism. Conservatism and the radical right accept a democratic framework, although their version of democracy is elitist. In contrast, right-wing extremists and fascists are anti-democratic. Fascism is an intensification of right-wing extremism that openly practises the attempt to overthrow democracy and the institutionalisation of terror. Franz L. Neumann (1936, 35) defines fascism as "the dictatorship of the Fascist [...] party, the bureaucracy, the army, and big business, the dictatorship over the whole of the people, for complete organization of the nation for imperialist war". Fascism refuses "groups with an independent existence of their own, groups which come between the state and the individual" (35) such as independent trade unions, meeting points, oppositional movements and parties. Fascism is based on the assimilation of all groups and organizations. In fascism, "the state is everything, the individual nothing" (36). Fascism robs workers of their rights and implements the terroristic rule of capitalist interests.

Fascism is anti-democratic and therefore sees dictatorship and top-down-leadership as the best organisation principles of society, the economy, the political system, and culture. Fascism is nationalist. It is a political form of fetishism that mythologises the nation as biological or cultural collective. Nationalist ideology tries to distract attention from actually existing class structures. Fascism scapegoats constructed enemies and is therefore often racist, xenophobic, or anti-Semitic. Fascism sees violence, imperialist conquer and war as appropriate means for solving political conflicts. It idealises the soldier as the ideal citizen and is thereby also patriarchal. Taken together, these features make fascism a type of character structure, ideology, practice, movement, structure, and society that enforces capitalism with terroristic means. For August Thalheimer (1930), fascism is "a form of open capitalist dictatorship". Clara Zetkin (1923) writes that fascism is "an asylum for all the politically homeless, the socially uprooted, the destitute and disillusioned".

11.2 Neoliberal Fascism

In *The Road to Serfdom*, the leading neoliberal theorist and ideologue Friedrich A. Hayek (1944/2001, 60) claims that socialism and fascism are "inseparable manifestations of what in theory we call collectivism" that do not "recognise autonomous spheres in which the ends of the individuals are supreme". As a consequence, Hayek rejects the notions of the "common good" and the "general interest" (60). He argues that only a neoliberal society that he terms a spontaneous order, where society and its institutions are organised as markets and are based on the commodity form and capital accumulation, secures democracy and freedom. Augusto Pinochet's neoliberal, military fascist regime in Chile already showed in the 1970s that the assumption that capitalism brings about and is the foundation of democracy is mistaken. More than 45 years after Pinochet's coup-d-état in 1973, the rise of new authoritarian forms of capitalism shows once more that Hayek was wrong.

Actions such as Trump's plan to build a wall at the US-Mexican border and the resulting government shutdowns aimed at forcing through this project, the travel ban for citizens from Muslim-majority countries, the separation of children from families at the US-Mexican border, his attempt to dismantle the legal protection of Dreamers from deportation, etc. are examples of the ideologically motivated cruelties of the Trump regime and what Giroux based on Rob Nixon terms slow violence (83–86). Over time, an accumulation of such cruelties can reach a tipping point where the system is negatively sublated and democracy is abolished.

Not everyone will agree with Giroux on his answer to the question of whether or not countries such as the USA have turned into fascist societies. But this question should not distract us from acknowledging the importance of Giroux's insight that neoliberalism and capitalism have authoritarian and fascist potentials. A key contribution of Giroux's (2019) book is the creation of the notion of neoliberal fascism, a formation "in which the principles and practices of a fascist past and neoliberal present have merged" (43) and that connects "the worse dimensions and excesses of gangster capitalism with the fascist ideals of white nationalism and racial supremacy associated with the horrors of the [fascist] past" (47). Giroux's category reminds us of Horkheimer and Adorno's insights that liberalism and capitalism have inherent fascist potentials, that fascism is a terroristic version of capitalism, that fascist potentials have not ceased to exist after the end of the Second World War, and that "whoever is not willing to talk about capitalism should also keep quiet about fascism" (Horkheimer 1939/1989, 78).

How has neoliberalism's radical individualism become combined with the repressive collectivism of nationalism and authoritarianism? The answer is that neoliberalism and individualism are not opposed to but just the flip-side of repressive collectivism. Trumpism tries to compensate for the social void that its advancement of neoliberal individualism creates by fostering repressive collectivism. Giroux's book contains many insights into how this negative dialectic operates, to which one needs to add a systematic analysis of this logic's different levels. Society is a totality of social relations organised in the three intersecting realms of political economy, the political s repressive collectivism is organised as the combination of radical neoliberal policies and protectionism. On the one hand, these policies favour the rich and US corporations, advance an economic version of Social Darwinism with all-out competition in the economy where only the most powerful survive and others face precarity, debt and ruin. Neoliberal political economy constitutes an antagonism between austerity and precarity. On the other hand, protectionist policies are advanced that are directed against international free trade arrangements and favour the interests of US capital.

At the level of ideology and culture, we find the combination of hyper-consumerist, narcissistic individualism, the cult of leadership, and nationalism. The nationalist moment propagates the ideological unity of US capital and US labor and advances the racist and xenophobic scapegoating of immigrants, refugees, people of colour, Muslims, and foreigners.

At the level of politics and the state, there is the combination of a neoliberal state that deregulates the economy, privatises and commodifies everything, and gives wide freedoms to corporations with a repressive state that polices the poor and advances law-and-order politics as well as racist immigration policies.

11.3 Trump the Spectacle

Friedrich A. Hayek (1988, 53) wrote: "Rationalists tend to be intelligent and in-tellectual; and intelligent intellectuals tend to be socialists". The conjuncture of neoliberalism and right-wing authoritarianism has advanced an irrational, emotional, anti-intellectual culture that forestalls socialist ideas and thereby ideologically justifies and cements capitalism. In such a political culture, the billionaire capitalist Donald Trump can successfully pretend to be a working-class hero. Trump signifies the end of the division of labor between the capitalist class and politicians and the rise of the 1%'s *direct* rule of the state. Right-wing authoritarians try to appeal to the working class by crude manners, proletarian habitus, and simple, dichotomous language. But in reality, these ideologues oppose the interests of the working class. When in power, they often implement laws that give tax breaks to corporations and the rich and harm the working class by dismantling the redistributive effects of the welfare state and public services. A tweet by Boris Johnson is revealing in this respect: "We are sup-porting business and cutting tax".[1]

Ideological language and communication operate at the level of the institutionalisation of collective political anxiety through propaganda. But given that communication is the process of creating social relations, ideological communication also operates as mediating process at all other levels that constitute conditions for the emergence of fascism. Giroux's (2019) book analyses Trump's use of ideological language and po-litical communication under neoliberal conditions. Language is "the starting point for tyrants to promote their ideologies, hatred, and systemic politics of disposability and erasure" (31). Words matter because they are "pedagogical tools to define social relations" (19). "Fascism begins not with violence, police assaults, or mass killings, but with language" (70).

One of Trump's infamous but typical tweets reads: "The FAKE NEWS Media […] is not my enemy, it is the enemy of the American People!". Trump tends to dismiss criticism as "fake news". He identifies his person with the American people in order to argue that any criticism of him is anti-American. The term "fake news" has become a right-wing propaganda term that Trump uses for rejecting criticism and vilifying his critics. Given the corruption of this category, it is better to speak of lies that are presented as real and as news as "false news". Right-wing authoritarians replace reason by ideology, facts by fiction, rationality by emotionality, truth by lies, complexity by simplicity, objectivity by prejudice and hate. Far-right political communication is not best characterised as post-truth politics, but as propaganda and ideology that tries to create false consciousness by simplification, dissimulation, manipulation, diversion, and outright lies. Giroux argues in this context that we do not live in a post-truth world but in a "pre-truth world where the truth has yet to arrive" (54).

The Cambridge Analytica Scandal has shown how the far-right uses data breaches, online data collection and targeted ads for trying to manipulate elections. "Alt-right" platforms such as Breitbart, InfoWars, Daily Caller, Philosophia Perennis, Unzensuriert, Westmonster, etc. are projects that spread false news and far-right conspiracies. Political bots have partly automated the creation of political online attention. It has become difficult to discern whether it is humans or machines that create online content and attention. The culture of false news is one of the factors of Trump's political success.

With tens of million of followers, Trump had one of the world's most followed and most visible Twitter accounts (that was deleted in January 2021 after his followers' storm on the Capitol). In the book *Digital Demagogue: Authoritarian Capitalism in the Age of Trump and Twitter*, the present author analyses how Donald Trump uses Twitter in order to spread authoritarianism, nationalism, the friend/enemy-logic, linguistic militancy, and sexism (Fuchs 2018). An analysis of Trump's tweets shows that he uses first-person singular pronouns much more frequently than first-person plural pronouns. Erich Fromm argues that narcissistic, authoritarian personalities are prone to engage in destruction for the sake of destruction. Twitter's affordance as me-centered, narcissistic medium invites authoritarian political communication. Twitter and Trump are a match made in heaven. Based on Hannah Arendt, Giroux (2019) characterises Trump's tweets as evil banality (80–81). He writes that "Trump's infantile production of Twitter storms transforms politics into spectacularized theater" (14). This insight needs to be further developed and deepened. The culture of the spectacle was not invented by Trump, but is deeply ingrained in capitalist tabloid culture that tries to sell sensations for making profit.

What Guy Debord calls the capitalist society of the spectacle has turned political debate into superficial, personalised, high speed events that lack the time and depth needed for exploring the complexities of antagonistic societies. Reality TV has become the model of political communication. In political television debates, candidates are asked to give short answers that are often allowed not to be longer than thirty seconds. The capitalist culture of speed, superficiality, tabloidisation, and personalisation is part of the apparatus that has enabled Trump the spectacle.

Trump the Spectacle

The liberal media and Trump have a love/hate-relationship. Although these media are some of Trump's fiercest critics, they also have helped creating him by giving his ideology lots of public attention and voice, which has helped them to increase their profits. Many of Trump's election campaign speeches were live-broadcast on CNN. Thanks to the coverage of Trump, the *New York Times* significantly increased its number of subscribers in 2016. The Tyndall Report found that in 2015 Donald Trump received 23.4 times as much coverage in evening television newscasts as Bernie Sanders. The capitalist mainstream media have helped to make the political spectacle Trump. The capitalist media require Trump just like Trump requires the capitalist media.

When Trump took to Twitter to call Kim Darroch "a very stupid guy" and the "wacky Ambassador that the U.K. foisted upon the United States", the *New York Times* immediately ran a story titled "UK Envoy's Leaked Views Inspire More Insults in Trump Tweets". No matter how silly or insulting, Trump's tweets are what the mainstream media talk about. The liberal media thereby do not deconstruct Trump but help constructing him. A real deconstruction of Trump means that it is often better to ignore him instead of giving him public attention that he can instrumentalise for his political aims.

11.4 Alternatives

Henry Giroux's (2019) book takes inspiration from teachers who strike against terrible working conditions and young people who protest against racism, police violence, student debt, sexual violence and stand up for gun control, peace, environmental protection, social security, equality, prison abolition, etc. He argues for a broad protest movement that forms a "united front" (180) against neoliberal fascism, brings together the multiple interrelated issues, interests and struggles, and "connects the dots among diverse forms of oppression" (183). Such an alliance needs to be an anti-capitalist non-violent movement for democratic socialism (179–180).

Giroux stresses the importance of critical pedagogy as intellectual weapon in the struggle against neoliberal fascism. Practising such a form of pedagogy requires strengthening public institutions that advance the formation of "knowledgeable citizens who have a passion for public affairs" and are enabled to develop "critical consciousness" (97). "Revitalizing a progressive agenda should be addressed as part of broader social movement capable of reimagining a radical democracy in which public values matter, the ethical imagination flourishes, and justice is viewed as an ongoing struggle. In a time of dystopian nightmares, an alternative future is only possible if we can imagine the unimaginable and think otherwise in order to act otherwise" (99). Giroux argues that commodified education whose aim is to advance the goals of capital tends to be anti-intellectual and instrumental, a pure training ground for the capitalist world. He makes the point that driving back authoritarianism needs critical education organised as tuition-free public service that cultivates informed citizens; promotes critical thinking, deliberative inquiry, a culture of questioning, dialogue, debate, thoughtful action, cultural production; and provides secure jobs for teachers.

Critical pedagogy needs to "sustain a culture of questioning" (121). The capitalist culture of speed and tabloidisation is the antidote of a democratic public sphere. For saving democracy and democratic communication, we not just require the decommodification of the public sphere, but also the deceleration of political communication. Club 2 and After Dark are debate formats invented in the European public service media tradition: a panel of five to eight diverse guests discusses a controversial topic in an uncensored debate that is set in a living room atmosphere without a studio audience. The programme is broadcast live and is open-ended. It ends when the discussants decide to go home. Reinventing democratic communication in the age of digital media requires a Club 2.0 – a combination of the classical Club 2 format and user participation via Internet platforms (see Chapter 16 in this book). A revival of the public sphere depends on the creation of new debate and news formats run on public service Internet platforms and platform co-operatives that challenge the dominance of Fox News, CNN, YouTube, Twitter, Facebook, etc. in the organisation of political communication. In order to saving democracy, we need to reinvent digital communication so that the combination of the digital tabloid and digital capitalism is replaced by the combination of the digital public and the digital commons. Challenging authoritarianism today requires the remaking of political culture and a radical reconstruction of the political economy of the media and the Internet.

It will be decisive for the future of democracy in the USA whether or not Bernie Sanders wins the Democratic Party's nomination and becomes US president and can instigate political foundations of a socialist transformation programme that is then carried further by the likes of Alexandria Ocasio-Cortez. Such victories will depend on the outcomes of broader social struggles. Henry Giroux's book is an important contribution to the development of the intellectual tools needed in the anti-fascist struggle for 21st-century democratic socialism.

11.5 Postface (Written in March 2021)

I wrote this chapter in 2019. It was published first in the *Los Angeles Review of Books* on 12 August 2019. As history has shown, Bernie Sanders did not make the Democratic Party's nomination and Joe Biden beat Donald Trump and became the 46th president of the United States. What followed after the November 2020 election was that Trump continued to repeat the claim that the election was rigged and to whip up the aggression of his followers in speeches, interviews, on Twitter and television.

On 6 January 2021, the US Senate and Representative House had a joint Congress session to confirm the electoral votes of the 2020 presidential election. Trump organised a rally nearby, where he repeated the false claims about the stolen and rigged election and called on his followers to march to Capitol (see the analysis in Chapter 14 of this book). What followed was that thousands of them attempted a coup and stormed the Capitol. Twitter, Facebook, and other social media platforms banned Trump.

In Section 11.2 of this work, I gave the example of Pinochet's coup-d-état in Chile in 1973 and the regime that was established as a form of neoliberal fascism. I argued that Trump has the mindset and ideology to bring about such events but that until 2019 the USA had not become a neoliberal fascist dictatorship. The events of 6 January 2021 confirm Henry Giroux's analysis about Trump and neoliberal fascism. The storm on the Capitol was the attempt to establish a neoliberal fascist regime, the attempt that the Trump presidency, as I wrote, reaches "a tipping point where the system is negatively sublated and democracy is abolished". US democracy was saved. But Trump and neoliberal fascism are not gone. He and other fascists will continue to haunt the world and will try to conquer power by all means.

Note

1 https://twitter.com/BorisJohnson/status/870739025426096128.

References

Ali, Tariq. 2018. *The Extreme Centre. A Second Warning.* London: Verso. Revised edition.
Fuchs, Christian. 2018. *Digital Demagogue: Authoritarian Capitalism in the Age of Trump and Twitter.* London: Pluto Press.

Giroux, Henry A. 2019. *The Terror of the Unforeseen*. Los Angeles, CA: Los Angeles Review of Books.

Hayek, Friedrich A. 1988. *The Fatal Conceit: The Errors of Socialism*. London: Routledge.

Hayek, Friedrich A. 1944/2001. *The Road to Serfdom*. London: Routledge.

Horkheimer, Max. 1939/1989. "The Jews and Europe." In *Critical Theory and Society: A Reader*, edited by Stephen E. Bronner and Douglas Kellner, 77–94. New York: Routledge.

Müller, Jan-Werner. 2017. "Müller." In *What is Populism?* London: Penguin.

Neumann, Franz L. 1957/2017. "Anxiety and Politics." *tripleC: Communication, Capitalism & Critique* 15 (2): 612–36.

Neumann, Franz L. 1936. *The Governance of the Rule of Law. An Investigation into the Relationship Between the Political Theories, the Legal System; and the Social Background in the Competitive Society*. Dissertation. London: London School of Economics.

Thalheimer, August. 1930. On Fascism. https://www.marxists.org/archive/thalheimer/works/fascism.htm.

Zetkin, Clara. 1923. The Struggle Against Fascism. https://www.marxists.org/archive/zetkin/1923/06/struggle-against-fascism.html.

Chapter Twelve
Authoritarian Capitalism, Authoritarian Movements, Authoritarian Communication

12.1 Studying Political Communication in Turbulent Times

We live in times of rapid political and social change that are highly complex and unpredictable. The 2008 crisis of the capitalist economy constituted a societal watershed. Rebellions, uprisings, occupations, revolutions, and counter-revolutions have become more frequent in the years since the crisis. Austerity measures, as well as short-sighted, uncoordinated responses to the the plight of refugees and to wars, have resulted in crises of national and transnational state power. In respect to ideologies and worldviews, socialism, nationalism, and right-wing radicalism have been strengthened. New technologies and popular culture have been embedded into these changes.

Paolo Gerbaudo's (2017) book *The Mask and the Flag: Populism, Citizenism and Global Protest* is a response to these societal, political, and academic challenges. Paolo suggests that the term populism should not simply be seen as signifying characteristics of right-wing radical movements, but should rather be understood in terms of people-power, grassroots empowerment, self-government, participatory democracy, and the common interest that aims at benefiting all those opposed to a particularism that benefits the few, the rich, and the powerful at the expense of the many. He argues that left-wing populism is a long-standing tradition, a tradition that has resurfaced in new forms in recent progressive social movements.

Certainly, as Paolo Gerbaudo concludes (2018, 752), the "future will tell whether the populist potential of social media will only favour right-wing populists as Donald

DOI: 10.4324/9781003256090-12

Trump who are currently in the lead or whether a more progressive and hopeful form of populism, such as the one championed by the likes of Podemos, Jeremy Corbyn and Bernie Sanders, will prevail". But history is not pure chance, but chance with necessity that can be influenced to a degree so that certain options for future developments become more likely and others less so. It is in this context that in my recent work I have become interested in a specific set of negative-dialectical questions that address another way of how critical research can inform left-wing movements. I ask: why is it that right-wing authoritarian populism in recent times has become much more popular than left-wing movements? How do right-wing authoritarian movements communicate? Why is it that right-wing political communication strategies seem to garner and result in mass support? Engaging with these questions has convinced me that authoritarianism and authoritarian capitalism, rather than populism, are key critical theory categories for understanding, explaining, and intervening into the political conjuncture that we are currently experiencing.

12.2 Right-Wing Authoritarianism

The far-right is successful in using social media for political communication. The far-right's use of the Internet has been much less studied than progressive movements' communication. W. Lance Bennett and Alexandra Segerberg's book The *Logic of Connective Action* (2013) mentions Occupy 70 times. It does not mention the Golden Dawn, Jobbik, the National Front, UKIP, Svoboda, Nigel Farage, the FPÖ, the Sweden Democrats, the Finns Party, Marine Le Pen, Geert Wilders, etc. a single time. The *Encyclopedia of Social Movement Media* (Downing 2011) presents 600 pages of analyses of "alternative media, citizens' media, community media, counterinformation media, grassroots media, independent media, nano-media, participatory media, social movement media, and underground media" (xxv). The focus is on all sorts of progressive, left-wing media, from the likes of the Adbusters Media Foundation to Zapatista media. The editor John Downing admits that "much less examination of media of extreme right movements occurs in this volume than there might be" (xxvi), but he does not explain why this might be the case, why it is problematic, and how it could be changed.

My argument is that we should not just study what we like, but also what we really dislike. Critical research is not a Facebook or Twitter "like" button, but must try to impart insights that can inform changes in the world. This does not simply require construction and positivism, but also the analysis of negative dialectics that hinder, and at the same time require, determinate negations, positive negations of the negative.

Contrary to the other contributions to this Crosscurrents section, I do not find the concept of populism theoretically meaningful. Its uses are too confused, meaning that the term requires constant explanation when employed in academic research. In the broadest sense, populism is the movement of making something popular, such as in popular culture. Etymologically the term "popular" stems from the Latin word *popularis* that designates that something is prevalent in the public (Williams 1983, 236). In a more political understanding, populism means the movement of making something appealing to the people. The problem of this second meaning is that by the people one can refer to (a) all humans, (b) all citizens, (c) the nation and those belonging to it. There is a variety of meanings of the term "the people" as the *populace* that ranges from universalism on one end to nationalist particularism on the other end. Populism as political movement goes back to revolutionary movements in 19th-century Russia (Labica 1987, 1026). But the term has also become associated with nationalist and right-wing extremist forces and ideology that try to appeal to prejudices, conceive of the people as an "undifferentiated unity" so that classes and their antagonisms are "denied and downplayed" (Labica 1987, 1028). Populism is therefore often associated with *"demagogy*, which has moved from 'leading the people' to 'crude and simplifying agitation'" and with "rightist and fascist movements which exploit 'popular pre-judices'" (Williams 1983, 238). In addition, populism is also used as a term for a particular style of politics that uses tabloidisation, scandalisation, entertainment, ridicule, simplification, one-dimensionality, and banalisation. Using a term such as "left-wing populism" is confusing because it can have many meanings: it can mean a political strategy that aims at ownership and control of society by all (self-management), a left strategy that uses popular culture, one that denies the existence of classes in a class society, one that uses tabloid politics, or one that resorts to traditionalist, nationalist, or xenophobic rhetoric and prejudices.

Whereas for Gramsci (2000) the "national-popular" as populism has to do with popular culture, organic intellectuals, the cultural dimension of class struggle, the popular university, and the formation of a collective socialist will, Hitler (1926) in *Mein Kampf* understands populism as the popularisation of the anti-Semitic Nazi movement: "Later on the National Socialist Movement presented the Jewish problem in a new light. Taking the question beyond the restricted circles of the upper classes and small bourgeoisie we succeeded in transforming it into the driving motive of a great popular movement". That both Gramsci and Hitler embraced the notions of the popular and of populism shows that these are not well-suited terms for a socialist strategy. Populism is not a clearly delineated, but rather a politically confusing term.

Instead, the notion of authoritarianism is a more suitable concept for explaining the Trump phenomenon, as I have discovered in the research for my forthcoming book *Digital Demagogue: Authoritarian Capitalism in the Age of Trump and Twitter* (Fuchs 2018 for a preliminary prolegomena see Fuchs 2017a, 2017c). The critical theory of authoritarianism advanced by the Frankfurt School and related authors on fascism, Nazism, and the authoritarian personality has been very helpful in this regard and particularly works by Franz Leopold Neumann, Erich Fromm, Theodor W. Adorno, Herbert Marcuse, Leo Löwenthal, and Willhelm Reich. Seen as a totality, the body of works of these authors has the advantage that by combining political economy, ideology critique, and critical psychology it enables an integrative analysis of society. Furthermore, it combines the social sciences and humanities, social analysis and philosophy, empirical social research and sociological theory. These authors start from Karl Marx's notions of alienation and Georg Lukács' (1923/1972) concept of reification. They see exploitation, domination and ideological manipulation as types of instrumental reason, as forms of asymmetric power that instrumentalise labour power (exploitation), citizens (domination) and consciousness (ideology).

A first important insight of the Frankfurt School authors is that political economy and ideology critique are not enough to fully understand right-wing authoritarianism. The combination of both can explain why right-wing authoritarianism emerges in particular contexts, but not why individuals and groups follow it. Wilhelm Reich (1972, 5) argued that the Left and Left analysis in the period form 1918 until 1933 only focused on "*objective* socio-economic processes at a time of crisis" and failed "to take into account the character structure" and the "social effect of mysticism". In order to produce proper understandings, critical theory and critical empirical research need to combine political economy and ideology critique with critical psychology. The success of far-right authoritarian populism is not just a matter of political-economic crisis and nationalist ideology. A significant dimension is that it appeals to people's everyday affects, emotions, desires, instincts, and drives.

Franz L. Neumann is one of the rather forgotten thinkers of the Frankfurt School. His works managed to combine political economy, ideology critique, and critical psychology in the critical analysis of authoritarianism (see Neumann 2017/1957, 2009/1944; Fuchs

2018, 2017c) Neumann (2017/1957) argues that destructive collective anxiety that generates large-scale support for far-right movements, groups, parties, institutions, and systems can emerge when six conditions coincide: (a) the alienation of labour; (b) destructive competition; (c) social alienation; (d) political alienation in respect to the political system; (e) the institutionalisation of anxiety; and (f) destructive psychological alienation and persecutory anxiety.

These categories can be applied to an analysis of the links between current forms of neoliberal capitalism and the rise of right-wing authoritarianism. Neoliberal capitalism has resulted in the intensification of labour's alienation, the destructiveness of competition, the great fear of social decline, political apathy, and a lack of trust in the political institutions of democracy and politicians. Neoliberalism is a politics of social anxiety (precarious labour and precarious life) that can backfire and turn into fascist politics of political anxiety. In this political void, nationalist and xenophobic far-right movements and their authoritarian leaders have not only stoked fears by constructing scapegoats, but have also promised alternatives in the form of nationalism, strong leaders, and authoritarian rule. They advance persecutory anxiety by creating and supporting the unleashing of aggressions in collective forms, and direct these at scapegoats. Contemporary societies can come to tipping points where quantity turns into new qualities that may take on the form of authoritarian capitalism and the undermining of democracy. Neoliberal capitalism has experienced its own negative dialectic of the enlightenment and has increasingly been sublated into authoritarian capitalism (Fuchs 2018, 2017a).

However, authoritarianism is multi-layered. It can operate at the levels of (a) an individual's psychology and behaviour; (b) groups/movements/parties; (c) institutions; or (d) society. We must distinguish between right-wing authoritarian personalities, groups, institutions, and society. These levels are nested, meaning that an upper level always contains and requires all necessary preceding levels. Each level is a necessity, but not a sufficient condition for the next level. There is not deterministic or automatic development from one level to the next, only the possibility of emergence under specific conditions.

In my analysis of the Frankfurt School's critical theory of authoritarianism, I have identified four elements of authoritarianism that Frankfurt School scholars seem to agree on: (a) authoritarian leadership; (b) nationalism; (c) the friend-enemy scheme; and (d) patriarchy and militarism. Nationalism is the construction of fictive ethnicity that tries to unite people around the ideological belief in a commonality organised

Right-Wing Authoritarianism

through elements such as blood, traditions, language, origin, and/or culture. Nationalism has a necessary outside, from which it distinguishes itself. The friend-enemy scheme constructs scapegoats, typically minorities, that are presented as society's ills and as the causes of social problems. The inclusive form of the friend-enemy scheme argues for the inferiority of the enemy group in order to exploit it, and the exclusive form constructs the enemy as inferior for the purpose of deportation, imprisonment, or extermination. In authoritarianism, "[h]atred, resentment, dread, created by great upheavals, are concentrated on certain persons who are denounced as devilish conspirators". In such situations, the "fear of social degradation [...] creates for itself 'a target for the discharge of the resentments arsing from damaged self-esteem'" (Neumann 2017/1957, 624).

Right-wing authoritarianism is a type of political fetishism that idolises the nation as a mythical collective that is directed against perceived outsiders who must be contained, purged, or eliminated, in order to achieve greatness. Its ideological role is that it distracts attention from, and dissimulates, the complex structural causes of capitalism's social problems that have to do with class structures and social domination. Nationalism tries to construct an ideological unity of capital and labour in the form of the national collective that is said to share a national interest that is under threat by foreigners and foreignness. The world is presented as a struggle between nations, a view that fetishises and naturalises the nation and disregards the realities of class conflicts and power inequalities. There is a difference between right-wing authoritarianism, right-wing extremism, and fascism. Whereas right-wing authoritarianism violates democracy, opposition is still possible and to a certain extent tolerated, whereas right-wing extremism propagates and practises direct violence against opponents, and fascism institutionalises it in the form of a system of terror. Authoritarian capitalism is a form of capitalist political economy, in which the principles of right-wing authoritarianism – authoritarian leadership, nationalism, the friend/enemy scheme, militarism, patriarchy – are, to a specific degree, practised by the state in order to organise capitalism and assert capitalist interests. In authoritarian capitalism, nationalism, political fetishism, and scapegoating are politically practised as ideology put into legal form in order to distract attention from class contradictions.

Authoritarianism involves the belief in, and the practice of, hierarchic social structures dominated by the leadership principle. Leadership is applied as a principle of totality that has no respect for individuality in the organisation of the political system, the capitalist economy, the army, the family, and the cultural organisation. Erich Fromm pioneered the study of the authoritarian personality. He describes the right-wing authoritarian leader and his followers as sadomasochistic personalities characterised by the simultaneous "striving for submission and domination" (Fromm 1942/2001, 122). A sadomasochistic individual "admires authority and tends to submit to it, but at the same time [...] wants to be an authority himself and have others submit to him" (141). Under the accumulated experience of particular conditions, the psychological striving for freedom and solidarity is suspended by negative dialectics of superiority/inferiority, love/hate, construction/destruction, submission/aggression. One psychological dimension of authoritarianism is that it is a form of collective narcissism The vision of the strong leader produces the psychological "enlargement of the subject: by making the leader his ideal he loves himself, as it were, but gets rid of the stains of frustration and discontent which mar his picture of his own empirical self" (Adorno 1951, 140). "The narcissistic *gain* provided by fascist propaganda is obvious" (Adorno 1951, 145). An authoritarian leader presents himself as superman and ordinary, as a "great little man" (Adorno 1951, 142). The image of the superman allows projection and submission – the sado-masochistic desire to be a superman and to be dominated by a superman.

Militarist patriarchy combines the gender division of social life with the fetishisation of the male soldier as the ideal human being. Competition, egoism, violence, and, in the final instance, physical destruction, war, and imperialism are seen as natural features of the human being and as appropriate solutions for social conflict. According to Theweleit (1987, 272), "Under patriarchy, the productive force of women has been effectively excluded from participating in male public and social productions". In patriarchy, leaders are typically male. The friend/enemy-scheme in the final instance leads to wars. Patriarchy entails militarism; the glorification of the male soldier, surveillance, the police; imperialism, and warfare. The figures of the soldier and the policeman are also bound up with nationalist ideology. The soldier and the policeman are in nationalist ideology seen as the defenders of the nation against foreigners and enemies. Authoritarians "destroy others to create themselves; they destroy things in the alien object-world and metamorphose into killing-machines and their components: a 'baptism of fire.' *Wreaking revenge* is their way of becoming one with themselves" (Theweleit 1989, 382). Militarist ideology and practice aims at annihilating the perceived enemies.

Speaking of right-wing authoritarianism implies that there is also left-wing authoritarianism. Stalinism was the best example of left-wing authoritarianism. It employed a socialist rhetoric and language, but used the leadership principle, nationalism, militarism, patriarchy, and a repressive state apparatus for the organisation and defence of a state-capitalist regime (James 1986). Only Stalinism's rhetoric was socialist. The Stalinist bureaucracy acted as a collective capitalist controlling the economy and exploiting waged and unwaged labour. In addition, the Stalinist economy was ideologically legitimated by a protestant ethic of toil, the idealisation of manual labour and abstinence (Marcuse 1958). Thus, the opposite of Stalinism is not "left populism", but democratic socialism.

Frankfurt School-authors' analysis of right-wing authoritarianism remains crucial today for understanding phenomena such as Donald Trump and their use of digital media.

12.3 Trump, Social Media, and Right-Wing Authoritarianism

There is an academic dispute about the causes of support for right-wing authoritarianism. The culturalist hypothesis assumes that such support is the result of a cultural and generational gap between the older and younger generations and the rise of post-material values (Inglehart and Norris 2016). The socio-economic hypothesis ascertains that the support of right-wing authoritarianism has to do with socio-economic inequalities, class structures, de-classification, and fears of social degradation (Bornschier and Kriesi, 2012; Lubbers, Gijsberts and Scheepers 2002; Oesch 2008, Roodujin, 2016; Werts, Scheepers and Lubbers 2012).

Taken together, there is ample evidence of certain tendencies, namely that voters of far-right parties live in rural areas, are older, are active or unemployed blue-collar workers, and live in areas that have become de-industrialised. Also unemployed, routine service workers, and small business owners show a certain tendency to vote for far-right parties. Fears and realities of social degradation and declassification generated by neoliberalism, post-industrialisation, transnational capitalism, and computerised automation play an important role. The generational gap that was amply observed in the Brexit referendum is not a different, but related phenomenon: the rise of the knowledge-based society has brought about higher levels of occupation for the younger generation, which comes along with different social experiences, realities, and moral values than in the parent generation. The younger generation faces new forms of self-determination combined with precarity that together with its educational status makes them overall more likely to support left-wing over right-wing forces. Especially blue-collar workers experiencing the key factors that Neumann (2017/1957) described (see the previous section), including economic, social, and political alienation, are prone to right-wing demagoguery.

The question of who supports right-wing authoritarianism is not new. Classical critical theories have often made the mistake to characterise right-wing authoritarianism and fascism as petty bourgeoisie movements. In contrast, more recent empirical research has shown that for example the Nazis had significant support of blue-collar workers both in respect to its membership and voters (Falter 1991, 2016; Fischer 1996). Nationalist ideology enables far-right parties to act as popular parties that promise something for every group in the name of the nation.

Authoritarian populism appeals to the emotions partly via public communications, including entertainment formats and social media. Therefore, it is not a coincidence that Donald Trump's two favourite media are reality TV and Twitter. Authoritarian politicians are convinced that one cannot "get at the masses with arguments, proofs, and knowledge, but only with feelings and beliefs" (Reich 1972, 83). Today, this circumstance is most often referred to as post-truth politics.

It is not an accident that Trump's preferred media are reality-TV and Twitter. Trump's capital accumulation is not simply real estate and casinos, but Trump the brand. Trump is a narcissistic self-branding machine that generates rent and profits for products that hold the Trump label. Trump is "the personification of the merger of humans and corporations – a one-man megabrand, whose wife and children are spin-off brands" (Klein 2017, 10). *The Apprentice* embodies the ingredients of social-Darwinist survival of the fittest, competition, militarism, patriarchy, and hyper-individualism. Twitter is based on a culture of high speed, superficiality and brevity. It supports simplistic, brief 140-character, propaganda messages transmitted at high speed that allow Trump to live out narcissism and feelings of leadership. In turn, the platform allows his supporters to admire their leader and express their hatred for the scapegoats. Trumpism is a political model that combines Trump's self-branding with the logic of *The Apprentice* and Twitter (Fuchs 2018, 2017a).

Among the reasons of the success of the authoritarian Right is that the simplicity and aggressiveness of its ideology appeals to those who feel politically left alone, disenfranchised, disappointed, and anxious. Media-savvy right-wing leaders "instrumentalize such disenchantment in text, image and talk, via many discursive and material practices" (Wodak 2015, 182). Social media is, just like the beer tent, the pub, and the public assembly, a space in which right-wing authoritarianism is communicated. Right-wing authoritarianisation is based on the Haiderisation and the Berluconisation of politics (Wodak 2013) – two forms of far-right authoritarian politics using entertainment and media publicity that were pioneered by Jörg Haider in Austria and Silvio Berlusconi in Italy.

Right-wing authoritarian communication is a semiotic strategy that publicly communicates right-wing authoritarianism's four elements. Based on critical theory, we can study how right wing authoritarianism is communicated in public, such as on social media. For the book *Authoritarian Capitalism in the Age of Donald Trump and Twitter*, I have used Frankfurt School theory as foundation for the analysis of Trumpism and Trump's communication strategy. For the empirical analysis, I collected all postings from Trump's Twitter-account @RealDonaldTrump for the time period between the start of the Republication National Convention (July 18, 2016) and Trump's inauguration (January 21, 2017). I used TAGS (Twitter Archiving Google Sheet), which is a plug-in to Google Docs. The data collection resulted in a total of 1,815 tweets that were the foundation for a Critical Discourse Analysis that used the Frankfurt School's critical theory of authoritarianism as its foundation. CDA combines text-immanent critique, socio-diagnostic critique, and prospective critique (Reisigl and Wodak 2001, 31–35). It critically theorises and analyses *texts* in their *contexts* and aims at advancing *prospects* for progressive changes of society. Critical social media discourse analysis can in contrast use "small data" analysis that provides a deep critical analysis of meanings.

Consider the following two examples:

Donald J. Trump: "It is time for DC to protect the American worker, not grant amnesty to illegals. Let's Make America Great Again! donaldjtrump.com"

(Twitter: @realdonaldtrump, 23 April 2015)

Donald J. Trump: "We should be concerned about the American worker & invest here. Not grant amnesty to illegals or waste 7 billion US-Dollars in Africa"

(Twitter: @realdonaldtrump, 1 July 2013)

In a nationalist manner, Trump communicates the need to "make America great again". National greatness is said to have come under threat by illegal immigrants, Africans, transfer of taxes to foreigners, and development aid. Americanness and the American interest are identified with the American working class, while un-Americanness is identified with immigrants and the developing world.

There are two semiotic chains, one of negative associations (amnesty, illegals, waste, Africa) and one of positive associations (protect, invest, concern, workers, America, greatness) that are combined with each other. The implication suggested is that immigrants and the developing world threaten the American worker and therefore the American interest. Political action by, and support of, Trump would therefore be needed in order to "make America great again". What is missing in the picture is U.S. capitalism that in reality not only exploits U.S. workers, but also migrant workers and workers in developing countries.

12.4 Conclusion: Towards Chaplin 2.0, Brecht 2.0, Verfremdung 2.0, Critical Data Visualisation, Slow Media, and Critical Public Sociology

One of the problems of the Left is that it has lost its appeal to blue-collar workers who fear or experience social degradation, and who are, despite automation, computerisation, and de-industrialisation, large enough in numbers to tip election results towards the right and the far-right. This is especially the case when voter turnouts are low, the Left is disorganised, factionalised, and weak, and when social democracy imitates neoliberalism and entrepreneurialism in an attempt to appeal to the new "middle class".

Corporate media monopolies and the logic of the acceleration, spectacularisation, and tabloidisation of the media are part of the reason why we see a rise in right-wing authoritarianism. The Left therefore needs to struggle for media reforms that advance slow media, non-commercial media, public interest media, a public-service Internet, the digital and communicative commons, and platform co-operatives (Fuchs 2018, 2017b).

Part of the problem of the Left is that it has more problems in appealing to the psyche, emotions, affects, and desires of those who feel politically anxious and disenfranchised than the Right does. It would be wrong to imitate the communication strategies and elements of right-wing authoritarianism. But the Left can also not leave political psychology entirely to the Right. Those who feel politically anxious and disenfranchised need to express their desires for love and hate. The key question is then how the Left can manage to turn a disenfranchised group's love for the authoritarian leader and nationalism into a love for participatory democracy and socialism, and its hatred of immigrants and foreigners into the hatred of capitalism and inequality. Part of the problem is that prejudices can often not be countered by rational arguments and citing statistical data, because they operate at the psychological level of hopes and fears that are the psychological material of post-truth politics. The solution then is not that the Left gives up the use of well thought-out arguments and debates. On the contrary, the point is to understand the complexity of the world and come up with proper responses that are supported by visual and argumentative strategies that bring the problem to the point.

Critical visualisations of data, studies, and statistics can form one important element of how to popularise progressive thought so that it challenges right-wing authoritarianism's prejudices, nationalism, scapegoating, and leadership ideology. An interesting way of responding to right-wing authoritarianism's irrationality is by political humour, satire, and parody. Horkheimer and Adorno (2002, 60) wrote about the "ambiguity of laughter": "If laughter up to now has been a sign of violence, an outbreak of blind, obdurate nature, it nevertheless contains the opposite element, in that through laughter blind nature becomes aware of itself as such and thus abjures its destructive violence". Humour is part of oppression itself, but may also be turned into challenging oppression. Left critique can be simultaneously enlightening, humorous, and serious. There is much to learn in this respect from Charlie Chaplin and Bertolt Brecht. The Left 2.0 requires Charlie Chaplin 2.0 and Brecht 2.0 for the age of social media and big data. The right-wing authoritarian spectacle staged via social media and reality TV needs to be challenged by the Brechtian epic and dialectical theatre 2.0, and the Boalian theatre of the oppressed 2.0.

Chaplin described the communicative approach of his movie *The Great Dictator* (1940): "Pessimists say I may fail – that dictators aren't funny any more, that the evil is too serious. That is wrong. If there is one thing I know it is that power can always be made ridiculous. The bigger that fellow gets the harder my laughter will hit him" (Van Gelder 1940).

Brecht speaks of *Verfremdung* as opposed to *Entfremdung* (estrangement, alienation) as principle of the dialectical theatre. "Verfremdung estranges an incident or character simply by taking from the incident or character what is self-evident, familiar, obvious in order to produce wonder and curiosity. [...] The V-effect consists in turning the object of which it is to be made aware, to which one's attention is to be drawn, from something ordinary, familiar, immediately accessible, into something peculiar, striking and unexpected" (Brecht 2015, 143, 192). *Verfremdung* is a negation of the negation that creates feelings, emotions, and affects of curiosity, surprise, and wonder. *Verfremdung* is the alienation of alienation and the estrangement of estrangement. By *Verfremdung 2.0* we mean equivalents of the Brechtian dialectical principle in the digital age.

Consider the following example:

> "I am happy to introduce my new FBI Director, John Miller. Incredible guy. Very impartial. You can trust him".
>
> [Image of a disguised Donald Trump]
> (Twitter: @realdonaldrumpf, 10 May 2017, https://twitter.com/ realdonaldrumpf/status/862142415460814849)

This tweet is a humorous comment on Trump's firing of FBI director James Comey. Meme and social media culture are in such cases turned into a left-wing strategy. For characterising such strategies, we do not need the term left populism, but can rather speak of left cultural politics or critical cultural politics. The term left populism in contrast risks association with a politics that is nationalist or xenophobic, does everything necessary, and does not shy away from any tactic in order to appeal to as many people as possible.

However, it is also the task of the intellectual in the difficult times we live in to be a critical, public intellectual who practises a critical, public social science. Franz L. Neumann, who as a Jewish socialist intellectual had to flee from Nazi Germany to Britain and the USA, and who perfectly understood right-wing authoritarianism like only few others did, has brought this task of a critical public sociology to the point in his essay *Anxiety and Politics* (Neumann 2017/1957, 629):

> "Hence there remains for us as citizens of the university and of the state the dual offensive on anxiety and for liberty: that of education and that of politics. Politics, again, should be a dual thing for us: the penetration of the subject matter of our academic discipline with the problems of politics [...] and the taking of positions on political questions. If we are serious about the humanization of politics; if we wish to prevent a demagogue from using anxiety and apathy, then we – as teachers and students – must not be silent. [...] We must speak and write."

Conclusion: Towards Chaplin 2.0, Brecht 2.0, Verfremdung 2.0, Critical Data Visualisation, Slow Media, and Critical Public Sociology

References

Adorno, Theodor. 1951. "Freudian Theory and the Pattern of Fascist Propaganda." In *The Culture Industry*, 132–57. Abingdon: Routledge.

Bennett, W. Lance and Alexandra Segerberg. 2013. *The Logic of Connective Action. Digital Media and the Personalization of Contentious Politics.* Cambridge: Cambridge University Press.

Bornschier, Simon and Hanspeter Kriesi, ed. 2012. "The Populist Right, the Working Class, and the Changing Face of Class Politics." In *Class Politics and the Radical Right*, edited by Jens Rydgren, 10–29. Abingdon: New York.

Brecht, Bertolt. 2015. *Brecht on Theatre*, edited by Marc Silberman, Steve Giles and Tom Kuhn. London: Bloomsbury Methuen Drama. 3rd edition.

Downing, John D. H., ed. *Encyclopedia of Social Movement media.* Thousand Oaks, CA: Sage.

Falter, Jürgen W., ed. 2016. *Junge Kämpfer, alte Opportunisten. Die Mitglieder der NSDAP 1919-1945.* Frankfurt: Campus.

Falter, Jürgen W. 1991. *Hitlers Wähler.* Munich: C. H. Beck.

Fischer, Conan, ed. 1996. *The Rise of National Socialism and the Working Classes in Weimar Germany.* Providence, RI: Berghahn.

Fromm, Erich. 1942/2001. *The Fear of Freedom.* Abingdon: Routlege.

Fuchs, Christian. 2018. *Digital Demagogue: Authoritarian Capitalism in the Age of Trump and Twitter.* London: Pluto.

Fuchs, Christian. 2017a. "Donald Trump: A Critical Theory-Perspective on Authoritarian Capitalism." *tripleC: Communication, Capitalism & Critique* 15 (1): 1–72.

Fuchs, Christian. 2017b. *Social Media; A Critical Introduction.* London: Sage. 2nd edition.

Fuchs, Christian. 2017c. "The Relevance of Franz L. Neumann's Critical Theory in 2017: "Anxiety and Politics" in the New Age of Authoritarian Capitalism." *tripleC: Communication, Capitalism & Critique* 15 (2): 637–50.

Gerbaudo, Paolo. 2018. "Social Media and Populism: An Elective Affinity?" *Media, Culture & Society* 40 (5): 745–53.

Gerbaudo, Paolo. 2017. *Populism, Citizenism and Global Protest.* London: Hurst & Company.

Gramsci, Antonio. 2000. *The Gramsci Reader*, edited by David Forgacs. New York: New York University Press.

Hitler, Adolf. 1926. *Mein Kampf.* Volume 2. Online version.

Horkheimer, Max and Theodor W. Adorno. 2002. *Dialectic of the Enlightenment.* Stanford, CA: Stanford University Press.

Inglehart, Roland and Pippa Norris. 2016. *Trump, Brexit, and the Rise of Populism: Economic Have-Nots and Cultural Backlash.* Harvard Kennedy School Faculty Research Working Paper Series RWP16-026. Cambridge, MA: Harvard University.

James, Cyril Lionel Robert James. 1986. *State Capitalism and World Revolution.* Chicago, IL: Kerr.

Klein, Naomi. 2017. *No Is Not Enough: Defeating the New Shock Politics*. London: Allen Lane.

Labica, Georges. 1987. Populismus. In *Kritisches Wörterbuch des Marxismus, Band 6*, 1026–9. Hamburg: Argument.

Lubbers, Marcel, Mérove Gijsberts, and Peer Scheepers. 2002. "Extreme Right-Wing Voting in Western Europe." *European Journal of Political Research* 41 (3): 345–78.

Lukács, Georg. 1923/1972. *History and Class Consciousness*. Cambridge, MA: MIT Press.

Marcuse, Herbert. 1958. *Soviet Marxism*. New York: Columbia University Press.

Neumann, Franz. 2009/1944. *Behemoth: The Structure and Practice of National Socialism, 1933–1944*. Chicago, IL: Ivan R. Dee.

Neumann, Franz. 2017/1957. "Anxiety and Politics." *tripleC: Communication, Capitalism & Critique* 15 (2): 612–36.

Oesch, Daniel. 2008. "Explaining Workers' Support for Right-Wing Populist Parties in Western Europe: Evidence from Austria, Belgium, France, Norway, and Switzerland." *International Political Science Review* 29 (3): 349–73.

Reich, Wilhelm. 1972. *The Mass Psychology of Fascism*. London: Souvenir Press.

Reisigl, Martin and Ruth Wodak. 2001. Discourse and Discrimination. *Rhetorics of Racism and Antisemitism*. London: Routledge.

Rooduijn, Matthijs. 2016. "Closing the Gap? A Comparison of Voters for Radical Right-Wing Populist Parties and Mainstream Parties Over Time." In *Radical Right-Wing Populist Parties in Western Europe*, edited by Tjitske Akkerman, Sarah de Lange, and Matthijs Rooduijn, 53–69. New York: Routledge.

The Democratic and the Authoritarian State. Glencoe, IL: The Free Press.

Theweleit, Klaus. 1989. *Male Fantasies. Volume 2: Male Bodies: Psychoanalyzing the White Terror*. Minneapolis, MN: University of Minnesota Press.

Theweleit, Klaus. 1987. *Male Fantasies. Volume 1: Women, Floods, Bodies, History*. Minneapolis, MN: University of Minnesota Press.

Van Gelder, Robert. 1940. "Chaplin Draws a Keen Weapon." *New York Times*, September 8.

Werts, Han, Peer Scheepers, and Marcel Lubbers. 2012. "Euro-Scepticism and Radical Right-Wing Voting in Europe, 2002–2008: Social Cleavages, Socio-Political Attitudes and Contextual Characteristics Determining Voting for he Radical Right." *European Union Politics* 14 (2): 183–205.

Williams, Raymond. 1983. *Keywords*. New York: Oxford University Press. 2nd edition.

Wodak, Ruth. 2015. *The Politics of Fear: What Right-Wing Populist Discourses Mean*. London: Sage.

Wodak, Ruth. 2013. ""Anything Goes!" – The Haiderization of Europe." In *Right-Wing Populism in Europe: Politics and Discourse*, edited by Ruth Wodak, Majid Kosravinik, and Brigitte Mral, 23–37. London: Bloomsburg.

Chapter Thirteen
Why There are Certain Parallels Between Joachim C. Fest's Hitler-Biography and Michael Wolff's Trump-Book

13.1 Joachim C. Fest's Analysis of Hitler

Demagogues, who are entangled into history's negative dialectics, attract a massive amount of public attention, including in the form of monographs. The Library of Congress, the world's largest library, lists in its catalogue around 3,300 books that have "Hitler" in its title. Joachim C. Fest's (1974) Hitler-biography, first published in German in 1973 and in English in 1974, is one of the most widely read books about Nazi Germany.

Fest portrays Hitler as having had a distorted psychological character: "The phenomenon of Hitler demonstrates, to an extent surpassing all previous experience, that historical greatness can be linked with paltriness on the part of the individual concerned. For considerable periods his personality seemed disintegrated, as if it had evaporated into unreality" (Fest 1974, 9). "There is surely a psychological link between this sense of being an outsider and the readiness to employ a whole nation as material for wild and expansive projects, even to the point of destroying the nation" (Fest 1974, 14). "Unlike the Fascist type in general, he was not seduced by history but by his own educational experience, the shudders of happiness and terror that had been his in puberty" (Fest 1974, 758). "Nervous weakness compensated for by superman poses: in this, too, Hitler revealed his link with the late-bourgeois age, with the period of Gobineau, Wagner, and Nietzsche" (Fest 1974, 759). "The purpose of all the ceremonies and mass celebrations was obviously to engage the popular imagination and rally the popular will into a unitary force. But beneath the surface it is possible to discern motives that throw light upon Hitler's personality and psychopathology" (Fest 1974, 517).

DOI: 10.4324/9781003256090-13

So Fest characterises Hitler in terms of "paltriness", "outsiderhood", "unreality", "shudders of happiness", "nervous weakness", and "psychopathology". He reduces the explanation of Nazi-fascism to Hitler as individual and to an alleged mental illness. Because Nazi-fascism is for Fest all about Hitler, it also disappeared in his explanation with Hitler's death: "Almost without transition, virtually from one moment to the next, Nazism vanished after the death of Hitler and the surrender". The repeated surges of neo-Nazism cannot be explained based on such an approach.

Also many other individuals experience difficult family situations and career disappointments, but such experiences do not regularly lead to the involvement in and planning of the systematic, industrial annihilation of 6 million Jews. Psychological explanations are insufficient and disregard the ideological and political-economic aspects of fascism. Consequently, Fest gives relatively little attention to the Shoah.

Ian Kershaw argues in his book *Hitler, the Germans, and the Final Solution* that Joachim C. Fest (1974) and Alan Bullock (1952) wrote in their Hitler-biographies little on "the persecution, the murder, of the Jews and on the war itself – both completely inextricable from the history of Nazism" (Kershaw, 2009, 18). Hermann Graml in one of the first reviews of Fest's book criticised that "Fest with his method suppresses the large part that certain economic circles – and other conservative groups such as the army and churches – played in the collapse of the Weimar Republic and therefore at least indirectly in the rise of the Nazis"[1] (Graml 1974, 88). Reinhard Kühnl in his book *Faschismustheorien* (*Theories of Fascism*) characterises the type of approach that Fest advances as explaining fascism from "the thought, will and actions of the fascist leader"[2] (Kühnl 1990, 53) and ignoring that "the leader cannot lead without [...] an alliance with specific political forces and interests against others"[3] (Kühnl 1990, 55).

13.2 Michael Wolff's Analysis of Trump

Trump is a far-right demagogue, but comparing him to Hitler or Nazi-fascism (see for example http://trumpandhitler.com) downplays the singularity of the Shoah. It is for certain that the phase of US politics under Trump will be particularly remembered in history. The possibility that this era will be remembered (in case remembering will still be possible) as starting a nuclear war cannot be ruled out, although it is more likely that South Korea and China will seek a diplomatic solution to the North Korea crisis because South Korea has no interest in being involved in a nuclear war and China does not want to see one in its backyard. History books about will certainly also involve chapters and passages about Trump's use of Twitter. The Trump era may end in disasters, in impeachment, after four years, or (more unlikely) after eight years. Only history will tell.

One year after Trump's presidency started, the first books about his political rise have been published. Michael Wolff's (2018) *Fire and Fury: Inside the Trump White House* has thus far attracted the widest public interest. Trump certainly does not like the book, which is why some of his tweets claim that it is "[f]ull of lies, misrepresentations" and that "Michael Wolff is a total loser who made up stories in order to sell this really boring and untruthful book".

Wolff's account is journalistic, not academic. But there are nonetheless parallels to Fest's approach. Wolff repeats Fest's mistake of individualising and psychologising far-right politics. Trump is characterised as being silly and psychologically unstable: Trump "didn't process information in any conventional sense – or, in a way, he didn't process it at all" (Wolff 2018, 113). "Some believed that for all practical purposes he was no more than semiliterate" (Wolff 2018, 113–114). "'He's not only crazy,' declared [Trump-friend] Tom Barrack to a friend, 'he's stupid'" (Wolff 2018, 233). "In truth, he was often neither fully aware of the nature of what he had said nor fully cognizant of why there should be such a passionate reaction to it" (Wolff 2018, 249). "Rex Tillerson [...] had called the president 'a fucking moron.' [...] For Steve Mnuchin and Reince Priebus, he was an 'idiot.' For Gary Cohn, he was 'dumb as shit.' For H. R. McMaster he was a 'dope.' The list went on" (Wolff 2018, 304).

Wolff characterises Trump as a psychologically unstable tabula rasa that can be politically moulded into any direction. There would have been a battle between Steve Bannon on the one side and Ivanka Trump and Jared Kushner on the other side (whom Wolff considers not just to be married, but to also form a political unity that he refers to as "Jarvanka") about who had been better able to politically manipulate Trump. Bannon would have tried to create a far-right president, "Jarvanka", a centrist one. Trump's government "represented a deeply structural assault on liberal values [...] But from the start it also was apparent that the Trump administration could just as easily turn into a country club Republican or a Wall Street Democrat regime. Or just a constant effort to keep Donald Trump happy" (Wolff 2018, 177). "Bannon and his ilk had made him the monster he more and more seemed to be" (Wolff 2018, 243).

The parallel between Fest's and Wolff's approach is that both reduce far-right demagoguery to an individual's psyche and leave out the importance of ideology and

Michael Wolff's Analysis of Trump

FIGURE 13.1   The author's book about Trump's use of Twitter.

political economy. Trump's ideology was militarist, nationalist, authoritarian, etc. before and during his presidential campaign and has remained so after it. He is not an ideologically isolated individual, but represents the far-right within the Republican Party that has been strengthened since the rise of the Tea Party movement in 2009. He is not a political tabula rasa, but represents the political economic project of trying to make the billionaire class faction identical with the ruling political elite (Figure 13.1).

13.3 *Digital Demagogue*

The book *Digital Demagogue: Authoritarian Capitalism in the Age of Trump and Twitter* (Fuchs 2018) takes a completely different approach. It combines political economy, ideology critique, and political psychology for explaining the emergence of authoritarian capitalism and its ideology, organisations, movements, and individuals.

Digital Demagogue's analysis shows that Trump certainly has an authoritarian character structure. But such a character structure does not develop simply because of early childhood or teenage experiences or because of a psychological predisposition, but is embedded into the broader political economic formation and ideological formations that form structures of feelings and experience that shape socialisation over long periods of time. And given the social character of these structures, authoritarianism does not produce single authoritarian individuals, but authoritarian movements with leaders and followers who are all small leaders envisioning themselves as big leaders controlling political, economic, and ideological power.

There is no automatic link between economic position and political consciousness. Voting, supporting, or joining authoritarian movements is not just a matter of class structures and ideological efforts, but also has to do with the history of an individual's personal, economic, political, and cultural socialisation that makes him or her more or less affectually prone to far-right propaganda. Right-wing authoritarianism often intensifies in and after political-economic crises, but also involves conscious ideological projects that try to speak to human's hopes, fears, desires, and aggressions.

Individualising psychological explanations, as advanced by both Fest and Wolff, fall short of explaining the causes and dynamics of right-wing authoritarianism. A theory of authoritarianism needs to combine political economy, ideology critique, and political psychology. As part of the analysis of the dialectic of object and subject it also needs to integrate structures and practices of communication, including the use of social media.

Notes

1 Translation from German.
2 Translation from German.
3 Translation from German.

References

Bullock, Alan. 1952. *Hitler: A Study in Tyranny*. London: Odhams Press.
Fest, Joachim C. 1974. *Hitler*. Orlando, FL: Harcourt.
Fuchs, Christian. 2018. *Digital Demagogue: Authoritarian Capitalism in the Age of Trump and Twitter*. London: Pluto.
Graml, Hermann. 1974. "Probleme einer Hitler-Biographie." *Kritische Bemerkungen zu Joachim C. Fest. Vierteljahreshefte für Zeitgeschichte* 22 (1): 76–92.

Kershaw, Ian. 2009. *Hitler, the Germans, and the Final Solution*. New Haven, CT: Yale University Press.

Kühnl, Reinhard. 1990. *Faschismustheorien. Ein Leitfaden*. Heilbronn: Distel Verlag. Updated edition

Wolff, Michael. 2018. *Fire and Fury: Inside the Trump White House*. London: Little, Brown.

Chapter Fourteen
How did Donald Trump Incite a Coup Attempt?

On 6 January 2021, supporters of Donald Trump stormed the Capitol after a Trump rally. This chapter asks: how did Donald Trump incite the storm on the Capitol on 6 January 2021)?

The presented research analyses parts of a dataset consisting of Trump's most recent 8,736 tweets as well as Trump's speech given at the rally that preceded the storming of the Capitol.

The chapter shows how Trump's speech and use of Twitter triggered violence and that the coup was the consequence of a long chain of events that unfolded as a consequence of Trump's authoritarian ideology, personality, and practices.

"Congress shall make no law respecting an establishment of religion [...] or abridging the freedom of speech, or of the press", says the US Constitution's First Amendment. The First Amendment does not protect speech that incites lawlessness that is imminent and likely, which includes the advocacy of crime and violence. How did Donald Trump incite the violence that erupted when his followers stormed the Capitol on 6 January?

Between 19 December and 6 January, Trump seven times announced the "Save America"-rally he held in Washington DC on the day his followers stormed the Capitol. In the first announcement, he tweeted, "Be there, will be wild!" (see the tweet below).

Donald J. Trump: "Peter Navarro releases 36-page report alleging election fraud "more than sufficient" to swing victory to Trump washex.am/3nwaBCe. A great report by Peter. Statistically impossible to have lost the 2020 Election. Big protest in D.C. on January 6th. Be there, will be wild!"

(Twitter: @realdonaldtrump, 18 December 2020)

"To be wild" is a circumlocution for the use of violence. The call to attend the meeting went viral among Trump's followers on social media (Barry, McIntire and Rosenberg 2020). Far-right groups such as the Proud Boys, QAnon conspiracy theorists, The Oath

DOI: 10.4324/9781003256090-14

Keepers, or Three Percenters joined (Hill 2021). Some Trump followers brought guns, Molotov cocktails, or pipe bombs (Porter 2021).

In the two months between the day after the US presidential election and the coup attempt, the US president unleashed a constant stream of a total of 1,718 tweets, claiming the election was rigged and fraudulent. Using TAGS (Twitter Archiving Google Sheet) and Discovertext, the present author collected all Trump-tweets between 2 June 2020 and 8 January 2021 when Twitter shut down Trump's account, which resulted in a dataset consisting of 8,736 tweets. In these tweets, Trump constantly repeated the message that "they are trying to STEAL the Election. We will never let them do it" (4 November), until Twitter first temporarily and then permanently blocked his account. The block took effect after he had tweeted about the riots, "These are the things and events that happen when a sacred landslide election victory is so un-ceremoniously & viciously stripped away from great patriots who have been badly & unfairly treated for so long" (6 January). Conducting a word frequency analysis using NVivo showed that "ballot" (153), "fraud" (140 mentions), "fake" (77), and "rigged"/"rigging" (67) were among the most frequently utilised words in Trump's post-election tweets (see the resulting word cloud in Figure 14.1).

Trump built up a high level of aggression among his followers step-by-step using social media, speeches, interviews, press conferences, etc. He is a highly mediated far-right politicians who cannot survive politically without having networked communication technologies at his disposal.

Trump's strategy to undermine the election results culminated in the events that un-folded on 6 January. His 71-minute-long speech at the "Save America"-rally triggered the coup attempt that followed (Trump 2021). What did Trump say in this speech?

Using NVivo, the present author analysed a transcript of Trump's speech. Besides references to the election, among the most frequent words (see the word cloud in Figure 14.2) Trump used were "illegal"/"illegally" and "fight"/"fighting"/"fights". The main message the speech conveyed to the rally's attendants was that the election result was illegal and that therefore they had to fight.

Just like on Twitter, Trump also in this speech over and over repeated the false claim that the election was stolen from him and his followers:

> "Hundreds of thousands of American patriots are committed to the honesty of
> our elections and the integrity of our glorious Republic. All of us here today

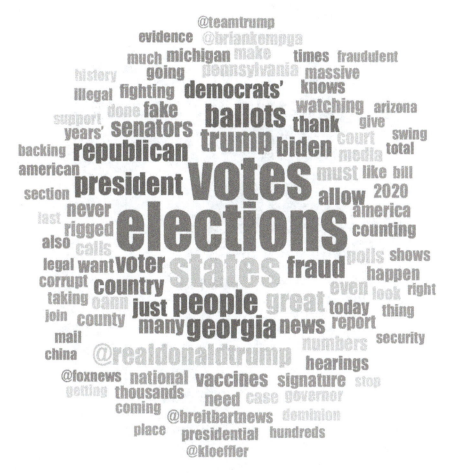

FIGURE 14.1 A word cloud of the text of all 1,718 tweets that Donald Trump posted between 4 January 2020 and 8 January 2021.

do not want to see our election victory stolen by emboldened radical left Democrats, which is what they're doing and stolen by the fake news media."

(Trump 2021)

"Our country has had enough. We will not take it anymore and that's what this is all about. To use a favourite term that all of you people really came up with, we will stop the steal."

(Trump 2021)

Trump here uses what scholars such as Ruth Wodak in Critical Discourse Analysis call nationyms, words that refer to the nation (Reisigl and Wodak 2001, 50). In the Trump-speech,

FIGURE 14.2 A word cloud of the transcript of Donald Trump's speech at the Save America-rally on 6 January 2021 in Washington, D.C.

example nationyms are "American patriots" and "our country". Trump combines the use of nationyms with the friend/enemy-scheme in order to construct a difference between "us" and his enemies who he claims have stolen the election and are the "radical left", the "Democrats", and "the fake news media".

Trump infers from his claims that something must be done, namely that his followers must act to "stop the steal". After the US election, #stopthesteal has been a popular social media hashtag used by Trump followers. Trump himself used the hashtag seventeen times in his post-election tweets and thereby helped crafting and popularising it.

In his speech, Trump frequently described his opponents as "weak" and urged his followers to be "strong". For example, he spoke of "weak Republicans", "weak congresspeople" ("we got to get rid of the weak congresspeople"), or "the weak ones". Somatonyms are words or phrases that refer to features of the body (Reisigl and Wodak 2001, 48–49), such as bodily weakness or strength. Trump utilises somatonyms in order to construct a binary between strong friends and weak enemies.

The friend/enemy-scheme was popularised by fascist thinkers such as the Nazi legal scholar Carl Schmitt. He wrote that the concept of the enemies implies "to repel and fight them physically" (Schmitt 2007, 49). Extermination and war are the friend/enemy scheme's logical consequence. Following on from the use of the friend/enemy-scheme and the strength/weakness binary, Trump referred in his speech no less than twenty times to "fight", "fights", and "fighting". In one instance, he imitated a boxer using his fists to symbolise how to fight. Here are some example usages from the analysed speech (Trump 2021):

- "you have to get your people to fight. If they don't fight, we have to primary the hell out of the ones that don't fight";
- "We're going to have to fight much harder";
- "And now we're out here fighting";
- "But it used to be that they'd argue with me, I'd fight. So I'd fight, they'd fight. I'd fight, they'd fight. Boop-boop";
- "And we fight. We fight like Hell and if you don't fight like Hell, you're not going to have a country anymore";
- "Together we are determined to defend and preserve government of the people, by the people and for the people".

By utilising the image of the fighter, Trump communicated to his followers that a battle had been going on that now reached its climax. The crowd responded to this image by chanting at the rally, on its way to and inside of the Capitol, "Fight for Trump! Fight for Trump! Fight for Trump!". Trump's lawyer Rudy Giuliani had earlier in a pre-speech called for "trial by combat", to which a Trump supporter dressed in military gear reacted, "He just said, 'Trial by combat'. I'm ready! I'm ready!" (CNN 2021).

Starting from the false claim that the election was rigged and building up hatred against his identified enemies, Trump's speech culminated in calls that his followers should together with him march to the Capitol:

"After this, we're going to walk down and I'll be there with you. We're going to walk down. We're going to walk down any one you want, but I think right here.

We're going walk down to the Capitol, and we're going to cheer on our brave senators, and congressmen and women. We're probably not going to be cheering so much for some of them because you'll never take back our country with weakness. You have to show strength, and you have to be strong."

(Trump 2021)

Trump's fans followed this call and the result was the attempted coup. Although Trump once said that "everyone here will soon be marching over to the Capitol building to peacefully and patriotically make your voices heard", given his rhetoric at the speech, the repeated false claims that the election was rigged, and four-year-long hate tirades against his enemies, it is no wonder that his followers forced entry into the Congress building, chanting slogans such as "Hang Mike Pence!" (Evon 2021) or screaming "Tell Pelosi we're coming for that bitch (TMZ 2021). Tell fucking Pelosi we're coming for her". Twitter stopped the Pence slogan when it trended (Pengelly 2021).

In previous research, the present author provided evidence that Donald Trump is a right-wing authoritarian who frequently utilises and practises top-down leadership, the friend/enemy-scheme, nationalism, law and order politics, and militarism (Fuchs, 2018a, 2018b, 2021, chapter 9). It was not a single speech by which Trump incited a coup. The speech at his rally was a trigger of a coup attempt that was incited by a long chain of events that unfolded as a consequence of Trump's authoritarian ideology, authoritarian personality, and authoritarian practices. Donald Trump's authoritarianism has made the world a more dangerous place, where the rise of new fascist societies has become an actual threat, and has brought the USA close to the brink of a civil war.

References

Barry, Dan, Mike McIntire, and Matthew Rosenberg. 2020. ""Our President Wants Us Here": The Mob That Stormed the Capitol." *New York Times*, 9 January 2021, https://www. nytimes.com/2021/01/09/us/capitol-rioters.html.

CNN. 2021. "CNN Newsroom Transcript." *CNN*, 8 January 2021. http://edition.cnn.com/ TRANSCRIPTS/2101/08/cnr.17.html.

Evon, Dan. 2021. "Was "Hang Mike Pence" Chanted at Capitol Riot?" *Snopes*, 9 January 2021, https://www.snopes.com/fact-check/hang-mike-pence-chant-capitol-riot/.

Fuchs, Christian. 2021. *Social Media. A Critical Introduction*. London: Sage. 3rd edition.

Fuchs, Christian. 2018a. *Digital Demagogue: Authoritarian Capitalism in the Age of Trump and Twitter*. London: Pluto Press.

Fuchs, Christian. 2018b. "Authoritarian Capitalism, Authoritarian Movements and Authoritarian Communication." *Media, Culture & Society* 40 (5): 779–91.

Hill, Becs. 2021. Active Far-Right Groups in the Capitol Riots. https://www.talkingaboutterrorism.com/post/active-far-right-groups-in-the-capitol-riots.

Pengelly, Martin. 2021. ""Hang Mike Pence": Twitter Stops Phase Trending After Capitol Riot." *The Guardian*, 10 January 2021, https://www.theguardian.com/us-news/2021/jan/10/hang-mike-pence-twitter-stops-phrase-trending-capitol-breach.

Porter, Tom. 2021. "One of the Trump Supporters Who Stormed the US Capitol Was Carrying 11 Molotov Cocktails and an Assault Rifle, Prosecutors Say." *Business Insider*, 8 January 2021, https://www.businessinsider.com/trump-supporter-arrested-at-capitol-had-11-molotov-cocktails-feds-2021-1?r=DE&IR=T.

Reisigl, Martin and Ruth Wodak. 2001. *Discourse and Discrimination. Rhetorics of Racism and Antisemitism.* London: Routledge.

Schmitt, Carl. 2007. *The Concept of the Political.* Chicago, IL: The University of Chicago Press.

TMZ. 2021. "Capitol Coup: Rioters Were Hunting For Pence, Pelosi … Threats of Violence, Hanging." *TMZ*, 9 January 2021, https://www.tmz.com/2021/01/09/rioters-wanted-hurt-nancy-pelosi-hang-mike-pence-capitol/.

Trump, Donald. 2021. Transcript and Video of the Trump-Speech at the Save America-Rally. 6 January 2021, https://www.rev.com/blog/transcripts/donald-trump-speech-save-america-rally-transcript-january-6.

Chapter Fifteen

Boris Johnson Takes His Brexit Demagoguery to the Social Media Sphere

15.1 Introduction

On 28 August 2019, UK prime minister Boris Johnson prorogued British Parliament, which means that its current annual session will come to an end earlier than expected. This will leave just a few days in early September for the opposition to attempt to block a "no-deal" Brexit by passing emergency legislation and/or trying to force out Johnson by a vote of no-confidence.

Labour Party leader Jeremy Corbyn described Johnson's move as "a threat to our democracy" and spoke of a "constitutional outrage" and a "smash and grab of our democracy by the Prime Minister".[1] Chanting "Stop the coup", thousands protested in Central London and other cities after Johnson's suspension of Parliament. The fight over a no-deal Brexit between Johnson's government and Parliament will enter a hot and decisive phase when the British Parliament reconvenes after its summer recess on 3 September.

15.2 Brexit's Long History

Johnson came to power as part of a revolt of the most right-wing factions in the Conservative Party against former prime minister Theresa May, whom they saw as secretly wanting to remain in the European Union (EU). The members of these groups assumed that she was not tough enough in the negotiations of a withdrawal agreement between Britain and the EU.

DOI: 10.4324/9781003256090-15

Johnson argues that the EU has to drop the so-called "backstop", an aspect of the withdrawal agreement that leaves the UK in the EU Customs Union in case no solution can be found that allows preventing a hard border between Ireland and Northern Ireland. Johnson says that if the EU does not change its position on the backstop, then Britain will leave without an agreement on World Trade Organization terms and with "no ifs, no buts" on 31 October. He speaks of wanting to use alternative technological arrangements instead of a physical border between Ireland and Northern Ireland, but such means do not exist. They are mere techno-deterministic fantasies.

Johnson's political plans include further reducing corporation tax and lowering the income tax rate for those who earn more than £80,000 per year.

Many observers believe that behind the scenes, Johnson is preparing for a general election and will try to blame the EU, the British Parliament, and anti-Brexit members of Parliament for the breakdown of negotiations in order to mobilise voters. At the same time, in light of the G7 summit, Johnson and President Trump have both talked about wanting to establish a free trade deal between the United States and the United Kingdom. Such a deal could result in the privatisation of public services, the further deregulation of working conditions, and the lowering of food and consumer standards.

On 27 August, leaders of the opposition parties met in order to plan for passing emergency legislation during the first two weeks of September, when the British Parliament will sit after its summer recess and before another break during which the British parties' annual conferences will take place. Under Corbyn's leadership, the Labour Party, the Scottish Nationalists, the Liberal Democrats, the Welsh party Plaid Cymru, the Green Party, independent members of Parliament, and potentially some Tories who oppose Johnson's position on Brexit plan to pass a law that would stop a no-deal Brexit.

On 28 August, the Johnson government got the Queen to prorogue Parliament. Prorogation is the period between the end of one parliamentary session (one parliamentary year) and the start of the next one that is opened by the Queen's Speech. Johnson's prorogation of Parliament reduces the time available to the opposition to try to block a no-deal Brexit.

The prime minister's move indicates that he is scared of the opposition blocking his no-deal Brexit plans, and that he wants to circumvent these plans by minimising the time available to parliamentary business before 31 October. An unplanned "no-deal" rupture between the UK and the EU without a withdrawal agreement would very likely bring back a physical border between Ireland and Northern Ireland, which could flare up and bring back the "Troubles in Northern Ireland" or, as the more pessimistic observers argue, be the trigger of a war in Europe.

There are only speculations about what consequences a "no-deal" Brexit would mean for Britain. The British and the EU economy are highly interlinked via imports and exports.[2] In 2018, 78.2 percent of the UK's import value of pharmaceutical products, including human blood and medicines, were coming from EU countries.[3] In 2018, medicinal and pharmaceutical products accounted for 6.7 percent of the value of all British imports from the EU.[4] A leaked government memo revealed that the Johnson administration expects food and medicine shortages in the case of a no-deal Brexit (Mason 2019).

Johnson's demagoguery has also extended to social media.

15.3 "People's PMQs" as Ideology

On 14 August 2019, Johnson broadcast the first "People's Prime Minister's Question Time"[5] via 10 Downing Street's Facebook page that at that time has around 630,000 followers.

At 11 am, a message was posted that called for users to ask questions: "Get ready for the first ever #PeoplesPMQs later today. Put your questions to the [prime minister] by commenting on this post". At 12:15 pm, the broadcast started. In the 75 minutes that were available to post questions, a total of 956 comments were made. The broadcast lasted for 11 minutes. Johnson answered eight questions, which means he devoted roughly 80 seconds to each selected comment.

The eight questions focused on the topics of leaving the EU, the British Union, preventing Parliament from blocking Brexit, restoring the British people's faith in politics, the alienation of rural communities from Westminster politics, mental health services, knife crime, and political heroes.

The selected questions allowed Johnson to present himself as the savior who will deliver Brexit on 31 October and thereby give a voice to, as he said in the broadcast, "people in towns and regions of the U.K. feeling that they weren't being heard". He presented himself as the leader who will make Britain flourish, implement tough law-and-order policies, and, like Pericles of Athens, is a "powerful articulator of the idea of democrac".

During the People's PMQs, no critical questions were selected that scrutinised Johnson's position on Brexit, his worldview, political convictions or actions. There was very little time for the preparation of questions. For example, the following comment was not taken up:

"I require weekly infusions of human immunoglobulin to keep me alive. Human [Immunoglobulin G] cannot be stockpiled as it is a plasma product. Human [Immunoglobulin G] also cannot be produced in the UK due to the British population being at risk from [Variant Creutzfeldt-Jakob disease]. What cast-iron guarantees can you give me, and the thousands of other patients in the UK who require this lifelong and life-saving treatment that supplies would not become difficult to obtain if no deal happens. If there was a shortage of this product, then the health of thousands of citizens could be at risk. Cancer patients also frequently require Human [Immunoglobulin G] during chemo as their immune systems deplete."

The format of People's PMQs does not encourage citizens to come together to discuss politics and then together formulate comments and inputs; it advances individualistic, superficial, high-speed political communication. If we understand political communication as engaged dialogue of several individuals on equal grounds, then Johnson's social media format is not at all a form of communication, because it does not allow for real dialogue.

The People's PMQs is highly instrumental. It gives the prime minister's social media team the power to select questions that allow him to present himself as positively as possible. There is no independent selection of questions that fosters critical scrutiny.

Further, the communication style of short questions and short answers is typical of demagogic politics. Such a politics accelerates superficial political communication, advances tabloidisation, does not provide sufficient time for in-depth discussion, and ultimately represents an informational space that does not foster dialogue and debate. The People's PMQ more resembles an emperor talking to his entourage than a democratic conversation.

Moreover, the selected questions were partly edited. For example, the question, "What are you going to do to protect our Union of Nations" reads in full: "Now we are leaving the [Common Agricultural Policy], do you think it's now time for more a green high tech revolution in farming? If so what policies do you have for this? Plus what are you going to do to protect our Union of Nations".

In his answers, Johnson not only presented himself as the voice of the British people who will deliver Brexit, but also communicated a deep division between those wanting Brexit, whom he described as the British people on the one side, and the EU and anti-Brexit members of Parliament on the other side. "There is a terrible kind of collaboration, as it were, going on between people who think they can block Brexit in Parliament and our European friends", he said. Johnson uses the word "collaboration" in the context of the highly contentious political topic of Brexit. He fosters resentments by appealing to the meaning of the word as "traitorous cooperation with an enemy".[6]

True, deliberative democracy fosters engaged political conversations and debates as foundations of informed decision-making. Participatory democracy extends democracy from elections to other realms, such as the economy and public institutions, and allows those who are affected by decisions and organisations to take part in these organisations' governance and decision-making processes.

Given its instrumental, accelerated, individualistic, demagogic, and tabloid character, Johnson's use of social media in his People's PMQs neither advances deliberative nor participatory democracy but rather, authoritarian plebiscitary politics. The plebiscitary state is based on pseudo-participation, where citizens are allowed to selectively and occasionally voice their opinions and vote on questions and matters that were selected by a charismatic political leader.

The People's PMQs exemplifies this pseudo-participation, where political voice is handled in a highly selectively and instrumental manner that allows a political leader to worship himself in a self-congratulatory manner.

15.4 Social Media and the Public Sphere

In his 1932 book *Legality and Legitimacy*, the fascist German legal theorist Carl Schmitt (2004) saw "plebiscitary legitimacy" as "the single type of state justification that may be generally acknowledged today as valid" (90). He was aware that the plebiscitary state advances tendencies of the "authoritarian state" and the "total state" (90). Further, Schmitt argues that plebiscitary politics means "authority from above, confidence from below" and requires "a government or some other authoritarian organ in which one can have confidence that it will pose the correct question in the proper way" (90).

In the age of social media, demagogic authority from above does not mean control of what questions are asked, but control and selection of the questions and the pieces of information that gain public visibility. Digital plebiscitary communication is a political instrument that controls and manipulates attention and visibility in the online public sphere.

In his classic work *Structural Transformation of the Public Sphere*, German sociologist and philosopher Jürgen Habermas argues that, at the time of absolute monarchies, the public sphere meant that the emperor "displayed himself, presented himself as an embodiment of some sort of 'higher' power" (Habermas 1991, 7). Representation meant the repeated presentation of authoritarian power to the public and of an "aura" that "surrounded and endowed" this authority (Habermas 1991, 7). For Habermas, the feudal public sphere is a pseudo-public that is based on the "staging of the publicity" (Habermas 1991, 8).

The People's PMQs advances the digital re-feudalisation of the public sphere. Political voice is stage-managed in a selective manner and instrumentalised in a digital spectacle that is designed to present the charismatic aura of a single person. Re-feudalisation means to "procure plebiscitary agreement from a mediatised public by means of a display of staged or manipulated publicity" (Habermas 1991, 232).

In the first People's PMQs, Johnson pointed out that Pericles is one of his political heroes. Pericles was a Greek army general and statesman who lived in the fifth century B.C. In his book *Pericles of Athens*, historian of ancient Greece Vincent Azoulay (2014, 33) points out that many of his contemporaries saw Pericles as "despicable demagogue" (134) who "had the most astonishingly great thoughts of himself" (33) and possessed the "ability to turn black into white – and, in particular, to persuade his listeners that he had won a fight when, in fact, he had lost it" (43). Pericles's speeches were criticised for their "tyrannical haughtiness" (47). His "self-glorification attracted virulent criticism" (34).

Johnson's People's PMQs can, in some sense, indeed be seen as having some Periclean aspects. It is an example of the use of social media for political, digital, and authoritarian demagoguery and the feudalisation of the public sphere.

15.5 Right-Wing Authoritarianism and the Media

The right-wing use of the means of communication for creating a pseudo-public sphere has a longer history. In his book *The Psychological Technique of Martin Luther Thomas' Radio Addresses*, critical theorist Theodor W. Adorno (2000) analyses how the

Christian demagogue Martin Luther Thomas used radio to spread far-right propaganda in the United States in the 1930s.

Following in the footsteps of this tradition, Rush Limbaugh moderated a right-wing talk radio show from 1984 until his death in 2021. Glenn Beck, Sean Hannity, and Alex Jones are among those who built on Limbaugh's right-wing use of broadcasting. The creation of Fox News in 1996 gave the reach of right-wing media a further boost.

The rise of the Internet and social media has brought a new level of interactivity to the public dissemination of right-wing propaganda. For example, far-right Canadian YouTuber Andy Warski's channel has around 250,000 followers, and far-right UK Independence Party member Carl Benjamin's Sargon of Akkad channel has more than 950,000 subscribers (see Holt 2017). Such videos often reach several hundred thousand views and achieve thousands of comments. False news sites such as Breitbart operate their own platforms and are active on multiple social media sites such as Facebook (Breitbart: 3.8 million followers), Twitter (more than 1.1 million followers), Instagram (480,000 followers), and YouTube (135,000 subscribers).

With almost 65 million followers, President Trump's Twitter profile is the far-right medium with the largest audience. In the book *Digital Demagogue: Authoritarian Capitalism in the Age of Trump and Twitter*, I analyse Trump's politics and his use of Twitter (Fuchs 2018a). An empirical analysis showed that top-down leadership, nationalism, the friend/enemy-scheme, and militant patriarchy are key ideological features of Trump's use of Twitter. Right-wing demagogues are at the same time self-centred and pretend to represent the people's interests.

Johnson and Trump's uses of social media are the latest development in and expressions of right-wing media use that advances pseudo-participation as the means of instrumental reason, where right-wing leaders maintain the ultimate voice and control communication power in the public sphere.

15.6 What is to be Done Against the New Right-Wing Radicalism?

In contemporary capitalism, the rise of new authoritarianism and new nationalisms is the result of the negative dialectic of neoliberal capitalism and the new imperialism. The commodification of everything – entrepreneurialism, privatisation, deregulation, financialisation, globalisation, deindustrialisation, outsourcing, precarisation, and the new individualism – has backfired, extended, and intensified inequalities and crisis tendencies, which created a futile ground for new nationalisms and right-wing radicalism.

How should the left best counteract against nationalism and right-wing authoritarianism? German philosopher Theodor W. Adorno suggests that it is wrong to practise a left-wing populism that imitates the tactics and strategies of the far right. Progressive media and communication should not "fight lies with lies", but "counteract it with the full force of reason, with the genuinely unideological truth" (Adorno 1968/ 2020, 49–50).

What we need is not a demagogic and authoritarian Internet, but rather a public service Internet with public service formats that advance the power of critical reason against ideology (see chapter 16 in this book and Fuchs 2018b).

Notes

1 https://twitter.com/jeremycorbyn/status/1166709007345750016.
2 https://www.trademap.org/Country_SelProductCountry_TS.aspx?nvpm=1%7c040%7c%7c %7c%7cTOTAL%7c%7c%7c2%7c1%7c1%7c1%7c2%7c1%7c2%7c1%7c%7c1.
3 Data source: https://www.trademap.org/Country_SelProductCountry_TS.aspx?nvpm=1%7c04 0%7c%7c%7c%7cTOTAL%7c%7c%7c2%7c1%7c1%7c1%7c2%7c1%7c2%7c1%7c%7c1.
4 Data source: https://researchbriefings.files.parliament.uk/documents/CBP-7851/CBP-7851.pdf.
5 https://www.facebook.com/10downingstreet/videos/2422897891153638/?__tn__=-R.
6 https://www.lexico.com/en/definition/collaboration.

References

Adorno, Theodor W. 2000. *The Psychological Technique of Martin Luther Thomas' Radio Addresses.* Stanford, CA: Stanford University Press.

Adorno, Theodor W. 1968/2020. *Aspects of the New Right-Wing Extremism.* Cambridge: Polity.

Azoulay, Vincent. 2014. *Pericles of Athens.* Princeton, NJ: Princeton University Press.

Fuchs, Christian. 2018a. *Digital Demagogue: Authoritarian Capitalism in the Age of Trump and Twitter.* London: Pluto Press.

Fuchs, Christian. 2018b. *The Online Advertising Tax as the Foundation of a Public Service Internet.* London: University of Westminster Press. Open access version: 10.16997/book23

Habermas, Jürgen. 1991. *The Structural Transformation of the Public Sphere. An Inquiry into a Category of Bourgeois Society.* Cambridge, MA: MIT Press.

Holt, Jared. 2017. "Sargon Of Akkad" Cites White Nationalist Propaganda, Reveals His Alt-Right Sympathies. Right Wing Watch, 13 December 2017. https://www.rightwingwatch.org/post/sargon-of-akkad-cites-white-nationalist-propaganda-reveals-his-alt-right-sympathies.

Mason, Rowena. 2019. "Brexit: Leaked Papers Predict Food Shortages and Port Delays." *The Guardian*, 18 August 2019. https://www.theguardian.com/politics/2019/aug/18/brexit-leaked-papers-predict-food-shortages-and-port-delays-operation-yellowhammer.

Schmitt, Carl. 2004. *Legality and Legitimacy*. Durham, NC: Duke University Press.

References

Chapter Sixteen
Slow Media: How to Renew Debate in the Age of Digital Authoritarianism

The rise of a new global, digital, and mobile form of capitalism has, since the 1970s, accelerated the pace of our lives. We produce more, consume more, make more decisions, and have more experiences. This acceleration is driven by the underlying principles that "time is money", "time is power", and "life is short".

In the realm of media and communication, we are confronted by fast-paced global flows of information on the Internet that we constantly access from everywhere via our smartphones, laptops, and tablets. Commercial platforms such as Facebook, Twitter, and YouTube are digital tabloids that circulate high-speed flows of often-superficial information that is consumed with short attention spans. The primary goal of social media's information acceleration is the sale of targeted ads. And digital authoritarianism, fragmented publics, fake news, bots, filter bubbles, and a narcissistic "me" culture have all proliferated alongside this high-speed communication (Fuchs 2018a).

Today's social media are in fact anti-social media (Fuchs 2018b) that undermine political communication and understanding. In 2019, a House of Commons committee inquiry into disinformation and fake news concluded that the negative implications of social media should "allow more pause for thought" (House of Commons 2019, 88).

There is a desire for something different. Research conducted by my team in the EU project netCommons (see https://www.netcommons.eu/) showed that almost 90% of 1,000 Internet users who participated in a survey said they were interested in using alternatives to the dominant, commercial platforms (Boucas et al. 2018).

In a similar vein to "slow food" – which was created to counter the negative implications of fast-food culture, and which became part of the wider slow life movement – Sabria David, Jörg Blumtritt, and Benedikt Köhler propose a "slow media" manifesto (see http://en.slow-media.net/manifesto).

DOI: 10.4324/9781003256090-16

Slow media takes the speed out of information, news, and political communication by reducing the amount of information and communication flows. Users engage more deeply with each other and with content. Slow media does not distract users with advertisements, it is not based on user surveillance, and is not undertaken to yield profit. It's not simply a different form of media consumption, but an alternative way of organising and doing media – a space for reflection and rational political debate.

Club 2.0: Slow Debate

Club 2 was a debate format broadcast on television by the Austrian Broadcasting Corporation between 1976 and 1995. Viewers could watch a live, uncensored, and controversial debate between diverse participants in a small studio with no studio audience. Club 2 was, in this sense, the original slow media. It was not interrupted by advertisements and used unlimited airtime. In Britain, After Dark, a version of Club 2 produced by OpenMedia, aired from 1987 until 1997.

In the age of user-generated content, I propose an updated version of Club 2 that would bring together live television and the Internet, broadcast via a non-commercial video platform (Fuchs 2017). Club 2.0 would be based on a public service, not-for-profit version of YouTube that is free of advertising. Users – named and registered – would generate discussions to accompany a live TV debate uploaded to the video platform.

Limiting the number of registered and active users – and how many videos and text comments they can make during debates – would control the pace of online discussion. Instead of a maximum length to comments (and videos) as one gets on Twitter, there would be a minimum. Groups of users in schools, universities, companies, associations, local communities, neighbourhoods, council houses, churches, civil society, unions, and other contexts could co-create videos in advance of an episode.

At certain points of time during the live broadcast, a user-generated video would be chosen and broadcast, which would, in turn, inform the studio debate. Ideally during a debate lasting two or three hours, a number of user-generated videos would be selected.

At a time when sustained political communication of people who disagree has become almost impossible, new visions for slow media point to how we can create a fresh culture of political debate and renew the public sphere (Fuchs 2014). See https://www.parliament.uk/globalassets/documents/speaker/digital-democracy/Digi026_Christian_Fuchs.pdf.

Decelerating the logic of the media is incompatible with the principles on which the commercial digital monopolies are based.

Turning vision into a reality requires structural changes in communication. And slow media requires that we reinvent the Internet as a public service Internet (Fuchs 2018c) with platform co-operatives (see https://en.wikipedia.org/wiki/Platform_cooperative).

The commercial Internet is dominated by digital capital, digital monopolies, "fake news", filter bubbles, post-truth politics, digital authoritarianism, online nationalism, digital tabloids, and high-speed flows of superficial content. Public service Internet and platform co-operatives are the vision of a commons-based, democratic Internet and a true digital public sphere.

References

Boucas, Dimitris et al. 2018. Alternative Internet's Political Economy Survey Analysis and Interpretation of Data. netCommons EU Project Report: https://www.netcommons.eu/sites/default/files/d5.4_survey_v1.0.pdf.

Fuchs, Christian. 2018a. *Digital Demagogue: Authoritarian Capitalism in the Age of Trump and Twitter.* London: Pluto Press.

Fuchs, Christian. 2018b. "Socialising Anti-Social Social Media." In *Anti-Social Media: The Impact on Journalism and Society*, edited by John Mair, Tor Clark, Neil Fowler, Raymond Snoddy, and Richard Tait, 58–63. Suffolk: Abramis.

Fuchs, Christian. 2018c. *The Online Advertising Tax as the Foundation of a Public Service Internet.* London: University of Westminster Press. Open access version: 10.16997/book23.

Fuchs, Christian. 2017. "Towards the Public Service Internet as Alternative to the Commercial Internet." In *ORF Texte No. 20 – Öffentlich-Rechtliche Qualität im Diskurs*, 43–50. Vienna: ORF. http://zukunft.orf.at/show_content.php?sid=147&pvi_id=1815&pvi_medientyp=t&oti_tag=Texte.

Fuchs, Christian. 2014. "QTube – Citizen-Generated Videos for Questions to the Prime Minister." In *An Idea Submitted to the Speaker's Commission on Digital Democracy.* https://www.parliament.uk/globalassets/documents/speaker/digital-democracy/Digi026_Christian_Fuchs.pdf.

House of Commons. 2019. *House of Commons Digital, Culture, Media and Sport Committee: Disinformation and "Fake News": Final Report.* https://publications.parliament.uk/pa/cm201719/cmselect/cmcumeds/1791/1791.pdf.

References

Part III

Conclusion

Chapter Seventeen
Conclusion: What is Digital Fascism?

This book has addressed the question: how is fascism communicated on the Internet? It has outlined theoretical foundations of digital fascism and has presented case studies that study how fascism is communicated online.

The reader will thereby have gained a better understanding of a variety of aspects of and theoretical insights into digital fascism. In the conclusion, based on the findings of this book, we will give an explicit definition of digital fascism. For doing so, we need to first ask: what is fascism? (Section 17.1). Based on this discussion, we will then address the question: what is digital fascism (Section 17.2)?

17.1 What is Fascism?

A critical theory of fascism must ask itself in what relationship fascism stands to capitalism. Classical Marxist definitions of fascism often characterised fascism as a particular type and stage of capitalist development. Let us have a look at two examples.

Georgi Dimitrov, who was the Communist International's general secretary from 1935 until 1943, defines fascism as "the open terrorist dictatorship of the most reactionary, most chauvinistic and most imperialist elements of finance capital" (Dimitrov 1972 [1935], 8). Dimitrov sees the fusion of finance capital, terrorism, dictatorship, and imperialist warfare as characteristic of fascism.

Leon Trotsky gave a comparable definition: "fascism is nothing else but capitalist reaction; [...] The historic function of fascism is to smash the working class, destroy its organizations, and stifle political liberties when the capitalists find themselves unable to govern and dominate with the help of democratic machinery" (Trotsky 1996, 14, 34). "The mission of fascism is not so much to complete the destruction of bourgeois

DOI: 10.4324/9781003256090-17

democracy as to crush the first outlines of proletarian democracy" (Trotsky 1971, 367). For Trotsky, fascism is just like for Dimitrov the most reactionary form of capitalism that uses terror for destroying socialist organisations and their struggle for socialism.

Such definitions ignore the important role that nationalism and exterminatory racism and xenophobia have historically played in fascism. For example, in the case of Nazi-fascism such approaches understand anti-Semitism as "peripheral, rather than as a central moment" (Postone 1980, 98). They also overlook that fascism often contains particular forms of one-sided anti-capitalism such as the hatred of finance capital because it is seen as being Jewish in character. For example, Hitler did not see an antagonism between capital and labour, but between "Jewish finance-capital" on the one side and German labour and German capital on the other side, which is why he spoke of the "exploitation of German labor power in the yoke of world Jewish finance" (Hitler 1941, 906) via financial mechanisms such as loans. Hitler's propaganda minister Joseph Goebbels (1925) argued that the Jew is "the creator and bearer of international stock-market-capitalism, the main enemy of German liberty". Hitler (1941, 288) wrote that the "fight against international finance and loan capital has become the most important point in the program of the German nation's fight for its independence and freedom". "The Left once made the mistake of thinking that it had the monopoly on anti-capitalism or, conversely, that all forms of anti-capitalism are, at least potentially, progressive" (Postone 1980, 115).

> By breaking interest-slavery we mean the elimination of the tyrannical money-power of the stock market in the state and economy, which exploits the productive *Volk*, making them morally contaminated and incapable of national thinking.

The Nazis wanted to advance "breaking interest-slavery" (*Brechung der Zinsknechtschaft*), a political demand that goes back to and that Hitler took up from the fascist economist Gottfried Federer who also wrote the Nazi Party's programme. By breaking interest-slavery, the Nazis understand "the elimination of the tyrannical money-power of the stock market in the state and economy, which exploits the productive *Volk*, making them morally contaminated and incapable of national thinking" (Goebbels 1925). The whole concept is based on the assumption that there is a "sharp separation of the stock exchange capital from the national economy" (Hitler 1941, 287).

The Nazis saw finance capital as parasitic and Jewish and industrial capital as productive and German. They propagated a simplistic and one-dimensional form of anti-capitalism that moralises, dualises, and personalises capital (good German industrial capital vs. evil Jewish finance capital). Finance capital is biologised as being Jewish and opposed to a fictive national interest of German capital and German labour. Moishe Postone points out in this context:

> "This form of "anti-capitalism", then, is based on a on the abstract. The abstract and concrete are not seen as antinomy where the real overcoming of the abstract – of the value dimension – involves the historical overcoming of the a well as each of its terms. Instead there is the one-sided attack on abstract Reason, abstract law or, on another level, money and finance capital. [...] The manifest abstract dimension is also biologized – as the Jews. The opposition of the concrete material and the abstract becomes the racial opposition of the Arians and the Jews. Modern anti-Semitism involves a biologization of capitalism – which itself is only understood in terms of its manifest abstract dimension – as International Jewry."
>
> (Postone 1980, 112)

Orthodox Marxist definitions of fascism have overlooked the importance of nationalism and racism as ideological dimensions of fascism. In contrast, an opposite extreme are liberal definitions of fascism that ignore capitalism or deny a relation between capitalism and fascism. Let us have a look at some of these definitions.

The historian Roger Griffin established a widely cited and used definition of fascism:

> "Used generically, fascism is a term for a singularly protean genus of modern politics inspired by the conviction that a process of total political, social and cultural rebirth (palingenesis) has become essential to bring to an end a protracted period of DECADENCE, and expressing itself ideologically in revolutionary and forms of deeply antiliberal and mythically charged NATIONALISM (ultranationalism) which may often embrace overt notions of racial superiority."
>
> (Griffin 2003, 231–232)

For Griffin, nationalism, racism, and anti-liberalism are the three key features of fascism.

There are no aspects of terror, militarism, patriarchy, authoritarian leadership, and capitalism in this definition. The historian Stanley G. Payne approves of Griffin's definition and defines fascism as "a form of revolutionary ultranationalism for national rebirth that is based on a primarily vitalist philosophy, is structured on extreme elitism, mass mobilization, and the *Führerprinzip,* positively values violence as end as well as means and tends to normatize war and/or the military virtues" (Payne 1995, 14). Payne sees nationalism, authoritarian leadership, and violence as features of fascism. Such a definition does not allow a distinction between fascism and Stalinism.

The historian Walter Laqueur sees nationalism, hierarchy, the leadership principle, and violence as key features of fascism: "a 'fascist minimum' such as the common belief in nationalism, hierarchical structures, and the 'leader principle'. All fascisms were antiliberal and anti-Marxist, but they were also anticonservative, inasmuch as they did not want to submit to the old establishment but to replace it with a new elite. Fascism rested on the existence of a state party and, to varying degrees, on a monopoly over propaganda and the threat and use of violence against opponents. Such a 'fascist minimum' is far from perfect, but it is sufficient for most purposes" (Laqueur 1996, 90). Also in Laqueur's definition, the relationship of capitalism and fascism remains unclear.

The political theorist Roger Eatwell defines minimum features of fascism. This is what he calls the fascist minimum. Fascism is an

> "ideology that strives to forge social rebirth based on a holistic-national radical Third Way, though in practice fascism has tended to stress style, especially action and the charismatic leader, more than detailed programme, and to engage in a Manichaean demonisation of its enemies. [...] Nationalism: The belief that the world is divided into nations is central to fascism [...] Holism: Fascism is based on a view that the collective predominates over individual rights and interests. This helps to explain its hostility to liberal democracy. However, the principle also has an individual aspect in the sense that it portrays man as a victim of alienation, divided from other members of the true community and as incapable of finding fulfilment within existing socioeconomic structures. [...] Radicalism: [...] Fascism involves the desire to create a new political culture, partly through mobilisation and sometimes through cathartic violence. Although the idea of rebirth figures prominently in propaganda, there is no reactionary or populist desire to return to a former society or mythical past (though there is a desire to preserve aspects of the past). Fascism is an alternative form of modernity, though it synthesises the optimism of most modernists with the pessimism of conservatism. The Third Way: Fascism is hostile to both capitalism and socialism, but draws on aspects of both. It sees capitalism as too

individualistic, too dominated by the short run and ultimately not loyal to the community. It sees socialism as too internationalist and based on false views of equality. [...] It syncretically seeks to draw on what is seen as the best of capitalism (the naturalness of private property, its dynamism) and socialism (its concern for the community and welfare)."

(Eatwell 1996, 313–314)

For Eatwell, the key features of fascism are nationalism, charismatic leadership, collectivism, violence, anti-liberalism, and a self-understanding that propagates a Third Way beyond both capitalism and socialism. It remains unclear what the relationship is between capitalist society and fascism.

The problem of liberal definitions of fascism is that by ignoring the relationship of fascism and capitalism they cannot explain why fascist movements exist in capitalist societies and do not "explain why fascist movements, however great their rhetorical anti-conservatism, *always* relied on conservative forces to gain support and aim at power – never on those of the left" (Thompson 2011, 88).

Both the reduction of fascism to capitalism and the ignorance of capitalism in definitions of fascism are inadequate. A critical theory of fascism should neither underestimate nor totalise capitalism as explanatory feature and characteristic of fascism.

The historian Ian Kershaw, author of a widely-read widely read biography of Hitler (Kershaw 2008), gives an enumerative characterisation of fascism.According to Kershaw, important features of fascism include hyper-nationalism, racism, authoritarian leadership, the friend/enemy-scheme (anti-Marxism, anti-socialism, anti-liberalism, anti-democratic, patriarchal values, militarism, violence, and terrorist extermination of identified enemies). Other than authors such as Griffin, Payne, Laqueur, or Eatwell, Ian Kershaw provides some indications about the relationship of fascism and capitalism without reducing the one to the other:

"hyper-nationalist emphasis on the unity of an integral nation, which gained its very identity through the "cleansing" of all those deemed not to belong [...]; stress upon discipline, "manliness" and militarism (usually involving paramilitary organizations); and belief in authoritarian leadership. Other features were important, indeed sometimes central, to the ideology of a specific movement, but not omnipresent. Some movements directed their nationalism towards irredentist or imperialist goals, with devastating effect, but not all were intrinsically expansionist. Some, though not all, had a strong

What is Fascism?

anti-capitalist tendency. Often, though not invariably, they favoured reorga-
nizing the economy along "corporatist" lines, abolishing independent trade
unions and regulating economic policy by "corporations" of interests directed
by the state. This amalgam of ideas, with varying emphasis, was generally
consonant with the aim of establishing mass support for an authoritarian
regime of an essentially reactionary, non-revolutionary kind. Some of the
radical Right [...] wanted [...] a nationalist, authoritarian government. [...]
Fascism sought a revolution not in terms of social class, as Marxists
advocated, but a revolution nonetheless – a revolution of mentalities, values
and will. [...] Whether the shift was to the conservative or to the radical
Right, it was advertised as essential to protect and regenerate the nation. As
class conflict intensified [...] national unity was advanced as the essential
bulwark to the threat of socialism. [...] It touched the interests of those who
felt threatened by the forces of modernizing social change. It mobilized those
who believed they had something to lose – status, property, power, cultural
tradition – through the presumed menace of internal enemies, and especially
through the advance of socialism and its revolutionary promise of social
revolution. However, it bound up these interests in a vision of a new society
that would reward the strong, the fit, the meritorious – the deserving (in their
own eyes)."

(Kershaw 2016, 228–230)

Kershaw argues that fascism tries to mobilise those who fear they might lose
status, property, power, or culture through the promise of a revolution. Fascism
arises in the context of crises of capitalist society. It presents itself as a solution to
such crises. The solution it poses does, however, not want to overcome class society, but rather constructs socialism as one of the enemies of the nation. Kershaw
does not explicitly stress the ideological dimension of fascism, namely that it
distracts from and denies class conflicts in capitalism, but he points out that fascists stress national unity as opposed to class conflicts and want to preserve the
existing social order, i.e. capitalism.

Max Horkheimer writes that "whoever is not willing to talk about capitalism should
also keep quiet about fascism" (Horkheimer 1939/1989, 78). This statement should be
understood in a double sense: (a) capitalism is the context of fascism. Economic,
social, political, and ideological crises of capitalist society and their intersection increase the likelihood that fascist movements emerge and that a fascist society

emerges; (b) fascism plays an ideological role in capitalism. Fascism as ideology distracts from the role that capitalism and class play in social problems by scapegoating constructed enemies of the nation who are presented as causing society's problems. The implication is that fascists advocate terror against constructed enemies instead of challenging the systemic causes of society's problems. Fascism does not challenge but practically deepens class society and capitalism. Fascism is a particular form of capitalist society.

Horkheimer and Adorno analyse the dialectic of the Enlightenment, the "self-destruction of enlightenment" (Horkheimer and Adorno 1947/2002, xvi) that results in "the reversion of enlightened civilization to barbarism" (xix). Capitalism's structures of exploitation and domination turn against liberalism's Enlightenment values and in the 20th century resulted in Auschwitz. "After the brief interlude of liberalism in which the bourgeois kept one another in check, power is revealing itself as archaic terror in a fascistically rationalized form" (68). Horkheimer and Adorno argue that capitalism on the one hand propagates Enlightenment values that aim at advancing freedom, equality, and solidarity, but on the other hand advances possessive individualism and freedom of private property that undermine equality and solidarity so that the capitalist antagonism between private property of capital and inequalities creates fascist potentials.

The concept of fascism underlying the book *Digital Fascism* is based on critical theorists such as Erich Fromm, Theodor W. Adorno, Max Horkheimer, Herbert Marcuse, and Moishe Postone. Fromm and Adorno characterised the fascist as the authoritarian personality. The levels of the psyche and ideology are two important dimensions of fascism, but fascism not only operates at the level of the individual and groups but at all levels of society. Fascism is neither an individual ideology and practice nor a type of society; it is a feature of class societies that can exist at different levels, namely at the levels of individual consciousness and practices, the ideology and practices of groups and organisations, institutions, and society as a whole. Fascism is a practice, ideology, social movement, mode of organisation, and a mode of capitalist and class society. The mentioned critical theorists do not give explicit definitions of fascism, but their theoretical approaches provide indications of how to define fascism.

Any social group, social system, and society has (a) organisational principles, (b) an identity and practices that bind together and relate individuals and give certain meanings to their existence, (c) relations and definition of relations to the outside world, (d) ways of how problems are solved. No matter at what level it is organised, proponents of right-wing authoritarianism are convinced of and propagate (a) top-down authoritarian decision-making and the leadership principle as organisational principle, (b) nationalism (the belief in the superiority and primacy of a biologically or culturally defined nation over other humans) as identity principle, (c) the construction of the friend/enemy scheme that polarises and explains the world as an antagonism between the nation and groups that threaten the nation (such as immigrants, refugees, socialists, liberals, Marxists, religions that are different from the nation's dominant religion, which implies that fascism is often racist, xenophobic, anti-socialist, anti-liberal, anti-Semitic, etc), and (d) militant patriarchy that sees the soldier as the ideal citizen, advances patriarchal values that want to confine women to subordinate roles in society, and believe in violence (including law and order policies, war, and terror) as the ideal means for solving conflicts and answering to society's problems. These four features are characteristic of right-wing authoritarianism. Figure 17.1 shows a model of right-wing authoritarianism.

Right-wing authoritarianism responds to political-economic crises with ideologies that speak to disenfranchised individuals' psychology. Those who feel politically anxious have an ambiguous relationship to love and hate. They seek for an alternative and identity that promises them hope and they want to express their anger and aggression. Figures like Trump on Twitter and in other forms of public communication institutionalise anxiety by offering opportunities to these individuals for loving the nation and the leader and expressing hatred against scapegoats. Right-wing authoritarianism works on the level of psychological anxieties, desires, emotions, affects, and instincts. It often does not use rational arguments, but post-truth political psychology and ideology.

Conservatism is a form of right-wing authoritarianism that accepts the existence and framework of democracy and practises the four principles of authoritarianism within democratic societies. It does not support terror but rather propagates law and order policies. Right-wing extremism is an ideology, a political movement, and not a type of society. It shows the tendency to accept and favour violence against constructed enemies but its attacks are mainly limited to political style, ideology, communication, and symbols. Fascism can operate at the level of consciousness, groups, organisations, institutions, and society as a whole. Fascism organises and institutionalises violence and terror as political means; it is a terrorist and exterminatory form of right-wing authoritarianism that aims at establishing a society built on terror against identified enemies that aims at their extermination, institutionalises the practice of the leadership principle, nationalism, the friend/enemy-scheme, and militant patriarchy. Fascism is a response to the antagonisms and crises of capitalist societies and class

Right-Wing Authoritarianism (RWA)

Individual ⇔ Group ⇔ Institution ⇔ Society

RWA's social role: Deflection of attention from structures
of class, capitalism and domination

Authoritarian Leadership
(in economic, political and cultural systems)

"WE"=

Leader

↓

People

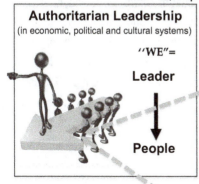

Nationalism
(political fetishism, constructs fictive ethnicity)

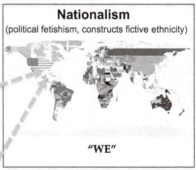

"WE"

Friend/Enemy-Scheme

Der Marxismus ist
der Schutzengel
Wählt   des Kapitalismus
Nationalsozialisten Liste 1

"THEY"

Authoritarian, Right-Wing
Extremist, Fascist Ideological
Practice

Patriarchy & Militarism

"WE" ⟵⟶ "THEY"

Anti-Fascist,
Socialist
Praxis
Communication

What is Fascism?

FIGURE 17.1 A model of right-wing authoritarianism.

societies. It tries to mobilise those who are afraid of social decline by promising a
better society where the national collective rules, benefits its members, and terrorises
and eliminates the constructed enemies who are blamed for society's ills. By scapegoating constructed enemies for society's problems and abstracting from these problems systemic causes and propagating nationalism, fascism plays an ideological role

in class societies. It distracts from the connection of society's problems to capitalism and class relations. Bourgeois theories of fascism often abstract from, ignore, or downplay the double role of fascism in capitalism and class society, namely fascism's ideological role in capitalism and capitalism's fascist potentials. Orthodox leftist concepts of fascism in contrast often underestimate, ignore, or downplay aspects of the friend/enemy-scheme, nationalism, racism, xenophobia, anti-Semitism, and extermination in fascism and reduce fascism to capitalism. Fascism operates on different levels of society, namely the individual, the group, institutions, and society. Fascism on one level does not automatically lead to fascism on the next level, but each upper level presupposes the existence of fascism on the lower levels. For example, a fascist society is based on fascist institutions, groups, and individuals but is more than the sum of fascist institutions, groups, and individuals.

We can define fascism as anti-democratic, anti-socialist, and terrorist ideology, practice, and mode of organisation of groups, institutions, and society that is based on the combination of (a) the leadership principle, (b) nationalism, (c) the friend/enemy scheme, and (d) militant patriarchy (the idealisation of the soldier, the practice of patriarchy, the subordination of women, war, violence and terror as political means) and the use of terror against constructed enemies, aims at establishing a fascist society that is built on the use of terror and the institutionalisation of the four fascist principles in society, tries to mobilise individuals who fear the loss of property, status, power, reputation in light of the antagonisms as its supporters, and plays an ideological role in capitalist and class societies by blaming scapegoats for society's ills and presenting society's problems as an antagonism between the nation and foreigners and enemies of the nation so that fascism distracts attention from the systemic roles of class and capitalism in society's problems and from the class contradiction between capital and labour. Fascism often propagates a one-dimensional, one-sided, and personalising "anti-capitalism" that constructs the nation as political fetish and an antagonism between the unity of a nation's capital and labour on the one side and a particular form of capital or economy or production or community on the other side that is presented as destroying the nation's economic, political, and cultural survival.

We want to now briefly discuss examples of critical theory approaches that have influenced the development of the understanding of fascism underlying this book.

Frankfurt School critical theorist Franz L. Neumann (1936, 35) defines fascism as "dictatorship of the fascist (National Socialist) party, the bureaucracy, the army and big business – dictatorship over the whole of the people, for the complete organization of the nation for imperialist war". Neumann here identifies some core characteristics of fascism:

1) Fascism is based on authoritarian leadership;
2) Fascism is nationalist; it propagates that "employers and workers work together in perfect harmony" (Neumann 1936, 39) although class society and the division of labour continue to exist;
3) Fascism is a dictatorial form of capitalism;
4) Fascism uses militaristic means (such as war, terrorism, and imperialism).

A feature that is missing is that (5) fascism uses the friend-enemy scheme for creating imagined enemies and scapegoats in order to distract from social problem's foundations in class inequality and power asymmetries.

The historian, political economist, and philosopher Moishe Postone (1980) argues that the analysis of fascism should not be reduced to its definition as "a terroristic, bureaucratic police state operating in the immediate interests of big capital, based on authoritarian structures, glorifying the family and using racism as one means of social cohesion" (101). He stresses that extermination is a central feature of fascism. In the case of Nazi Germany, the Shoah – the project of the extermination of the Jews that is symbolised by Auschwitz – is a central defining feature. "*No analysis of National Socialism which cannot account for the extermination of European Jewry is fully adequate*" (105).

Postone has given special attention to the analysis of Nazi-fascism and anti-Semitism as the form of the friend/enemy-scheme that dominates in Nazi-fascism and has brought about the Shoah as terrorist project of extermination. He sees Nazi-fascism and Auschwitz based on Horkheimer and Adorno as the consequence of capitalism and characterises Auschwitz as negative factory:

> "A capitalist factory is a place where value is produced, which "unfortunately" has to take the form of the production of goods. The concrete is produced as the necessary carrier of the abstract. The extermination camps were not a terrible version of such a factory but, rather, should be seen as its grotesque, Arian, "anti-capitalist" negation. Auschwitz was a factory to "destroy value", i.e. to destroy the personifications of the abstract. Its organization was that of a fiendish industrial process, the aim of which was to "liberate" the concrete from the abstract. The first step was to

What is Fascism?

dehumanize, that is, to rip the "mask" of humanity away and reveal the Jews for what "they really are" – "Müsselmänner", shadows, ciphers, abstractions. The second step was then to eradicate that abstractness, to transform it into smoke, trying in the process to wrest away the last remnants of the concrete material "use-value": clothes, gold, hair, soap."

(Postone 1980, 114)

The political theorist Daniel Woodley (2010) discusses features of a critical theory of fascism. He builds a critical understanding of fascism on the works of Karl Marx and Moishe Postone (1980, 1993, 2003) and interprets fascism as a political version of fetishism concept. Woodley sees fascism as "a populist ideology which seeks, through a mythology of unity and identity, to project a 'common instinctual fate' (uniform social status) between bourgeois and proletarianized groups, eliding the reality of social distinction in differentiated class societies" (Woodley 2010, 17). Woodley (2010, 76) writes in this context that "the social function of fascism is to create a unity of social forces incorporating propertied interests, lower-middle class voters and plebeian elements".

Fascism aims at creating a particular model of society:

"[F]ascism must *itself* be understood as a political commodity: Fascism is not simply a subjectively generated, reactive strategy – a desperate attempt by atomized individuals to overcome the disenchantment and inauthenticity of modernity – but an aesthetic innovation which transcends existing patterns of differentiation and political subjectification to disrupt established narratives of history and progress. [...] the fetishization of communal identities which conceal the true nature of the commodity as a structured social practice, bridging the gap between the specificity of the nation-state (as the nexus linking culture and power) and the rationalization of circuits of capital."

(Woodley 2010, 17–18)

17.2 What is Digital Fascism?

Digital fascism means the communication of fascism online as well as fascist groups' and individuals' use of digital technologies as means of information, communication, and organisation. Fascism is a particular, terrorist form of right-wing authoritarianism that aims at killing the identified enemies by the use of violence, terror, and war.

Digital fascism means that fascists utilise digital technologies such as computers, the Internet, mobile phones, apps, and social media in order to (a) communicate internally so that they co-ordinate the organisation of fascist practices and (b) communicate to the public the leadership principle, nationalism, applications of the friend/enemy scheme, and threats of violence as well as the propagation of violence, militarism, terror, war, law-and-order politics, and extermination directed against the constructed enemies and scapegoats in order to try to find followers, mobilise supporters, and terrorise constructed enemies.

In digital fascism, fascists make use of digital technologies for trying to advance violence, terror, and war as means for the establishment of a fascist society. Scapegoats that ideology constructs and against whom it agitates online include socialists and immigrants. The scapegoats that fascist ideology constructs and against whom it agitates online include immigrants, socialists, liberals, intellectuals, experts, and democrats.

In their goal to advance fascist society, digital fascists make use of digital technologies and their particular features. There is a number of key characteristics of digital fascism:

- **Fascist convergence:**
  Networked computer technologies enable to convergence of one-to-one and the convergence of information-, communication-, and production-technologies in one digital platform. As a consequence, fascist digital communication is based on converging forms of communication and the convergence of activities. The convergence of social roles on social media supports fascist ideology's spreading on the Internet.

- **User-generated fascism and fascist prosumption:**
  Networked computers are not just information and communication technologies but also means of production. The computer is a means of communication and a means of production; it enables consumers of information to become producers of information, so-called "prosumers" (productive consumption), which resulted in the emergence of user-generated content on the Internet. Digital fascism utilises these digital capacities in the form of user-generated fascist content and fascist prosumers who are active on social media platforms.

- **Interactive and multimedia fascism:**
  The Internet is interactive and multimedia-based: users change the status of Internet applications by entering commands and navigate in individual forms through combinations of digital texts, images, sounds, videos, and animations.

What is Digital Fascism?

Digital fascism utilises the interactive and multimedia capacities of networked computing.

- **Hypertextual, networked fascism:**

  The World Wide Web is a network of interlinked online texts, sites, and platforms. Digital fascism makes use of this networked character of the WWW so that there are fascist networks, platforms, and communities on the Internet. The social media and fascist ideology and practices spread on mainstream sites and platforms.

- **Fascist co-operation:**

  The networked computer supports online collaboration. Digital fascism makes use of the co-operative potentials of the Internet so that fascists co-operate in their goal to establish fascist societies.

- **Fascist tabloidisation:**

  The Internet enables the combination of piece of information that are devoid of context (decontextualisation). It supports the blurring of the boundaries between the real and the virtual, reality and fiction, truth and ideology. Internet communication operates with high-speed flows of vast amounts of information. The logic of tabloidisation shapes the Internet in the form of the accelerated production, distribution, and consumption of often superficial and sensationalist information. Digital fascism makes use of tabloidisation on the Internet in order to spread fake news, post-truth culture, algorithmic politics, and filter bubbles.

- **Fascist surveillance:**

  On the Internet, private, semi-public, and public information converges. This means that fascists on the one hand are enabled to collect private, semi-public, and public data about their enemies that enters their practices. On the other hand, fascist activities can also be traced, documented, and tracked online. Fascist surveillance means the online surveillance of and by fascists.

Gáspár Miklós Tamás (2000) argues that fascism is not limited to German Nazi-fascism that organised the Nazi state in the years from 1933 until 1945 and to Italian fascism (1922–1943), but changes historically. He characterises contemporary fascism as post-fascism, by which he understands a "cluster of policies, practices, routines, and ideologies" that constitute an unclassical form of fascism that shares with classical fascism the "hostility to universal citizenship" and the distinctions between nation/enemies and citizens/non-citizens. "Post-fascism does not need stormtroopers and dictators. [...] Cutting the civic and human community in two: this is fascism". Post-fascism argues for installing and practices the constructed enemies' "suspension of [...] civic and human rights". Tamás utilises Ernst Fraenkel's (1941/2017) notion of the dual state: there is one part of the state, the normative state, that defines and guarantees rights for regular citizens; and another part of the state, the prerogative state, that discriminates, oppresses, marginalises those who are defined as non-citizens and enemies of the state. "By the Prerogative State we mean that governmental system which exercises unlimited arbitrariness and violence unchecked by any legal guarantees, and by the Normative State an administrative body endowed with elaborate powers for safeguarding the legal order as expressed in statutes, decisions of the courts, and activities of the administrative agencies" (Fraenkel 1941/2017, xxiii).

Post-fascism utilises all means necessary to destroy defined enemies and to construct and attack them as scapegoats for society's problems so that there is a distraction from the actual material causes of these problems. Classical fascism operated in the context of the crisis of financialised, industrial, state monopoly capitalism. Contemporary fascism has operated in the context of the crisis of financialised, digital, neoliberal capitalism. Classical fascism used stormtroopers and monopolised, state-controlled broadcast media (such as the *Volksempfänger*). Contemporary fascism, among other means, uses troll armies and social media in order to attack defined enemies. Classical fascism was strictly organised top-down based on the leadership principle. Contemporary fascism fetishises the leader and more combines fascist leadership with networked, decentralised organisation. Classical fascism openly opposed democracy. Contemporary fascism often disguises itself as and claims to be democratic. Classical fascism defined the enemy primarily in terms of race and biology, while contemporary fascism defines the enemy based more on culture and religion. Both classical and contemporary fascism construct conspiracy theories about a union of socialists, liberals, experts, and minorities (Jews, immigrants, refugees, people of colour, Muslims, etc.) that are said to rule the world. Classical fascism often racialised this proclaimed union, whereas contemporary fascism constructs such a union as one of "globalisers", "metropolitan elites", "political correctness", "cultural Marxism", etc. Classical fascism operated based on the central organisation of propaganda and lies for which it utilised broadcasting and mass events. Contemporary fascism also spreads propaganda and lies, but combines a central ideological apparatus with the organisation of user-generated post-truth, user-generated fake news and filter bubbles that spread fascist ideology. Both contemporary and classical fascism appeal to human consciousness by combining emotions and ideology.

Right-wing authoritarianism and fascism involve a high degree of polarisation. It is difficult to convince those who believe in racism, nationalism, authoritarianism of the problems these worldviews entail. Rational debate is often not possible and not welcome. In the long run, only a society that strengthens equality and overcomes exploitation and domination can undermine the roots of fascism. In the short term, only reforms that redistribute wealth and power coupled with the advancement of the general level of education and critique of and deconstruction of false news, post-truth culture, and ideology can help to weaken fascism and digital fascism. The digital means of information and communication are not just tools that help spreading but also tools for challenging fascist ideology.

References

Dimitrov, Georgi. 1972. *Selected Works. Volume 2*. Sofia: Sofia Press.

Eatwell, Roger. 1996. "On Defining the "Fascist Minimum": The Centrality of Ideology." *Journal of Political Ideologies* 1 (3): 303–19.

Fraenkel, Ernst. 1941/2017. *The Dual State*. Oxford: Oxford University Press.

Goebbels, Josef. 1925. *The Little ABC of National Socialists*. Online version.

Griffin, Roger. 2003. Fascism. In *The Blackwell Dictionary of Modern Social Thought*, edited by William Outhwaite, 231–4. Malden, MA: Blackwell. 2nd edition.

Griffin, Roger. 1993. *The Nature of Fascism*. Abingdon: Routledge.

Hitler, Adolf. 1941. *Mein Kampf*. New York: Reynal & Hitchcock.

Horkheimer, Max. 1939/1989. "The Jews and Europe." In *Critical Theory and Society: A Reader*, edited by Stephen E. Bronner and Douglas Kellner, 77–94. New York: Routledge.

Horkheimer, Max and Theodor W. Adorno. 1947/2002. *Dialectic of Enlightenment. Philosophical Fragments*. Stanford, CA: Stanford University Press.

Kershaw, Ian. 2016. *To Hell and Back: Europe, 1914–1949*. New York: Penguin.

Kershaw, Ian. 2008. *Hitler: A Biography*. New York: W.W. Norton & Company.

Laqueur, Walter. 1996. *Fascism: Past, Present, Future*. Oxford: Oxford University Press.

Neumann, Franz L. 1936. *The Governance of the Rule of Law. An Investigation into the Relationship Between the Political Theories, the Legal System; and the Social Background in the Competitive Society*. Dissertation. London: London School of Economics.

Payne, Stanley G. 1995. *A History of Fascism, 1914-45*. London: Routledge.

Postone, Moishe. 2003. "The Holocaust and the Trajectory of the Twentieth Century." In *Catastrophe and Meaning. The Holocaust and the Twentieth Century*, edited by Moishe Postone and Eric Santner, 81–114. Chicago, IL: University of Chicago Press.

Postone, Moishe. 1993. *Time, Labor, and Social Domination. A Reinterpretation of Marx's Critical Theory*. Cambridge: Cambridge University Press.

Postone, Moishe. 1980. "Anti-Semitism and National Socialism: Notes on the German Reaction to "Holocaust"." *New German Critique* 19 (1): 97–115.

Tamás, Gáspár Miklós. 2000. "On Post-Fascism." *Boston Review*, June 1, 2000.

Thompson, Willie. 2011. *Ideologies in the Age of Extremes. Liberalism, Conservatism, Communism, Fascism 1941–91*. London: Pluto Press.

Trotsky, Leon. 1996. *Fascism: What It Is and How to Fight It*. New York: Pathfinder.

Trotsky, Leon. 1971. *The Struggle Against Fascism in Germany*. New York: Pathfinder.

Woodley, Daniel. 2010. *Fascism and Political Theory: Critical Perspectives on Fascist Ideology*. Abingdon: Routledge.

Index

CPSIA information can be obtained
at www.ICGtesting.com
Printed in the USA
LVHW040447190423
744686LV00004B/244